**Free Spirits**

# Free Spirits

*Spiritualism, Republicanism, and Radicalism in the Civil War Era*

MARK A. LAUSE

UNIVERSITY OF ILLINOIS PRESS
*Urbana, Chicago, and Springfield*

© 2016 by the Board of Trustees
of the University of Illinois
All rights reserved
Manufactured in the United States of America
1 2 3 4 5 C P 5 4 3 2 1
♾ This book is printed on acid-free paper.

Library of Congress Cataloging-in-Publication Data
Names: Lause, Mark A., author.
Title: Free spirits : spiritualism, Republicanism, and radicalism in the
   Civil War era / Mark A. Lause.
Description: Urbana : University of Illinois Press, 2016. | Includes
   bibliographical references and index.
Identifiers: LCCN 2015050880 | ISBN 9780252040306 (hardcover : alk.
   paper) | ISBN 9780252081750 (pbk. : alk. paper)
Subjects: LCSH: Spiritualism—United States—History—19th century.
   | Republicanism—United States—History—19th century. |
   Radicalism—United States—History—19th century.
Classification: LCC BF1242.U6 L38 2016 | DDC 133.90973/09034—dc23
   LC record available at http://lccn.loc.gov/2015050880

# Contents

Acknowledgments  vii

Prologue  America's 1848: Republican Spirits in Revolt  1

**PART I. THE SOUL OF A REPUBLIC**

1  Free Democrats to the Republicans: Radical Spiritualists and the Antislavery Insurgency  23

2  The Mystical Union: The Republican Medium of the National Destiny  44

3  Father Abraham: President Lincoln and the Spirit of the Union  65

**PART II. THE PROMISE OF A REPUBLIC**

4  Liberty: Toward a Rational Spirit of Freedom  89

5  Equality: Race and Gender  106

6  Fraternity: Reconstructing a Movement and the Nation  125

Epilogue  Long Shadows: The Legacies of Civil War–Era Spiritualism  145

Notes  161

Index  217

*Illustrations follow page 86*

# Acknowledgments

Since I bought a used copy of Hardinge's history roughly thirty-five years ago, a considerable number of students of this subject—mostly contemporaries or near contemporaries—have generated an impressive literature. Without their carefully marked trails, I believe it would have been nearly impossible to navigate safely through mountains of often tediously repetitive accounts of conversations with dead people. I am terribly grateful to whoever makes the decisions at Google, the Internet Archives, and similar digitalization projects for access to hundreds of often hefty tomes for free. However, a dedicated group of collectors and scholars functioning as the International Association for the Preservation of Spiritualist and Occult Periodicals made a sustained and unique effort to make PDFs of newspapers (and much else) available through their site at www.iapsop.com. Earlier I had encountered one of them, John B. Buescher, who had for years shared what he knew freely through the website spirithistory.com, since absorbed into iapsop.com. Although we have never actually met, we have had a long association online, and without his knowledge, insights, and suggestions this study would certainly be far weaker, should it exist at all. At critical points in this study, the Langsam Library of the University of Cincinnati had retained enough staff to sustain an interlibrary loan service that proved essential and expert in running down the occasional odd volume not otherwise available. Over the past two decades I have presented elements of this work in various forms and benefited greatly from the feedback of numerous colleagues, most consistently from Prof. Janine

Hartman, with whom I have shared an interest in this subject since graduate school. The staff at the University of Illinois Press has been superb from start to finish, particularly crucial in forcing upon me the kind of constrictions that have focused this study and made it as useful as I hope it will be. To all of these, I am deeply grateful. Most fundamentally, my wife, Kathy, has provided the kind of consistent anchor and patient support without which such projects as this would never have gotten beyond a spirit's whisper.

# Prologue

## America's 1848

### *Republican Spirits in Revolt*

> Almost simultaneously great revolutions have convulsed the four quarters of the globe, and the human race have been strangely moved and quickened in destructive or productive activities. While Europe awake at the shout of trampled millions, suddenly roused to demand freedom, and to hurl down blood-cemented thrones, and dynasties hoary with age and crime, Asia to her center felt a renewing spirit, and the Chinese Empire arose against its Tartar oppressors, filled with a new religion, a new policy, and a promise—on the tongue, at least—of the social and political regeneration of a mighty people.
> —"Present Aspect of the World,"
>   *Spiritual Telegraph*

So it was that American spiritualists located their origins in the tumultuous year of 1848. As republicanism began moving people from Paris to Prague and the visions and voices of Hong Xiuquan inspired what became the Taiping Rebellion, Americans confronted the hard realities that their much-touted system of checks and balances actually sanctioned unaccountable power where it was based on unlimited accumulations of wealth, particularly when it involved the legal ownership of other human beings. July saw the national convention for women's rights at Seneca Falls, and the following month former president Martin Van Buren's "Barnburner" Democrats hosted a gathering of what became the Free-Soil Party. At both Seneca Falls and Buffalo, stenographers recorded claims to represent the views of the nation's founders, and the reporters tapped those claims across the country on the new telegraph. Not far from there, departed spirits spoke to the world through the "Rochester rappings" as a "spiritual telegraph."

Spiritualists chose to locate the birth of their movement over a long, dark 1848 night in upstate New York, though it had many precedents and complex theological roots. Moreover, it assumed many of its defining characteristics, such as mediumship and the séance, only after 1849. The impact of spiritualism as a movement on the social and political course of the nation in a particularly critical period of American history merits reconjuring.

## The Fox Sisters and the Birth of the Movement

The mundane truth is that spiritualism grew from the boredom of two youngsters who started entertaining each other with bodily noises. Fourteen years before, the already sizable Methodist family of John and Margaret Fox of Rochester had added Maggie and her sister Katie three years later. The eldest son, David, farmed in rural Arcadia and told his father that the nearby hamlet of Hydesville needed a blacksmith, so John moved his family to a house there in December 1847.[1] Stories that the house had been haunted for eighteen months and "charged with the aura requisite to make it a battery for the working of a telegraph" surfaced only much later.

The two youngest girls missed the lights of the reasonably sized town of Rochester. In their boredom, they discovered that popping the joints of their toes on the wooden floors made sounds that resonated through the small cottage, leaving the source largely undetectable. On March 31, 1848, they tried this around their parents and playfully denied that they had made the sounds. To their amusement—and perhaps to their horror—they learned just how credulous adults could be. Convinced that they were listening to the spirit of a dead man, the parents brought in select neighbors for consultation, and the Fox sisters suddenly found community expectations sweeping them irresistibly on to where they knew not.[2]

From the onset of the raps, interested parties other than the girls read their own fears and desires into them. Frightened family members converged on David's farm at Arcadia, and their mother clung to her Bible as a talisman. The first neighbors who crowded in to hear them asked questions that led the noises to identify themselves as the efforts to communicate by the disembodied soul of a murdered peddler. Stories circulated (much later) that human bones and a peddler's pack were found in the cellar walls, but contemporaries needed no such confirmation.

Their eldest sister, Ann Leah, quickly took charge. By some accounts, the girls shared their secret with Leah, who had a well-developed survivor's sense. Married when she had been Maggie's age, Leah already had several children of her own, before her abandonment by her husband. She advised her two younger siblings to remain silent, and some taps began to be heard briefly in association with her own daughter Lizzie.[3] On one level, though, the sisters got what they wanted, when their parents took them back to Rochester early in the summer.

Yet the stories supposedly followed the family to Rochester, where they quickly found some noteworthy well-wishers and promoters. Although initially skeptical, Isaac and Amy Post accepted the claim, partly due to their distaste for the joyless salvation of Calvinism. Isaac even proposed that a listener could point to letters on an alphabet board, creating a "spiritual telegraph" to the beyond, and Eliab Wilkinson Capron then wrote a history of these early experiments, "entirely without any action of his mind." The Posts had a great need to believe because they had lost children, as had Ira B. Davis, a tough-minded New Englander living in New York who took solace from the regular presence of a daughter who had died in infancy.[4] Only later did they hit on the idea that the entranced voice of the medium provided an even more readily understood means of communication.

The prospect of so great a breakthrough appealed to people who had been repeatedly trying to make breakthroughs in other areas. The Posts had been Progressive Friends, Davis a secularist and socialist admirer of Charles Fourier. What became the unprecedented boom of unrestrained capitalism in America had already impoverished much of the population in selected parts of the country and created serious social and cultural dislocations. A generation before the spiritualists, British social critic Robert Owen had denounced organized religion as a key problem. The series of communitarian ventures overseas and in the United States had some striking successes but obviously failed to thwart the triumph of the capitalist ethos. Although he continued to work for social and political change back in Britain, the prospect of working for a moral change through spiritualism brought even the veteran critic of religion to the cause. In the years just before Hydesville, Fourier's more mystical critic of capitalism won even more followers across the country, fostered by such prominent journalists as Horace Greeley.[5]

Spiritualism owed a special debt to two of these radical newspapermen. Eliab Wilkinson Capron came to Rochester from Auburn, New York, and he remained an "infidel" and a Fourierist. Another Auburn freethinker and printer, Henry Danforth Barron, joined Capron in Rochester and helped launch the new movement, though he soon moved on to the West. With the Posts, they got the Fox sisters to demonstrate the rappings in public on November 23, 1848, some months after the first knocks in Hydesville. Local critics scoffed unmercifully at the noise, and the local clergy, who had a tenuous-enough hold on the souls of a diverse and fluid American community, muttered about orthodox cries of witchcraft and demonology. At one point, in Katie's absence, Maggie made a noble twelve-day attempt to desist from making the sounds that would be invariably translated into spirit communication, but the expectations of the adults around her became too strong for her to deny them cooperation.[6] Paradoxically, as the hostility of some churchgoers' suspicions cut into Leah's supply of piano students, the family looked increasingly for support from those wishing to communicate with the dead.

Yet spirit communication remained a relatively private matter for another year. On November 14, 1849, the organizers arranged to get a variety of prominent local gentlemen and several reporters to Rochester's Corinthian Hall, including one from Horace Greeley's nationally important *New York Tribune*. Believers had coaxed respected local figures to investigate the manifestations and explain them. When they declined to offer an explanation, the audience appointed a second committee that included both the fifty-year-old judge John Worth Edmonds and former Antimasonic congressman Frederick Whittlesey. None reportedly could explain the source of the rapping.[7]

No sooner had the movement become more public than it began spreading, largely because so many local clergymen had become disaffected with the drive toward denominationalism. Auburn, the home of Capron and Barron, already had Thomas Lake Harris's "Apostolic Circle" and quickly acquired Uriah Clark, a Universalist long interested in mesmerism and healing. Clark not only became a national proponent of the cause but also sustained his own *Spiritual Clarion* and later became involved with the *Spiritual Telegraph*. The Reverend Russell Perkins Ambler brought a delegation from Springfield to Rochester that returned to form its own circle there and foster another at Albany.[8]

The repercussions of the second Rochester meeting in the winter of 1849–50 galvanized local networks across the Northeast.[9] Groups coalesced at Binghamton, Ithaca, Westford, Scott, Scipio, Courtland, Port Byron, Waterloo, Macedon, and other places, with another year adding circles at Greece, Sennett, Fleming, Kellogsville, Ballston Spa, Saratoga, Glenn Falls, and Syracuse. Despite the initial success of a local Christian mob in preventing Maggie from taking the platform at Troy in May, local spiritualists persisted and organized a presence in the community.

It spread across New England. In addition to Ambler's group at Springfield, Andrew Jackson Davis had a "Harmonial Brotherhood" at Hartford. At Stratford, LeRoy Sunderland launched a circle that briefly sustained the *Spiritual Philosopher* or *Spirit World,* which provided Gothic novelist and radical George Lippard a platform for the Brotherhood of the Union and also published P. J. Proudhon. By then, followers functioned at Chicopee, Fitchburg, Greenfield, Templeton, Plymouth, Quincy, and Worcester in Massachusetts, as well as Bridgeport, Norwich, Waterford, and Willimantic in Connecticut, with Winsted and Stamford hosting meetings. Groups formed at Providence, Rhode Island, along with Moretown and other towns in Vermont. Fostered by Jeremiah Hacker's *Pleasure Boat* of Portland, circles developed there and elsewhere in Maine. Circles of unspecified location existed in New Hampshire and doubtlessly others.

Formal organization appeared at Philadelphia in October 1850, according to Dr. Henry T. Child's later account of the Philadelphia movement in the *Religio Philosophical Journal.* By then, locals who had observed spirit communications included radicals, such as Theophilus Fisk and a veteran of the earlier movement among female mill hands, Sarah Bagley. By 1854 their meetings became interesting enough for the departed father of one participant "to imitate all the exercises of a company of royal dragoons, to which he belonged previous to his death." The following year, Thomas Price briefly provided them with a monthly publication, the *Index.* Those interested at Georgetown and Morristown plausibly represented local variants of the Philadelphia circles. Titusville particularly became "a stronghold of the belief," and the movement also appeared at Corry and even at the college town of Meadville under Dr. John Newcomer. As early as 1851, circles began to take form at Allegheny and Pittsburgh.[10]

Across the Midwest, various intentional communities and local congregations led by renegade clergy provided a ready-made audience for spiritualism. In Indiana Pennsylvania-born Quaker abolitionist Kersey Graves, a schoolteacher turned lecturer, supported the antislavery Liberty Party and became interested in language reform and socialism. Graves joined the "Union Home" and the subsequent communities at Harveysburg and possibly the Highland Home at Zanesfield. These associations linked Graves with John Otis Wattles and his brother Augustus Wattles at Cincinnati. The movement there quickly assimilated the new eastern techniques. By the fall of 1850, Dr. Joseph Rodes Buchanan, medical educator and editor of the *Journal of Man*, hosted regular séances in his home and at the Franklin rooms on Vine Street. Reflecting the persistent reality of the local group, Buchanan became the promoter of "psychometry," the ability to know the nature of an object simply by its feel.[11]

The strength of the movement in the "burned-over district" of New York spilled over into the "Firelands" of the Western Reserve of northern Ohio. There, the spiritualists channeled Tom Paine to assure them that "the Infidelity, as they are called on the earth, will be the first to embrace the truth, having no opposing creeds or prejudices to prevent them." When St. Timothy's Episcopal Church in Massillon tried Abby Warner, "an orphan girl, and so destitute of education that she could neither read nor write," for her mediumship, local spiritualists waged a vigorous defense. Periodically active there were William Denton and his sister Ann Denton Cridge and her husband, Alfred Cridge.[12]

Early on, individuals familiar with the developments at Rochester brought the movement into the Midwest. Ohio groups started not only at Ravenna and Salem but also at Amherst, Cardington, and Painesville, as well as in Ashtabula County and Willoughby in Lake County. To the south, spiritualists organized at Columbus and Dayton and in the shadow of mysteriously suggestive ancient Indian earthworks at Marietta, Circleville, Chillicothe, and Newark. Thomas L. Nichols grafted another radical community off the internal disturbances in Antioch College and established a spiritualist Memnonia Institute. Jonathan Koons and John Tippie established special "spirit rooms." In Indiana Cincinnatian E. C. Posten established the "Posten Circle" at Laporte, while the Greensburg circle included Senator Charles Cathcart and Congressman James Bradford Foley, both Democrats destined not to survive the decade in office. The movement also spread into Michigan, seeding circles at Battle Creek, Tecumseh, and Adamsville, with others at Niles and Sturgis.[13]

Amherst, Ohio, had an important little group of national significance. The young New Jersey–born Henry Steel Olcott reported that it limped along until a female clairvoyant "competent to control the circle" emerged. There, too, healing medium Seldon J. Finney emerged as a local leader and spokesman. Olcott went east to work on Greeley's *Tribune* and became an active spiritualist there, which dulled none of his work on scientific agriculture, which included running a farm school at Mount Vernon and promoting sorghum. Finney, in turn, went to Illinois and became one of the most important wartime voices of the movement.[14] Both attained a national, if not international, stature.

A strong movement emerged in Illinois. Groups coalesced early at Waukegan, Rockford, Maquon, and Dixon, the first two with monthly publications, the *North-Western Orient: A Monthly Miscellany* and the *Spirit Advocate.* As elsewhere, radicals such as abolitionist and land reformer Seth Paine found spiritualism a unifying set of ideas. By 1859 spiritualists predominated in some small communities, such as El Paso, where they peopled most of its six dwellings. By then Koons had moved from Ohio to Jefferson County, Illinois. Prominent and wealthy Chicagoans such as Ira B. Eddy, the president of the Bank of Chicago, and Nathan H. Bolles, a real estate mogul, embraced the movement, though the family and partners of the former had him carted off to Connecticut and the Hartford Lunatic Asylum when he decided to invest in Paine's cooperative bank. Paine, Ira Porter, and Bolles secured his release and a speedy sanity hearing before a judge, who ordered Eddy's immediate release. The movement won a similar case when the family of John J. Glover at Quincy sought to prevent his leaving much of his estate to the movement.[15]

Wisconsin became a banner state. Local spiritualists began regularly meeting in Milwaukee's Hope Chapel, but strong centers emerged from Watertown to Wilson's Grove in Iowa, as well as the old Ceresco community of the Fourierists in Fond du Lac County.[16] Individuals without number strove more quietly to find understanding and live their lives in the pores of the pervasive alienation that had already begun to subsume American life.

By 1850–51 advocates of an eastern-style spirit communication made early efforts at scattered points in Oregon, Nebraska, Idaho, and Utah. The more numerous settlers on the Pacific Coast replicated spiritualism with other accoutrements of civilization in these outposts, and believers began functioning at Salina and San Francisco.[17] Spiritualism, in short, became a national movement in a very brief period of time.

Spiritualism represented a kind of cultural frontier unbounded by the geographic frontier. Dorus M. Fox—an uncle of the Fox sisters—later documented the case of one John Brown, no relation to the John Brown of Kansas and Harpers Ferry fame. After being shipwrecked as a young man near Galveston, Brown fought in the Texas War for Independence and became a mountain man and hunter in various parts of the West, as far north as the headwaters of the Columbia and Yellowstone Rivers. Familiar with the living legends of the region, such as Kit Carson and Jim Bridger, he married Maria Louisa Sandoval at Taos, where they settled before the arrival of the United States there. With the California Gold Rush, he headed to the coast, coming to rest at San Bernardino, where, in 1853, he became a justice of the peace . . . and a spiritualist.[18] Just as Brown had found new opportunities off the beaten path physically, he expected to find them spiritually and intellectually as well.

## The Evolution and Standards of the Movement

The movement quickly evolved to where it generated its own histories by Capron, Barron, Clark, Leah Fox Underhill, and Emma Hardinge Brittan, all of which described its alleged origins in 1848. The most voluminous of these, that of Hardinge, demonstrates the attraction of the year. A native of London's East End, Emma Floyd had tried her hand as a singer, actress, and pianist before dabbling in occultism and formulating ideas of a secret "brotherhood" protecting knowledge of the cosmic verities. Taking on the name "Hardinge"—alleged revenge upon a man who had convinced her that they had been married while she had been "magnetized"—she showed her flare for showmanship that made her *Modern American Spiritualism* a real masterpiece of the genre. Actually a resident of the socialist community at Modern Times, Hardinge had been particularly aware of the revolutionary implications of 1848.[19] All offered compilations of anecdotes about individual encounters with spirits, many of them repeated from volume to volume.

Spiritualism certainly had deep roots in the community. Waves of evangelical revivals, known as the "Second Great Awakening," had been rolling out of the Northeast across the country for decades. Not scientific inquiry and reasoned argument but an emotional recognition of the need of each individual for that leap of faith moved this powerful wave across much of the nation. This grew in part from the absence of an established clergy, and a similar consideration in terms of medicine created the need for practical and accessible healing arts. Spiritualism sanctioned the work of those inclined to treat the health of the body and the soul while lacking in formal, institutionally acceptable training.[20] Not surprisingly, it encouraged a suspicion of dogma and orthodoxy of all sorts.

So, too, the movement assimilated important intellectual and theological precedents in various currents of the Christian revivals that spread across the burned-over district of upstate New York and into New England. The same impulses that gave rise to Mormonism and other sects had radically transformed Quaker, Unitarian, and Universalist currents in the region. Ralph Waldo Emerson described spiritualism as a variant of Swedenborg's ideas, and

John Humphrey Noyes treated it as "Swedenborgianism Americanized." In the process, it tended to assimilate the spirit communication common among sects such as the Shakers.[21]

Then, too, there already existed strands of spiritualist ideas and practices. Known as "No-God, No-Government, No-Money, No-Meat, No-Salt and Pepper Collins," John Anderson Collins had been a particularly active abolitionist ally of William Lloyd Garrison until an 1841 trip to England opened his eyes to the condition of the growing working class in industrializing Britain. Because America steamed not far behind, Collins returned a confirmed socialist, setting up his own community at Skaneateles in 1843 with members who began experimenting with spirit communications.[22]

The "Auburn Circle" of Thomas Lake Harris had also begun exploring the questions. Along with James Leander Scott, the local Unitarian minister and the editor of the *Cayuga Chief,* Harris exercised strong control over their group of thirty followers. However, the news from Rochester began bringing hundreds into their gatherings and provided the raw material for a new "Apostolic Circle."[23]

Most immediately, though, Andrew J. Davis, the "Poughkeepsie seer," had developed trance skills coupled to a talent for medical diagnoses. The well-read contemporary saw flashes of Galen of Pergamon, Anton Mesmer, Emmanuel Swedenborg, Charles Fourier, and others, but even they tended to doubt whether an unlettered rural mechanic would have the wherewithal to utter such ideas. Encouraged by figures such as the Reverend Samuel Byron Brittan, Davis began touring several years before the Rochester rappings, even as the learned man began transcribing his trances and publishing a series of massive volumes largely unread today. Davis channeled the "Harmonial" philosophy of those spirits who knew no inequality of race, gender, or class.[24]

Not just trances but actual rapping sounded in Cincinnati years before Rochester. As William Turner Coggeshall later wrote, John P. Cornell, Augustus and John Otis Wattles, along with others of these investigators formed a "True Brotherhood" or "Spiritual Brotherhood" in the spring of 1845. In or around the circle worked stove maker Josiah Warren, who had followed Robert Owen into declaring a "mental independence" from marriage, private property, and the state. The group formed the core of the local Fourierist movement, which reorganized a community upriver from the city as "Utopia," launched several land-reform organizations, and sustained Warren's "Labor-for-Labor" cooperative stores in the city as well. Joseph Rodes Buchanan, one of the members of Cincinnati's old Spiritual Brotherhood and publisher of his own *Buchanan's*

*Journal of Man,* also became a prime mover in the Eclectic Medical College there.[25] An entire category of mediums focused on the healing arts.

At the same time, a similar community of occultists and mesmerists farther west supported the *St. Louis Magnet*. The circle took in a range of eclectic healers and the former head of West Point General Ethan Allen Hitchcock, known as "the father of American alchemy." Such proslavery Southern partisans as Dr. Joseph N. McDowell passed through its ranks, and over time it would also include trade unionists such as Thomas Gales Forster as well as James H. Blood, who later presided over the local association before he went off with Victoria Woodhull.[26]

Even earlier, Phineas Parkhurst Quimby, the son of an impoverished Yankee blacksmith, encountered his first lecture on mesmerism in 1838. Interested in healing, he came to believe that the patient's state of mind had actually caused the malady. His massages and water cures aimed to foster a state of mind that could eliminate illness of all sorts.[27] Typical of the kind of ideas that developed significant local followings, Quimby's approach persisted until, years later, one of his followers, Mary Baker Eddy, recast them into a "science of Christ" as the cornerstone of her Christian Science.

The case of Sojourner Truth demonstrated even older roots. Born into slavery in Ulster County, New York, before the turn of the century to captured African parents, the woman who became known as "the Lybian Sibyl" found herself sold and resold several times. As Isabella Baumfree, she carried her slave name into a marriage that produced five children. Escaping with an infant daughter in 1826, she later became the first black woman to file suit successfully against a white man for custody of a young son. A few years later, she became the housekeeper of Robert Matthews, who declared himself a living prophet operating under various names: Robert Matthias, Jesus Matthias, Matthias the Prophet, and Joshua the Jew Minister. Later, she adopted the name "Sojourner Truth" and joined a socialist community at Northampton, Massachusetts, where she worked alongside a wide range of white radicals, including Henry Clapp, the future innovator of "bohemian" life in America, and future spiritualist Giles B. Stebbins. From there she became involved prominently with both the abolitionist and the women's rights movements and became the "near neighbor" of prominent spiritualist Warren B. Chase.[28]

Indeed, the informality of the new spiritualist movement also assimilated a small but vital network of freethinkers that had functioned for decades. The "infidels" at New York had organized episodically since Tom Paine's last days in the city early in the century, and the 1838 blasphemy trial of Abner

Kneeland had inspired a movement at Boston, during which Horace Seaver left the ministry. With Josiah Mendum, he took up the *Boston Investigator*, primarily to fight religious orthodoxy, opening its columns to all sorts of reform. For decades Ira B. Davis—no relation to Andrew Jackson Davis—had been "what the world called an infidel," who "not only discarded the doctrine of immortality, but was at a loss to believe even in the existence of a Great First Cause."[29] Such figures saw sectarian religion as innately conservative but naturally encouraged spiritualist criticisms when it came.

What drew many of them was the spiritualist offer of demonstrable evidence for what people in that civilization dearly wanted to believe: the survival of death by the individual, particularly their children and their existing human ties. Trial by committee reflected the civic mechanisms by which Americans then established a collective opinion. Any public meeting with such a purpose would appoint a committee to formulate resolutions or declare sentiments and return to the group with the results of their deliberations. After appropriate debate, discussion, and revision, these motions would be adopted as giving the sense of the body. The acceptance of such an approach as the means to prove spirit communication provided a common measure of truth for a distinctive movement. Certainly, a deeply rooted resentment and skepticism about scientists, clergymen, jurists, and community leaders fueled this leap.[30]

On the other hand, the spiritualist challenge to explain the rapping often backfired. In February 1851, Stephen Albro's Unitarians sponsored the Fox sisters before impaneled University of Buffalo officials, who produced a very skeptical report. By April the press openly discussed the fact that the girls made the raps by popping their toes, and Maggie seems to have early admitted as much to a woman at Arcadia. Massachusetts-born Reverend Charles Chauncey Burr replicated the rapping so successfully that he resumed his old title and took to the stage himself, joined in May by his brother Heman in Rochester's Corinthian Hall, where it had all started. When the path of the Burr brothers crossed with that of Maggie and Katie in Cleveland, Leah enlisted Joel Tiffany, a spiritualist attorney, to go after the Burrs for damages to the Fox family.[31] As the Buffalo group grew into a constituency that could support its own weekly *Age of Progress*, the question of manifestations remained hotly contested.

Many serious spiritualists mistrusted the showmanship. Charles Partridge, a preeminent leader of the movement in the city, thought manifestations revealed nothing about the truth of spiritualism, so he "never encouraged spiritual manifestations in promiscuous assemblies. He thought that if these influences are from Spirits at all (and he most firmly believed they were), it is reasonable to suppose that a Spirit might conjoin with Spirit or a human organization better where there is a great degree of harmony." One New York spiritualist acknowledged his "apprehensions that if manifestations were encouraged at the public Conference, impositions would be practiced by some professing to be mediums, and presented some reason for entertaining those apprehensions."[32]

These concerns shaped the most important feature of the movement, the séance, from the French term for a "seated session." On one level, the séance represented a compromise between private consultation and public performance, depending largely on the tastes and talent of the spirit medium. At its most benign, the séance adopted reassuring rituals and practices to make their ideas more acceptable to churchgoers. The Fox sisters began their sessions, disarmingly, with a prayer followed by a hymn, and Leah used the piano to add theatrical elements.[33]

The séance also required a new self-created profession that involved the seemingly technical standardization of the presentation of spiritualism. Taking place in the domestic sphere of the parlor, female mediums prevailed. Spiritualists explained this in terms of their purity of purpose and passive natures, which allowed for their self-sacrifice.[34] Still, in a society where a woman had few rights apart from those that her father, brother, husband, or son would permit, females undertook this process of creating and shaping mediumship. The most active and successful mediums developed a creative sensitivity to the audience sufficient to permit ongoing adjustments as to the proportions needed to keep the listeners and viewers themselves entranced. Regardless of any overt intentions, it challenged not only the underlying paternalism of orthodox Christianity but also the constitutional and legal standards that left women little better off than chattel.

Many found themselves controlled by Indian guides; a spirit from a long, unknown past before the arrival of the whites; or by the affable Ben Franklin, a fit conveyer of the unseen energies. A Mr. King became a regular, originating among the Shakers, who apparently called him "John King." Nearby Ohio mediums noted his presence in séances at Cleveland, Columbus, and Athens, and the name began appearing at séances from California to England, often with a Mrs. King, whose spirit acquired the first name "Katy" during the investigation of a haunted house.[35] By the 1870s, early theosophists noted the presence of the Kings among the spirits regularly in touch with them.

The venue proved sufficiently public to justify making claims but not so public as to open to serious scrutiny, so they often became arenas of even greater showmanship, albeit on a much more intimate scale. For some, the rappings evolved into modest movements of the table, which became greater until large tables jumped violently, often galloping across the room. At Williamsburg one man jumped onto such a table and rode on it. Olcott described "dramas . . . enacted by five or six mediums who were controlled to speak different languages, and to imitate the customs of different tribes and nations, showing the different stages of man's progression." Born to a working-class Scot family said to have "second sight," Daniel Dunglas Home found his demonstrations of levitation opened doors on both sides of the Atlantic. Jonathan Koons's "spirit rooms" outside Athens, Ohio—and those of Tippie and others—brought visitors into a spiritualist Disneyland, offering dramatic validation for the believers through a complex network of mechanisms and showpieces. Not surprisingly, spiritualism had a fascination for "the theatrical profession" and for musicians, such as George F. Root and the Hutchinson Family singers.[36]

In short order, the spirits began writing on walls, playing musical instruments, moving furniture, taking control of the writing hand to scrawl messages, and performing a wide range of functions. Spiritualism encountered and absorbed older techniques. St. Louis had a "snapping doctor" or "color doctor" operating out of a shanty and using what we would later call auras. A Waukegan medium wrote on her arm with the point of her finger, it remaining "for some minutes illegible, but soon it begins to appear in raised letters that can be both seen and felt distinctly."[37]

A rapid and eclectic growth became possible because no organization formed to establish and maintain standards. By August 1852, the movement had become strong enough regionally to sponsor a convention at Boston. It elected the Reverend Adin Ballou president, and prominent male mediums and female mediums took opposite sides of the platform. John Murray Spear, A. J. Davis, and LeRoy Sunderland and others discussed plans for organization by state and city. After some debate, though, they postponed the idea of a "Massachusetts Association of Spiritualists."[38]

The following year, Universalist renegade Spear tried for a more coherent model. A protégé of Hosea Ballou, Spear became the close colleague of Theodore Parker and William Lloyd Garrison, but, at nearly fifty, he broke with the church to speak on behalf of an "Association of Electrizers," led by the spirits of Benjamin Franklin, Thomas Jefferson, and others. In 1853 he took his followers to near Jamestown, New York, and founded Kiantone, a community of "New Communists." Later, inspired by the impact of the sewing machine on the lives of working people, especially women, Spear set on a "New Motive Power" at High Rock, overlooking Lynn, Massachusetts. With support from Alonzo

Newton, Caroline Hinckley, John Orvis, and Julia Branch, Spear projected a new secret society of spirit communicators and anticipated a mechanical "New Messiah" to free people from the drudgery of labor.[39]

## The Scale and Significance of the Movement

The explosion of interest in spiritualism continued through the 1850s, against the backdrop of sectional tensions and the impressively simultaneous eruption of the new Republican Party. In May 1854, editor Clark of the *Spiritual Telegraph* "knew of only a score or so of places open for spiritual lecturers in the whole country," but, in 1861, he had since personally spoken "in nearly fifteen hundred places in the Northern States between the Penobscot and the Mississippi." He had started as one of "only about a dozen" stumping the country to alert it to the reality of spirit communications, but, by the time of the Civil War, the movement had "about one thousand speakers, nearly four hundred of whom are in the field or ready to take it whenever their services were demanded." One of them, Warren B. Chase, gave three or four talks a week, some to crowded town halls, courthouses, theaters, and churches. In some places, this happened with remarkable speed. At Watertown, Wisconsin, the tiny audience of 20 in 1852 became hundreds over the following year, with as many active mediums as there had been listeners.[40]

In the decade leading up to the Civil War, the records counted 25 to 30 million Americans, noting that only about 1 in 7 adults—representing, with family members, perhaps 3 or 4 million—belonged to a church. By 1855 some spiritualists claimed 2 million believers, and the estimates continued up to 5 or 6 million by 1860. Simultaneously, spiritualist publications made more modest estimates by states, totaling 780,000 in 1857 and 1,537,000 by 1860.[41] Either set of numbers would have made spiritualism a significant force.

Of course, anyone who believed in the possibility of spirit communication to and from "the other side" might consider themselves (or be considered) a "spiritualist," and nobody who did not would want to do so. Then, too, no spiritualist believed each and every claim of spirit communications. William J. Young complained of having had "enough of the treachery of dark circles and tieings and untieings by the 'spirits' to make me chary of all possibly illusive statements that affix my attention, and can have no faith without demonstration, and can conceive of no crime equal in magnitude to intentional deception by professional mediums or their imitators." He personally insisted that he had never seen any manifestation that "cannot be proven to be not of mortal origins."⁴² Still, that did not prevent him from describing himself as a spiritualist or being seen as such by other spiritualists.

These varying categories of intensity of belief made American spiritualism something of a layered movement. Various *professionals* made a living—or part of a living—based on their promotion and publicizing claims of spiritualism that formed the defining core of the movement. The *Banner of Light,* with its heavy bias to the East Coast, regularly listed the schedules of 250 to 300 speakers, which lends some credence to Clark's claim that the movement nationally had 400 speakers on the road regularly to promote the movement, with at least as many more on the circuit. At least eighty-three communities in antebellum New York fielded one or more "missionaries."⁴³ In addition to the many full- and part-time lecturers, these professionals also included publishers and promoters of various sorts.

In addition, there also existed a large number of what we might call *semiprofessionals.* At one point, the *Cincinnati Daily Times* discussed the movement's expansion in that community. There had been "but few believers" in 1851 when the local Brotherhood of the Union began doing public work, but, in short order, Hardinge cited an observer who noted at least fifty-nine séances in a single night, with many more "embosomed in private limits" or held only occasionally. The paper counted 310 functioning mediums active in the city.⁴⁴ Extrapolating a proportion of even the lower figure for urban communities across the nonslaveholding states suggests thousands of functioning mediums and other leaders prominent in their communities with a regular clientele.

None of these professionals or semiprofessionals would have amounted to much were it not for the less vociferous *active experiencers,* or, to use the contemporary term, "investigators." Cincinnati needed several hundred mediums because of the demand generated by 1,200 participants. Chase's diary records three or four talks a week over many years, making possible a crude estimate of the audience those hundreds of speakers could reach.⁴⁵ If that record were relatively normal and he had an average audience of 50 persons—we know that many audiences were actually in the hundreds—he would have reached 150 persons a week, or more than 7,500 a year. If 800 of Clark's thousand speakers kept such a schedule, they would have reached a potential audience of well over 6 million listeners—or, more realistically, 500,000 attending bimonthly activities. Such tangible participation reflected some credulity, though surely at different levels.

Then, too, for every person regularly attending public or semipublic activities, there existed perhaps two or three *seekers.* These people might attend private séances or privately consulted mediums and clairvoyants. They attended meetings, participated in séances, or quietly consulted fortune tellers, but felt no need to testify as to the veracity of spiritualism in their lives. They dabbled in these activities in hopes of finding something to validate their hopes for a loved one who had passed over or was in an afterlife. Their level of participation provided a crude measure of the extent to which they neared the perception of the experiencers. "An intelligent gentleman" attending one New York gathering said that, although he had attended "300 to 400 circles, he did not feel fully competent to instruct the meeting."[46] On one level, they believed in the possibility, if not entirely the reality, of spirit communication and remained unwilling to make a regular public confession of their belief.

Some modest version of the numbers spiritualists claimed seemed within the reach of reason in the North and West. Certainly, like any movement, spiritualism remained continually in flux. Depending on various factors, individuals would flow in and out of the movement or from one layer to the next. Then, too, as external or internal conditions changed, the various layers of the movement fluctuated, moving at different rates.

However, the numbers suggested for the South ranged into nothing but wishful thinking and fiction. Certainly, a spiritualist in Bayonne would have responded to outrageous misrepresentations of their strength (or that of their neighbors in Newark). Then, too, the relative strength of the estimated numbers in Massachusetts and Connecticut had to be largely truthful. No such considerations restrained the absurd 1857 estimate of 57,000 spiritualists in the slaveholding South or the 100,000 said to be there three years later.

The fiction became essential to the aspirations of moderate spiritualists to represent themselves as a national rather than a sectional movement. "We think Spiritism is not at all confined to Boston, or the Yankees," declared the *Banner of Light*. "We hear of it in New Orleans, in Texas—in fact, there may be found believers in all the Southern States." Then, too, spiritualists could discuss the presence of cothinkers in Baltimore, Washington, Wheeling, Moundsville, Louisville, and St. Louis, just as they had in northern cities. The early movement in Baltimore combined figures such as the uncompromising abolitionist J. E. Snodgrass with the conservative defender of Southern standards "Colonel" Washington A. Danskin.[47]

John B. Wolff organized small homegrown circles at Wheeling and Moundsville. Most dramatically, though, Harris and Scott later brought their followers from Auburn, New York, to Mountain Cove in western Virginia. The group published the *Mountain Cove Journal* and a series of tracts, including a strange account, *The Spiritual Pilgrimage of Thomas Paine,* in which the unorthodox critic of Christianity undergoes a posthumous conversion.[48]

Certainly, individual spiritualists who ventured into the South found no great numbers. Judge John Edmonds headed south in late 1852 "for the benefit of my health," and Thomas L. Harris went to Charleston, South Carolina, with the intention of traveling west to Montgomery, Alabama, and New Orleans, Louisiana. Chase reported that, in 1860, he delivered 184 lectures in thirteen states, two of them—Maryland and Missouri—slaveholding. When Hardinge went there to hold public meetings, she faced threats in South Carolina and Tennessee. A later correspondent may well have been right in declaring, "There has never been, perhaps, a single Spiritualist lecturer, or even a liberal preacher in all East Tennessee." The legislatures of Alabama and South Carolina actually prohibited séances and other spiritualist gatherings in those states.[49]

There existed a smattering of other small clusters across the South. The railroad carried the movement south of St. Louis into Jefferson County, where Lewis C. Hootee, the organizer of the school system, and other professional men became spiritualists. Later in the decade, the movement clawed its way to some respectability in Mark Twain's Hannibal. Neighbors viewed Ohio-born schoolteacher John Russell Kelso eccentric for his hostility to tobacco and alcohol and his radical predispositions on almost every question. At the same time, Dr. James E. Spencer, a St. Louis practitioner of electrical medicine, transformed a small group from the Reformed Christian Church of DuPage County, Illinois, into vegetarian Angelites organized into a Harmonial Society, which established a colony a few miles north of Maysville, Arkansas, where it became a version of Virginia's Mountain Cove. In 1859 it established the Harmonial Healing Institute and published the monthly *Theocrat*.[50]

At Columbus, Georgia, Lewis Feuilleteau Wilson Andrews, the son of an Old School Presbyterian minister, converted to Universalism and published the *Georgia Citizen* as well as the *Christian Spiritualist* in 1860. So, too, in Nashville, Campbellite minister Jesse Babcock Ferguson became a Universalist and had talked as early as 1844 about breaking down the barrier between the surrounding material world and the "invisible world." He edited the *Christian Magazine* and served as the pastor of the congregation that Senator Andrew Johnson sometimes attended. Galveston supposedly had spiritualists as early as 1850 and had a weekly circle meeting by mid-1853, entranced by the fourteen-year-old Ada Bruno, the adopted daughter of a local dentist. Locals wrote the national spiritualist press from Galveston and from the steamer *Sarah* on the Mississippi River, near Vicksburg.[51] Neither Andrews nor Ferguson saw spiritualism as antagonistic to slavery.

Nevertheless, the ruling classes below the Mason-Dixon line almost always placed spiritualism alongside socialism, secularism, woman suffrage, diet reform, and other "isms," including abolitionism. "The necromantic, and other arts of divination, now rising into favor, have extended beyond the circles of mere mountebanks and deceivers," warned the *Southern Literary Messenger*, "and the diablerie of spiritualism has spread through the much wider and less manageable classes of arrant zealots, weak-minded enthusiasts, and gullible dreamers." Spirit communication represented merely the "new fantasy" sweeping "the North—which, like ancient Egypt, and Libya, is a land fruitful of monsters—of the access of the spiritual frenzy being not limited to merely mental insanity, but resulting in confirmed physical lunacy, and ultimately terminating in death."[52]

In this, as in other areas of southern history, New Orleans offered a remarkable exception. There, African, Caribbean, and French influences created a uniquely hospitable environment for spiritualist ideas and practices. The movement in someplace like New York or Paris would have understood how Charles Testut, the Franco-Caribbean Freemason and socialist, embraced the cause, but would have struggled with the mediumship of "an orphan girl between thirteen and fourteen years of age," who materialized medallions representing "the Virgin Mary." Although "the Catholic clergy have seemed to me the most hostile to the new faith," the girl was herself a Catholic, though she exercised her talents "indiscriminately in the presence of Catholics, Protestants, and those of no religion."[53]

In 1855 the new spiritualist circle subsumed an older "Association for the investigation of all questions coming under the head of Animal Magnetism, Psychology, etc." Members included several distinguished gentlemen, such as the Honorable Felix Garcia, president of the senate of Louisiana. When the circle's leader, Joseph Barthett, looked to the future, he established connections with an Afro-Creole, Dr. J. B. Valmour, and steamboat captain James Wingard to issue *Le Spiritualiste*, the pages of which were filled entirely with testimonies and commentaries by the departed. Barthett claimed about five thousand local believers, who awaited an upcoming tour by Hardinge "with a great deal of interest, and a good time is in store for all in the coming winter—the progressive ball will be put fairly in motion." In addition to Valmour, Constant Reynes became one of the most popular local mediums. The entire local movement benefited greatly from the influence of the Caribbean.[54] Surely, black mediumship in the South likely did not ease the suspicions of planters about spiritualism.

\* \* \*

The aspirations of the white men of wealth who owned and ruled antebellum America had carried the nation to where it found itself in midcentury. Orestes Augustus Brownson denounced spiritualism as a conscious attempt to harness religious faith for atheistic purposes by "seers and seeresses, enthusiasts and fanatics, socialists and communists, abolitionists and anti-hangmen, radicals and women's-rights men of both sexes." Southern proponents of slavery would take little comfort from a closer look at spiritualism generally.[55] As the ruling concerns hurled American civilization toward the abyss, other disembodied voices began speaking in often thunderous tones through the young, females, people of color, and the working poor, whose own voices were but faintly recorded for posterity.

The scale of spiritualism alone inspired great expectations for its impact on the wider society into which they hoped to inject a new moral sensibility. One adherent noted that "each nation on the globe has sooner or later developed its own form of religion." Theodore Parker pointed out that "in 1856, it seems more likely that spiritualism would become the religion of America than in 156 that Christianity would be the religion of the Roman Empire, or in 756 that Mohammedanism would be that of the Arabian population."[56]

However one looked at it, this did not bode well for the prospects of the established order.

## PART I

# The Soul of a Republic

The mystic chords of memory, stretching from every battle-field, and patriot grave, to every living heart and hearthstone, all over this broad land, will yet swell the chorus of the Union, when again touched, as surely they will be, by the better angels of our nature.

—*Abraham Lincoln, first Inaugural Address, March 4, 1861*

# 1
## Free Democrats to the Republicans
*Radical Spiritualists
and the Antislavery Insurgency*

In early 1854, while Warren B. Chase had been out on a speaking tour, news of the Kansas-Nebraska Bill reached his neighbors back at Ripon—what had been the socialist community of Ceresco, peopled largely by spiritualists. Befitting the location, as many women as men attended the gatherings that condemned the bipartisan opening of the West to slavery and declared themselves absolved of old party allegiances and in favor of an altogether new party. They suggested adopting "a cherished name with our foreign population of every nationality." Specifically, they proposed to call themselves "*Republicans, Republicains, Republikaner, Republicanos*—or by some modification of it in all European countries, and this name meets them here like an old friend." Horace Greeley helped sell the idea nationally. While later historians ascribed to the party "a thousand birthplaces" in the Northern protest meetings against the Nebraska Bill, those at Ripon detonated many of them.[1]

Although spiritualists later sought to identify their movement with 1848, the year of revolutionary upheavals in Europe and of the Free-Soil electoral protest led by former president Martin Van Buren against Southern domination of the Democratic Party, in reality spiritualism flowered as Van Buren and kindred politicians trailed back into their party, leaving the insurgency to the most stalwart radical elements who reorganized as the Free Democratic Party, in which spiritualists became ubiquitous. These political shifts brought antislavery political leaders to Washington, providing the movement with its first strong foothold there. By 1854–56 spiritualism grew with the rise of sectional tensions. Kansas became the catalyst for a major shift in Free Democratic circles as well as politics generally. Spiritualists, particularly in the upper Midwest, made vital decisions that marked the emergence and triumph of a new Republican Party.

## The Free Democrats

Nonslaveholding states had accepted the national dominance of the Democratic Party for a generation, and Southern slavery remained the party's preoccupation. Spiritualism, even at its least political and most commercial, tended to validate the judgments of the insurgents. The Vermont or Wisconsin farmer suspicious of slavery and its influence experienced a kind of feedback loop, encouraging an examination of those suspicions that transformed them into an increasing hostility. Doing so among the increasingly like-minded fostered concerted action. Spiritualist mediumship, in general, translated the abstract ideals into concrete practice.

More important, the spiritualists provided a sizable number of those whose break with the politics of the past had become permanent. As Van Buren and his followers went back to the Democrats, thousands from Vermont to Ohio reorganized as Independent Democrats or Free Democrats.[2] This happened simultaneously with the explosive growth of spiritualism and in those areas that experienced the most explosive growth of spiritualism at the same time.

The abolitionist *National Era* reported grassroots meetings and conventions across New England and as far as Ohio, but found it "impossible to publish the proceedings of all the Independent Democratic meetings which are sent to us." The 1849 Massachusetts state convention consisted of what the *Spirit of the Age* called "the elements of the former Workingmen's party." It reflected the assumption that "no social injury could result to the white race from the oppression and servitude of the black." Urging "universal reform," it warned that any party "professing to represent the interests of Labor, which leagues itself with an aristocracy, enslaving the colored laborer at home, as a means of wealth, and preaching democracy abroad as a means of power, degrades Labor everywhere." It also warned of an "alliance between the champions of Southern free Labor and certain conservative interests of the North, as for instance that of manufacturing capital." They insisted that "a party of consistent progress and reform must grow up, representing the religious hope and the best wisdom of the people of all sections." "Labor is universally dishonored," it declared, adding that "the first step for its elevation must be the limitation and extinction of Slavery."[3]

As some of the more privileged of the antislavery radicals who had clung to the insurgency—men such as Samuel Gridley Howe, Thomas Wentworth Higginson, and George Frisbie Hoar—clung to the Free Democrats, they found themselves regularly in the company of plebeian militants. The *Boston Herald* scoffed that they remained a relatively isolated third party, discussing its problems as those of "a workingmen's party." "If the workingmen had sufficient money and leisure, we should counsel the formation of a workingmen's party, to exist, at least, until labor received an equal attention with capital at the hands of our Legislators." Internal factionalism "does more to keep any proper industrial reform out of our Legislative arena, than all other causes." "Our mechanics and working men have too long trusted others. They must now depend upon themselves."[4] What the Democratic press meant by this, of course, was that workers should assert their independence by ignoring the more radical of their number and supporting the party.

Philadelphia Free Democrats called all those opposed to the Whig and Democratic Parties to meet at the courthouse on June 28. George Lippard spoke, and much of the meeting's leadership came from veterans of those cooperative ventures of his Brotherhood of the Union. William B. Thomas presided, with other speeches by August H. Duganne, Charles Goepp, William J. Mullen, and John Sheddon. A well-known spiritualist, Sheddon had been in the Chartist movement before immigrating, where he became an "able and powerful advocate" of land reform. Listeners described his stock speech for the Free Democrats as "beyond description," one "not soon to be forgotten by the workingmen."[5]

Spiritualists made implicit claims to Lippard himself, and he certainly never disabused them of it publicly. He had sought out the Fox sisters when he got to Rochester and "almost fainted away" when he received "three blows, from an unseen hand, upon his shoulder." He left credulous of spirit communication, and his work regularly showed the influence of spiritualist ideas. However, Lippard had a Gothic penchant for old-fashioned Christianity, enjoying a long friendship with trenchant critic of spiritualism Charles Chauncey Burr. In his declining illness, Lippard responded to two visiting spiritualists by referring to the small bust of Christ on the mantel: "That's the spirit I believe in."[6] Nevertheless, his close identification with the movement reflected his hostility to orthodoxy.

The prominence of spiritualists among the Free Democrats became even more pronounced in the West. Spiritualists and Free Democrats such as Joshua R. Giddings and John C. Vaughan turned up at midwestern gatherings of peace organizations and antislavery societies. Early on, Oliver Johnson, the editor of the *Anti Slavery Bugle* at Salem, Ohio, embraced spirit communications in principle. Joel Tiffany, who had defended the Fox sisters against the Burrs, had come to Cleveland to assist Giddings at the *True Democrat*. Then, too, the antislavery press reprinted Fourierist materials and cited the "striking similarity in the policy of the Monopolist classes the world over." Ohio Free Democrats also adopted radical land measures because "the use of the soil is as sacred as their right to life itself."[7]

The Free Democrats veered into even more radical directions in Wisconsin and Michigan. The politically more conservative judge John W. Edmonds found his 1854 "tour thro' the West" an eye-opener. His discussions with people there convinced him that, as he later wrote Abraham Lincoln, "the Anti Slavery sentiment would yet control the election of President."[8]

Chase, who had earlier taken the demand for woman suffrage into the territorial constitutional convention, helped rally those Wisconsin insurgents unwilling to follow the politicians back into the Democratic Party. Illegitimate and raised in a Yankee orphanage, Chase pursued the demons of success into a fine middle-class respectability, but remained the consummate outsider, the self-described "Lone One." Even as he organized a socialist community at Ceresco, he became prominent in state politics, running for governor in 1849 as a Free Democrat. Although the advent of spiritualism in the region found him middle-aged, he took to the road to campaign on its behalf. The two endeavors kept him on the road so continually that he once carried his baggage five miles through the rain and mud to Nemah. "If this was not a tramp life," he recalled, "I do not know what could be."[9] Hundreds had similar experiences.

The figure of Chase also loomed larger as the National Industrial Congress began holding its annual gatherings of social radicals from across the country in the Midwest. What was left of Cincinnati's Spiritual Brotherhood hosted the meeting of 1849, which called for "the Brotherhood of the Race" before cholera struck the city and scattered the event. The next year, Chase called to order the 1850 session at Chicago. "All truth whether social, religious, political, physiological, and psychological constitutes unity," it declared, "and no fragmentary reform can be carried out without going hand in hand with all other reforms." It called for women's equality and explicitly denounced slavery.[10] When the assembly returned east, gathering at Albany in 1851, the first black delegate requested and gained admission. The emergence of a spiritualist movement coincided with the more coherent and unified social critique of antebellum reformers focused on slavery.

In May 1852, for example, the Milwaukee Land Reform Association, "composed of 300 members," elected delegates to the upcoming National Industrial Congress scheduled for Washington, D.C. Few doing so back east may have been officeholders or men of influence, but the Wisconsin gathering included Congressman Charles Durkee, as well as the transplanted Henry D. Barron, then editing the *Waukesha Democrat*. When the National Industrial Congress gathered that summer in Washington, Congressman Durkee took the chair and presided.[11]

On August 10, roughly two thousand Free Democrats assembled at Pittsburgh's Masonic Hall. Senator Henry Wilson presided, and the list of vice presidents included a number of prominent participants in the spiritualist movement, including Chase, Sheddon, Gerrit Smith, Giddings, J. E. Snodgrass, and Frederick Douglass. They selected Senator John P. Hale and Congressman George W. Julian to run for president and vice president. However, the remarkable convention cast three ballots to nominate Smith for president and, as vice presidential candidates, three each for abolitionist land reformers James H. Collins and George Henry Evans.[12]

Most important, the Free Democrats sustained their party beyond the presidential campaign. As speakers such as Chase took to the road as full-time missionaries for the spiritualist movement, they linked it to radical antislavery politics. Events in the state capital drew Chase back to Madison in January 1853, where he provided some assistance to the antislavery forces, became an officer of the Wisconsin State Agricultural Society, and discussed spiritualism with the governor. At the height of the campaign, he reported a single spiritualist in an audience of twenty. Returning the next July, he found as many active mediums out of an audience of hundreds. He reported that they were bathing one man "with the electro-magnetic fluid," which had cured him of his "violent convulsions."[13]

Particularly in Wisconsin, the agitation proved very productive. After one tour, Chase stopped to visit Henry D. Barron, then living at Waukesha. Too, such national figures such as Cora L. V. Scott toured the state, along with her mother. By 1854 at least some of the Free Democrats and their allies in the Wisconsin Legislature discussed sending socialist Chase to the U.S. Senate, but he had no interest in leaving his work for spiritualism at that point. Instead, the legislature chose Durkee, also a spiritualist, leaving Chase free to tour the East Coast.[14]

## New York City

New York City illustrates the parallel development and convergence of spiritualism and antislavery politics. Despite its studied homespun simplicity—or, more likely, partly because of it—spiritualism gained a broad following in the metropolis. "What," wondered the stupefied diarist George Templeton Strong, "would I have said six years ago to anybody who predicted that before the enlightened nineteenth century was ended hundreds of thousands of people in this country would believe themselves able to communicate daily with the ghosts of their grandfathers?"[15] With an unexpected alacrity, insights promoted as humble, unlearned, and rural in their origins also captivated Strong's friends and neighbors in the most cosmopolitan and sophisticated center of American civilization.

Some in New York had been interested in earlier versions of spirit communication. By 1849 the *Univercoelum and Spiritual Philosopher* came into the orbit of Davis's admirers. Having absorbed the *Christian Rationalist* and, later, the *Harbinger* of the Fourierists, the paper published prominent writers from Ralph Waldo Emerson to George Lippard, but always remained more concerned with the socialism of Fourier than the trances of Davis. In 1849, before his death, John P. Cornell, the Cincinnati radical who owned the controlling interest, transferred it to the *Christian Socialist,* and it continued as the *Spirit of the Age.*

Some New Yorkers readily welcomed the Fox sisters in 1850. Families of publishers such as the phrenologists Lorenzo N. Fowler and New Hampshire–born Horace Greeley had also lost children. Then approaching forty, Greeley had spent half of his life in New York City after a difficult and hardworking youth and become the printers' printer. Grating against the irrationality of the world he found there, he became naturally drawn to ideas that offered some hopes for a rational human order, which had earlier interested Eliab W. Capron, Barron, and others in Fourierism.[16]

The proslavery and socially reactionary Democratic *New York Herald* openly scoffed at spiritualists as "a singular collection of dupes and fanatics, resembling more a congregation of lunatics than a company of rational creatures." Yet on the Fox sisters' first visit, Captain Isaiah Rynders took the girls under his wing to introduce them to the leading lights in that Democratic community. A rabid white supremacist, founder of the Empire Club, and participant in overseas expansionist ventures, Rynders also headed an underworld organization of "sluggers" for Tammany Hall who kept its critics intimidated.[17]

On the day the Fox sisters arrived in the city, they gave a persuasive demonstration of their powers at a private home. Their audience included historian George Bancroft and novelist James Fenimore Cooper, as well as poets William Cullen Bryant and Nathaniel P. Willis. Reporting for the *Tribune* was George Ripley, another key Fourierist leader. Greeley encouraged their plans to give public sittings and urged Leah to charge not one dollar a sitting but five dollars, to "keep the rabble away." Supporters were so eager to keep them in the city that Judge John W. Edmonds offered to pay for the education of Maggie and Katie. Broadway theaters cranked out a new song, "The Rochester Rappings at Barnum Hotel." On September 30, when the Fox girls left the city, various groups determined to continue the meetings and experimentation.

A "New York Circle" took shape on November 14, only a year after the movement's Rochester debut. In addition to those mentioned, Andrew J. Davis's old friend Stephen B. Brittan became increasingly interested in establishing a paper for the movement. He started the *Spiritual Age* with W. S. Courney in 1857, but it bounced from shop to shop before merging into A. E. Newton's *New England Spiritualist* and becoming the *Spiritual Eclectic,* which was published as late as 1860.

In the end, Brittan's joint publishing venture with wealthy New York match manufacturer Charles Partridge bore fruit. Rubber manufacturer Horace H. Day—who had yet to lose his legal battle with Charles Goodyear—worked with Judge Edmonds to make spiritualism acceptable to their peers. Edmonds had observed the Fox sisters upstate and privately attended séances at the home of Leah Fish as "an inquirer and by no means a believer," before declaring himself a proponent, determined to make it more respectable and acceptable to other professionals.[18]

Over the next few years, circles proliferated in the city. Some favored the model of the church congregation under a single pastor, such as Thomas Lake Harris, then passing through the city. Reportedly, "a large body of the congregation who call themselves Christian Spiritualists, being better pleased with Mr. Harris than any of their other speakers, have desired for some time to make him their regular minister." Certainly, though, even the self-defined Christians in the movement found it necessary that the faith be "revised and corrected."[19] Many spiritualists, however, seemed to prefer the structure of a lyceum, providing a platform to diverse speakers.

The Fox sisters returned in the winter of 1851–52 to find a movement that had largely superseded them. Leah leased a brownstone at 78 West Twenty-Sixth Street near Madison Square, and they resumed afternoon and night demonstrations. Maggie had grown to womanhood and taken up with a handsome fellow celebrity, Arctic explorer Dr. Elisha Kent Kane. Despite their own continued ecumenical approach to the spirit world, the reactionary Rynders had faded from the scene, having become less concerned about communications with spirits than translating as many Spaniards and Cubans as possible into that state.

The local spiritualists and their associates became consistently involved with the Free Democrats. Gerrit Smith, Frederick Douglass, and others participated in the state convention, along with William Lloyd Garrison and Ernestine Rose. The party ran land reformer David Marsh for governor of the almshouse and spiritualist Horace Dresser for judge of the supreme court. Their local Free Democratic League repeatedly tried to coalesce a national organization. All sorts of veteran radicals associated with the spiritualists pitched into this effort, including health reformer Russell T. Trall.[20]

The Free Democratic League in town participated alongside the local Brotherhood of the Union in a coalition with émigré revolutionaries around the Universal Democratic Republicans of English Garibaldian and spiritualist sympathizer Hugh Forbes. The ideas penetrated the "bohemian" circles of hard-bitten newspaper writers such as Mary Sargeant Neal Gove Nichols, who had interviewed Edgar Allan Poe before marrying Thomas L. Nichols, or Marie Stevens Case Howland, a mill hand turned schoolteacher living at Modern Times. Emma Hardinge and other spiritualists resided there, under the general take-it-or-leave-it theoretical leadership of Stephen Pearl Andrews, Josiah Warren, and Edward N. Kellogg, articulating their versions of socialism, anarchism, and greenbackism. Through radical circles, spiritualism enticed the newly transplanted bohemian culture of New York—Henry Clapp, Edward F. Underhill, Fitz-James O'Brien, George S. McWatters, and other friends of Walt Whitman—who could alternately write scathing exposés of spiritualism and attend séances themselves. Clapp went so far as to attend and speak at the 1858 Free Convention at Rutland.[21]

Another important group coalesced around the *Spiritual Telegraph,* another at Lamartine Hall under Dresser, with more groups popping up in Brooklyn, Williamsburg, and Greenpoint, as well as across the river in Jersey City. George Wilkes's *New York Police Gazette* estimated a February 1855 citywide mass meeting in the Broadway Tabernacle as having brought out "over five thousand persons" and estimated "not less than *forty thousand Spiritualists* in this city." The number of mediums in the city had reached 55 by 1855 and 231 by 1859. By then Brooklyn alone had fifty circles.[22]

The more radical and bohemian figures tended to attend what became the largest and most diverse of the spiritualist platforms in the city. It began with regular Sunday meetings at Stuyvesant Institute, then "Hope Chapel," but soon settled at Dodworth Hall. Allen Dodworth, a musician with the Philharmonic, opened his place as a dance studio, at 806 Broadway, just north of the Grace Street Church. On October 15, 1853, Harris gave the inaugural talk there, after which Judge Edmonds declared himself "ready to commence his public labors in this city, where he had never yet attempted to lecture on the subject under consideration." The spiritualists continued to meet there "every Tuesday evening, till further notice." Andrew J. Davis gave regular lectures there, and participants included Sarah Helen Whitman, the former fiancée of Edgar Allan Poe. It drew the most radical figures in the city, including Joshua King Ingalls, Lewis Masquerier, and other leaders of the working-class National Reform Association. There, too, Major George Washington Raines of the U.S. Army reported the positive "result of a scientific investigation of spiritual phenomena."[23]

A few years later, former ministers Russell P. Ambler and Harris caused a "disturbance" that split the Dodworth gatherings. The former had become something of a force in the movement. With a printer named Apollos Munn, he had launched the *Spirit Messenger* in 1850 and kept it going into 1853, when it was reorganized as the *Journal of Progress* and then the *Reformer,* itself absorbed by the *Messenger of Light.*

Harris's self-described "Christian spiritualists" went off to hold meetings of their own at Academy Hall, while Ambler's remained at Dodworth's. Then, too, the old disagreements among Universalists over whether universal salvation required the soul's active self-development after death resurfaced among the spiritualists. Over the coming year, those who remained would regularly host Warren B. Chase and other prominent Republicans. By 1857 Harris launched the *Herald of Light,* which he left in 1859 to go to London, the paper limping on into the summer of 1861.[24]

These successes at New York City, in turn, proved to be a springboard for the spiritualist initiatives at Washington, D.C., and their plans to influence national policies.

## The Spirits in the Councils of the Nation

Katie Fox toured earlier to the national capital, and in 1853 she and Maggie took up residence in a lodging house on F Street. At various points, Harris, Ambler, and French of Pittsburgh spoke there as well. As in New York, some surprisingly conservative figures participated, such as General Charles C. Hamilton and General Waddy Thompson, former senator from South Carolina, proponent of Seminole removal, and an ambassador to Mexico.[25]

By the winter of 1853–54, the chief statistician for the U.S. Postal Service hosted gatherings in his home. The *Spiritual Telegraph* thought Cranston Laurie "among the most interesting mediums" in the city. His father, the Reverend James Laurie, a Scotsman, ministered to the local Presbyterians before his demise. At one point, he reported the death of one of his father's friends in Glasgow before news had arrived. Laurie already had two daughters "in the spheres."[26]

Others took up the cause at Washington as well. In May 1853, New Hampshire–born Dr. Charles Hartwell Cragin turned to spiritualism after his wife's death. Cragin had worked at Richmond, Virginia, and gone to California during the Gold Rush before settling in the capital and taking on various local offices, including postmaster. Veteran newspaperman and old-time union printer Augustus F. Cunningham took up spiritualism after having been a radical freethinker and Owenite. He went on to publish the *Old Dominion* at Portsmouth, Virginia, with Theophilus Fisk.[27]

The size of the gatherings in Washington expanded with sectional tensions. In December 1853, "several ladies and gentlemen" hosted a Philadelphia medium, who channeled various spirits, including "a Camanche Indian chief" and a prospector who drank himself to death in California, whose name was subsequently identified. Early in the new year, Capron visited from New York, and the spirit of Ben Franklin joined them, perhaps in deference to the presence of Congressman Giddings and a reporter from the U.S. Senate.[28] By this time, Giddings and other antislavery congressmen participated, while the Waddy Thompsons had gone by the board.

Prominent political figures and government officials came to the fore. Yankee-born upstate New York congressman Augustus Porter Hascall—formerly one of the leading lights of the Antimasonic Party—had been among the movement's earliest political allies. Senator Nathaniel P. Tallmadge arrived among these Washington spiritualists from Wisconsin. The New York native had risen politically there before being appointed governor of Wisconsin Territory, from which he returned in 1853 a confirmed spiritualist in a group that included Lewis C. Hootee, briefly in the capital from Missouri; Henry Clay Preuss, the author of *Fashions and Follies of Washington Life;* and a "physician well known here" who began holding circles in his office. U.S. Supreme Court justice John McLean reportedly became convinced by early summer, as had the widow of General Alexander Macomb Jr. and Chief Justice Joseph Williams of the Iowa Supreme Court. John Russell Bartlett, "the well-known Mexican Boundary Commissioner," embraced the manifestations. After one lecture, Colonel Thomas Jefferson Whipple of New Hampshire declared it had been "superior, as a rhetorical effort, to any speech which has been made in Congress on the Nebraska bill." Also testifying as to the wonders of spiritualism was Captain Abner Doubleday of the U.S. Army, then in Washington.[29]

The tensions of that spring seem to have driven many more people to the spirits. One defined the core of the movement as the "probably upwards of three hundred families in Washington who are experiencing in their midst these remarkable manifestations." A new "Washington Conference" leased the Temperance Hall on E Street near Ninth and began holding larger gatherings, including "a crowded one" in mid-April. These events coincided roughly with the first reports from the Crimean War.[30]

On two nights in January 1854, Laurie's daughter Isabel set the mood, banging out martial tunes on the piano, inspiring Napoléon Bonaparte to take possession of her father. "I see flying squadrons," he said, "banners trailing in the dust, riderless horses; carnage, slaughter, and death. Blood flows like torrents, and the destroying sword flashes like the lightening of the Almighty God. The rattling drum and the soul-stirring trumpets call the rally; but there is no use—no rally—they fly!" As government began working through the future of slavery in the western territories, cabinet officials and civil servants listened to the Napoleonic imaginings, rather sickly premonitions of American disaster. Elsewhere, New York spiritualists fretted over the image of "military companies parading the streets," with their young men "marching in rank and file, preparing for the coming future." Others described "images of battle, pictures of forming squadrons, chivalrous combat, and gallant assault."[31] Events had begun to smudge the medium with the message.

All this interest among those with government connections fueled hopes for a series of spiritualist petitions to Congress. The petition was the brainchild of the grandly named Society for the Diffusion of Spiritual Knowledge. John Henry Watson Toohey and Hardinge launched its paper, the *Christian Spiritualist*. It soon involved such figures as radical industrialist Howard H. Day and John

Shoebridge Williams, prominent earlier at Springfield, Illinois, among other places.

Most famously, the group petitioned the first session of the Thirty-Third U.S. Congress, while Congressman Elihu B. Washburne of Illinois submitted such a memorial in February 1854, and New York's Thomas T. Flagler presented a broader petition. This moved Tallmadge, Edmonds, and others focused on organizing a memorial calling "for the appointment of a Scientific Commission to which this subject shall be referred, and for such an appropriation as shall enable the Commissioners to prosecute their inquiries to a successful termination." Although collected on very short notice, the petition aptly reflected the sectional nature of interest in spiritualism. New York, Ohio, and Massachusetts provided more than 53 percent, with some impressive numbers from specific places across the North. In contrast, the southern states on the Atlantic Coast—Virginia, the Carolinas, Georgia, and Florida—accounted for only twenty-two names, with Mississippi and Alabama adding another twenty-eight. In late March 1854, Tallmadge met with Senator James A. Shields, who gave Tallmadge the impression that he favored the measure and would introduce the memorial.[32] In part, the spiritualists sought an official vindication for their "proofs" and for the resulting claims about the scale of their movement.

On April 17, Shields took the floor to present the memorial, speaking of "an occult force . . . in direct opposition to the acknowledged laws of matter and transcending the accredited powers of the human mind." Some senators laughed aloud, and laughter punctuated the reading of the memorial. Upon finishing, Shields himself ridiculed the proposal, referring to Rosicrucian spirit communications and Cagliostro, and the Senate duly tabled the matter. Proponents denounced the Senate's insult to the twelve thousand signatories to the petition, and Tallmadge wrote a letter to the local press, claiming, in effect, that Shields had misled him. Shields responded on April 19, Tallmadge sent another rejoinder on April 20, and Tallmadge reported to the Washington Conference the next day. Capron reminded the government that "the carpenters and fishermen of the world are the ones to investigate new truths and make Senates and Crowns believe and respect them. It is in vain to look for the reception or respect of new truths by men in high places."[33]

The spiritualists claimed that they had been circulating the petition "in every part of the Union" for two weeks, but the results reflected sectional realities. New York's *Spiritual Telegraph* described its popularity among "great numbers of all classes—not excepting our merchants, officers of insurance companies, bank directors, the masters of art, science, and law, as well as the teachers of theology and religion," and the state provided nearly a third of the nearly twelve thousand signatures.[34]

The problem owed as much to the context in which the Senate heard the petition as to its content. Washburne and Flagler—Whigs straining toward a break with the party in favor of what would become the Republican Party—treated the subject respectfully, while Shields, a Democrat, used it to goad the opposition after recent developments. The rubbishing of the memorial alongside the passage of the Kansas-Nebraska Bill created the convergence with the Republican Party, even though spiritualist organization remained very amorphous. Earlier, various local or regional attempts, such as Cincinnati's True Brotherhood, sought to harness the model of masculine fraternalism into a useful shelter for occult knowledge.[35] Perhaps the gendered nature of mediumship precluded any such simple fraternal order.

By June Washington saw an orthodox counteroffensive. A Methodist minister—probably one Reverend Mr. Reese from the church on Ninth Street, challenged them, and the Reverend John Bovee Dods began suggesting that the mediums, though sincere, were encountering not spirits but their own imaginations.[36] Still, people looking for answers in Washington—or anywhere else in the country—wanted what the mediums offered, and their need reached beyond reason.

The absence of organization proved more telling, as vastly larger numbers came to identify themselves as spiritualists. Horace Greeley and his *New York Tribune* began taking an increasingly skeptical account of the movement, particularly after the involvement of many spiritualists in the so-called free-love scandal of 1855 in New York City. Many, such as Pascal B. Randolph—after formulating his version of Rosicrucianism—realized that the lack of organization left the movement forced to accept whatever wild claims might be made by any self-described medium. Frustrated, Randolph sought to disassociate himself from the movement, though he later attended the Utica convention and reversed himself to suggest that the movement's members should not break ranks. He urged organization "for mutual protection—from the tricks of impostors, and whitened sepulchers having nothing of Spiritualism, except the stolen name—things beautiful without, but foul within."[37]

The Society for the Diffusion of Spiritual Knowledge formed officially in June. With Tallmadge presiding, other officers included Judge Edmonds, General Edward Fitch Bullard, industrialist Horace H. Day, Gilbert Sweet, and George T. Dexter. Some of the signers certainly came from beyond New York City, but signatories such as Laurie from Washington and Missourians

Peter E. Bland and A. Miltenberger could have no real hand in the leadership of such a group. Then, too, prominent Fourierists Chase and Benjamin Urner also lived at a distance and likely owed their inclusion less to their radicalism than their prominence as, respectively, a Wisconsin politician and a Cincinnati insurance man.[38]

Editors of the *Spiritual Telegraph* were little short of furious. The new society claimed to be inclusive and national, they complained, but "we had no knowledge of the recent meeting until its deliberations were over, and the organization formed." Moreover, although the group sent reports on the organization to the *Herald*, the *Evening Post,* and other papers, it provided the *Spiritual Telegraph* with "no reliable information."[39]

The old land reformer Ingalls sketched the shortcomings very succinctly. "Notwithstanding its claim to nationality," he noted, "there was no call for the organization circulated among the Spiritualists even of New York city," and nine of the twelve trustees were from the city. At the heart, though, he detected a "Titlomania" essential to the society's character. Tallmadge "owes his election, not to the intrinsic virtue of the man, but to the circumstance of his having filled certain political offices." Ingalls imagined Chase's reaction "when he learns that the accident of his once being in the senate of his adopted State has been elevated to a Vice-Presidency of this national society." Ingalls described two kinds of organization, a union growing from "a spontaneous concert of action" and an order centered on one mind, such as the Jesuits of Ignatius Loyola.[40] Such a concert of action had yet to inspire a union.

Some substantive organization appeared within very specific constituencies. John Murray Spear, John Orvis, John Allen, Ellen Lazarus, Stephen Pearl Andrews, and other veterans of the Fourierist movement sought to translate the drive for fraternalism into the oddly named ultrafeminist Order of Patriarchs and, toward the close of the decade, the Sacred Order of Unionists. Spear's attempt to sexualize the machinery of the Industrial Revolution and creating a perpetual motion machine alienated many, likely helping inspire Randolph to contemplate sex magic. Before this, in 1855, he went to London, representing Spear's group in Robert Owen's World Convention.[41]

## The Materialization of the Republicans

On May 25, only a few weeks after Shields and other Democrats mocked the spiritualist petition, they forced the Kansas-Nebraska Act through the Senate. The bill authorized a territorial reorganization of these places with an eye toward statehood. In the process, it accepted the Democratic argument for "popular sovereignty," whereby settlers in those territories would themselves have the option of whether to establish the legal enslavement of Africans and their descendants. The doctrine represented a Northern Democratic attempt to compromise the increasing insistence of the Southern wing of their party that slavery could not be restricted anywhere. The legislation, in effect, dissolved older agreements that slavery would not be permitted in the territories above the Missouri Compromise line. Leading critics of the "Nebraska Bill" included senators with ties to spiritualism themselves or through their families—Hannibal Hamlin, William H. Seward, Charles Sumner, Benjamin F. Wade, and Isaac P. Walker.[42]

The decision effectively ended a generation of faith in Democratic reformism. The news particularly horrified the residents of the former Wisconsin phalanx at Ceresco, recently renamed Ripon. The men and women in these meetings replicated the bipartisan policies on slavery in the territories, absolved them of old allegiances to the Democrats and Whigs, and urged formation of a new party with "a cherished name with our foreign population of every nationality."

Republican state organizations followed quickly in Michigan, a state that long vied with Wisconsin for the honor of starting the new party. The 1854 state platform embraced the Free Democratic leaders, while opening the door to antislavery Whigs and others. It represented particularly the work of Vermont-born Jacob Merritt Howard, a former Whig congressman and a spiritualist.[43] Spiritualism provided the third-party insurgency that became the Republican Party, a deeper open-ended theology of "free labor," and a deep faith in the national rebirth in a second American Revolution.

Actual participation in the free-state movement to Kansas followed. Edward Daniels led several hundred armed men from the Ripon area into Iowa, on their way to the territory. A Boston-born geologist and an Oberlin graduate, Daniels had taught school at the Fourierist community and served briefly as Wisconsin's first state geologist before taking on his duties with the Kansas Aid Society. When the group crossed the border from Iowa, U.S. dragoons disarmed them. Another geologist, spiritualist lecturer William Denton, chose to test the psychometric abilities of his sister Annie with a piece of limestone from the bluffs at Quindaro, the multiracial Kansas settlement that had provided radicals a vital point of entry into the territory.[44]

Yet the spiritualists entering Kansas lent the contested territory a good deal of its radicalism. John Tippie—of spirit-room fame back in Ohio—turned up in Lynn County, Kansas. When the antislavery forces prevailed and Kansas moved toward statehood, Justice Williams of Iowa gained an appointment to the territorial supreme court in Kansas. Refugees of the original Brotherhood of the Union at Cincinnati turned up in Kansas because the flash flood on the Ohio River in 1849 washed away their community at Utopia. Augustus and John Otis Wattles had nothing to hold them when Congress opened Kansas to the possibility of slavery. At different times, the spirits told William Coggeshall the same thing they had Augustus Wattles, both being informed by the spirits that their brothers had died while on California trips. Coggeshall described John O. Wattles as "a spontaneous clairvoyant."[45]

The shadow of the Kansas troubles fell darkly across some spiritualists in the South, contributing to a general intellectual crisis. While still admiring his Democratic father, John Russell Kelso turned from the old party and never went back. By the 1860 election, when the local Southern Rights faction of the Democratic Party threatened to sweep the district, Kelso attended their meeting and waited until "the last secession harangue" before introducing Unionist resolutions condemning the conduct of state officials as treasonable. As the crowd fell into a dangerous stunned silence, an eight-year-old boy hurried forward, took his teacher's hand, and led him to safety.[46] Thereafter known to local Unionists, Kelso provided a vital organizing center to Unionists in southwestern Missouri.

By the fall of 1856, the new party fielded John C. Frémont as its presidential candidate. Its vote not only outstripped the Free Democrats of four years before but even surpassed the old Free-Soilers. *Nichols Monthly* noted, nervously, "Never has a vote for president been so sectional."[47]

Among the spiritualists, local gatherings gave rise to state conventions, which began to assume a regional character. As these turnouts grew larger, they became increasingly political. A Vermont body, for example, passed resolutions on temperance, diet, tobacco and dress reform, educational reform, parental reform, and "the emancipation of women from all legal and social disabilities—that she may fulfill the noblest mission, and be fitted to become the mother of noble offspring, as she cannot while a menial or a slave." In addition to "universal peace," it declared for "the abolition of all slavery—whether chattel, civil, mental or spiritual—because freedom is the birth-right of man, and the indispensable condition of his best development."[48]

Spiritualists also participated in related gatherings of abolitionists, Progressive Friends, and others. Chase recalled addressing a three-day gathering of "near two thousand" at Berlin Heights, hosted by the free-love socialists and drawing "many skeptics, and mostly Spiritualists, from all the region round about." They met with "no chairman, no business committee, no resolutions" and had "no signs of rowdyism, or prejudice, or even of bad behavior on the grounds." Frank and Cora Barry "sang beautiful words beautifully, and harmony, peace and love prevailed till the grounds were deserted."[49]

The spiritualists called what became a mass, broadly based "Free Convention" gathered at Rutland, Vermont, in June 1858. When it became known that Andrew Jackson Davis would be there, the railroad arranged for special trains to help bring an audience that reached three thousand participants. On the first day, Davis showed up, wearing a black skullcap and accompanied by an entourage of a half-dozen female mediums.[50] Having the status of something like a rock star, he moved through a virtual who's who of antebellum social reform.

Nationally, the broadly discussed 1858 "Free Convention" at Rutland inspired further attempts to assemble such numbers but failed. September saw an attempt to hold a more politicized gathering at Utica and another at Worcester, which met with "failure—not more than a dozen persons being present at one time" through the first day. Most notably, Mrs. Branch took the floor again, scandalizing reporters with her suggestion that the state declare all children legitimate. After another attempt at St. James Hall at Buffalo, a "fifth session" took place at Utica on September 16–18. This was to be "a Free Convention" as "the mouthpiece of Human Liberty—the platform whence issue the mandates of unlimited Progress. Spiritualists, Materialists, Jews, Christians, Reformers—all, east, west, north, south—will hereby consider themselves cordially invited." The efforts staggered on into a fifth session at Utica in September 1859, with a three-day meeting at Magnetic Springs, Kiantone in Chautauqua County, as well as a meeting at Ellensville that Frederick Douglass attended.[51] In part, of course, the constituencies to which these meetings appealed remained closely focused on the emerging Republican coalitions.

The push for national organization deepened. A local convention at Plymouth in September 1859 projected a convention at Cleveland for the following January, but the October raid on Harpers Ferry and its impact required a postponement into early June 1860, when Providence hosted a convention around that time.[52]

Behind the drama that unfolded in Kansas and at Harpers Ferry were those spiritualists ready to support armed abolitionism and armed abolitionists who had moved toward spiritualism. Garrison, Thomas Wentworth Higginson, Abby Heywood, and George Luther Stearns were among the more prominent figures spanning both spiritualism and the most militant wing of the antislavery movement, though Congressman Robert Dale Owen might well belong on the list.[53] After his execution, they sang of John Brown's disembodied spirit marching on and bringing much of the country along in its wake.

John Brown's Virginia raid struck with the vengeful spirits of the past and the demands of the future. It certainly galvanized the thinking of William E. Coleman, a sixteen-year-old Richmond librarian. By that time, he had become quietly hostile to slavery and "became interested in the various reformatory movements of the age, including the woman's rights, labor and other sociological reforms," including "rationalistic spiritualism." He greeted the news of Harpers Ferry as a first step toward abolition and became what was later described as the first Republican in the city.[54]

Brown's entire operation certainly involved spiritualists at various levels. A veteran Garibaldian whom the eastern abolitionists sent to advise Brown, Hugh Forbes attended spiritualist functions in New York City before going west. Several of Brown's active collaborators in the Harpers Ferry raid sympathized with the movement, notably Aaron Dwight Stevens, who became a particularly proselytizing believer. Spiritualists also predominated in the John Brown commemorative meetings that noted his execution in Virginia. At Cleveland Toohey presided, sharing the platform with, among others, Mrs. Hannah F. M. Brown and black abolitionist Charles Henry Langston in praise of Brown's initiative. Among other things, their meeting resolved that the country faced an "irrepressible conflict" between slavery and freedom and that Brown's execution "will bring confusion upon his enemies, and do more to overthrow the bulwarks of Slavery than a long life of philanthropic deeds, with a peaceful exit."[55]

After weeks of planning a rescue attempt, one of their comrades, Dick Hinton—who likely shared the views of his spiritualist wife—read a letter from another spiritualist, James Redpath, who "thought it was time that slavery should be abolished, by political parties, if possible—if not, then by armed parties of insurrectionists." In the summer of 1860, another spiritualist, the aged John Pierpont, presided over a convention of angry abolitionists gathered to discuss a political reorganization of the movement.[56] Once hanged, Brown's body lay "a-mouldering in the grave," while his soul went marching on as yet another of the unseen agencies of revolutionary change.

Other spiritualists strove to locate Old Osawatomie within an American revolutionary tradition:

Did he believe that governments are instituted among men to secure this with other rights? So did they. Did Brown believe that when any government fails to secure the enjoyment of these rights, revolution is both the right and duty of the government? So did they. Did Brown believe and proclaim that "resistance to tyrants is obedience to God?" They proclaimed the same. Did Brown employ arms against the established government? Washington did the same. Did he endanger his own life, and sacrifice the lives of others, in the cause of Freedom?

Hannah F. M. Brown added that Washington had been a slaveholder, while Brown had not been; the former had fought for a very limited idea of liberty, while Brown gave his live for "universal freedom. The associates of Washington were Patritians [sic], those of Brown were Plebeians."[57] Knowing that such views had come to be expressed across the North must have unnerved Southern leaders.

At the same time, deeply radical forces came to the fore within spiritualist meetings. "Human history is but the record of a perpetual struggle for social equality," explained Dr. Maximilien Leopold Langenschwarz, a German Jewish Forty-Eighter, to a New York City spiritualist gathering.

> All that has been advanced upon this topic may be true, but it is not new. It is but the old story. Communism has been tried and may do very well with the few, perhaps; but somehow it has in it a constitutional tendency to self-destruction. Talking is of no use. His remedy for social wrongs is *revolution*. He is a man of great tenderness of spirit; he would not harm a fly that kept at respectful distance; but he holds the right inalienable, to kill everything that he don't like. He must kill the vipers. His model Reformer is John Brown. He would make every despot a head shorter.[58]

Such revolutionary émigré leaders had already begun to participate in coalitions such as the Universal Democratic Republicans and with groups such as the Brotherhood of the Union and the Free Democratic League.

By then the subject of "social equality" captivated the New York Spiritual Conference, where the old Fourierist and land reformer Ira B. Davis issued a Fourth of July call for "all who felt disposed to consider the subject" to meet to consider how to "remove the terrible evils which arise from the inequality of condition, induced by the unequal distribution of *all* the goods of *this* life, which is the inevitable result of the present methods of life." Further meetings invited "all men and women interested in such a cause." Davis proposed "an order of mutual protection" that would organize workers' cooperatives that might supersede capitalism. The *Herald of Progress* reported on the continuation of these meetings through August and probably into September, when a Commonwealth Association emerged under Davis's leadership.[59]

That new Commonwealth Association of Davis and Young, in turn, called for a National Industrial Congress to meet on November 20 in New York City. There "various questions connected with Labor and Land Reform were thoroughly discussed." The *Herald of Progress* summarized their resolutions:

> That the present system of commerce is false—that the laborer should receive the full net product of his labor—that all intermediates between producers and consumers are non-essential; they should exchange with each other the products of their own labor—that the legal recognition of paper currency should cease—that land monopoly is an evil—that the public lands should be given to actual settlers—that a homestead exemption law should be passed—that women are entitled to an equal voice with men in the administration of government, and to the same freedom of industrial pursuits, and the same compensation enjoyed by men.[60]

Their position made the elimination of slavery not only an absolute moral imperative but an unavoidable civic duty.

On the eve of the 1860 election, some spiritualists in eastern cities confronted what seemed to be the growing irrelevance of nonresistance. "I have a toothache; that is positively bad to me," declared Pascal B. Randolph, in opposition to the morally ambiguous writers. "There is no good about it at all." Lysander Spooner agreed that acknowledging the relationship between good and evil did not require confusing them. "So long as the desire remains to devour widow's houses," insisted Jacob Edson, "there must be contention and resistance, which are of the animal spirit; and for the animals gratification, which is evil and only evil, and that continually so long and so often as it is continued and repeated." Dr. William J. Young described the inadequacies of a blind faith in the spirits to create a just world. "It has been advanced here, that the tendency of wealth to concentrate will cure itself. He looks upon the doctrine as a fallacy. The facts are the other way. At the South the nabobs not only own the land, but the laborer as well; and unless a power that is mightier than avarice is speedily invoked, by the time the continent of North America is under parchment titles, Slavery will be universal."[61]

Such views became widespread enough to shape the outcome of the election. The Republicans carried Vermont, Massachusetts, Maine, Rhode Island, Michigan, Wisconsin, New Hampshire, and Connecticut. Four years later, they also carried New York, Pennsylvania, Iowa, Ohio, Indiana, and Illinois, as well as California, placing Lincoln in the White House.

\* \* \*

Spiritualism exploded onto the scene simultaneously with a mass Republican Party and in the same regions. From 1857 through 1860, spiritualism cultivated multiple centers, fielding full-time lecturers and touring mediums in twelve of these fifteen states. Between 1857 and 1860, the most moderate of the spiritualist claims are that their numbers leaped from 357,000 in New England and New York to 715,000. Such numbers imply that many, if not most, Republicans in New England and New York dabbled to some extent in spiritualism. The same years saw numbers go from 200,000 to 360,000 for Wisconsin, Michigan, and Ohio, all decisive in the origins of the Republican Party. By then—as far as Northern states were concerned—the *Banner of Light* may not have gone too far in asserting that "the sun shines upon few hamlets, either in the Atlantic or Western States, where may not be found many believers in the *facts* of Spiritualism and the general principles of the Spiritual Philosophy."[62] Yet it grew most dramatically in places where people sought answers to the questions raised by the Kansas crisis and the *Dred Scott* decision.

More important, perhaps, the more moderate antislavery positions of the Republicans suited the concerns of the more respectable spiritualists who rejected absolute and universal ideas of right and wrong. As in dealing with the world of the spirits, communication of ideals with the flawed material world required a medium, to regulate what could be accepted. Such was a view shared by Abraham Lincoln, William H. Seward, Salmon P. Chase, and other Republican leaders. Then, too, spiritualism provided a particularly deterministic and fatalistic response to the sectional "irrepressible conflict." Their talk of cosmic balances and spiritual trade-offs represented a wonderfully bourgeois resurrection of the traditional anthropomorphized Judeo-Christian God, balancing accounts in ways that seem incomprehensible to us mere mortals.

All of this found an almost messianic expression in the rapid emergence of a mass party movement and its aftermath.

# 2

## The Mystical Union

### *The Republican Medium of the National Destiny*

"Even now, Mammon holds a divided empire," observed one spiritualist. "Things temporal are giving place to things eternal; the age is entering upon a new experience; it is taking lessons in a higher school; let us be hopeful and *patient;* for, in the development of man's spiritual nature, lies the sure destruction of every evil, the cure of every ill." In December 1860, Warren B. Chase wrote, "The union of two worlds is growing closer, as I anticipate the union of all States will after the convulsion of the political storms are over, and the second sober thoughts of the people come to the rescue of right, duties, and obligations of justice."[1] The mystical Union represented a spiritual republic, representative of all the souls involved in the working out of a common destiny.

The emergence of the Republicans and the crisis of civil war forced spiritualists to final reckoning with antebellum nonresistance. These same processes also pressed spiritualism into an even more coherent national force. Without any real organization regulating the process, spiritualists poured their hearts and hopes into the survival of a federal union imbued with an almost mystical importance, the embodiment of what the departed had invested in the country and a gift to the future. In addition, the spiritualists concentrated their efforts on lending an increasingly public voice to the departed, particularly those falling in the war.

## Reluctant Warriors

Not all spiritualist were Fourierists, abolitionists, and land reformers, and a sizable minority remaining stoically antipolitical and skeptical about reform, politics, and the Union. Yet this ambivalence itself had very different origins. "Our radicalism aims to be conservative—our conservatism to be radical," wrote one spiritualist. "Each is the natural half and twin of the other."[2]

Yet as in any cultural or religious trend, there existed a current that ultimately held innately reactionary positions on virtually any proposal for change. Asaph Bemis Child's *Whatever Is, Is Right* articulated a spiritualism that scorned discontent and agitation. The middle-aged Vermont-born Bostonian shared the demographic and social faith of many antebellum radicals and acknowledged much of the injustice and irrational features of the present order. No less than orthodox Christians, some spiritualists talked about a flawed human nature, though Child did not see it as flawed. He did not stand alone in the belief that the drive for equality would produce more trouble than it would solve. If nature produced an inequality, it seemed unnatural to try to change it.[3]

Hudson Tuttle translated Child's quiet Yankee conservatism into a full-blown noisy midwestern antiradicalism. Early in his career, his essay "The Social Relation of Spiritualists" complained bitterly that "the universal grasp of Spiritualism has gathered the floating rubbish of the sea of mankind, as well as heaven born truths." It had been "basely prostituted to purposes of quacks." With undisguised scorn, he complained that "the Land Reformer was sure the spirits were Land Reformers. The advocate of Woman's Rights was equally sure that they advocated his hobby. The Reformer whose specialty was the abolition of Capital Punishment was sure the hosts of heaven were on his side. And the Socialist resented the imputation of their opposing him and his." He came notoriously close to sharing Orestes A. Brownson's complaint that spiritualism had become a stalking horse for "modern philanthropy, visionary reforms, socialism, and revolutionism."[4]

Then, too, the pervasive nature of American racism allowed some spiritualists to discuss political issues with absolutely no regard for the rights of people of color. William Smith Waite, a Yankee Jacksonian transplant to Illinois, warned spiritualists "to moderate their ardor sufficiently to take a cool and comprehensive view of the existing state of the public mind on this subject." He argued that the South had rescued the African from "the hopeless ignorance and horrible despotism which prevail in his native clime" and disagreed with "the immediate and unconditional emancipation of slaves." Waite urged reliance upon "a generally pervading moral influence" to work "upon the mind of the master."[5]

Through Cora Hatch, the spirit of Jefferson scolded the radicals, "If you can benefit the African, or any other alien race, it is your duty to do so; but to introduce any outside people into our midst and make them a bone of contention among us, is entirely beside the question; and the consideration of slavery should be excluded from your legislation altogether." Another suggested that "inasmuch as God permits slavery, He sanctifies it, upholds it, and it is a part of His governmental law." "The slaves are not entitled to freedom," insisted Daniel Tarbell, "and cannot enjoy it till they obtain it themselves." "The African does not only differ in color, but in mental organism." Abolition, ran another argument, would "take away from them the few privileges they have so long enjoyed without molestation, particularly without giving them any warning." Black America would face "universal abject poverty or their sale into slavery."[6]

Others simply mistrusted the political and social leadership of the nonslaveholding states. Jeremiah Hacker, the curmudgeon Yankee reformer who had edited Maine's *Pleasure Boat* for many years, blasted the pretensions of the North. "Both ends of the nation are rebels against God—rebels against Spiritualism—both are equally guilty of slavery; for while the South held slaves, the North bought the productions of slavery, and the partaker of stolen goods, knowing them to be stolen, is just as bad as the thief. The North and South have both rejected the counsels of God—have denied him and forsaken him and he has left them to punish each other, and has no more to do with them now while fighting than the man in the moon has, nor can true Spiritualists have." "The war sprung naturally from the corrupt state of the public mind—is just as natural as fermentation in a compost heap; but the public mind had no right to be in that corrupt state which produced the war."[7]

A related skepticism about institutions inspired others. "Our first work should be individual reformation," suggested Cora A. Syme, "and the seeking of right conditions and relations." This also became the message of Amanda Melvina Fitzallen Spence, whose essays "Spirits as Cultivators and Workers with Mankind" ran through the early months of the war. "It has been said by one wiser than I, 'All parties that seek supremacy by the sword shall lose that for which they contend.'" Another writer refuted the idea that war would necessarily strengthen "the Old by infusing into it larger elements of Force," but expected it would accomplish nothing because "Force will be tried by both sides only to find how perfectly powerless it is to unite hearts and hands."[8]

"War is terrible, even for liberty and right," declared Cora L. V. Hatch. At the war's start, she thought the motives for mass slaughter boiled down to "but one impelling principle, not patriotism, not religion, not justice, not the country, but mere ambition. For we do not know of one warrior of ancient times who had not for his highest motive self-aggrandizement" or "who did not desire to supersede the ruler and ascend the throne." "All sectarians and dogmatics," Andrew Jackson Davis had declared, "do unavoidably, from the nature of their creeds, fall into the iron or force age," as opposed to that of reason and justice.[9]

Some insisted that they had no choice but to accept the transformation of the Union into "two Confederacies" and encourage "a peaceful separation of dissatisfied States" as a "most Christianlike mode of *settling* differences that could really be settled in no other way." Even after the secessionists fired on Fort Sumter, a few correspondents blamed the entire crisis on "some of the Abolitionists [who] call for the stirring up of a bloody negro insurrection among the blacks of the Southern States." Disavowing desire for slave rebellion, the *Banner of Light* claimed, "We are no advocates of it nor apologists for it." As late as February 1862, it urged what it called "moderation."[10]

Nevertheless, things changed quickly. John Otis Wattles had long complained that "the world is a great bone-pile, cemented with blood, over which the Gods of War and Gain drive their rattling chariots," but he wound up an ally of John Brown in Kansas. Christian spiritualist John H. W. Toohey conceded that "the dogma of 'Whatever is, is right'" had been "suggestive of the largest charity, but our better consciousness must pronounce it false, however specious its sophisms may seem. We need to erect the most elevated ideal of right, and govern all our aims and acts according to that standard." "There is a right and a wrong, as well as a high and a low," declared Frank L. Wadsworth. "We have no business to fold our arms in passive ease or stultification, and say, 'Whatever is, is right.'"[11]

Chase thought some of his fellow spiritualists "tangled in the web of absurdities and contradictions, and cannot see it through the meshes of metaphysical philosophy, to the clear regions of divine and celestial light and life beyond." "*To me*, they are *not* all right or wrong; and as I feel the difference, I must have a term to express it." The firing on Fort Sumter changed everything, and Chase turned toward New England and the stronghold of the anti-institutionalists and nonresisters.[12]

"The aristocracy of the Southern confederacy," warned a rather representative Northern speaker, "regard the laboring classes as the 'mudsills' of society.

They exist for the Government; not the Government for them; and want of property and intelligence must forever shut them out from the place of authority." In making this argument, they had only to cite the vast literature from the secessionists themselves: "The evil of Northern institutions is in the fact that all can vote, while the security of the South is, that the power of the country is wielded by the intelligent classes, who have a permanent interest in the well-being of society."[13]

Chase made the radical position even more explicit. The preoccupation with maintaining slavery meant there would be no effort to better the lot of poor whites, either. The masters "despise labor because it is done by blacks and they have no means of education—hence they are idle and ignorant." Acceptance of secession would prove "inconsistent with the real liberty of the slaveholder himself, binding him down, as it really does, to the mere raising of certain products of the soil; and keeping his soul in the bondage of fear, and of the moral corruption which fear always engenders." He also challenged the "fallacious" assumption that "a great barrier raised by Nature between the black and white races" justified secession. As S. B. Brittan complained, "The leaders of the Southern Rebellion have never been willing to make a frank and open appeal to the People." Freed from the need to defend the paper's decision, secessionists even began returning copies of the *Banner* to the North, as though it were an abolitionist publication. "The time will come when the South will feel most thankful for the success of the North in this war, for she has the greatest interest in our success," suggested Chase. Union victory would be "of the highest importance to the nation, and especially to the South, that it be completely subdued, and the government fully maintained over all the states, and ultimately over this continent and its islands."[14]

Then, too, as the war rolled over the nation, spiritualism tended to a final fatalistic sense of prophecy. Some now claimed to have gotten warnings of the impending crisis and conflict from the spirits. The spirit of Andrew Jackson, said some, had prophesied war in 1856. One spirit recalled that "we predicted civil war in this country. We heard the cannon's roar, and knew the hour was near at hand. Had we then uttered such sentiments as we have tonight, half of the audience would have left the house." Franklin L. Crane, a Kansas spiritualist, conjured the prophecies of Nostradamus about the American war.[15] When necessary, spiritualism eased the transition from war resister and pacifist to an eagerness to trample out the vintage where the grapes of wrath were stored.

In May 1861, the spiritualists at Dodworth's Hall discussed the warnings made a decade before by the spirit of John Quincy Adams and others. "With sad hearts they look down on the land they love, and see what fearful strife the institution of slavery will engender, at no distant day, and that it will lead to dismemberment and civil war. Shall we remain dumb and insensible to the cries of three millions of our bleeding, persecuted, and down-trodden fellow-men?" Spiritualists held that "those same principles of harmony which bind us together will cause us to answer gently the cry of the distressed—will lend us to the house of the sick man, and teach us to moisten his lips and bathe his fevered brow; and such will be the duty of Spiritualists in the time that is to come." Do not ask that "this contest, be smoothed over, as so often before in the earlier stages, nor seek to arrest it till the work of Revolution is completed; but yet see to it that, in our part of the performance, we are governed by no evil passions." The meeting closed with the usual collection to "be applied to the relief of the family of a volunteer who, under the impulse of patriotism, had left them entirely unprovided for."[16]

As to the chance of averting war, spiritualists—like Republican leaders—tended to believe in "the latent union feeling in the Southern States, which is supposed to be overawed by the tyrannic haste of ambitious leaders." Secessionists not only strove to suppress Unionism in Maryland, Kentucky, and Missouri but had largely done so in eastern Tennessee, western Virginia and North Carolina, and northern Alabama, "that entire Allegheny region, flanked on the west by the Cumberland mountains, and on the east by the Blue Ridge, where only freedom can live and free men can dwell and prosper." Even after the war began, some spiritualists continued to believe that Southern Unionism had the potential of ending it. "If the principles of the North, and its institutions were made known to the soldiers of the Southern army, every regiment in the South would disband in twenty-four hours. They have been prejudiced against the North and they have been taught we are their enemies, and would place the negroes over them. They have been deceived, cheated, defrauded; for if the truth were known to them, they would be with us at once. We are to pity them—not despise them."[17]

## National Organization

War may have generated more in terms of spiritualist impulses, but its initial impact left something of a shambles of what had never been a very well-organized movement. Most obviously, it left chaotic ruins of its press. The *Banner of Light* survived the dislocations of the war, but the *Herald of Progress, Christian Spiritualist,* and *Spiritual Telegraph* did not. In addition, the preexisting community at Hopedale launched the *Progressive Age,* which evolved into the periodical *Spiritual Reformer.* In Iowa M. M. Daniels started the *Rising Tide,* and Frances H. McDougal launched the *Golden Gate* at Sacramento.[18]

Spiritualist activity continued unabated across New England and the Northeast, clustering there in the cities, but appearing across the countryside of the Midwest as well. "I counted seventy-five country wagons that came," reported Stevens Sanborn Jones of an event in northern Illinois, held "in a most beautiful grove, near the village, well fitted up with stand and seats, but not half enough of the latter." L. K. Coonley, touring the Midwest, described the preoccupation of the movement. "All was for 'Union and the War.'" Near the start of the war, the existing associations sponsored a conference at Sturgis, Michigan, of the "western lecturers," who appointed a vigilance committee to call future gatherings.[19]

A conference of eastern spiritualists also appointed a committee at Quincy to represent New York, Pennsylvania, and New Jersey. Perhaps inspired by the newly important national concerns, it called a convention for August 1861 at Oswego's Music Hall. John H. W. Toohey of the *Christian Spiritualist* and the other prime movers hoped to use the convention to establish the defining parameters of the movement. "The conditions of our country," they later acknowledged, "have prevented the attendance of many of you whose presence we had joyfully anticipated."[20]

Toohey and Uriah Clark opened the convention, though politics or its terminology quickly pitted them against each other. Clark worried that the idea of freedom had become too abstract and general, professing "so much general liberty, we had but little individual left." Toohey mistrusted the general ideological cant about individualism, which, he believed, encouraged "individuals who seem to ride over all individuality except their own, and who recognize no laws admitted for the general good." The two later seemed to recognize that their disagreement actually turned on an issue of terminology.[21]

The convention set aside Saturday for an excursion across Lake Ontario into Canada. A large steamboat left in midmorning, getting fourteen or fifteen hundred persons to Stone Mills by midafternoon. Canadian spiritualists doubled the total of the gathering and had a speakers stand prepared at a nearby grove. That evening the convention had "a moonlight and all-night sail back to Oswego." Those who wished stayed up all night, singing, telling stories, and talking. They landed in Oswego at dawn.[22]

True to their original purpose as healers, spiritualists explored medical and health issues, anticipating "a new era in the treatment of disease" based upon "spiritual laws and spiritual influences." Moving into a realm where one could expect such insights to matter, William Spence, a Kentuckian, and his wife, Amanda M. Spence, had launched their own "Psychological Institute for the Insane." The convention also discussed the prospect of developing "harmonic children." Urging "the necessity of our recognizing the great movements of the age," they implored each other to avoid being "sensitive and squeamish" in confronting "popular prejudice."[23]

Despite these achievements, the Spences remained very critical of institutions. Amanda thought that "too much corruption has pervaded in every department of government, religion and society. We have professed to be a Christian people and government, advocating the principles of peace and fraternity, but the whole country is now involved in an appalling war." She saw "these dark, troublesome and discordant times" threatening to pull mediums "back into the world, and the spirit-world shut from their sight."[24]

So, too, A. J. Higgins articulated the widespread suspicions about "the enormous robberies of the people by political demagogues," with the political rewarding of military commissions and army contracts. "The war thus far had developed no object for war," he complained. "Slavery is to be upheld, and he thought the no object policy must eventuate in the rebels taking possession of the Capitol, before the people of the north will be aroused to the importance of declaring for the entire abolition of slavery."[25] The dynamic of the conflict would change all of that.

These questions bore directly on the fate of the Union. Henry C. Wright, "the oldest pioneer" present, spoke on "the Mission of Spiritualism in the present crisis of our country." "In the midst of our country's crisis, we are called to meet the one grand issue, shall slavery or liberty rule?" With their countrymen, he argued, spiritualists took up "the great mission of our nation in maintaining the principles of the Declaration of Independence." "Never let your hat go off before tyrants, without your head goes, too," he said. "Whoever talks or fights against liberty or for slavery, is a traitor to God and humanity."[26]

There, too, the issues of the war proved unavoidable. "Many volunteers were present," according to reports, and Mrs. S. A. Coonley read a poem, "Southward Ho!" L. K. Coonley offered "a review of Reformers of Ancient and Modern times" that appeared in the *Rising Tide* of Independence, Iowa. With a thinly veiled reference to the White House, Mrs. Cora A. Syme declared, "The humblest log cabin was prophetic of the order and union of the world." "Our fragmentary efforts would prove measurably fruitless; concentration and union were needed." Whereas some continued to urge personal "regeneration," Clark agreed that the effort had, thus far, been too focused on "externals," that is, institutional "social laws and customs." However, he suggested that "when this great revolution shall have wrought out its disintegrating and union influences, the people will be the better prepared to stand forth in the light and liberty of the opening spheres and hail the millennial morn of earth and heaven."[27]

Although the convention decided to take no steps toward a national union of spiritualists, what became one of the strongest wartime components of the movement began to take form. That fall what was becoming the Religio-Philosophical Society of St. Charles, Illinois, opened its three-day annual "festival" west of Chicago. S. S. Jones assured all and sundry that "no resolve shall be put to vote approving or disapproving of contested matters of opinion or faith; nor for any purpose, further than is essential for the transaction of the ordinary business of the Festival." The northern Illinois movement provided a microcosm for the kinds of disputes that existed at the national level. Judge William A. Boardman of Waukegan took up Dr. A. B. Child's argument that "what is, is right," while others pointed out that it remained "difficult to tell what is right or what is wrong. It was evident that all things must develop; and therefore must be right in each stage of progress."[28]

## The Union

For spiritualists, the American Union became a mystical expression of "the radical brotherhood that sends its lightning-like impulses from heart to heart." When word of the firing on Fort Sumter reached the office of the *Banner*, the staff consulted the spirits, who assured them that "the fort will be taken back again." Indeed, the weight of all the past efforts to build a federal Union brought forth shades of not only Zachary Taylor but also Andrew Jackson, who "is in Washington with Old Abe." John H. Randall called the Union "an impregnable fortress, that can withstand all the assertions and sneaking insinuations aimed at it by the corrupt and perfidious hierophants of this present age." "The raising of American Flags is an universal practice, now-a-days," reported the *Banner*. "The streets are fluttering with them. Staffs are decorated with them." "The children of our time may live to be grey and decrepit, and never again see what their eyes have seen during the week beginning with April 13 and ending with April 20." Sumter changed everything, and "We are all one man here, on this subject."[29]

Increasingly, Northerners began to focus on the work: "A few despotic tyrants in the South, swaying through passion and prejudice, the minds of the ignorant poor whites, contest the palm of government with twenty millions of freemen, whose commerce whitens every sea, and whose mechanic arts spread civilization everywhere." The Democrats who had "control of the government machinery in the Southern States" created "a regularly concerted *plan,* a conspiracy, not merely *to go out* of this Union, but to *overthrow* the Union, and afterwards reconstruct something more to their own purposes on its ruins." The *Banner* accepted the idea of change but insisted that "the rebels shall not force them upon us with arms in their hands and at the mouths of loaded cannon." They accepted war because "no single remedy less violent is likely to prove efficient in curing the present disease." The secessionists had "fatally misconstrued" the country's mood. "War is a terrible thing; but there are other things still more terrible," such as a "prosperous iniquity, base servility, legalized wrong, and consent that this wrong may be perpetuated to future generations." Peace required "substantial justice and equality among all its people. Such are the laws of human nature—such its instinctive abhorrence of injustice—that it cannot long rest under the burden of a conscious wrong."[30]

Through the first year of the war, spiritualists showed growing enthusiasm for its prosecution. As medium Lizzie Doten put it in a revised version of "John Brown's Body" and "The Battle Hymn of the Republic":

> We have joined another army
> > In the service of the Lord,
> And every one enlisted
> > With a full and free accord,
> Not for sake of pay or bounty,
> > For his love is our reward,
> As we go marching on.[31]

By then the meaning of the spiritualist song differed little from the mystical idealism sung by the rest of the Unionists.

For this reason, spiritualists generally threw themselves into the war effort. The *Banner of Light* reported that its printers had left for the war and noted that the first identifiable spiritualist killed in the war died of wounds received in June 1861 at Big Bethel, on the Virginia coast. "Many a son is off with the troops, fighting battles for the government, which men declare can be preserved in no other way; they will give thanks in their hearts, and pray Heaven that another return of this festival may find them safe at home with those they best love. But they are not forgotten in their extremity; millions of hearts are with them in their struggles, and the hopes of a whole people centre in their success and safety."³²

Judge John W. Edmonds admonished them all. "On the battle-field, let the spiritualist remember the forebearance and love which his faith teaches him; even though smarting under the shock of violent bereavement, let him implore forgiveness for the enemies who know not what they do." In addition to stories about Ellsworth's premonition, spiritualists reported that a soldier of the Sixth Massachusetts had written of having a vision of being attacked in the streets of a city months before it happened in Baltimore. The experience of combat also generated a seemingly endless supply of near misses, fortuitously intuitive movements, and other oddities for which spiritualists could provide a ready supernatural explanation.³³

The fierce realities of the conflict became apparent in its first weeks. On a July Monday in 1861, news reached a sitting circle that a fight had taken place along Bull Run, and a visitor asked for confirmation of the Federal Army's defeat. The medium asserted that the news accounts must have been "incorrect" or "partially correct." Union ranks may "suffer more terribly than they have any conception of," and the army might experience "a partial destruction," while "many, very many shall lose their physical bodies," but the medium assured them that *"there shall be no defeat of the Union Army!"* When the news finally came, the *Banner* called it "a strange 'defeat'" in which "both armies run away from each other fast as legs and horse could carry them!"³⁴ Amid all the slaughter and mayhem for Sullivan Ballou and his comrades, though, the defeated Unionists unexpectedly failed to abandon their project of reuniting the country.

At the height of the Civil War, a Federal colonel sent a letter home from the front. He complained that "sectarian religion does not stand by a man—does not build up the spirit—does not build up the moral nature in this place, where, more than in all others, is needed high moral power." When he met a fellow officer who, "amid all the temptations of camp life keeps himself in the path of integrity, I am almost sure that man at home was called an infidel."³⁵ Such an upending of the modern no-atheists-in-foxholes view of war testifies to the as yet unchurched nature of the society that faced the Civil War and the variations in their approach to the experience.

The *Banner* also wrote of a "regiment of spiritualists," likely the Fourteenth Massachusetts. It identified the commander as a "well known Spiritualist and medium," as well as "the grandson of two of the most heroic patriots and officers of the revolutionary army; he is both a college and a military graduate, and has served in all capacities up to a field-officer." His second in command, also a spiritualist, "has commanded one of the divisions of the Massachusetts Militia," while "the Adjutants, Captains and Lieutenants are mostly Spiritualists." It added that the chaplain would be Fishbough, "well known to all old Spiritualists." Elsewhere, "Mr. Clark of Washington, whose advertisement appears in another column holds a Captain's commission and seeks a company entirely made up from Spiritualist ranks."[36]

Samuel Byron Brittan's own underage son had already tried to run away to the army, but the editor retrieved him and kept him at home until they negotiated an agreement that allowed the lad to join Captain W. D. Porter as his master's mate on the gunboat *Essex*. As it approached Fort Henry on the Tennessee River, Confederate guns struck the boiler, scalding and blowing Porter overboard, leaving young Brittan among the forty killed. As might be expected from the demographics of the movement, numerous Federal officers were also ardent spiritualists. Most obviously, perhaps, was Dorus M. Fox, an uncle of the sisters, who had gone to Michigan as a young man and reached well into middle age before joining and winning command of the Ninth Michigan and, later, the Twenty-Seventh.[37]

One of the more prominent early spiritualist casualties of the war was likely Major Sullivan Ballou. The Ballous, a prominent family in the New England movement, publicized several versions of the letter, one resurrected by Ken Burns's 1990 documentary series *The Civil War*. "O Sarah! If the dead can come back to this earth and flit unseen around those they loved, I shall always be near you; in the gladdest days and in the darkest nights . . . always, always, and if there be a soft breeze upon your cheek, it shall be my breath, as the cool air fans your throbbing temple, it shall be my spirit passing by. Sarah do not mourn me dead; think I am gone and wait for thee, for we shall meet again." The publicity around the letter had all the more importance when it became known that the victorious Confederates had mutilated his corpse on the battlefield.[38]

The war touched the lives of spiritualists everywhere. As Confederate sympathizers recruited and organized in southern California, the old "wizard' John Brown formed a local Unionist company and transformed a church under construction into a makeshift fort. John R. Kelso in southwestern Missouri found that the slaveholding elite manipulated "the gross ignorance and the absurd prejudices that prevailed among the poorer classes of the South." At one point, he listened as "a poor fellow, who never could have owned a decent horse, much less a slave," complained about the Yankee attempt to free "our niggers." They feared what they called "nigger equality," after which the "buck nigger" would take the "white girls." He added that these were "about the only arguments ever advanced." In the face of continual intimidation, he became the first Union volunteer in the country and organized others to fight for the Union, after which the secessionists burned out his family.[39]

Aside from participation in several major battles, Kelso became a notoriously ruthless counterinsurgency officer, cultivating a terrifying reputation that would best serve his purposes. There he "might have been seen any day, when just in from a scout or off duty, pacing up and down the veranda of his hotel with his book in his hands, generally studying aloud. When in camp he paced back and forth in front of his tent with his book in his hand." Indeed, after "the most fatiguing scout or march," he "stretched himself upon the ground on his blanket with his head slightly elevated against a tree or on his saddle, with his book in his hands, earnestly perusing its pages until the bugle-call sounded the march." The 1883 county history went further, reporting that he "frequently engaged in the study of mental philosophy and the subtleties of metaphysics while lying in the brush by the roadside waiting, to 'get the drop' on a 'rebel,'" that "he could lie at the side of a road in ambush, with a Latin grammar in one hand and a cocked pistol in the other, awaiting the passing of his intended victim; Kelso's attention being distracted from the book for only the time it took to shoot." Living and functioning near the Indian Territory, he cultivated the rumor that he had Indian blood, which particularly terrified.

Southerners who resisted secession, including most of the spiritualists among them, risked the fate of Kelso's family. Just beyond Kelso's corner of Missouri, the Harmonial Vegetarian Society in nearby Benton County, Arkansas, still had thirty-eight members left in 1860, but the Confederate military commandeered the lands in 1861 as a training camp. They also arrested the remaining members of the community, whose activities likely contributed to rumors of the massive Peace Society said to exist in the county.[40]

Then there was Harris's much-touted colony at Mountain Cove in western Virginia. From the war's start, British-born Wilfrid Wylley followed the Federal troops into the hills, reporting back with letters to the *Banner*. He wrote how their columns "toiled on, up the deep valleys and over the rugged mountains of western Virginia." He rode with them "beside the Kanawha, the survivors of the gallant band—decimated by disease and battle—sing again." This would have led them right through Mountain Cove on that very river. "Oh, this mystery of living and dying! Who, though skilled in the lore of every age—who can penetrate its secrets?" Harris had abandoned the colony sometime earlier and then crossed the Atlantic, where he announced his abandonment of the entire idea of spiritualism. As of the 1860 Census, though, some of the Northern-born colonists remained at Mountain Cove. Like many of their neighbors, the young men of military age dealt with early secessionist control of the area by melting into the woods or escaping across the Ohio River, where they joined Union regiments. Another voice for spiritualism in western Virginia, John B. Wolff, had already slipped away and would turn up later at Denver.[41]

Spiritualists carefully followed the reporting of the conflict. "Whoever reads of a battle fought, invariably places a large interrogation point upon it, and tucks it away in his vest pocket for future reference." Success in war, they came to realize, represented work "engineered by knowledge, professional skill on the part of officers, and experience, it makes its way against all the odds which can be brought against it." They joined the legions of admirers of those "men who lead and command and direct to-day, and who were born for the country, to lead and command and direct in the immediate future." The spiritualist papers reported the fierce realities of the war. They also published and reprinted accounts of their activities, such as Frederick L. N. Willis's eulogy to his comrade and fellow spiritualist Captain John L. Hackstaff. Many such followed over the course of the war.[42]

By the spring of 1862, the Confederacy west across the mountains from Virginia began to unravel. The arrival of the Federal armies in Tennessee liberated a wave of Unionist activities by those who had been unable to restrain the secession of their state government. Meanwhile, the editor of the *Richmond Examiner* reportedly turned on the enterprise, and one of the elder statesmen of the Confederacy had barely escaped capture in Alabama. The *Banner* reported hopeful rumors that the Confederacy was about to fall. Spiritualists and other Republicans had always looked hopefully for Southern opposition to secession to destroy it. Talk of "New Virginia" and a free state inspired hope "among the border States in good time, that will bring about a new set of economical views, and therefore their release from the incubus, and loss of unprofitable slave labor." The spiritualist press covered the work of D. S. Fracker of the Sanitary Commission at Wheeling. A slaveholding Unionist spoke against slavery at Gallatin, Tennessee, and some North Carolinians proposed to take that state out of the Confederacy. "The very men who went into this war, as they insisted, for the sake of ridding themselves of what they styled 'meddling abolitionists,' are now become the foremost abolitionists themselves." Georgia officials also began to shake loose from their Confederate allegiance.[43]

Spiritualists witnessed the intensification of the fighting after its first indecisive year. The individual most identified with the care of the wounded, Clara Barton, remained a lifelong spiritualist. Arriving in the wake of Shiloh in April 1862, a horrified Dr. C. D. Griswold called for volunteers to care for the wounded, noting the presence among them of mediums. In July 1863, Quaker-born Dr. Henry T. Child, one of the founders of the Philadelphia movement, hurried to Gettysburg. "The spirit world is populating rapidly with revolutionary minds," they noted, "and what their influences will be upon the coming destiny of this country, it is difficult to determine, but it may be safely concluded that ultimate good will be the result."[44]

Not a battle of any size was fought that did not claim the lives of spiritualists. William Berry, one of the printers from the *Banner*, fell at Antietam. Fredericksburg took the life of chaplain Arthur B. Fuller, the brother of Margaret Fuller. By 1864 such losses became commonplace, the *Banner* noting, for example, the movement's loss of R. S. Alcoke. "With the knowledge he possessed of the bright future," the wounded and suffering believer lay unattended for three days on the field at Cold Harbor.[45]

Spiritualism made for courage in the field but often left its converts ill-suited to military life. In the fall of 1863, Damon Young Kilgore left his teaching post to serve as an assistant quartermaster and took with him as a clerk James Martin Peebles, whose innate hatred of war finally yielded to his Unionist and antislavery politics. Peebles wrote compassionately about the "erring yet sincere" Southerners they encountered and returned home physically and mentally drained by the experience.[46]

Peebles's experience was not unusual. N. Frank White, a trained draftsman as well as a spiritualist, joined the U.S. Balloon Corps, but decided after its dissolution "to doff the regimentals which become him so well, and return to his old occupation as a lecturer in the field of Spiritualism." John H. Randall helped recruit "liberal and moral men, especially my acquaintances among the readers of the *Banner*," but returned from the war broken in health. So, too, Yankee-born James Harvey Blood took command of the Sixth Missouri from Peter E. Bland, himself one of the spiritualist petitioners to Congress, leading it in one of the assaults on the Confederate works at Vicksburg. Service left him reclusive as he returned to St. Louis, won election to public office, presided over the local spiritualists, and took up with Victoria Woodhull, then on the verge of a notoriety all her own.[47]

Yet spiritualists managed to do all of this without becoming uncritical supporters of the institutions necessary to the war. Here and there, the old antebellum nonresistance bobbed to the surface again. Young Ezra Hervey Heywood, just a few years into the abolitionist movement, could not see how killing a man would be morally preferable to enslaving him. Like many of the other abolitionists, he ardently believed in spirit communication.[48] Of course, what everyone faced was not simply a matter of weighing moral abstractions.

The war reshaped some of the discussions within the movement over questions such as "social relations." "Let us try to help and build up each other, and to remove the obstructions in society which prevent the harmonization of man," one participant urged. "Free Love and Secession are agitators or firebrands thrown into society to awake thought and examination everywhere," they acknowledged. "The wild national commotion will purify the age." Wiser allies on the other side declared themselves "Unionists in the fullest sense; we are with you of the Free North, and will aid you in the struggle to maintain your rights against the tyrannical usurpation of the South; and we acknowledge no secession save that from the lower form of government to the higher—a rule of secession which is sought to be revered by Southern tyrants, who will be subjugated, and their oppressive institutions overthrown by the moral and physical power of your freemen."[49]

## The Spirits' War Commentaries

From the onset of the conflict, in the *Banner of Light* the spirits offered a running commentary on the war and its experience at free public weekly meetings. For all of their shortcomings, these commentaries reflect a spiritualist dialogue with what they perceived to be the essentials of their society. They sensed the departed evaluating their decisions as a matter of course. "Do you suppose the spirit of old John Brown—the first martyr in the present struggle—sleeps? He who laid down his life in behalf of the slave, so sure as he retains his individuality, so sure does he look anxiously on the strike."[50]

At these public forums, the mediums sought the spirits of national leaders past. These included Daniel Webster, Henry Clay, John C. Calhoun, Thomas H. Benton, Charles C. Pinckney, John and John Quincy Adams, Thomas Jefferson, Alexander Hamilton, James Otis, and John Hancock, as well as "the long line of statesmen who inhabit the summer-land of immortality—do they sleep? Never. Surely as they exist, do they mingle in the affairs of the nation." Those of Webster, Clay, and John Quincy Adams turned up in the free circles, as did Stephen A. Douglas and Andrew Jackson, all having shed their partisanship with their bodies. Sam Houston returned to recant some of his negative remarks about spiritualism before his own death. Most surprisingly, perhaps, Calhoun, "our departed, misguided brother," had undergone a miraculous rethinking about liberty and race after his death.⁵¹

Deceased family members of the secessionists sometimes returned to berate them. Zachary Taylor showed up to berate his son-in-law Jefferson Davis, and the mother of Georgia governor Joseph E. Brown sought to dissuade him. "I know you think you are right," the dead mother of a Confederate soldier told him. "I know you believe you are fighting for freedom. I know you think you have been terribly wronged by your brethren of the North. But I, your mother, ask you to look into your own heart, and see if you have done right by all God's children yourself." One of Robert E. Lee's daughters reminded him that she had warned about slavery. The daughter of a Confederate colonel—and the half-sister of a young mixed-race slave—explained that slavery, what her father had "considered a blessing to the South, is its greatest curse."⁵²

Then, too, passing over often seemed to give the spirit a new perspective on the world. Confederate general Felix K. Zollicoffer had developed Unionist sympathies. Most remarkably, perhaps, the pious "Stonewall" Jackson returned, announcing "new thoughts, new desires, upon a new highway, and a new army to lead. Thanks be to the Eternal, that army, like its Almighty Father, knows no North, no South, no banner with its stars and stripes, save the banner of Eternal Truth." By the later months of the war, he had begun to take a kind of social worker's interest in the case of one family. Uniquely, the spirit of Ben McCulloch stuck to his guns, insisting that "we don't change much in dying." In the midst of war, spiritualists talked of seeing "the group of Rebel Generals passed away from the smoke of battle," counterparts to "Lyon, Ellsworth, Sumner, Kearney, and a host of others in council on the affairs of the republican party."⁵³ Their preliminary sightings presaged the postwar white idealization of national reconciliation.

Such commentaries confirmed the spiritualist faith in white Southern Unionism. Not only did they encounter the shades of civilian Unionists butchered by the secessionist authorities. Unionist sentiments also continued in the army, where a North Carolina sergeant found himself in the guardhouse for his sentiments. "The idea of people of the same country pitting themselves against each other without the slightest cause," he complained after his death. "Well, I was a fool to do it, and so are all the rest."⁵⁴

Of greater interest, spiritualists gave voice to dead children consoling their parents and to "our poor soldiers, who lay down their bodies on the field of battle," returning "to tell their tale of hardships and wrongs by the swindling contractors, by unskillful surgeons, and the manner of their exit." There, one could read of a battle in which thousands died and then check on the safety of a loved one by attending one of these open public readings. The spirits that returned reflected what mediums believed mirrored the broad spectrum of experience. "Say to my friends that I died without fear," said the spirit of William Madigan, vice president of the National Typographical Union, "and am content. I hope soon to be able to make a lengthy report from my new home." Those who died in prison had mixed responses, some expressing their bitterness.[55]

First and foremost, the spirits sanctified the necessity of the war and reassured listeners of its necessity. The Civil War tore spiritualism from its ideological hostility to violence and an institutional skepticism of the military. Armed struggle was "sometimes necessary and inevitable, and our present war should be put through in defiance of all Copperheadism." "War may be a necessity," confessed one spiritualist, "but war and Christianity are not compatible." They raised the issue repeatedly. "Are the Spirits in Favor of War?" "I used to wonder when I was on earth why the spirits hadn't power to stop the war," asked one of its casualties, "or why they hadn't prevented its beginning at all? I see a little further now than I did then."[56] The high cost of the war in blood and treasure required great results to justify them.

Race sparked a strange argument among the spirits. One aspect of this had been the lessons of race. The interestingly named "Major Christian," an unrepentant Confederate spirit, confronted one of the mediums, who asked, "Is there any slavery in the spirit-land?" The departed simply insisted that "the negro is just as distinct from the Anglo-Saxon race as you are from your Newfoundland dog." "I see them there!—black and white—enlisting side by side in this sacred war for freedom! There are statesmen who supported Slavery while mortal!" The spirits of dead African Americans turned up very regularly. "I groaned for liberty," declared one South Carolina man, "and my soul felt that it was prisoned in the flesh." He described himself "Benjamin, Major Christian's thinking negro. I shall be known by that title." Another victim, self-described as "racially mixed," had been shot for "having assisted in liberating some of your men and also of having done something for those who were sick among us." One declared himself "here to speak for meself."[57] He did not, of course, but the mediums tried their best.

At least one of the mediums realized how far short their efforts fell, as the spirit of a black soldier became confrontational over the issue, asking whether spiritualists had rules "up here, admitting colored folks to the gallery only, do you?" His had been the spirit of one of the black volunteers of the Fifty-Fourth Massachusetts. Another of the dead black soldiers told the medium that he remained aware that whites did not care much for black people. "In the spirit-world," he reminded the gathering, "a black man is considered just as good as a white man, and how devilish foolish it looks to see a white man here feel better than a black man."[58]

Indians, always a favorite among mediums, sent their spirits to second the appeals of the living for spiritualist assistance. In the fall of 1863, not long after the death of Seminole war chief Billy Bowlegs, a Union officer in the Indian Territory, his spirit joined those of King Phillip, Tecumseh, Osceola, and others for "an Indian Council in Spirit Land." They not only reminded the living of their debt to the Native peoples but also declared that their living successors would not succumb to and assimilate into white society.[59]

War had its own logic that took the course of history out of human hands. It represented "a conflict which has for years existed and gathered strength in the *minds* of men, nay, in the superior forces which lie back of the men, moving and wielding them, as instruments, according to their states." In the storm of history, one described "the benumbing influence of a sort of paralysis, at the thought that we are all drifting upon rocks and shoals, with no pilot to call upon who is competent to help us safely out of our great dangers." Viewed in the social and historical context, "all persons are 'possessed,' in one way or another."[60]

By forcing the issue over the planters' peculiar version of property rights, secession moved the hitherto undiscussable future of slavery to the top of the agenda. War would be both "*a scourge for our national vices* and *the instrument of restoring health and purity.*" It would purge the government of "the miserable wire-pullers and politicians" and draw out "the moral and intellectual qualities of men *who have hitherto sought the shade,* and can only be brought out in great emergencies." "In this eventful revolution, what the patriots of the past failed to accomplish," wrote a Washington correspondent, "their descendants will perform, with the timely assistance of invisible powers." In the end, civil war would create "a virtuous, a veracious Republicanism, worthy to be the joy and the crown of the whole world."[61]

The Southern elite sustained "the character of the feudal ages" through a "monopoly of wealth and education," while keeping the rest "in poverty, below labor, in idleness and ignorant of the first rudiments of science and literature." This left them particularly good material "for mobs, for rebellion, for guerrilla warfare, for political excitements and social or military revolutions, and the corrupt politicians and ambitious demagogues arouse them and collect them into mobs or armies to carry out their schemes." War would place the nation on "the eve of a much firmer brotherhood than we ever knew before." "In the grand contest between the North—the exponent of liberty—and the South, the representative of tyranny," declared one spiritualist, "we of the North have not only superior intellectual and physical resources, but a just source of inspiration from the spirit-world which will direct us onward to a victory whose value to humanity will far surpass our brightest anticipations."[62]

Increasingly, spiritualists saw possibilities in the changes a national mobilization might engender. With admirable optimism, if not a grasp of history, one spiritualist insisted that "no nation has ever been successful in war, that I know of, where improvement, justice or liberty have not been the purpose of the contest." One of the spirits assured them that, however stormy the war, it would be "the harbinger of a beautiful morning. You cannot always see the hand as kind, that showers blessings upon you."[63]

The dynamic of the war for union made it a war of slave liberation, for free labor, and, perhaps, more. "War brings with it temporal injustice," said John G. Kaulback, a lifelong Fourierist and cooperationist in May 1861, "but does away with greater and more cruel injustice." A few weeks later, the *Banner of Light* predicted that the conflict would end with the abolition of slavery. Already, D. J. Mandell had laid out a complete plan for rebuilding the federal Union along lines that would respect the rights of the individual human spirit. Andrew J. Davis, "our mutual friend," published this "Programme for the Nation" in August 1861.[64]

\* \* \*

Under the press of events, the *Banner* cultivated a sense that the war was "fast assuming the form of a Revolution, in party estimates, and no longer is open to the fling of mere Rebellion." "The few presses and public speakers still bluster about fighting to the last drop of blood and the last dollar of treasure." "We cannot be made to believe that any respectable portion of the free citizens of the North and West are ready to throw themselves into a personal and bloody conflict with millions of their Southern brethren with whom they are closely allied by ties of consanguinity and affection."

> We were told with a great deal of emphasis, during the canvass of last year, that with a new administration was certainly to arise a *new order* of things. We never saw a likelier chance to inaugurate it. We were continually assured that

the dry and rigid old formalities of law—whether so expounded in the Dred Scott Case by the Supreme Court, or in any other form of meaning—were to be somehow passed over, set aside, despised and trampled on by the new men, whose resources were claimed to be vast enough to cope with all the extemporaneous needs and problems of the age.[65]

From this perspective, resolving secession required addressing deeper social questions. "This war, like all other similar revolutions," explained Cora L. V. Hatch, "is the result of the impurities of your own country." America "had as good a lesson in the history of the Roman and Grecian Republicans as any nation could have; yet with that record before you, and even before the vision of those who framed the Constitution and laws, your country is drifting to the same position which those republics occupied." In contrast, the course of the Confederacy inclined "to monarchial government," with its focus on "the goal and aim of the American mind—wealth, wealth, wealth! With that wealth has come corruption, and with that corruption has come the war." An ultimate resolution required getting beyond "distinctive political subjects."[66]

# 3

## Father Abraham

*President Lincoln and the Spirit of the Union*

Abraham Lincoln believed in what he called his "doctrine of necessity," which Herndon described as "fatalism." After reading Robert Chamber's *Vestiges of the Natural History of Creation,* he became "a warm advocate" of its "doctrine of development of evolution," based on his understanding of social and political change. In the Declaration of Independence, explained Lincoln, America's founders had written of liberty and equality in 1776 not as utopians but "simply to declare the *right,* so that the *enforcement* of it might follow as fast as circumstances should permit." Society progressed as "the most enlightened souls" embraced greater liberties, which "in God's own time . . . will be organized into law and thus woven into the fabric of our institutions."[1] Like the spiritualists, Lincoln did not regard reasoned discourse, respect for biblical wisdom, and the folk traditions of spirit communications as mutually exclusive.

The reality proved far more complex. The peculiar leadership of Abraham Lincoln as the new president eased individual spiritualist misgivings about the war and the value of the Union. Under his presidency, these perennial radicals who had begun in revolt against the shams of church and state found themselves as thoroughly immersed as possible in the government's cause, making practices that had been outlawed in parts of the South commonplace in Washington, D.C., even among political leaders. More than this, the Lincolns themselves had become involved at the edges of the spiritualist movement in the city, though obviously closer at some times than others. In the end, the vast majority of active spiritualists came to see Lincoln and his policies as a medium-like conduit to the stated values of the departed founders and a prophet of the nation's future survival. It marked a particular contribution to the elevation of Abraham Lincoln from president to spiritual hero of the Republic.

## The New President

Lincoln's cousin Dennis Hanks thought that by his twenty-first year, Lincoln had experienced "an entire revolution" to become "the same boy in every particular that he subsequently exhibited to the world from 1831 to the time of his death." Yet the young man who honed his social graces and political skills at New Salem shared no more than the bare facts of his early life, adding that he thought it "a great piece of folly to make any thing out of my early life. It can all be condensed into a single sentence. . . . 'The short and simple annals of the poor.' That's my life, and that's all you or any one else can make of it."[2]

However, the paucity of written records or the printed word did not mean an absence of ideas. Lincoln's mother, one of "the Hanks girls," had been "great at camp-meetings" in 1806, and she, with her husband, formally affiliated with the Free-Will Baptists in Kentucky and the Presbyterians in Indiana. After her death, his father joined the Disciples of Christ, which represented something of a Presbyterian split that assimilated many Baptist congregations across Pennsylvania and the lower South. As he told Mariah Vance, the family's black housekeeper in Springfield, "Visions are not uncommon to me. Nor were they uncommon to that blessed mother of mine." His family had dreams and premonitions and knew others who seemed to have a "second sight" and dealt with ghosts, spells, and the supernatural as a matter of course.[3]

As he grew to adulthood, the ambitious and clever Lincoln inclined toward the ideas of freethought common among sections of the Kentucky and Virginia gentry. When he read Thomas Paine's *Age of Reason*, Comte de Volney's *Ruins*, and writings by Voltaire, he "assimilated them into his own being" and later even wrote "an extended essay—called by many a book—in which he made an argument against Christianity, striving to prove that the Bible was not inspired and therefore not God's revelation, and that Jesus Christ was not the son of God" and "intended to have [it] published or given a wide circulation in some other way." Years later, Lincoln told one confidant that he remained a non-Christian, though he claimed to have "carefully read the Bible."[4] However one describes them, his views remained quite unorthodox.

No orthodoxy barred Lincoln from consulting mediums and fortune tellers, who became more numerous around Springfield, Illinois, as the movement got under way. He did not discuss his interest in the subject widely, partly because the clergy of the orthodox denominations regularly mobilized their flocks against anyone associated with a perceived rival. Lincoln told one White House confidant that he had been "greatly annoyed by the report" of his interest in spiritualism. The president preferred speaking in the least offensive generalities, and even Herndon claimed to know nothing directly, but thought the Lincolns "did sometimes attend here, in this city, séances. I am told this by Mr. Ordway, a Spiritualist," he added, most likely referring to Nehemiah G. Ordway, a New Hampshire man who served the Lincoln administration later in the post office. He added that Lincoln's "close friend from Springfield, Dr. Anson Henry seemed to have understood and shared the interest of the Lincolns in the subject" before moving to Oregon.[5]

Lincoln himself told Mrs. Vance that, after the 1850 death of their first son, Eddie, he and his wife consulted "three good women who are in touch with the spirit world, and can straighten us out." A devout churchgoer, Vance thought her employers rather gullible for frequenting "fortune tellers" and "cheats." While the listings of Springfield mediums are scant in the East Coast *Banner,* they do include the antebellum notice of a Mrs. D. R. Judkins, identified in the census as Dorothy Judkins, the wife of a cooper from New Hampshire.[6] She was thirty-seven years old at the time of Eddie's death and was the most likely spiritualist consultant of the Lincolns.

The Sangamon Association provided another possible source for these spiritualist advisers. New York native the Reverend Theophilus Sweet headed the local congregation of Campbellites, the denomination of Lincoln's parents, when he became interested in Fourierism. They acquired a site for their community at Loami, southwest of Springfield, and John Shoebridge Williams brought the Integral Phalanx from Ohio. The groups merged and sustained a society for several years before dissolving in 1848, with the legal assistance of Stephen T. Logan, one of Lincoln's early partners. Their president Williams had resigned upon his daughter's death and a few years later reported that her spirit had contacted him. He attained a certain prominence back east, where he launched the short-lived periodical the *Spirit Manifestations*.[7] As with other Fourierist groups, many members of the Sangamon Association would have followed the trajectory of Williams, leaving any number of spiritualists among the clients of Lincoln's partner.

Certainly, midwestern believers already viewed Lincoln as one of them. A gathering of "the professed Spiritualists of Knoxville, Ill.," referred to him as "our worthy brother." When the president-elect reached Cincinnati in February 1861, William T. Coggeshall, the historian of the local movement about to take charge of the state school system under the victorious Republicans, joined the presidential train and helped thwart a plot to kill him. News of another such conspiracy came from the spirits through Charles Lenox Redmond, a free black abolitionist.[8]

The most famous plot threatening Lincoln had centered on Baltimore, and private detective Allan Pinkerton unearthed it. Gradually drawn into military intelligence operations, he later brought a largely obscure group of colleagues to Washington. However, contemporaries would have recognized Seth Paine, one of the most prominent spiritualists in the state, and Alfred Cridge, the spiritualist and psychometrist married to Anne Denton, the sister of William Denton.[9]

Warren B. Chase plausibly described Lincoln as "a personal acquaintance" for whom he actively campaigned. As Lincoln's party headed east, Chase finished a lecture tour on the coast and headed west, passing through Baltimore, in which he described strong Unionist sentiments, despite the prevalence of "the rebel element" in the local government. From there, Chase headed to Philadelphia to see Lincoln.[10]

There, medium Levi Conklin canceled his appointments to attend the Philadelphia ceremonies greeting the arrival of the president-elect. When he did so, he recognized Lincoln as someone who had attended his readings earlier. Conklin said that Lincoln brought a transcript dated March 23 of an exchange at New York over "K," who had left Wisconsin three days earlier and reported having died. Lincoln returned three days later, reporting that he had a telegraph from the brother-in-law of "K," stating that he had died. Conklin thought the story such a proof of spirit communication that he arranged to have it printed. The *Cleveland Plain Dealer* published it under the title "The President Elect Is a Spiritualist." Back in Springfield, Ordway mentioned Lincoln's spiritualist interests to Herndon. A Democratic campaign tract warned that the election of Lincoln "demonized" the country. In England a piece of sheet music was published that portrayed him holding a candle while violins and tambourines flew about his head. The piece of music was called "The Dark

Seance Polka," and the caption below the illustration of the president read "Abraham Lincoln and the Spiritualists."[11]

Lincoln's rhetoric often sounded spiritualist in tone. In his inaugural address, he appealed in familiar language to "the mystic chords of memory, stretching from every battle-field, and patriot grave, to every living heart and hearthstone, all over this broad land," when "touched, as surely they will be, by the better angels of our nature." As the president explained to one of his housekeepers who touted the importance of the Bible, "The same Bible says God is spirit. So if all things are created in his image and likeness, as the Bible says, and I believe that also to be a main truth, then his Son was spirit. Then we are spirit. We could go on and on and say the birds of the air and fish of the sea were spirit, and so on.... [W]hy couldn't we, or our loved ones, return after the state called death?" Much later, when Robert used spiritualism as proof of his mother's madness, she replied, "I am not EITHER a Spiritualist—but I sincerely believe—our loved ones, who have only, 'gone before' are permitted to watch over those who were dearer to them than life."[12] Yet these oddly contradictory disclaimers were hardly unknown within the movement.

Rather typically, one writer asserted that Herndon, an unabashed skeptic of such matters, "flatly denied" Lincoln's interest in spiritualism. In fact, Herndon stated publicly that he thought Lincoln inclined toward such beliefs, being "a kind of fatalist in some aspects of his philosophy, and skeptical in his religion." The president certainly believed his premonitions of his own untimely death. Herndon thought the president simply "had great—too great confidence in the common judgment of an uneducated people. He believed that the common people had truths that philosophers never dreamed of; and often appealed to that common judgment of the common people over the shoulders of scientists." As a result, Herndon thought his partner to be "in some phases of his nature very, very superstitious; and it may be—it is quite probable that he in his gloom, sadness, fear and despair, invoked the spirits of the dead to reveal to him the cause of his states of gloom, sadness, fear and despair. He craved light from all intelligences to flash his way to the unknown future of his life."[13]

Nevertheless, this is to say nothing more than that the president was a man of his age and circumstances. "The spiritualist epidemic was then commencing to rage in America," observed one visitor to wartime Washington from the heart of the new administration. "One heard of nothing but of spirits and mediums. All tables and other furniture seemed to have become alive, and you could not sit down upon a chair without a spiritual suspicion."[14]

## The Spirit of the President

As the president, Lincoln faced a proverbial army of "job seekers," some claiming spiritualist credentials. William O. Stoddard noted that so many wrote the president on behalf of the angel Gabriel and dead founders of the nation that he speculated as to whether "when any man goes clean crazy in these war-days he at once sits down and pens an epistle to the President."[15]

Subsequent writers automatically assumed that spiritualists generally fell into Stoddard's category of "crazy," but they did not. Growing up in Rochester himself, he had been familiar with the movement from the onset. When he moved to Chicago, he went to work on Seth Paine's paper and described the printers generally as believers. He attended numerous séances and readings in Chicago, concluding that the belief in spirit communication could make Paine into a great man, even as it made "wrecks" of others.[16] That is, an acknowledgment of fraudulent mediums did not preclude anyone from a belief in the possibility of spirit communication, a faith that merits the same kind of assessment as any other.

Few of these letters survive in Lincoln's own manuscripts, partly because Robert destroyed material he deemed embarrassing to his father. Francis L. Capen sent a letter to get work predicting the weather, on which the president scribbled that Capen "told me three days ago that it would not rain again till the 30th of April or 1st of May—It is raining now & has been for ten hours—I can not spare any more time to Mr. Capen." After Lincoln's friend Colonel Edward D. Baker died in battle, one I. B. Conklin wrote the president to assure him that he had "experienced a happy reality—a glorious change, by the process termed 'death.'" Most despicably, Charles J. Colchester—claiming to be the illegitimate son of an English duke—fastened relentlessly on Mrs. Lincoln after the death of her son Willie in February 1862. Far from catering to his wife's unrealistic hopes, the president simply sent an official from the Smithsonian to warn Colchester out of town.[17] These individuals seem to have had generally little or marginal contact with the movement.

This did not mean that Lincoln did not share Mary's deep desire for contact with Willie or rejected any and all who attempted to communicate with the spirits. That spring he spent several days at Fortress Monroe waiting for news of the campaign on the peninsula. While there, he asked Colonel Le Grand Bouton Cannon to read from William Shakespeare's *The Life and Death of King John*. Cannon came to this passage:

> And, father cardinal, I have heard you say
> That we shall see and know our friends in heaven:
> If that be true, I shall see my boy again;

"Colonel," the president interrupted, "did you ever dream of a lost friend, and feel that you were holding sweet communion with that friend, and yet have a sad consciousness that it was not a reality? Just so I dream of my boy Willie." On another occasion, he asked an officer, "Do you ever find yourself talking with the dead? Since Willie's death, I catch myself every day involuntarily talking with him as if he were with me."[18]

Indeed, this fitted his belief that unseen forces shaped our individual destinies and often offered us premonitions and dreams that demonstrated this reality. There was none more so, perhaps, than Lincoln's well-documented dream of having awakened in the White House to hear the weeping downstairs at his own funeral. That the singularly melancholic man with the "fatalist" faith won and wielded power during the heyday of the spiritualist movement seems an unlikely coincidence.

Certainly, Lincoln never hesitated to tap the talent he needed from spiritualists or occultists of any sort. For military expertise, he pulled out of retirement the noted eccentric and occultist General Ethan Allen Hitchcock. When conscription came, he also arranged a version of "conscientious objector" status for Shakers and others with elder Frederick W. Evans of Mount Lebanon. Some spiritualists, such as H. H. Day, took their place among others seeking government funds for technological innovations.[19]

The number of other government officials involved with the spiritualist gatherings proved truly daunting. Horton thought it became "notorious that many of the leading men of the nation are full believers." Gideon and Mary Jane Welles, who had lost children, had consulted spiritualists, but spiritualists expressed broader affinities as wider circles of the cabinet became more militantly antislavery. A cousin of austere secretary of war Edwin M. Stanton had mediumistic abilities, and, as such things supposedly ran in the family, spiritualists wondered if Stanton himself might have some direct association to the wisdom of the spirits. They included Congressman Robert Dale Owen (author of *Footfalls on the Boundary of Another World*), Judge Ebenezer R. Hoar, former congressman David E. Somes, James G. Blaine, and Schuyler Colfax. Although Mrs. Somes had become reclusive after the loss of her eldest son, Mrs. Lincoln asked her and her husband "to spend an evening at the White House, and asked them to bring along two young mediums." The first family expressed a special fondness for one of their spirit guides, "Miss Pinkie." General Daniel Sickles and other notables participated in this not-unusual White House gathering.[20]

Active spiritualists formed a network well integrated into the new administration. John Pierpont was a seventy-six-year-old Yale graduate and former Unitarian minister who, as a young man teaching in South Carolina, developed a lifelong hatred for slavery. He came back to work as a lawyer in Newburyport and then as a businessman. He eventually passed through Harvard Divinity School, but his reformism went beyond the respectable issues such as temperance to abolitionism, which made securing a pastorate difficult. Despite his age, he volunteered to serve as the chaplain of Colonel Henry Wilson's Twenty-Second Massachusetts Infantry, but poor health forced him to resign within two weeks. Pierpont stayed in Washington, accepting a clerkship in the Treasury Department.[21]

From his position in the Treasury Department, old Pierpont helped provide work and support for those passing through the city. Colburn remembered him as "a tall, slender man, straight and commanding in appearance, and over eighty years of age, with the quick step and alert manner of a boy." She thought he "had the absolute confidence of Mr. and Mrs. Lincoln" and became a conduit for information from the field about the conditions of the freed people. Along with others, he funneled information from workers in refugee camps across the country who urged government action to "make freedom a blessing to the freed," who often "suffered fearfully from insufficient shelter & clothing, from sickness, from want of occupation, & not least, from abusive treatment at the hands of army officers." Others present in the Treasury included Parnie R. Hannum and Stephen James Wilson Tabor, a Vermont-born Iowa editor, a relative by marriage of Lewis Masquerier, the aged land reformer.[22]

Also in the government sat the Connecticut-born Henry Clarke Wright out of his apprenticeship as a hatmaker into the Congregationalist clergy. By 1837 his radicalism carried him beyond abolitionism to women's rights and virtually anarchistic ideas. After going overseas for the peace movement, he had written *Defensive War Proved to Be a Denial of Christianity and of the Government of God*, returning to the United States during its war of conquest against Mexico. Like other radicals, Wright concluded that "slavery or the Republic must die," and the willingness of the Union to take up the challenge of war inspired him to see "the American Republic as the God-appointed Messiah of Liberty to the great family of Nations."[23]

Spiritualists also made great contributions to the war effort in such shadows. While Paine and Cridge worked in the Pinkerton Agency, Henry S. Olcott served the army by investigating fraud in government contracts. Cridge and Olcott later took positions in the Army Quartermaster's Department, as did George A. Bacon and William E. Coleman.[24]

Then, too, established political leaders, such as former Democratic judge John W. Edmonds, saw the president as a kindred spirit. He knew that "no man was ever placed in a more trying & responsible position than that in which you have been placed." Edmonds sent him "two Books & shall rejoice indeed if they can be of any service to you." Edmonds sent Lincoln copies of his *Spiritualism* and the *Sacred Circle* in hopes they would explain the government's "upward progress," which would lay "the foundations for a glorious future for our country & for freedom." "You & I may not remain on earth long enough to behold the full result of what you have begun," wrote Edmonds, "but we & all mankind will in the future behold it and rejoice."[25]

At some point in the summer of 1862, Nettie Colburn decided to go to the capital and would later write the most authoritative account of movement activities at Washington. While she was a child in rural Connecticut, her dying grandfather told her his dead wife had visited him. Encouraged by the joyous tears of her father, an ardent Republican, she pursued her mediumship "from my humble home in the ranks of the laboring people" into a new profession. When her father and four brothers left for the front, she and her cousin Parthenia Hannum followed to Baltimore, where Washington A. Danskin helped arrange her visit to the capital. So did Major George Chorpenning and his wife, he being the first to get a government contract to carry the mail across the Rockies, from Salt Lake City to San Francisco. Chorpenning had participated in the early war effort but became preoccupied with the legal battle over his postal contract. Perhaps because of Colburn's presence, the "brilliant company" that met weekly at the Chorpennings usually ended in a séance. There, too, she met Republican congressmen Henry L. Dawes of Massachusetts as well as Eben Clark Ingersoll, John Franklin Farnsworth of Illinois, "and many others, whose names I cannot now recall."[26]

Colburn brought a letter of reference from Danskin to Thomas Gales Forster. The South Carolina–born printer had served in the army of an independent Texas and been among the earliest and most ardent organizers of the National Typographical Union. At the time of Lincoln's election, he and his family boarded with fellow spiritualists in Cincinnati, but he soon came to

Washington to work as a clerk in the War Department. When entranced, Forster told Colburn that, beyond arranging leave for her brother, she had "other and greater work to do" in Washington, including contacting Lincoln. When she said that she thought the president would simply have her arrested as a lunatic, he urged her not to make such assumptions. Although he had not yet met the president, Forster had seen him many times and offered to accompany her, a suggestion that she "flatly refused."[27] Notwithstanding the title of Colburn's published recollections, spiritualism usually takes a back seat in her memory to her efforts to negotiate the arcane mysteries of the federal bureaucracy.

Certainly, Colburn's book did appear long after most of the principals had passed from the scene and could not refute its contents. Nevertheless, her book did not do what might be expected from a dishonest, self-promoting account. She did not slight the influence of other spiritualists in the community. It could have also emphasized her connection with the president rather than Mary Lincoln, but did not. Finally, the Lincoln she presented was never entirely credulous about manifestations and often appears as disparaging and teasing about them. Certainly, she did not include any of the absurd claims, such as that the spirits moved Lincoln to proclaim emancipation.[28]

Colburn's version of the famous story about Lincoln on the levitating grand piano is also far more plausible than it became in its repetition. Colonel Simon P. Kase later described a séance in which Colburn levitated a grand piano. He and Lincoln supposedly climbed onto the instrument but were unable to still its movement. The year made it impossible, and Belle Laurie Miller, who used the piano as a prop, might have been a more likely candidate than Colburn. Laurie's son remembered Lincoln observing Belle's dancing piano because the boy had been injured by a runaway horse earlier in the day, which placed it in late in 1862. He remembered Lincoln's quip, "Never mind, Cranston, if they break the table, I will give you a new one." Colburn placed the incident explicitly on February 5, 1863, and describes a much more skeptical president, who, unable to see the mechanisms moving the piano, attributed the movement to "an invisible power."[29]

By late 1862, Colburn had become something of a regular in the growing spiritualist circles in Washington, regularly meeting at the Georgetown home of Cranston Laurie, certainly an acquaintance of Nehemiah G. Ordway, the New England agent for the post office. Various paranormal talents already guided much of his family, including a married daughter, Belle Miller, who played the piano. James J. Miller, the inventor of a steam condenser and a government contractor, had married Belle Laurie. He thought the Lincolns became interested in the doings of the spiritualists "soon after his inauguration. Some senators were telling their experiences one day when the President expressed a curiosity to attend one of the Laurie séances; not that he had the least faith in spirit communion with mortals, but would like to investigate the jugglery practiced." This provided Colburn's first contact with the Lincolns, and it is probably important to note that Herndon's informant for Lincoln's continuing wartime interest in the subject, Frank B. Carpenter, had likely been acquainted with Laurie. The author of the *Inner Life of Abraham Lincoln*, Carpenter recalled not only Colchester but Forster, Lucy A. Hamilton, and a Cecelia A. Redmond.[30]

Shortly after Colburn's arrival, the organized spiritualists of the city fretted over the attempts of the unassociated self-described mediums to contact the Lincolns. One Lydia Smith wrote him, claiming to channel "the Father of the Universe the Creator of all things." Surely, this was the "woman by the name of Smith" who impressed local spiritualists as "half deranged. Her wild manner and disjointed sentences so decreased the size of her audience, that she found remaining none but a hooting mass of boys and a number of empty benches." Presenting herself a messenger of Christ, she offered to tell the president and six of his picked men "just what to do that will speedily terminate this Devilish war now existing in your midst. Now do as I tell you or if not you will have to suffer the consequences of not." It left the local spiritualists "exceedingly mortified," and they undertook a meeting in response featuring Pierpont, Colburn, A. E. Newton, and others.[31]

## From the Depths of the War

General spiritualist reactions to the crisis of secession and war had a certain clarity from the beginning. While viewing the election of Lincoln as the triumph of a representative American figure, the *Banner of Light* found his administration strikingly distinct. It expressed a growing "confidence in the sagacity and superior wisdom of Abraham Lincoln. It does appear to us as if Nature had kept him out of sight, and out of the destructive influences of public life, for this very hour. Had he been a politician all his days, he would have friends to reward and enemies to punish now; and that work must naturally have warped his mind and prejudiced his efforts in this great crisis." At the end of the war's first year, it continued to declare Lincoln "up with the age in all respects."[32]

Mrs. Lincoln pursued her interests in spiritualism rather rigorously and had become a regular at the Lauries. Senator Orville Hickman Browning noted a conversation with her in which she said that Mrs. Laurie "had made wonderful revelations to her about her little son Willy who died last winter, and also about things on the earth." Mrs. Elvira M. Dupuy, a Washington matron, also remembered meeting Mrs. Lincoln at the Lauries along with Nettie Colburn. The first lady also arranged to get jobs for Colburn and Hannum at the U.S. Treasury Building.[33]

The president, as well as his wife, sometimes attended these events, and the Lauries clearly had a relationship with both of them. Mrs. Laurie recalled intervening with the president over the case of a Maine soldier convicted of desertion. A friend of the soldier hurried to Washington with the explanation that he had overstayed his furlough because of his sister's death but had no way to reach Lincoln and been directed to the Lauries. One need not believe Mrs. Laurie's claim that the White House guards had orders "to admit Mrs. Laurie at any hour, day or night," to accept the notion that she had access and used it, as did others, to save the lives of soldiers facing execution. One evening, she said, she hardly got the words from her mouth when Lincoln, without speaking, motioned for a pen, jotted a reprieve, and told her "never fear to arouse me on an errand of mercy like this." Like Colburn, Laurie made no claims about his beliefs but thought him "warm hearted enough to be a Spiritualist."[34]

Young Jack Laurie later said that he had "very often seen Mr. Lincoln at my father's house engaged in attending circles for spiritual phenomena" through 1862 and 1863, with Mrs. Lincoln sometimes with him, surely inverting their likely levels of participation. He even recalled the president's attempt to become "partially entranced, and I have heard him make remarks while in that condition, in which he spoke of his deceased son Willie, and said that he saw him." Lincoln had been present when Colburn went into a trance, after which he told her that he had recognized the verbal styles as those of Daniel Webster. He became particularly fond of the spirit of "Dr. Bamford," an old-fashioned Maine Yankee, who talked to the president through her. Colburn's "first sitting at the White House" came early one December night in 1862, and she mentioned other visits into February and March 1863. Toward the end of this time, the Lincolns hosted a private séance at the White House, as the president took lunch.[35]

In May 1863, the Lincolns brought Colburn into the White House, just as the news of Chancellorsville had reached the president but had not yet become known in the city. This also seems to have been the incident when Colburn's reminiscences developed more fully. The Someses escorted her through the city to the White House, where "a servant, who was evidently on the watch for us, quickly opened the door and we were hurried up stairs to the executive chamber, where Mr. Lincoln and two gentlemen were awaiting our coming." She noticed the stripes on their pants, indicating they were military, as Mrs. Lincoln arrived. The president told her, "You need not be afraid, as these friends have seen something of this before." She entered into a trance and began writing. As she emerged, she heard the president saying that "every line she has drawn conforms to the plan agreed upon." When Somes and his wife rejoined them, he asked if all went well. Lincoln replied that "Miss Nettie does not seem to require eyes to do anything." As they left for the Chorpennings, Lincoln reminded them "not to mention this meeting at present."[36]

There simply exists no substantive reason to dismiss entirely these sources, though there are often multiple possible interpretations of their meaning. Expressions of astonishment at the spirits' awareness of sensitive information about the war could have been amazement at their acuity. Yet they could just as easily have reflected concern about the laxity with which sources in the government treated such information.

Some writers have challenged these accounts because Joshua Fry Speed, an old friend of Lincoln's, sent him a note, in October 1863, to suggest he would enjoy meeting "my very good friend Mrs. Cosby and Miss Netty Colburn her friend," both "very choice spirits themselves" who could provide "some relief from the tedious round of office seekers."[37] The date of this letter was used to question Colburn's recollection of an older association with the Lincolns. However, Speed, an irregular visitor to Washington, had not been there for a year and most likely encountered the charming mediums after the president did. Then, too, Colburn's involvement in earlier events, such as the local spiritualist concerns about Mrs. Smith, indicate that she had been present, on and off, for at least a year before Speed's letter.

In fact, around the time of Speed's arrival, spiritualist activity in the nation's capital had turned into other channels. The Lauries had moved to the suburbs, and a smaller version of the gatherings had briefly passed into the home of Mrs. Anna Mills Cosby before her own death. Cosby, by the way, was the daughter of architect Robert Mills, who had worked to complete the capital, and spiritualists attributed meaning to the project's completion. Almost surely, these figures brought Speed into the group, where he had met Colburn.[38] The May 1864 death of Mrs. Cosby and the move of the Lauries from the city reshuffled local spiritualist networks.

The war's last summer did not spare Washington or its spiritualist community. As Confederates moved on the nation's capital, the Second District of Columbia called out Missouri spiritualist Lewis C. Hootee to Fort Stevens. On July 12, the contending lines battled over a house belonging to one of the contributors to the *Banner of Light*. Mrs. E. D. E. N. Southworth had been close enough to hear the fighting "in her cottage with only her daughter and hired man for company," though a protective spirit joined them. "Eight cannonballs passed through it entirely, holes 3–6 inches in diameter, sides with bullet holes." Only minutes after the women fled the house, the Confederates arrived. The Reeves family returned to their home to find everything damaged, "except the library of spiritual books, which was unharmed," though a shell struck and compressed the file of the *Banner*. Reeves had "prophesied, some time ago, that his home would become memorable before the close of the war, and this appears to be a literal fulfillment of that prophecy. The Government has since purchased the grounds adjoining the Reeves estate for a Soldiers' Cemetery."[39]

By this point, the government that defended at Fort Stevens had expectations far different from those with which it had entered the war. The conflict had transformed a modest little central government into a massive entity engaged in unprecedented spending that had a transformative effect on the economy and society. "Orthodoxy of every stripe has been deprived of its peculiar authority by the events of this war," proclaimed the *Banner of Light*. "The process was going on for some time before actual battles began; but it required this very culmination of arms and violence to deal out the blow for which the creaking structure was waiting."[40]

By the summer of 1864, spiritualist efforts had come to focus on the freedmen. Bacon attempted an association with Laurie and Forster on its business committee. Pierpont, Forster, Colchester, Colburn and Hannum, Colonel Nathan W. Daniels, and others attended the wedding of Major George Chorpenning and Carrie V., daughter of the late Colonel Robert W. Dunlap of Philadelphia. "Closely confined to his desk in the War Department during the past two and a half years," Forster worried "that the channels which had been so widely opened to spirit influx might have become closed—that material care and social labors might have drawn the mind from higher contemplations—and that the instrument which had been so carefully attuned might no more be played upon by angel fingers." At the height of the struggle, his spirit guide, Professor Dayton, began to speak to Forster.[41]

Beneath fanciful tales about the Emancipation Proclamation or galloping pianos, the spiritualists made a very real contribution to addressing massive problems the war dropped on a people rather ill prepared to consider solutions. Spiritualism had a particular hold on those interested in the healing arts who found themselves quickly drawn into the war, which generated injuries and illness far beyond what the existing medical professionals had been addressing. Many, such as Napoleon Bonaparte Wolfe, had been "practicing the healing art *a la* Newton, with great success" before taking his commission as surgeon in a Pennsylvania regiment and going to war.[42] The accounts of C. D. Griswold at Shiloh or Henry T. Child at Gettysburg represent the experiences and contributions of many.

As the Civil War unfolded into a struggle for slave liberation, it also emancipated a radicalism in the Republican Party. Historians often discuss Radical Republicanism as a current among politicians with, perhaps, some popular support among some in the South. Spiritualism offers an insight into a wider view. Before the war's end, spiritualism, with its Republican base and its heavy dose of social radicalism, certainly provided a source for persistent calls for a thorough reconstruction of American civilization.

## Transcendence

Democratic appeals to white supremacism naturally alienated many spiritualists, who hoped for a consensus that slavery had "perished with the sound of the first gun in Charleston Harbor." The local movement had already supported the Republicans against New York mayor Fernando Wood, one of the richest men in the city. Then, in the summer of 1863, the Democrats responded by making an issue of the limited federal reliance on conscription to stir Irish animosity toward emancipation and blacks in what came to be remembered as the "draft riots." In their aftermath, John H. W. Toohey "spoke wisely and nobly in defense of the Irish in this country, and his address was full of patriotic and liberty-loving appeals, which brought down the house with thunders of applause." They also noted that the local *Journal of Commerce* and the *New York World* published forged presidential proclamations and blamed the *New York Herald* for forging an alleged Republican campaign tract advocating "miscegenation."[43]

Nor did spiritualists credit the constitutional complaints about the Lincoln administration. Regular contributors to the *Banner,* such as Dr. Horace Dresser, frankly discussed constitutional issues, such as the federal suspension of habeas corpus in key areas, but insisted that "tyranny never unlooses its grasp till its throat is seized by a stronger hand, and then at first tightens, if it can, to the death of its victim, unless forced to loose its hold to defend itself, as the rebel government now seems to be by its talk of freeing and arming its slaves." Spiritualists had already distanced themselves from Greeley's increasing hostility to radicalism. One reminded that their duty lay in the advancement "of general, universal laws, which are as fixed and unchangeable in their nature and action as Deity himself."[44]

Some of the opposition press and part of the regular army officer corps still talked of a coup as the best way to both reestablish the Union and thwart what they called the constitutional abuses of the Lincoln administration. General George B. McClellan, having built the Army of the Potomac, seemed to be cast for this role of "the man on horseback" to take charge of the nation. "This bold and desperate scheme, entertained by men who call themselves strict Constructionists of the constitution," declared the *Banner*, "would at once subvert the spirit and forms of public liberty, and set up the power of the army instead. . . . Thus did Rome fall, and thus have fallen at last all nations—great and small—that trusted their liberties with the keeping of military hands."[45]

Attacked by conservatives over emancipation, Lincoln also faced a revolt by radicals who wanted to run a more consistently antislavery candidate. Eventually, they hosted a Cleveland convention that nominated John C. Frémont for president and John Cochrane of New York for vice president. The Democratic *Boston Traveler* even suggested that the spiritualists would be "putting a Presidential ticket into the field."[46]

Most spiritualists scarcely disguised their sympathies for the president as he came up for reelection, though they strove to sound nonpartisan. In February 1864, the *Banner* suggested, "Wire-pulling and war do not go together." "If Mr. Lincoln is popular, let him remain so; if somebody else wants his place, let him wait," the paper suggested. "Nothing could come more awkwardly or dangerously for us than the Presidential election of this year." "We believe in effectively closing the rebellion, instead of clogging the wheels of government by turning the attention of the country to President-making," declared the *Banner*. "Save the country first—electioneer afterwards." As Congressman Joshua R. Giddings tried to rally the Radicals to Lincoln, the spiritualists gathered for their first national convention in three years.[47]

The national spiritualist convention of 1864 came as the war reached something of a stalemate and provided an important boost to a campaign that Lincoln himself thought might fail. A series of local and state conventions and conferences had led up to this. Boston spiritualists met in February, and New Yorkers held a three-day convention in April, while the Philadelphians played a major role in bringing discussions of a national convention to reality. Henry T. Child explicitly declared their purposes. "Our fathers perceived certain divine principles, on which they sought to establish our government, and which they enunciated in the immortal Declaration of Independence," "Liberty, the boon for which aspiring humanity has ever sought and prayed, but which has been too little understood, too often crippled in its flight by the sheers of conservatism and error—of ignorance and a false theology on the one hand, and carried forward into licentiousness on the other—will never be understood aright until harmonious men and women come to realize it physically, mentally, and morally."[48]

The convention met August 9–14 in Chicago's Bryan Hall, the largest in the city. Specifically, the convention sounded a call for the "perfect and entire equality of rights as between the sexes, including equal property, equal marital, equal parental, equal educational, equal civil, political, and equal religious rights; and, that we reject the absurd pretext, that sex, in any instance whatever, confers the slightest authority." In a scheduled address, Leo Miller urged the merits of Stephen Pearl Andrews's "individual sovereignty" and the importance of local association.[49]

The body decisively overwhelmed the tiny minority that had never warmed to the Republicans, Lincoln, or the Union war effort. From Daniel Tarbell of Vermont to Judge Albert G. W. Carter of Ohio, they had long mocked the pretensions of abolitionists and Unionists. Amanda M. Spence complained that "too much corruption has pervaded in every department of government, religion and society. We have professed to be a Christian people and government, advocating the principles of peace and fraternity, but the whole country is now involved in an appalling war."[50] Most, however, shared Lizzie Doten's sense that "if we allow ourselves to be gagged, it will be because Jeff Davis & Co. are among us."

Wright, the veteran abolitionist, dominated the Committee on the State of the Union. Its proposed resolutions minced no words, denouncing secession as a "denial of the democratic theory of the right of the people to decide who shall administer their public affairs, and, consequently, the substitution of the oligarchic rule." They added their hostility to the "enslavement of millions of the human family and their posterity," declaring that they would resist this "no matter how long the struggle, how great the cost, or how fearful the sacrifice." The convention urged the reelection of Abraham Lincoln "in whose veins run the blood of the common people." They declared that "however slow and circumspect, he has never taken a step backward, but has steadily proceeded onward in the right direction." They repudiated "any division on any pretext in favor of any other candidate," declaring it "incumbent upon all the friends of impartial justice and liberty, and of universal progress to use all the social, moral, religious and political influence . . . to secure the reelection of Abraham Lincoln in the impending Presidential canvass." Cincinnati's Judge Carter got a disproportionate number of Lincoln's critics onto the regular Committee on Resolutions, where they constituted a fifth of the twenty-five members, roughly twice their feeble strength in the convention generally. In the end, the convention voted 316 to 55 for its most pro-Lincoln measures.

The convention discussed organization. Initially, it divided over the name: the United States Spiritualist Union or the Spiritualist Brotherhood of the United States of America, with ten principles of spiritualism. However, Warren Chase successfully argued against a national organization without forming what would be constituent bodies. The circular of his committee "to the Spiritualists and Friends of Progress Everywhere" recommended "the immediate formation (without creeds or articles of faith), of societies or local organizations, for associate efforts by Spiritualists and all progressive minds everywhere." In the end, the convention sustained him 217 to 45.[51]

In the wake of the convention, the Religio-Philosophical Society at nearby St. Charles established itself as something of a flagship association. Its Stevens S. Jones praised "this august assemblage of free thinkers—this body of philanthropists—this assemblage of harmonial philosophers—this first National Convention of Spiritualists." His society boasted "no church, no creeds, no dogmatisms to inculcate or maintain. With us truth is omnipotent," he declared. For a period, at least, it seemed as though the model of the Religio-Philosophical Society would prevail, as spiritualists across the land of Lincoln organized themselves, spreading into adjacent states. The local association at Des Moines even adopted the same name, Religio-Philosophical Society. The new First Wisconsin Heavy Artillery had voted to make a female member, Ella E. Gibson Hobart, its chaplain. Although Lincoln supported the appointment, he left it to the discretion of the War Department, which eventually blocked it.[52] That her rejection is usually ascribed to gender and she herself later described herself simply as a Christian reflects the later marginalization of spiritualism rather than its prominence in the war years.

Wright reported on the convention to William Lloyd Garrison and the *Liberator*. "I have attended many Conventions of Abolitionists and friends of progress during the past thirty-five years, but never have I attended one in which justice, liberty, free labor, free institutions, free thought and free speech, and loyalty to God and man, have received a more enthusiastic support, and cunning, fraud, injustice, slavery and treason a more signal, triumphant and unmistakable defeat." This represented the first organizational support for Lincoln's renomination.[53]

Spiritualists pulled out all the stops in campaigning for Lincoln's reelection. Lizzie Doten proposed to address "the Issues of the Day, the War, and the November elections," from a woman's perspective, concluding with her declaration to stand by "the Union forever." The spirit of Colonel Baker took his place alongside Dr. Henry T. Child and sent his congratulations to his old friend in the White House. Victory, Baker assured the president, would make America "a Beacon light to all."[54] The movement greeted his second inauguration as a vindication of their sacrifices for the Union, emancipation, and a radical Reconstruction. Finally, they readily added the president to the iconography of martyrs sacrificed on the altar of liberty.

These appeals did not necessarily take place from exclusively spiritualist platforms. Nettie Colburn spoke alongside Congressman Henry L. Dawes. In her words, she "became entranced and addressed the audience for about fifteen minutes. The spirit controlling me stated . . . with unerring certainty, that Abraham Lincoln would be re-elected at the coming national election." She awoke to the applause of the audience, and Dawes congratulated her "in his kind way upon the manner in which I had been instrumental in closing the evening's exercises." By the October state elections, the trend seemed clear to spiritualists that Nettie's informant from the other side, along with many more of the spirits, would prove correct. Though close, Pennsylvania went Republican, as did Ohio and Indiana. In November the reelection of Abraham Lincoln represented not only a victory of party but also a popular declaration of support for the administration's implementation of emancipation, with the recruitment, arming, and use of black troops in the war. So, too, it represented a willingness to stay the course. "The present election," declared the *Banner*, "will long be reverted to as a great historical point in the career of the nation."[55]

The campaign generally made spiritualism indistinguishable from Radical Unionism in areas such as southwestern Missouri. Against the backdrop of the fall 1864 Confederate offensive, local Unionists—particularly those in uniform—turned to John Russell Kelso as their spokesman. Emancipation, wrote one spiritualist there, "grates hard on the feelings of the rich and influential portion of our inhabitants, but when they can be brought to realize that the law of progress requires personal sacrifice for the benefit of humanity, perhaps they will be more reconciled." In this "very exciting contest" in the Fourth Congressional District, Kelso ran against his former commander, a well-known and popular figure. In contrast, Kelso "had only come into public notice" with the war, but he "found time to make a canvass of the district." He lost in those areas that had been least contested, but Kelso's "hosts of friends and admirers, especially among the soldiers," gave him "a handsome plurality" of 3,841 to 3,548 for the incumbent Republican moderate, with only 400 for the Democrats.[56] In general, the Radicals triumphed in the election.

As Lincoln rode this wave of vindication, he encountered Nettie Colburn, who warned him of the "shadows" hanging over him. Lincoln joked about the threats to his life, adding that "nobody wants to harm me." "Therein lies your danger, Mr. Lincoln," she responded of his "over-confidence in your fellow-men." "I shall live till my work is done," he explained, "and no earthly power can prevent it. And then it doesn't matter." Within weeks of his second inauguration in March 1865, Federal forces successfully closed the circle on Petersburg and Richmond. In the field, Sergeant Edward T. Steele claimed that his spirit guide led him across the battlefield, "through a tremendous fire, to a point in the rebels' abatis where a narrow path was left for their pickets to pass through." His comrade Lieutenant Colonel John W. Crosby had also spoken of "his spirit-friends on these occasions, so much so that he lost all consciousness of fear, and the whizzing of musket-balls produced no more trepidation in him than the falling rain," but they had not saved him from being repeatedly wounded earlier or, ultimately, from being killed in action before Petersburg. Within hours, though, the Confederate government abandoned its capital to "a force of colored Union troops." Six days later, the largest and best-led Confederate army surrendered at Appomattox Court House.[57]

Only a few days later, the *Banner of Light* stopped its presses to insert an announcement: "Terrible National Calamity! Murder of President Lincoln!" The president had sincerely believed that he "had never made an enemy in his life, and supposed, in the thrust of his simple heart, that no living person harbored a thought of malice against him." "Who cannot feel now, looking back over the eventful history of this country for the last four years," asked the *Banner*, "that its guidance has been in other than human hands?" The news reached New York on April 15, and, before the day's end "several interested citizens" invited Emma Hardinge to speak the next day at the Cooper Institute. That same day, Chase spoke at Syracuse, while back across the country, to Illinois and beyond, spiritualists participated in or hosted commemorative meetings. Official Washington brought Olcott and his New York City detectives to investigate the assassination, and the three government commissioners coordinating the investigation included Britton A. Hill, an associate of many spiritualists over the decades and a future Greenback theorist.[58]

Devastated, Mary Lincoln sought consolation wherever she could. One account later said—and her son Robert claimed to believe—that "women spiritualists in some way gained access to her." However, Colburn had left for New England, and the regular soirees at the Laurie home had long since dissolved. Other sources say Dr. Anson G. Henry, an old family friend from Springfield, turned up to console her. "I believe our departed friends hover over and around us, and are fully cognizant of all that transpires, while we are not sensible of their presence," Henry later wrote, adding that he had "made Mrs. Lincoln a convert to this doctrine & it is fast becoming a great source of comfort and consolation to her. When I was to see her this evening she was comparatively joyous."[59]

With the earlier Illinois cases of Ira B. Eddy and John J. Glover behind him, Robert Lincoln had used spiritualism to make the case for his mother's alleged insanity when he tried to have her institutionalized. The very hint that his father had shared these interests would have directly undercut his position, and he responded to Colburn's book by getting former White House secretaries to go on record. Ward Hill Lamon insisted that the president had been "no dabbler in divination, astrology, horoscopy, prophecy, ghostly lore, or witcheries of any sort." John George Nicolay insisted that Lincoln never even attended a séance, "and if he ever did so it was out of mere curiosity." Not long after, Carl Sandburg and others blamed Mary's insanity on the influence of Mary's dressmaker Elizabeth Keckley and others, whose beliefs had "wrecked havoc" with the first lady's fragile feminine psyche.[60]

Nevertheless, the Lincoln administration left a legacy that included the logical possibility of a Radical Republicanism. Spiritualist Victoria Woodhull married Colonel James H. Blood, a war hero then presiding over the spiritualist association at St. Louis. So, too, Cora L. V. Scott Hatch married Colonel Daniels of the United States Colored Troops.[61] War and the legacy of Lincoln bound together the values of Unionism, abolition, women's rights, and more.

\* \* \*

Initially, spiritualists of all sorts, like the Republicans generally, tended to see Lincoln's successor, Andrew Johnson, as "a man of the people." Hardinge even suggested a Southern opponent of the old slavocracy might be better than "the too-merciful Lincoln" in dealing "with treason and murder." However, spiritualists scoffed at "a great cry against 'radicalism.'" The radical, they pointed out, "has been, in all ages of the world, a pioneer of civilization and human reform." As a group, they formed "the bone and muscle and life, of all enterprising movements and operation." In the duality of nature, "we actually know only a present; but it is ever to be enlarged, enriched, and expanded to the largest limit possible by the vast volume of the past, and illuminated, extended, made poetic and glorious, by the lights which stream down across it from the future."[62]

For the spiritualists, Abraham Lincoln embodied the spirit of the Union cause. His moral mediumship translated the demands of history that informed the course of the country. The spirit of the martyred president joined the ranks of Benjamin Franklin, John King, and the countless Indian guides reaching to us from the beyond. Nevertheless, appearances of Lincoln seem few and far between, partly because the spiritualists' familiarity with him made it more difficult for his disembodiment. Then, too, they surely realized that theirs would not be the only or most important effort to transform the dead president into an icon of American faith.

A postcard view of the cottage of the Fox family at Hydesville, where the spirits first made it through to contact the living. On the eve of World War I, after the later spiritualist movement became more institutionalized, it moved this cabin to Lily Dale and venerated it through images such as this one. In the 1950s, it was burned down.

Fox sisters, *left to right*—Maggie, Kate, and Leah. The caption describes them as the "original mediums of the mysterious noises at Rochester, western New York." Library of Congress.

Nathaniel P. Tallmadge, the New York transplant to Wisconsin who carried spiritualism into the government and sought to make it a political issue. Frontispiece, Charles Linton, *The Healing of the Nations, with an Introduction and Appendix by Nathaniel Pitcher Tallmadge*, 3rd ed. (New York: Society for the Diffusion of Spiritual Knowledge, 1855).

The career of Cora Lodencia Veronica Scott Hatch Daniels Tappan Richmond embodied the dilemma of the female medium. She constructed a remarkably creditable image of virginal ignorance and innocence. Like many, she was a woman of genuine intelligence, critical insight, and analytical abilities who had found a way to exercise these skills freely in a male world by effectively disowning those talents by ascribing them to immaterial spirits. This ubiquitous "publicity shot" was used, among many other places, as the frontispiece for Harrison Delivan Barrett, *The Life Work of Cora L. V. Richmond* (Chicago: Hack & Anderson, 1895).

William Denton, a geologist as well as a spiritualist and a psychometrist, first identified the bones of the La Brea Tar Pits as prehistoric.

Thomas Gales Forster, a South Carolina–born printer, had been both a prominent early member of the National Typographical Union and a noisy advocate of spiritualism and, later, the war for the Union. Frontispiece to Forster's *Unanswerable Logic: A Series of Spiritual Discourses* (Boston: Colby & Rich, 1887).

James H. Blood, St. Louis official and Union officer who took up with Victoria Woodhull. Benjamin R. Tucker Papers, Manuscripts and Archives Division, New York Public Library. Astor, Lenox, and Tilden Foundations.

Joseph Rodes Buchanan, a prominent advocate of "eclectic medicine," became one of the developers of psychometry, the science of identifying objects sight unseen. Among spiritualists, the Kentuckian became notable among the small minority of Democratic diehards uninterested in slavery and the war for the Union. Harvey W. Felter, *History of the Eclectic Medical Institute, Cincinnati, Ohio, 1845–1902* (Cincinnati: Alumnal Association of the Eclectic Medical Institute, 1902), 98.

John Pierpont, prominent old spiritualist and reformer, who spent the war in the civil service at Washington, after age removed him from the army. Nettie Colburn Maynard, *Was Abraham Lincoln a Spiritualist?* (Philadelphia: Rufus C. Hartranft, 1891), opposite 74.

Nettie Colburn, Abraham Lincoln, and others. Nettie Colburn Maynard, *Was Abraham Lincoln a Spiritualist?*, opposite 52.

John Sartain, the engraver associated with Fourierist and spiritualist circles, produced *Abraham Lincoln, the Martyr, Victorious* and successfully employed spiritualist themes to address the wider society's search for meaning in the president's murder. Not only did it spiritualize Lincoln (and Washington), but the presence of these figures in association with the spiritual world secularized and made more tangible the very traditional angelic imagery. Published by W. H. Hermans, Penn Yan Yates Co., ca. May 2, 1866. Library of Congress Prints and Photographs Division.

Tennessee Claflin, the sister and coworker of Victoria Woodhull. Tennessee Claflin C2 (young), Benjamin R. Tucker Papers, Manuscripts and Archives Division, New York Public Library. Astor, Lenox, and Tilden Foundations.

Victoria Woodhull. The spiritualist, suffragist, free-love advocate, and American publisher of the *Communist Manifesto*. Victoria Woodhull v2 (Sarony), Benjamin R. Tucker Papers, Manuscripts and Archives Division, New York Public Library. Astor, Lenox, and Tilden Foundations.

## PART II

# The Promise of a Republic

That the earth, like the air and light, belongs in common to the children of men, and on it each human being is alike dependent. Each child, by virtue of its existence, has an equal and an inalienable right to so much of the earth's surface as is convenient, by proper culture, to support and perfect its development, and none has a right to any more; therefore, all laws authorizing and sustaining private property in land for the purpose of speculation, and which prevent men and women from possessing any land without paying for it, are as unjust as would be laws compelling them to pay for air and light, and ought to be at once and forever repealed.

—*Proceedings of the Free Convention Held at Rutland, Vt., June 25th, 26th, 27th, 1858*

# 4

# Liberty

## *Toward a Rational Spirit of Freedom*

Henry C. Wright, a veteran abolitionist and spiritualist, spoke for almost the entire movement in addressing the president on emancipation. "God bless thee, Abraham Lincoln! With all my heart, I bless thee, in the name of God & Humanity." He asked but "this one favor—which I earnestly solicit—i.e. that you will write for me, & subscribe your name to it—with your own hand—this sentence in your late Message—i.e.—I shall not attempt to retract or modify the emancipation proclamation; nor shall I return to slavery any person, who is free by the terms of the proclamation, or by any of the acts of Congress'!" "Keep that pledge," he pleaded, "& the great heart of Humanity will give you its grateful homage. Be this the reward for my life-work—& for the life-work of the old tried Abolitionists; that you see to it, that the above pledge be made an actuality."[1] Lincoln responded through Wendell Phillips, who had been particularly fearful of the administration's backtracking.

Emancipation for spiritualists represented a generational landmark for liberty, which they saw as essential for the well-being of the human spirit. They generally saw this within a wider, rational, and scientific way of understanding the world and disbelieved a liberty that did not have its own concrete materializations in that world. The federal adoption of an end to slavery as a war goal generally overwhelmed reservations about the merits of the conflict. At the same time, they saw liberty as having clear social and economic dimensions. As such, they espoused a liberty that foreshadowed the emergence of postwar radical resistance to the power of capital.

## Toward a Science for a Changing World

The century ached for a broadly comprehensible explanation of an increasingly complicated world that might explain the place of liberty in the social universe. From its earliest days, spiritualism engaged the implicit tensions in the harmonial ideologies. Most obviously, it sought to explore, measure, and map Hamlet's "undiscover'd country, from whose bourn no traveller returns."

Unlike other "faiths," spiritualism proposed to place religion within a rational understanding of the natural, material world. Then, too, faith that human affairs formed part of the natural world fostered an assumption that scientific inquiry into the human condition might produce new insights with far-reaching implications. Most fundamentally, a generation before Karl Marx's socialism presented itself as a scientific approach to the human condition, spiritualism offered a strangely rational intellectual challenge to the fundamental hierarchies of civilization. The spiritualist embrace indicated their adoption of Benjamin Franklin as a spirit guide and the technological language of "the telegraph."

Their founding interest in the healing arts naturally appealed to such people as Juliet H. Worth Stillman Severance. After marrying John Dwight Stillman, she joined other Adventists in Iowa as a schoolteacher. Her broadening interests—which embraced not only abolitionism but also dress and dietary reform, temperance, and the water cure—brought her back to New York. There, she became a spiritualist, while earning her medical degree from Dr. Russell Trall's Hygeio-Therapeutic College. She divorced her husband, went to Wisconsin, and married Anson B. Severance, who ran a dance school at Milwaukee, while she opened her own medical practice between there and a budding spiritualist community at Whitewater. A militant freethinker and socialist, Severance catered to working women, hoping to educate for the preservation of health, particularly given the pressures of labor and motherhood.[2] The medical arts, then, kept spiritualism closely tied to the practicalities of science.

New technologies seemed to offer a way into understanding the spirit world. Interestingly, perhaps, spiritualism had some appeal for photographers, such as Isaac Rehn. The Pennsylvania Quaker taught chemistry, even as he pioneered techniques of photolithography. His partner got the "bromide patent" for the ambrotype process that took an image on a pane of glass rather than the burnished metal plate of the daguerreotype. Rehn also became associated with Seth Pancoast, the "sexual hygienist" and student of the kabbalah. Less scrupulous operators of the equipment, such as William H. Mumler, had already begun experimenting with the use of double exposures to create "spirit photographs."[3]

Spiritualism did not preclude original insights into specific problems. Born in England to Methodist parents, William Denton emigrated in 1848 to America with his sisters Elizabeth and Annie, the latter becoming the wife of Alfred Cridge. He began educating on geology and science alongside the Bible, as well as taking up slavery and women's rights. Associated with Warren B. Chase and veterans of Cincinnati's Brotherhood, such as John Otis Wattles, he married Elizabeth Foote, a compositor at the *Type of the Times*, run by the radical Longley family there. Their local concerns with "psychometry" inspired Denton to adopt it, and, years later, he found himself scouting for possible oil fields in southern California. There, he visited the asphalt quarry at Rancho La Brea, where workers kept encountering the bones of what they thought to be modern animals trapped only decades or centuries before. Denton, however, rightly identified them as the fossils of extinct animals, though his report generated little interest among scientists.[4] It is easy to dismiss this as a lucky guess, though a better explanation might be that this represented an intuitive leap unrestrained by the framework of widely accepted but mistaken assumptions.

Nor were these examples unique or even, for contemporaries, the most prominent. Albert Brisbane, the leading American exponent of the mystical anticapitalist ideas of Charles Fourier as well as a spiritualist, had also been a successful entrepreneur and inventor who tried to persuade the city to adopt pneumonic tubes underground as a mass-transit solution. One of the key financiers of the Christian Socialists, Horace H. Day had already begun his lifelong battle in the courts over his role in the vulcanization of rubber. Henry Steel Olcott came from Ohio to run the Westchester Farm School at Mount Vernon, New York, and became a promoter of sorghum and the associate agricultural editor of Greeley's *New York Tribune*. Then, too, John Murray Spear claimed to have invented perpetual motion with his "New Motive Power" at High Rock, overlooking Lynn.

Contemporary scientific interest in light, electricity, and other unseen forces groped beyond the merely mechanical measure of the visible, and some scientific thinkers certainly thought spiritualism might be part of some grand unified theory about the human place in nature. Robert Hare developed a "galvanic deflagrator," a battery that sparked combustions and introduced aspects of spiritualism to the "disciples of Faraday." Journalist Robert Chambers, whose *Vestiges of the Natural History of Creation* was a pioneer in discussing the idea of evolution, participated in Edinburgh phrenological circles, had a neighbor notorious for her belief in ghosts and spirits, and participated in séances. By 1859 he regarded skepticism about spiritualism as akin to reactionary skepticism about social and political reforms. His *Vestiges* turned the attention of James Clerk Maxwell as a student toward a broad range of popular ideas about the "dark sciences," such as spiritualism. One of the two codiscoverers of the theory of evolution, Alfred Russell Wallace became an ardent and lifelong spiritualist. Charles Darwin attended séances, but never accepted spiritualism, as did his "uncle Ras," Erasmus Alvey Darwin, or his cousins Francis Galton and Hensleigh Wedgwood.[5]

Despite private beliefs, scientists as a group balked at accepting spiritualist methods. When the American Scientific Association met in Washington in the spring of 1854, Hare announced that the local spiritualists had invited the Reverend Thomas L. Harris to speak there, but Professor Joseph Henry of the Smithsonian Institution objected to scientists providing spiritualists a platform. A few years later, Harvard simply dismissed Frederick Llewellyn Hovey Willis, a young divinity student who had adopted spiritualism. The university did this despite the protests of Thomas Wentworth Higginson and the Alcotts.[6]

The more radical spiritualists, of course, sought to extend the healing mission to the entire civilization. "Society is sick," declared one, "and, like any other patient, it wants help just where it is. It can't go into the country to be cured—it must be able to get off its sick bed before it can get there." "The world does not yet altogether realize that it is sick," said Ernestine L. Rose. For this reason, "to press our reformatory pills upon one who thinks himself in sound moral and social health, is but to create disgust both with our pills and us." When Americans faced "the fact of disease, then its nature," she thought, "we need not invoke the aid of spirits." Andrews thought "the whole world is verging into Spiritualism, and that Spiritualism is verging into Socialism, and from these two facts, he considers the desired result as certain." As one Yankee spiritualist declared, the movement hoped to see a state where "humanity is joined in one mighty phalanx to unfold and apply truth."[7]

As might be expected, visitors to Andrew J. Davis and attendees at his talks included figures running the gamut from Brisbane to a more skeptical but fascinated Edgar Allan Poe. Religious figures such as Gibson Smith, L. Prescott Rand, and William Fishbough became early allies.[8]

In this sense, spiritualism found the flexibility to embrace a range of reform strategies. The Fourierists had offered a plan of action for nearly a decade and found spiritualism a less arcane explanation of their proposals. Starting with

Henry D. Barron and E. W. Capron, the movement reached out to involve Brisbane, John Orvis, John Allen, and virtually every Fourierist of note in the country. As one of them, Ira B. Davis, argued, the logic of spiritualism made it "the duty of Spiritualists to investigate these evils of society."[9]

Along with the Fourierists came other prominent radicals. These included John Murray Spear, John A. Collins, Josiah Warren, Augustus and John O. Wattles, as well as the brilliant and original minds of Josiah Warren and Stephen Pearl Andrews. The latter believed, "There is, or was, in the Divine mind, a social science, and that it is possible for us to grasp it."

> It had been but recent that the bare idea that there is a science of society has obtained among thinkers. No one, for example, had supposed that commerce was amenable to scientific laws, or that there could be any certainty in finance. What a drunken Legislature at Albany could do, has been accepted as the ultimate possibility, and so society as a grand complex, has been left to God and these dunder-pates. No man has given as much attention to a single department of human interests, as a chemist would bestow upon an analysis of Croton water.[10]

Then, too, many leading spiritualists, such as D. H. Hamilton, went on to advocate remarkably radical social and political measures.[11] It was purely "anarchy in the house of God."

Andrew J. Davis had always hoped for a coherent "harmonial" sensibility that would employ reason to transform the human condition. "Harmonialists could meet on one common platform," he suggested, "and embrace with one fond, endearing clasp of brotherly affection the great race of man, without distinction of sect, color, or pecuniary advantages." Self-described Rosicrucian Pascal B. Randolph proposed to "look into the science of universal nature, and teach the world the language written by the mighty fiat of Omnipotence on its breathing pages." Young lawyer Leo Miller, who came to a spiritualist meeting to disprove its arguments, found them instead convincing, stayed for decades, and urged the movement to an ever more engaged radicalism.[12]

Even in its most conservative form, though, spiritualism entertained any and all ideas. Even mistaken ideas contributed to solutions. "Let those sneer at the '*isms*' of the day who will. . . . Every '*ism*,' if untrue, is but a false solution of that problem, and the attempt is to be respected, though it has failed, because it was sincerely and honestly made, and because it proves that the unfettered mind of the race is at work with unconquerable energy, digging for the great truth."[13]

"Independence is indispensable to the establishment of peace and happiness among men," so everyone should have the "enjoyment of equal rights, and bound together by mutual interest, there would be free scope for the growth of useful knowledge and fraternal love, which would ultimate in the realization of heaven upon the earth." Added another, "The subject has a stomach as well as the prince. Why should it not be filled as well? Universal intelligence, independence, happiness should be the aim of a great people; not the building up of private fortunes." The *Regenerator* spoke of social change as "a current of moral and mental magnetism rushing to the earth like lightening, as big as the river Amazon. *The earth must be free for men to inhabit.* Human rights shall be enjoyed, and each shall walk in the name of his own god, where there is none to make afraid."[14] Peering through this window into a new world seemed to offer the same view to the thousands who discovered their own mediumship.

## Emancipation

The cost of the war always seemed to demand more than the mere preservation of the government. "Slavery and Freedom cannot live together," insisted Leo Miller, who worked with Confederate prisoners at Camp Douglas, and "the history of the world—the rise and fall of kingdoms, nations, and empires, admonish us in a voice of thunder to beware—to see to it that this mighty element of discord and national death in our midst be removed far from us." Miller discussed what could result as "the new dispensation, or the approaching manhood of the race." L. Judd Pardee spoke on the country's coming "Reconstruction," which he explicitly took beyond a mere constitutional or legal proceeding, to the "the inauguration of a *Theocratic Democracy*." The maintenance of slavery had precluded any serious freedom of discussion or freedom of association for anybody, including white men. For that reason, if no other, it made peaceful change impossible and a serious republic inconceivable.[15]

Once they overcame their early confusion or reluctance about the merits of the war, even moderate spiritualists became unsparing in their criticism of its limited goals. As early as the summer of 1861, the *Banner* excoriated a Massachusetts officer for returning a runaway to slavery—"a deed more reprehensible than all else, and which native ignorance and stupidity can hardly excuse." "Not another government on earth, except it be Dahomey," the Reverend George B. Cheever told a New York audience, "holds or deals in slaves or upholds the rights of property in man—not even Spain." From the start of the war, black Americans themselves had made slavery a practical problem. "What is to be done with the thirty thousand negroes around Beaufort?" asked one spiritualist. Slave flight meant that the country generally now had to "either admit or deny the right of property in man."[16]

As the war escalated in the spring of 1862, the Lincoln administration remained "both satisfied and determined to keep the war going for no other cause than the restoration of the authority of the Constitution over the length and breadth of the land." At the same time, a Cincinnati mob attacked Wendell Phillips, indicating that attitudes remained unchanged among many whites in the North. "Twenty years hence, when slavery is extinct in this country, and all have come to see what a daunting curse it is to-day, when they fully realize what it has cost this government, in blood and treasure," declared C. D. Griswold, then on his way to Shiloh, "how the above record will shame every intelligent inhabitant of that city, when his attention is called to it, and he feels how deep a stain it is to wipe out!" "Honored above all men," he continued, "should be the man who wages a war for natural rights against the usurpation of power—the man who stands with the minority of men with God, contending against human wrong."[17]

For some weeks, the *Banner* devoted its columns to the discussion. By the summer, though, it came to new conclusions. "The Age," explained one piece, "is revolutionary and new." "The war now waged against the Government is confessedly a war for the extension and perpetuity of African slavery on this continent, as has been enunciated in the Satanic League of the States in rebellion." Warned another, "Let success attend their rebel arms, and slavery and the slave trade will become continental." As Wright succinctly told Lincoln: "Slavery or the Republic must die," and the willingness of the Union to take up the challenge of war inspired him to see "the American Republic as the God-appointed Messiah of Liberty to the great family of Nations."[18]

Lincoln proclaimed emancipation as a war goal in September 1862, scheduling its implementation with the new year. Spiritualists around the country joined other abolitionists in celebrations. "If the black man were to be liberated at once," they noted, "all would be the better for it, for justice always brings its reward." Nevertheless, they were certain that the war would "not stop short of the death of the monster Slavery, which is swallowing up the wealth of our land in an endeavor to sustain it."[19]

There were conservative, even racist, arguments for emancipation. Some argued that this would be the best means to keep blacks from coming north. "Our view is a wider one than that," declared one spiritualist. Opined another:

Who that does not respect and admire, even if he have neither will nor inclination to copy, the man who has subjected his lower faculties to the rational control of the higher, who walks erect and free, the slave of no lust or desire, at one with God's highest purposes, using even the vicissitudes of social life to the furtherance of his spiritual growth, and making every accident and incident of life, every relative success and failure contribute its portion towards the work of building up the beautiful character which he rightly esteems the great end and object of human existence?

Freedom required a struggle "to emancipate ourselves, daily and continually." "Every step from barbarism to civilization, from heathenism to Christianity, from despotism to democracy," said Theodore D. Weld, "has been a victory of the higher law, or rather of the one only law."[20]

After emancipation Wilfrid Wylley reappeared in the columns of the *Banner*. The British-born spiritualist wrote from northern Ohio about his recent tour of Canada to sense the reality of support for the Confederacy there. After returning to the news of emancipation, he declared himself ready "to buckle on once more the harness of toil, and go forward in the service of this the land of my adoption." He assured readers that "strong arms and resolute hearts are but waiting in the camps on the Potomac to make the words of our President words of truth for us all."[21]

By the fall of 1863, the government had fully embraced emancipation, but many spiritualists fully credited the slaves themselves and the many soldiers who went above and beyond the call of duty to assist them. One recalled that "virtue does not, as a general thing, come out of the palaces, but the cottages." "The rich and the respectable classes are always behind the spirit of the age," Frederick Robinson declared. Weighing down the thoughts of the colleges and learned professions, the ruling class constitutes "an ease-loving, pleasure-seeking, and fashion-hunting aristocracy. Clinging blindly to hereditary opinions, they are not prepared for new conceptions, and resist all progressive ideas." Instead, Robinson looked to "the aristocracy of labor—intelligent men and women, impelled to hard work, either of body or mind." In Europe they thought "the future area of freedom or tyranny depends more upon the people than upon the thrones and governments of the world."[22]

Spiritualists had some understanding of the violent, martial mechanisms that moved these changes. Perhaps for this reason, they praised General U. S. Grant with a remarkable consistency. "This man is a worker. He prays with his deeds, and not by his breath only." Being from the West, he had "been out of the immediate reach of the political marplots, which has left him larger scope for the exercise and display of his qualities as a commander in the field." They thought Grant "the man who has been providentially raised up to take active control of the war at this final stage of its progress, and finish it by the discomforture of armed rebellion." His "work is hard, but he will certainly do all that man can do."[23]

Emancipation even won over many hitherto conservative Unionists. One correspondent recalled speaking to one runaway slave who had "not the slightest trace of negro blood in a single feature or complexion, and hair straighter than you can generally find in the pure Anglo-Saxon." The man's father, a Confederate colonel, had sold him when he was fourteen. "I never was an Abolitionist," the correspondent continued, "but I am not in favor of white slaves in a white country, and that where we call our nation a white one."[24]

Refugee camps also became the scene of a major transformation in the nature of the war, as they became prime recruiting grounds for the new regiments of black soldiers being raised. As Wylley wrote, the Confederates had been "materially, fatally injured by the immense draft which has been made on their laboring and producing population by the President's proclamation, no one, I think, will have the hardihood to deny. The armies of the Republic have been augmented in a very efficient and profitable degree by these black troops, no one can doubt." "Emancipation is a success," he wrote, adding that "negro soldiers are a success; the substitution of free for slave labor is a success, as proved by the experiment made under the most inauspicious circumstances, at Hilton Head." "In superior to the civilization of the cavalier the fundamental principle of which is the 'capital should own labor,' and that 'civil and religious liberty' and 'popular education,' are affairs which concern the few who govern and not the many who are governed."[25]

Frederick Douglass, John M. Langston, Martin Delaney, and others recognized the logic of black military service in that time and place. White spiritualists became heavily involved in this process. Higginson, Nathan W. Daniels, George L. Stearns, and others understood that "if the negro race in this land are to be redeemed and elevated, it must be accomplished mainly through their own exertions. There is no doubt that this rebellion is furnishing them with the long desired opportunity which is to bring them release."[26]

Confederate policy gave black soldiers and their officers no quarter. Emma Hardinge later referred to "the sable martyrs that had perished at Port Hudson and Fort Pillow." Lincoln alluded to it while at the start of the fair in Baltimore. "He declared that, if it should be found that the butchery had really taken place at Fort Pillow as described, he would consider it his solemn duty to retaliate amply upon the rebels, although he could not then decide upon the most proper mode of applying the *lex talionis*."[27]

Many spoke of the elimination of slavery as the necessary prerequisite to the attainment of free labor. Phrenologist Orson Fowler thought the concentration of wealth and power to be at "the bottom of all the departments of human life—in politics, in property, and in religion. Marriage, as it exists, is a monopoly; indeed, it is the pivotal monopoly of the whole monopoly system." What he called "distributive justice must cast out the devil of monopoly." "Monopolies of heaven and earth must be destroyed and broken down," declared another spiritualist. "Equal rights of mankind to heaven and earth, individual sovereignty and universal equality must redeem the poor, and they only can do it." Ira Davis warned that reforms that did not strike at this problem would fail, but once they had gotten past slavery, the people, "having time and means to accomplish everything that the heart can rationally desire and possessing sufficient knowledge of the sad experience through which humanity has passed, would prevent a relapse into slothfulness or barbarism."[28]

Many spiritualists found Stephen Pearl Andrews's formulation of "individual sovereignty" a vital and logical extension of their faith in personal liberty. Andrews and his supporters placed self-directed activities by free people as the essential measure of a civilization's quality. He elaborated the social and political implications of this belief, the most immediate of which jibed well with the concerns of the movement.[29] A militant socialist, as well as an abolitionist, Andrews also viewed gross inequalities in wealth as an innate check on the liberty of the laboring majority.

## Liberty and Property

Oliver Wendell Holmes was not alone in his wishful thinking that the war "is at this very moment doing more to melt away the petty social distinctions which keep generous souls apart from each other, than the preaching of the Beloved Disciple himself would do."[30] In fact, while military service leveled social distinctions among the middling sort, it did, as it usually does, lock many of them into place.

War and massive government spending fostered monopolies. "The latest rage among the American people is for speculating in stocks," wrote the *Banner* after two years of war. Another year persuaded its writers that "the people of the country are to-day suffering vastly more from the effects of speculation than from those of the war. The Government really does not levy one-half the tax upon us, which we have to carry on our shoulders in consequence of the extortion of the speculators. *They* are the army which is fast eating out our substance." Spiritualists took some solace in the broad recognition of "grasping and unprincipled speculators." "The usurer, the monopolist, the hypocrite, the deceiver, all are haunted, though they wear so bold a front" in asserting their right to profit in the face of the wartime social conditions.[31]

"I cannot recollect any times within the scope of my memory that I have not heard some one or many complaining of hard times," wrote Chase from Lowell. However, he added, he could recall "no period in our history as a nation, when more money was paid for labor or service than at this time." Two years later, the *Banner of Light* also noted, "For a novelty, *prices* go up now-a-days and *labor* goes up with them. It has not always been so." The demands of the military made wages go up. "The armies must be fed, and those who stay at home must be fed; and it will take labor, and any quantity of it, to supply the demand." "Even *war* has its compensating advantages, just like any other evil."[32] With large numbers of workingmen going to war, labor became scarce, but wages did not go up enough to keep pace with prices, and they certainly did not go up for all workers.

All this had a dismal effect on the Union they hoped to preserve. By the spring of 1862, the *Banner* found ample confirmation that "a commercial people are in much greater danger of parting with their liberties than a people purely agricultural." The former gained their wealth "by *exchange,* and not by outright labor." Having "but one pursuit, and that engrosses them" in a "continual fever," commercial interests desired that "the existing order of things be kept permanent, if possible; and, in their wish to keep it so, they are too ready to pay almost any price, even at the cost of their real liberty." They constituted a "newly-blown element of society known as 'shoddy,'" after the quality of the merchandise they sold the government.[33]

In part, spiritualists reflected some of the cultural concern of the old established classes with the upstart nouveau riche of the war, those to whom "by common consent has been applied the characteristic title—Shoddy." "All the contract partiers of the war have come out in the Park in full force. So great has been the crowd and crush they have got their carriages tangled up in the general melee, and some of them have fallen to cursing and swearing." "We make at the Park as great a display of wealth as may be seen either in London, Paris or Vienna; but in those cities the people are well-behaved, orderly, dignified. Here the shoddyites—the great mushroom growth of the past two years—imitate the show, the pomp, the glitter of European society.

But its politeness, its refinement, its extreme decorum, our newborn great people have no conception of; and this is not to be wondered at." "Now he is a millionaire; and so on through the great array of carriage at the Park." The *Banner* continued, "Shoddy, shoddy, shoddy. The French call such people parvenus: the English, upstarts. We, with our usual originality, have coined our own term, and have added to our vocabulary the word shoddy."[34]

The federal government policed abuses only in a limited sense, though spiritualists contributed. Olcott had likely earned his reputation for discretion after he slipped into Virginia to cover John Brown's hanging for the *New York Tribune*. After the start of the war, he became a signal officer in the North Carolina campaign, a position that usually involved the gathering of intelligence. After being invalided home, Olcott received an appointment from the War Department to investigate bounty jumpers and war profiteers in New York.[35]

In the end, though, spiritualists saw a great paradox. Economic values tended to reduce all wealth to "money, property, or means for procuring the necessaries and luxuries of life or the gratification of selfishness, or ministering to our ideas of self-happiness." Respect for the market framed the concerns of "not only barrel-makers but preachers, doctors, lawyers, teachers, who could hardly be expected to favor the fostering of morality, health, justice, intelligence." Given this, what could foster the "equality of the race, good works—because they are the only sure means of real happiness, and consequently harmony"? Progress would "fully abolish governments, theologies and institutions" to embrace "the laws of Father God and mother Nature in their formation and being."[36]

In the public mind, monopolies regulated prices in the interests of business to the detriment of the laboring poor. Critics talked of "the heinous sin of conspiring to keep provisions, fuel, and the several necessaries of life, at a price where the poorer classes cannot by any possibility reach them." One voice declared, through the *Banner*:

> No community that permits its poor and, comparatively speaking, dependent class to be made poorer by extortioners, oppressors and thieves, ought to expect that existence in a state of health and wholesomeness is at all possible for itself. No society that allows one class of men to combine, merely because they have the power and facility, against the prime wants and the bare necessities of another and a helpless class, can well expect for a long time to stand. The poor must be provided for even before all the rest. The laborer is at the bottom of

our civilized possibilities; take him out of the scale, and the whole system will come down for want of support.

The more radical spiritualists suggested that a society that tolerated such things would be "not wholly civilized—for barbarians set us a better example than that—it is not able long to exist. It will soon be stung to death by its own scorpion vices." Whatever drained "the life-blood of our social existence," they added, "we cannot tolerate them and live."[37]

Impoverishment, believed some spiritualist commentators, did run deeper than a bankbook. They took issue with the "vain fancy that these whom they style the 'town's poor' within, are all the poor that live within the limits of the town. Oh, if we could but look into human *hearts,* how many there are, whom we all of us think to be happy, who are, indeed, embodiments of wretchedness." More deeply, may the truly impoverished "not likewise comprise a few of such as walk on thick carpets and still continue to sip their broth from silver spoons?"[38]

"Dollars are not the only things that count," complained such writers. "In gaining wealth," said one, "a country does not necessarily gain men." War had tended to "confound and confuse ordinary social limitations, make temporary chaos of all the old definitions and judgments and standards, put every man upon the sole resources of his highest inspiration, and his truest individual instincts." Conversely, "*real* poverty begins and betrays itself" not "in the outward garb, but in the inward man; not so much in the circumstances and accommodations of the life, as in the realness and truth of the action." "It is not money that evidences a nation's wealth, but labor," the discussion ran, tapping into antebellum Ricardian labor theories of value. "Labor is the only token of wealth. Take that away, and the springs of national life at once dry and disappear."[39]

Yet the most direct social impact of this became most evident among the working poor. Liberty could mean little where "millions are born paupers and are trespassers upon ground owned by others, from the cradle to the grave—mortgaged before they come into existence!" Charles Partridge found the entire social order hanging from "the complex superstructure of falsehood." Another insisted that "people cannot grow refined and intelligent until they have first secured something to live on. . . . Hence material wants must needs be provided for first."[40]

Benjamin N. Kinyon, a New York–born Mississippi lawyer who had fled to Des Moines, concluded that "three-fourths of mankind at least, in the civilized,

Christianized and governed States, are the victims of poverty." Their system left "the earth and its fruits, and all property . . . monopolized and held by the few; while the many are homeless, poor and heavenless." Poverty, he continued, "cannot be eradicated by the practice of the virtues of temperance, industry and economy" when institutions were "conceived in blasphemy against God, and are a continual warfare upon his divine laws, implanted in the constitution of his creature, man." "What, then, is the plain path of duty for the poor? It is to rise against a Church which shuts them out of heaven, and the State that denies their equality, and equal rights to land and all other property to supply the necessities of their organization."[41]

Through the *Banner*, spiritualists wondered about "this matter of Capital and Labor, their relative rights and privileges, and what sort of influence and power each is entitled to hold, which it will take not one generation of inquiries and experimenters only to solve, but will task the best thought and most ingenious experiments of many to clear up." A series in the *Rochester Express* by John T. Amos "advocates with vigor the claims of Labor, not merely to a living, but to valuable perquisites and enjoyments." "When men obtain property by their labor, then he declares they begin to be sought for in public places, and not much before then. Property gave such laborers as are now in office." Capital is the "Supreme Ruler."[42]

The economic course of the war had helped draw legions of women out of the home, exposing them to new health hazards and expenses, to which healers associated with the movement—such as Severance—began turning. At the same time, it raised issues about the ability and desirability of women to bear large families. Declared one observer, "No woman is happy or healthy, because health depends upon happiness, who has more children than she can care for tenderly. Her body is exhausted by actual labor, and her heart is broken with her inability to supply all their needs, physical, mental and moral, unless she is herself so nearly on the animal plane as to recognize only their animal wants."[43]

This process largely gendered the nature of poverty. "Women who never worked before, had a chord touched in their natures, which gave the ready response," said Lizzie Doten, striving to understand their experience as a voluntary aberration from their domestic nature. Moreover, women worked into the night at home, while a man might, "in the quiet of the evening, sit down and read his paper, or visit the reading room, or the club." The longer the war dragged on, the price of noninvolvement made neither the military recruitment of men nor the work of women entirely voluntary. Yet demographic forces left vastly larger proportions of females unmarried or widowed, living lives beyond whatever shelter a man might have provided. A new kind of radicalism—which included socialist men, such as Chase—took up the rights of poor women in ways that transcended the family to address larger questions about wealth and labor.[44]

Anxieties focused on women in the needle trades. Some of the more visionary spiritualists, such as John Murray Spear, hailed the sewing machine as the beginning of women's liberation, but the technology in a capitalist system simply reduced them further. Midwestern entrepreneurs proposed reforms that would move "the overcrowded labor-market in New York, more particularly in the sewing-women's line—and to supply the deficit in Milwaukee and the West." Some critics thought the laboring women of New York City to be "as wronged as masters at the South would not wrong even their slaves." Amos thought working conditions a "crime" that "must be expiated by the nation either by hastening to do justice or by sufferings not now thought of." Modern society had maintained the assumptions of woman's dependence while forcing her to "secure her independence, and the freedom she enjoys to make herself a position and an influence in society."[45]

Liberty for working women required action by the government. A typical gathering at Philadelphia brought to the platform Andreas Smolnikar, Alfred Henry Love, abolitionist Theodore Tilton, and the Hutchinson Family singers. They urged listeners to think beyond slavery to "the great burdens that rest upon the colored race on account of their color merely" and linked this to the plight of working women petitioning the government over low pay at the Philadelphia Arsenal. As H. F. M. Brown noted, when the nation needed them, "No one asked, or cared, whether the men were Jews, Mormons, Christians, or Hottentots—i.e., if they were *white* and war-worthy." The same forces moved women. "Would it not be well for the women of Washington to inaugurate a new society founded in Justice and Equality?" When the delegation from these women's groups got to Washington, they noted particularly the support of some "gentlemen in the Treasury Department," surely Pierpont, Tabor, and other spiritualists there. At Washington Chase spoke of "the Relation of Spiritualism to Governments; of Governments to the People," reflecting the sense that government and war contractors had reshaped economic and social realities.[46]

Wartime social conditions pushed many spiritualists toward a systemic critique of liberty in a system that failed to place "production, distribution and exchanges of wealth upon equitable principles." Kinyon gave considerable thought to the fact that "the earth and its fruits, and all property are monopolized and held by the few; while the many are homeless, poor and heavenless."[47]

This did not simply represent a backward-looking utopianism. Indeed, some spiritualists gave the new ideas of Karl Marx such a favorable reception because they, too, thought in terms of dialectical contradictions. While denouncing monopolies steaming forward by rail, a spiritualist such as John H. W. Toohey acknowledged that "railroads and other facilities for traveling and communicating, were now so efficient, the whole land was easily put into fellowship, and an interchange of thought and aspiration was ensuing." Stephen P. Andrews agreed. "We need more wealth; we need the right man in the right place—the scientific agriculturist to the land, the mechanic to the workshop, the thinker to his study—to every pursuit a master, and to the aggregate of their united industry and skill, the grand science of distribution."[48] In short, capitalism provided the mechanism for its own transformation.

* * *

At its most radical, spiritualism challenged the predisposition of the standard institutional "liberty" centered on the right of anybody to buy, sell, invest, or disinvest capital. In the same sense that freedom of the press meant different things to a newspaper owner and a consumer, this thoroughly capitalist idea of liberty tended to leave out entirely those who did not have any capital in the first place. As elsewhere, this unevenness gave rise to massive monopolies, a process that became very rapid in wartime. Inadvertently, it created a studied and willful blindness to the fact that "it makes a great difference, whether one is comfortably situated, and with slender means at that, or is perfectly wretched with the care of his accumulated means in the shape of stocks and bonds."[49] The spiritualist radicalization in the course of the war demanded another idea of human liberty.

Chase described what would be a new American order to emerge from the war. Over the course of the war, he gave hundreds of talks, noting that those on the war eclipsed those on spiritualism, weaving them into what may have been the clearest general statement of radicalism in the war, *The American Crisis; or, The Trial and Triumph of Democracy*. He proposed reconstruction based on "four great cardinal principles" of human rights. He resurrected the old national reform idea that everyone should have access "to land without extortionate prices, and the right of all families to homes exempt from forced sale or attachment." Implicit were also the "right and duty of all persons to labor, and the security of means to labor, and to the products, and to the credit of respect and honor," and the "right of every child to education, free to him or her as air and water, and the duty of governments to place it in the reach of all, and see that each has it." Finally, the government needed to ensure an equality not only of race but "of females with males, of course, involving voting, holding office, filling the professions and receiving like pay for like labor in every department or industry."[50]

A much broader and more sweeping sense of freedom began to take form.

# 5

# Equality

## Race and Gender

Liberty required an equality unprecedented in the history of civilization. Spiritualist Benjamin N. Kinyon pointed out that, in the so-called representative system of American government, six out of seven of its subjects could not vote if they wanted to do so. Women, children, and minors under the age of twenty-one "do not have this privilege, and so far as the Government is concerned, are as powerless as the serfs of Russia." If one figured in the four million slaves and others excluded, it left the vast majority of U.S. residents without even the most formal voice in the country's government. Kinyon and other spiritualists would have also added that class considerations substantively muted the voices of most who could vote. Later, Cora L. V. Tappan declared that "a government that has for nearly a century enslaved one race (African), that proscribes another (Chinese), proposes to exterminate another (Indians), and persistently refuses to recognize the rights of one-half of its citizens (women), cannot justly be called perfect." By the end of the war, the more conservative *Banner of Light* embraced much of what it had disparaged at its onset, aspirations "for a Government which shall act as a paternal providence over all its subjects, irrespective of race, color or sex," but three years of war had compelled it along with many readers to favor government action to ensure equal rights.[1] There could be no substantive reconstruction of America without revisiting the issue of equality.

This radical new egalitarian sensibility among the spiritualists reflected, in part, the relatively inclusive nature of the movement. For radical spiritualists—which, at least for a time, included most of them—emancipation had to lead beyond the absence of slavery toward black equality. They saw a complete and critical reexamination of U.S. policy toward the Indians as inseparable from emancipation and black equality. Having always advocated women's rights on one level, they became increasingly predisposed to a practical egalitarianism.

## Movement Diversity and Black Emancipation

A uniquely egalitarian sense of individual liberty underlay the spiritualists' view of society and reform. Ira B. Davis became an ardent and public proponent for "social equality," which he described as "equal rights as human beings; that is to say, equal opportunities, equal protection, sympathy and love, as between the members of one great family whose interests in all the affairs of life are mutual." Even moderate spiritualists looked toward "the creation of physical conditions which shall allow of the perfect exercise of this equality," an attempt "to bring the external into harmony with the internal." Augustus Wattles expected the boundaries between the material and spiritual world to fade "as we bring the body in subjection to the 'higher law' and holier demands of the Spirit."[2]

Isaac Rehn defended the pluralistic nature of the movement. He suggested that they would "justly expose ourselves to the contempt of the world when that time shall arrive in which we, as Spiritualists, having given such a mighty impulse to the cause of individual liberty, shall commence to barricade the way, because John Smith or Betsy Black claims the right to travel it, and carry their budget of isms on their backs." "When our cause becomes so feeble and impotent as to be incapable of maintaining its integrity because somebody latches his hobby upon it, we shall be justified in despairing of it as a power in the world."[3] Reality could look different from different perspectives, and, conversely, similar words could also convey different concepts.

In some quarters, spiritualism became a kind of secularist Western Christianity. From the early 1854 meetings in New York's Dodworth Hall, Ira Davis urged "a true social reform founded on real spiritual Christianity." Across the Atlantic, Gerald Massey would soon speak of Christ as "the Kingliest King." Gerrit Smith, an abolitionist, found religion as the basis for saying "a great many sharp, and a great many true things." In the end, so many came to the movement from a skeptical background that William Fishbough complained that the purpose of one convention seems to have been "mainly intended to degrade the bible to the level of any other book containing the records of an 'unprogressed age.'"[4] Yet the nature of the movement itself inspired Fishbough's complaint, which did absolutely nothing to change it.

Then, too, a rabbi's daughter, Ernestine Louise Polowsky Rose, became a regular at spiritualist gatherings on the East Coast. A native of Russian Poland, she became a freethinker and began traveling widely early in life. While abroad, she had become an Owenite socialist and married William Ella Rose, a craftsman. After coming to the United States in 1836, she quickly identified herself with abolitionism, women's rights, and freethought.[5] The movement, then, included individuals from Jewish and Catholic backgrounds.

Spiritualists tended to claim almost any and all non-Christian beliefs or practices "spiritualist," including the religious beliefs of Native peoples or black Americans or, at times, even the exotic faiths of Asia, about which a large literate community in the Western world had just begun to learn. For a while, the movement broadly took in a large number of traditional seers and fortune tellers who had always found a livelihood of some sorts, particularly in the prosperity of America, while also drawing upon non-Western religious traditions. As a movement of the unorthodox, it saw itself in such broad terms, particularly after its ecumenical successes among dissenting Christian currents and freethought. Observers noted—and adherents boasted of—the endemic "lack of harmony among Spiritualists. Converts to Spiritualism have been made from all classes—from the rankest infidel to the worshiping Christian."[6]

Some individual former Roman Catholics turned up in the movement. Irish-born John H. W. Toohey had begun life as a Catholic near the start of the century, but he had done so by way of lengthy sojourns with Baptists and the Universalists. Andrej Bernard Smolnikar, a self-defrocked Slovenian Benedictine priest, who began to use the name Andreas, brought his own eastern European Catholic mysticism to spiritualism. A true eccentric, he convinced the 1853 National Industrial Congress to give him fifteen minutes for "an important communication," though he was not a delegate. When the body of reformers refused to give him more time without seating him, Smolnikar produced his credentials, duly signed by Benjamin Franklin. Notwithstanding that body's refusal to recognize them, Smolnikar continued to pass on the warnings of the spirits about the efforts of mystical "secret enemies of true Republicanism."[7]

What spiritualism never conceded to traditional Christianity was the ecumenism of its spirituality, even making itself into an umbrella for views transcending traditional Western ideas. Amanda M. Westbrook Britt Spence believed that only some souls would attain immortality, while others would be either reincarnated or reabsorbed into "the grand ocean of being." The original ideas that Pascal Beverley Randolph called "Rosicrucian" incorporated tantric sex magic.[8] Of course, these ecumenical aspirations could also reflect the imperial appetite of its time.

The spiritualist discussion of race developed unevenly among these various kinds of spiritualists. Some complained, with abolitionists, of how white Americans generally gave much greater attention to the struggles for liberty abroad than to addressing the subjugation of black Americans or the Native peoples at home. As Parker Pillsbury said, they "are not the Greeks; they are not Poland. They are not Kossuth, Lamartine, nor Mazzini." "All these our country could bless; did bless, at least with sympathy, if not with more material aid," he added. "They are not Ireland, in famine, or we could send them whole cargoes of corn and commiseration." Radical spiritualists such as Charles Testut at New Orleans embraced the black struggle for freedom as part of a world revolutionary movement, his *Le Vieux Salomon* offering a fictionalized view of secret black American revolutionary societies that strove for much the same goals as whites in Hungary, France, or Italy.[9]

Increasingly, though, spiritualists took up the unvarnished language of racial equality. Though sometimes marred by appeals to white paternalism, John Pierpont, Henry C. Wright, Giles B. Stebbins, and others expressed an underlying egalitarian cast of mind characteristic of the movement's most articulate core. Wright saw spiritualism as "a religion for humanity," with "the most exalted ideas of man, the brightest hopes and encouragements," and with "the ideal of a better church, state and society, amid the evolutions which threaten all the old order of things," including abolitionism and other social reforms.[10]

Black Americans north of the Mason-Dixon line found spiritualism, with its faith in the underlying equality of peoples, almost irresistible. Prominent black leaders, such as Frederick Douglass, Sojourner Truth, Harriet Tubman, and others, regularly attended spiritualist meetings and conventions. Nevertheless, perhaps because most free blacks had disproportionately greater claims upon their time and labors, they never came into the movement as actively as whites. One black abolitionist, Samuel J. May, told another that he suspected William Lloyd Garrison to be a silent supporter of spiritualism.[11] Black Americans became disproportionately predisposed to be sympathetic as the movement gained momentum.

More unusually, Randolph became one of the movement's most original thinkers. Born to the mean streets of New York in 1825, he described his background as "Caucasian, aboriginal and the darker strain." Orphaned early in life, he made his own way through a childhood in the Five Points. Pursuing various means of making a living, he pursued his own education and self-improvement relentlessly. By 1853 he worked as a barber at Utica and had not only embraced spiritualism but also taken up a new occupation as a "clairvoyant physician and psycho-phrenologist." Chase thought him, "when well-controlled, the best and more profound speaker and reasoner he had ever met in his life." Making at least two trips abroad, he encountered sex magic and consciousness-expanding drugs, such as "hashish and cannabis indica." Like another of Spear's associates, New York bohemian artist Albert L. Rawson, Randolph took up the dress of the Orient and adopted these eclectic ideas under the exotic-sounding label "Rosicrucian."[12] Much later, British mystics would later take up Randolph's Rosicrucianism as part of their fringe Masonry, and, still later, respectable white American seekers after truth would encounter these exotic "Eastern" ideas clueless of the fact that they were the brainchild of a pot-smoking black American sex magician from Toledo!

Radical spiritualists appreciated Randolph's teachings, despite his reputation as a cantankerous eccentric. Not only did radical spiritualists such as Chase discuss his talents, but conservative spiritualists, such as Stevens S. Jones of the *Kane County (Ill.) Democrat*—and later the *Religio-Philosophical Journal*—praised his work as well. Randolph provides one of those rare examples demonstrating the spiritualist professions of faith in an equality of mediumship. Then, too, John H. W. Toohey quipped about "the difference between an Irishman and a negro as 'six of one and half a dozen of the other.'" He declared himself one of those "believing in the equality of 'the races,' and the individual 'right to life, liberty and the pursuit of happiness.'" By 1859 he embraced John Brown as the herald of a national resurrection.[13]

Many who had seen themselves as conservative pragmatists earlier realized that emancipation would be insufficient. History demanded suffrage, land, and government guarantees of black rights. Even the more conservative Unionists among the spiritualists realized that "social equality will perhaps never be attained in this world, for nature has made wide distinctions in the race; but equal rights are within our reach."[14] Even before the war, those uninspired by—and dismissive of—what they saw as utopian ideals saw merit in establishing equality before the law. This, however, would require government and society to take conscious measures to reconstruct themselves.

War first involved white spiritualists generally with large numbers of black Americans. They participated in the General Sanitary Commission and the Western Sanitary Commission to raise funds and helped staff hospitals and perform other functions that the army and the government generally opted not to perform. Although these bodies also provided reading matter to the troops, they tended to concentrate on the distribution of orthodox Christian tracts, with which literate soldiers would have already been very familiar. For this reason, Warren Chase's son Milton—a hospital steward in the Sixth Michigan—told his father that "copies of the *Banner of Light, Herald of Progress,* and *Investigator* are seized eagerly, and worn out in being read, while religious papers are often unopened save to kindle fires." Henry Strong of the Ninety-Third Illinois suggested that the "spiritualists of New England imitate Sanitary commission in distribution of tracts."[15]

Alongside soldiers there developed large encampments of displaced persons and refugees, increasingly black Americans fleeing slavery. They faced serious difficulties from the Indian Territory through the Mississippi Valley to the East Coast. A former missionary among the Ojibwe Indians complained that many officers "have no kind of sympathy with the negroes; would rather they were back in slavery than here; & will thwart any plans we may divise to better their condition, if possible. They are proslavery, secesh at heart, unprincipled." When Grant ordered refugees moved to the safety of Cincinnati, officers simply dumped them upriver in slaveholding Kentucky rather than across the Ohio. They urged "some self-supporting occupation—about the army—on fortifications—bearing arms, or, better than all when possible, the cultivation of the soil, where all might work & where schools & all due appliances for their improvement might be worked to the best possible advantage."[16]

War provided many white Americans from outside the South their first experiences with a variety of black Americans or obviously mixed race people. A white middle-class Victorian Yankee such as Nettie Colburn had never encountered anything like Thomas, the dignified servant of the secretary of the U.S. Senate. He and his daughter, "a very pretty mulatto girl" who played the piano, performed "Kingdom Coming." Nettie's spirit guide drew her into trying to help "an old colored friend" of Major George Chorpenning's black cook. Nettie took pride in having her talents "exercised, in the presence and for the benefit of the ruler of a great nation, while the latter part was given, in the same manner, to alleviate the misery of a poor old negro who represented one of his most humble adherents."[17]

Spiritualists had much to offer when the wartime government faced its most immediate test in its reaction to the crisis on its doorstep. The numbers of runaways opting for what protection Washington might give them grew from around four hundred in the spring of 1862 to roughly four thousand that fall and forty thousand by the war's end, with similar numbers in nearby communities and refugee camps. Free blacks and white well-wishers helped establish hospitals and other institutions among them. What they called "Lincoln Hospital" became "a great school" around which some seventy-five buildings clustered in a kind of "country village." During one visit, Chase crossed over to the freedmen's village at Arlington, where he got a tour from his old neighbor from Michigan Sojourner Truth, "looking as well and as young as when I first knew her, many years ago." She spoke "freely, as she should, for she is a power anywhere as all know who have seen her in public or private life." She reported on the conditions of the "several hundred colored people receiving rations, and some of them a little work." She told him that the surgeons sold the bodies of the dead, and she became "most scathingly severe on some of the officers connected with the freedmen's care, etc." She told him that "many are worse off than in slavery, and some even voluntarily return to it."[18]

Colburn later recalled her father's noting that Congressman Robert Dale Owen, a fellow spiritualist, headed the special committee to make recommendations to improve the lot of the freed people. Others who participated in séances, such as General Daniel Sickles, helped the government grapple its way toward what became the Freedmen's Bureau. Alfred Horton, George A. Bacon, and others labored tirelessly to meet the needs of the "thousands of worthy colored persons . . . anxiously waiting to be taught, and if we had more teachers and better accommodations, these golden opportunities would be joyously improved. I never saw before such general eagerness to learn; verily, some of them are hungry to know how to read." By the start of 1865, the Freedmen's Relief Association of Washington, New England Freedmen's Aid Society of Boston, and Pennsylvania Freedmen's Relief Association discussed the recruitment of two hundred teachers to begin classes for the twelve thousand children.[19]

By the spring of 1863, Horton thought that "the capital of the nation is more anti-slavery than was Boston two years ago." Spiritualism changed too, emerging from private homes once more into a more public venue, meeting in a boardinghouse on Ninth Street. They gave Dr. Francis J. Stratton, a clerk and patent officer, "probably the first Spiritual funeral held in public here." Horton contrasted their racial practices with that of a Methodist camp meeting that featured "a fence dividing the blacks from the whites—brothers of the same church, yet the distinction had to be kept up."[20]

Horton described free schools "inaugurated by Spiritualists" where "the colored people are treated with greater consideration, for it has been proverbial, where slavery has existed that the colored people have no rights which the whites were obliged to respect." One spiritualist thought it the duty of "all candid persons to put them on an equality with the whites. I do not think the war will end until every right of the blacks will be recognized." A spiritualist woman who had lost two sons and had two others in military hospitals began visiting black soldiers there as well. "The prejudice against the blacks is gradually giving way here," wrote Horton, "and soon it must in the North." Most immediately, he insisted, they needed to "educate all, blacks as well as whites, so that there shall be no more objections either here or in the spirit-world. But let us keep true to nature in all we do—educate rightly."[21]

However, the spiritualist closest to the Lincolns was surely Elizabeth Keckley, the former slave who became Mrs. Lincoln's dressmaker, friend, and confidante. Keckley brought the first lady not only to spiritualism but also to various projects to aid the freed people. Mrs. Lincoln wrote her husband after a bout of severe depression that "had it had not been for Lizzie Keckley, I do not know what I should have done." The following day, she sent him a note on "a very important item," Keckley's lack of success in raising money for the Contraband Association at Washington. Mrs. Lincoln quietly gave her two hundred dollars and wrote the president to send a check.[22]

"Slavery ranges in degree of degradation from serfdom to simple chattelism," explained Horace Dresser. "Color is but an accident of the condition."[23] Wartime conditions pushed many whites to think beyond slavery to address race, and the thoroughness with which they did so turned largely on their relationship to spiritualism.

## Native Americans

Like the Mormons, spiritualists felt a special kinship with Native peoples. Indeed, the "Indian guide" became a staple among mediums, which seemed logical, given the demographics of the continent. A civilization dominated by the whites appeared only recently in places like upstate New York. It seemed only reasonable that most of the spirits lingering around places like Poughkeepsie would be Indians. Perhaps, too, this represented a shadow of Jean-Jacques Rousseau's "noble savage," an essential template for a humanity uncorrupted by the trappings of civilization. Once beyond the realm of personal matters, the course of a trance or séance proved far more likely to turn on the assistance of the otherwise unidentifiable spirit of the wise Native than that of any whites, including Benjamin Franklin. Spiritualists also learned from—and acquired the power of—real indigenous shamans and medicine men. They noted Wau-chus-co, a "noted Indian Spiritualist and Clairvoyant," born near the head of Lake Michigan, who had been eight or ten when Ojibwe massacred English settlers at Fort Michilimackinac and had a prophetic vision of the Indian massacre of the whites at Fort Dearborn in 1815. In turn, such Native spiritual leaders often sought to appropriate what appealed to them in Christianity, with Wau-chus-co formally converting to Presbyterianism before his death in 1839 or 1840 on Round Island.[24]

On the eve of the 1864 spiritualist national convention, James M. Peebles added to his comments on slavery "if nothing can be done . . . in behalf of our forest brothers, the Indians." Spiritualist and Indian rights advocate John Beeson saw the question facing the nation as "whether the red race and the white race and the black race *have each at this day* the inalienable right to their complexion, to their language, to their religion, and to their freedom and to their homes, under the administration of a great Government."[25]

The few white advocates of Indian reform noted in the literature tended to make the plight of the Indians, like that of the poor, an argument for the serious reconstruction of the society. For many spiritualists, emancipation represented just one step in correcting antebellum injustices, particularly in terms of race. As one of them declared, "Our nation is struggling to consolidate life, and all because of injustice to the Indians and the Africans." "Humanity is waking: all races are demanding their rights," declared Peebles, "and no nation can long live, unless its foundation be based not only upon Justice, Equity and Equality, but cemented by those diviner principles of human brotherhood and universal love." "Our nation is now struggling for constitutional life, and all because of injustice to the Indian and the African."[26] Probably no comparable intellectual or theological current among American whites became so engaged with the plight of Native peoples.

Demographically, few spiritualists had any close connection to the dominant Southern faction of the Democratic Party, which had authored the removal policy and had long controlled and corrupted the remarkably lucrative Office of Indian Affairs. The architects of Indian destruction had gone on to engineer secession and sought "to fasten these outrages upon the North, and the present Government, and kindling a spirit of revenge which may lead them to take up arms with the rebellious States against the government." However, they surely engaged in wishful thinking in suggesting that their neighbors "in no wise sympathize as a people here at the North, with those outrages" and in hoping that the federal authority "will throw around them its strong arm of power to protect them in their rights." In fact, the federal armies opened the war by abandoning the Indian Territory to the tender mercies of the Texans and other secessionists who imposed treaties on their own terms over the nations there.[27]

Nevertheless, spiritualists persistently urged the issue upon the federal authorities, none more so than John Beeson. An English-born transplant from Illinois settled in Oregon, he had become an inadvertent casualty of the Rouge River War of 1855–56. While it raged, he infuriated other whites by taking the side of the Native people. Leaving his family in the West, he came east to publicize "the wrongs perpetrated by both Government and settlers on the Indians in that quarter," demanding, at the least, "a change of policy and treatment."[28] In short, Beeson and his supporters in the spiritualist movement proposed reassessing Indian policy with egalitarian goals.

In November 1858, a mass meeting at the Cooper Institute gathered "in behalf of the American Indians." A schoolmaster from the Indian Territory spoke of the "fine farms, good houses and furniture, with the frequent schoolhouse and church" there among people "on the whole as equal, and indeed superior in intelligence and civilization, to the neighboring white of Arkansas." By the end of that year, one writer in the *Banner of Light* spoke scornfully of "the very Christian termination" of the war in the Northwest. While participants in these eastern meetings often echoed that romanticized Rousseauian perception of Indians as "a spiritual people," their efforts assailed the "apathy which has so long rested upon us, inducing us to consent to their extermination."[29]

The next year brought another round of meetings in New England. The only overtly political resolution adopted by the Vermont state spiritualist convention in September 1859 expressed support for Beeson's efforts and the Indians in the West. Within days, Beeson, Wendell Phillips, and others met at Boston's Old South Church to plan a mass meeting in that city around the issue on October 10 at Faneuil Hall. That larger gathering sent "agents to the distant tribes, to assure the Indians of friendship, and to gain correct information of their needs; to issue suitable publications, and to aid in getting up a series of Mass Meetings in various cities, and as soon as practicable, convene a National Convention." It opted to work through existing missionary organizations among the Indians and endorsed Beeson's brilliant proposal that transcended the slavery question in the territories to declare a general moratorium on the admission of any new states "monopolized by our [white] people" until it admitted Indians their rights. Through 1860, as the sections tore the country apart, spiritualists continued to speak, write, meet, and pass resolutions urging justice for the Indians.[30]

Through the first weeks of the war in May and June 1861, Beeson toured with Larooqua, a young woman of the Penobscot tribe who provided songs to accompany his speeches on the conditions of the Indians of the West. They spoke at Boston and Clinton Hall in New York, where the old land reformer William J. Young joined others. At Philadelphia that first Thanksgiving of the war, former Whig governor James Pollock and Republican congressman William Darrah Kelley, a member of a committee of the House dealing with Indian issues, joined Beeson, and Larooqua offered her "very sweet and solemnly thrilling" version of a Native funeral song.[31]

Certainly, though, the spiritualists spearheaded a Republican predisposition to revisit what had been U.S. Indian policy for a generation. As the war began, Lincoln talked about the need to revisit the entire policy of the whites toward the Native peoples and appointed a three-man commission to make recommendations. After Augustus Wattles, the transplanted Cincinnati spiritualist, had testified in Washington about conditions in Kansas, the new administration appointed him to make recommendations on Indian policy, along with George E. H. Day of Minnesota and Dr. Elijah White, an Oregon missionary.[32] Events subsumed much of this effort, though.

In the absence of living advocates, though, Indian spirits told whites what they already knew.

> The white brother has asked for his red brother. He comes from his home of light o'er wood, and mountain, and river, to speak to the white brother of the Indian's old home. When my people first came to this land, where then were your people? They came to us few in numbers; we gave them what they asked—food and lands. We asked only their friendship in return. When they grew to be a great people, they fain would make us slaves, like those they brought in big canoes across the mighty waters; but we said, *No, never, never!* Will a red man be a slave? Tell your Great Chief he never can bind us down by force.

Whites, the spirit conceded, had "taught them many arts, but they have brought much evil also."[33]

Beyond the idealizations, though, spiritualists seemed aware of Indian sentiments on the issue, however unconsciously. One spirit fulminated so much that the *Banner* got only bits of his comments. "The red man looks into the future, and he sees the white man, looking strong now, weak," the spirit declared. "The white man says, 'I will rear a tree of liberty,' but he knows nothing of liberty." "Every Indian mound that rises from the Mississippi to the furthest lake," it continued, "will answer with a voice of thunder, that the ashes of the Indians are full of the magnetism of hate to the white man." "On the earth I fought for what I called my home and my rights," declared the spirit of Tecumseh. "In this better land I do not have to fight. The Great Spirit here gives us equal rights with pale faces. Here we live in harmony; here we are not driven about by a race calling themselves *civilized*."[34]

The agitation of Beeson and the spiritualists continued after the desperate 1862 Indian revolt in Minnesota and its brutal repression exposed any self-delusion that Northerners had not been involved in the oppression of Indians. In its aftermath, the Federal Army turned its attention to a crusade to exterminate not only those Indians that had risen but also the related Sioux people of the Dakotas. Hearing of the repression of the Winnebagoes, one spiritualist said simply, "No wonder the avenging hand of Justice is laid heavily upon the nation at this time for its manifold sins." After some concern that whites in the affected area would stop reading the *Banner* because of the position it took, Beeson promised five new subscribers "for every 'Banner of Light' dropped by Minnesotians, because of kind words relative to the red man." Late in 1863, as the conflict had become very explicitly a war for slave liberation, spiritualists again pointed west, urging for "ample justice . . . to our red brethren."[35]

The more the story of Minnesota became known, the greater the protests became. "For the accursed love of gold," Cora Wilburn pointed out, "their annuity was withheld by the scheming Indian agent, the *white brother* appointed by the Government to watch over their interests." Then it had been "because of their imitation of the vices of civilization that they committed the horrible deeds now constantly called up in accusation against the entire race." Beeson, in turn, strove to educate other spiritualists about Indian religious beliefs, particularly those of the threatened Sioux.[36]

March 1864 saw one of the most remarkable meetings of the war. Spiritualists and their allies occupied Congress in a meeting on behalf of the Indians. On behalf of those in the war-torn Indian Territory, a missionary declared that "their fields are laid waste, their cattle carried off, and they left in the most destitute condition. The women and children were driven to pick up the grains of corn and oats left after feeding the Union horses." They—if not Congress—actually listened to the fact-finding report of Augustus Wattles, George E. H. Day, and Elijah White of Oregon, the commissioners appointed to investigate Indian affairs and make proposals for change. Their experience confirmed Beeson's claim that "the frauds practiced upon the red man, are not, as yet, for some cause, permitted to come before the public."[37]

Beeson recalled when Confederate general Dabney H. Maury had visited New York before the war "as a self-elected representative from Arizona." Speaking before the Historical Society, he had described the Navajo as "'savages that must be either fed or killed,' for our people were rapidly taking possession of their fertile valleys." Other Confederates in the region quite openly discussed ethnic cleansing. Despite the secession of Maury and his kinsmen, Beeson complained that under the Union administration, New Mexico Indians had witnessed "the most cruel and unjust war of extermination against them carried on this last summer."[38]

Finally, in late 1864, news of the Sand Creek massacre reached the East. After Colorado troops "surprised and butchered nearly the whole of the inhabitants composing an Indian village," and their commander had been only suspended, the *Banner* suggested that he be "suspended by the neck." "No wonder the Indians retaliate," it continued.[39] Even federal authorities repudiated the perpetrators.

The dynamic of the spiritualist campaign for Indian rights during the war echoed through the rest of the century, though government responses shaped it into an ever more desperate paternalism. Ultimately, egalitarian change never took place, though the Grant administration made determined efforts to establish peace on the plains, if only to silence the agitation.

## Women

Notwithstanding its intellectual roots among the mystical musings of Andrew J. Davis and others, spiritualism became a movement through the Fox sisters and quickly became a cultural current largely dominated, in some ways, by women. Although the movement generally withdrew into the séance, it never gave up the kind of public lecture–hall advocacy that had provided a platform to few women—notably Frances Wright—daring to speak on secular subjects. As the movement evolved, this predisposition toward a gendered public space never quite became complete. Still, the *New York Herald* reported that, when women tried to speak, "the masculine mediums . . . would belch forth sounds that would frighten the inmates of a mad house."[40]

Paradoxically, the case of Cora Lodencia Veronica Scott Hatch Daniels Tappan Richmond demonstrated how a clever female medium could work the expectations of a crowd. Her upstate radical blacksmith father became interested in the "Practical Christianity" of Adin Ballou's Hopedale community in Massachusetts and took his family to Wisconsin. She became a promising young healer at fifteen and masked an eclectic intelligence behind a face framed in ringlets, conveying innocence through what Henry James described as a perpetual look of surprise. This carefully constructed image of an almost virginal vulnerability defined the incident that won her national prominence. While on the road in New Haven, she encountered and sought the help of Dr. William Britten—not yet Emma Hardinge's husband—in fleeing her own spouse, Dr. Benjamin Franklin Hatch, an opportunistic cad past fifty, who married her and pocketed her earnings. The case galvanized the outraged spiritualists of New York City who advised and managed her 1859 suit for divorce, rescuing the young damsel in distress.[41] She had her audience select a committee that chose a random subject on which the spirits would take control of Cora and deliver a creditably learned lecture to an audience legitimately impressed and confident that the young woman before them could not have been discussing such subjects with that kind of facility.

An almost unspoken consensus within the movement transformed its assumptions about spirit communication into a sweeping worldview that challenged some of the fundamental assumptions that had informed the course of the wider society. In July 1848, within weeks of the arrival of the Fox sisters back in Rochester, Amy Post and Eliab W. Capron joined Elizabeth Cady Stanton and others at the historic national women's rights convention at Seneca Falls. All became early advocates of spirit communications to other participants in the Seneca Falls convention, including Edward Fitch "Ned" Underhill, the pioneering stenographer, drawn into spiritualism as well as militant socialism and Republicanism. The *Spiritual Telegraph* published one call for women's rights signed by the most prominent advocates of the day, including Lucy Stone, Antoinette L. Brown, Elizabeth Oakes Smith, Elizabeth C. Stanton, Paulina Wright Davis, Mrs. Clarina I. H. Nichols, Rose, and Lucretia Mott. The *Telegraph* headed its account "Let Them Be Heard."[42]

Gender became inseparable for the press in presenting both issues of women's rights and spiritualism. The more conservative press mocked the very notion of men sitting in a public meeting listening to a woman, famously calling the men present at Seneca Falls "hermaphrodites."[43] In part, while women spoke publicly, they tended to shrink from open conflicts, generally preferring to leave the lecture hall to the domination of the men.

Beyond Seneca Falls, spiritualists played a direct role in legislative reforms favorable to women. In Indiana Owen's son Robert Dale Owen—both of them spiritualists—got protection for the property rights of married women through the Indiana Legislature and into law. William Batchelder Greene carried the issue of woman suffrage into the state constitutional convention, waging a one-man battle to get the issue heard. Chase did much the same in the organizing conventions for the state of Wisconsin.[44]

One writer found "the *fundamental* source of inequality" in the subjugation of women. "Genius is of no sex," it stated, "and does not *ask* for homage, but commands it." Although "not concerned about the SOCIAL destiny of woman," the author insisted upon her equality: "I would not ask that she be made *leader* or dictator, unless she possess the requisite qualifications for that position, and if so, I would ask that she be allowed to *take* that position, not as a menial or a subordinate, but as an equal." In part, this followed the approach of the antebellum radicals, such as the land reformers, who, in 1850 declared that "woman's rights are the same as those of men on all subjects, including rights to liberty, property, self-government, the elective franchise, and eligibility to office."[45]

Sensitivity to women's role in the movement certainly compelled spiritualists to consider and address their concerns. The burden of wartime impoverishment fell most heavily upon women. The situation might be improved if "some of our philanthropic merchants would bestir themselves." "This is a question which will press upon public attention with more and more force, as wealth accumulates in this country and the population of our cities and towns becomes denser every year. Even with this civil war's bloody exactions, it is found by the last popular vote that the several loyal States show an increased population over that of four years ago." So it was that American cities saw the rise of large new "overcrowded and foul tenements," bearing resemblance to those of London or Paris.[46]

Among themselves, spiritualists fostered a new role for women in every aspect of life, though its content ranged as widely as did the language of "free love." Most asserted the merits of "free love" as opposed to the restrictive institution of marriage, but the press loved telling the most embellished version of these tales, and critics of spiritualism loved them. During the divorce of Cora L. V. Scott from her husband, the *Boston Herald* described him as a spiritualist widower claiming to be a physician while seducing the young woman and taking her as his third wife. The *New Orleans Daily Picayune* reported that a woman in the audience rose to confront one female medium. She claimed that the speaker had "alienated from me the affections of my husband, who now resides with her. He has left me and my children for no other reason that

I can discover, but because he loves this woman better. I never injured her, but she has injured me and mine." The medium "blushed scarlet."[47] These made for good sales for conservative papers, but the truth or relevancy of many of them remains in doubt.

More generally, leading spiritualists seem disproportionately to have practiced what they preached. Davis married three times, the first wife dying and the second agreeing to an amicable divorce before his final marriage in 1885. This subject he regularly addressed without the benefit of mesmerism, as in *The Penetralia, Being Harmonial Answers* (1856) and *The Philosophy of Spiritual Intercourse* (1856). James Arrington Clay, perhaps most well known for his divorce in public defiance of the law, also associated with the spirtualists.[48]

More important, spiritualist women proved no more reluctant to divorce. Davis's second wife, Mary Fenn Love, went to Indiana to divorce her husband on the grounds of incompatibility. Out of Cleveland, Hannah Francis Morrill Brown, a New Hampshire–born mill hand who took up the pen after moving to Ohio to advocate for spiritualism, women's rights, and radical reform generally, not only divorced her husband but also allied herself with the Berlin Heights community, largely founded around the idea of "free love." Moreover, by 1858–60, she edited the *Agitator* to espouse such views publicly. After divorcing Dr. Benjamin F. Hatch, Cora L. V. Scott Hatch went on to marry Colonel Nathan W. Daniels, Samuel Forster Tappan, and finally William Richmond, eventually landing in Chicago's Rogers Park, where she reigned as the movement's matriarch well into the twentieth century.[49]

Critics called "free love" a rationalization for unbounded sexual promiscuity. "That is not Liberty which liberates the intellect, and enslaves the affections," responded Andrew Jackson Davis without repudiating this interpretation. "That is not Liberty which emancipates the African from bondage, and refuses freedom to the unhappily married; that is not Liberty which frees the wrongly-married, and withholds from woman the rights of property and citizenship." Their advocacy of "free love" took many forms, some of which involved sexual freedoms of all sorts.[50]

October 1855 also saw radicals in New York City use that expectation to engineer a cleverly managed scandal over a "free love" club. This provoked the mayor's office to send in his police to cart off alleged members of the club. In the end, the case of the municipal authorities deflated in an embarrassing crisis that contributed to the Democratic loss of the municipal government.[51]

At its minimum, though, spiritualists tended to agree with Robert Owen's dramatic indictment of the institution and asserted the independence of love from marriage. They made a vital distinction between the reality of human affections and the nature of the institution, asserting the priority of the former, often under the rubric of "free love."[52] Beyond this, what they meant by this term seemed to range from opposition to arranged marriages of any sort to advocacy for property rights for married women, ease of divorce, and all the way to asserting complete freedom of sexual relations.

Even the most socially conservative spiritualists found themselves critical of the institution of marriage. "The degradation of prostitution is a phantom of materialism that belongs to self-righteousness," declared Dr. Asaph Bemis Child. It came from "the fictitious distinctions of self excellence; prostitution, so-called, in reality, is an undisguised condition of life; and open expression of the elements of existence that are spontaneous and natural, and that are antagonistic to material glory." It existed on a continuum for working-class women, and he painted a horrid and accurate portrait of the lot of women in the needle trades. "The midnight lamp reflects the hectic flush, her aching, tired shoulders—these in silence proclaim her suffering. Every pain she bears cuts asunder a thread of love that binds her soul to earth, and it shall mount on wings to spirit-love, to soar away in freedom, sooner for her suffering."[53]

Emma Hardinge proposed a movement campaign to rescue "fallen women" enslaved by their poverty. The realities of the war and wartime conditions had also driven legions of women in any large city into prostitution. For many working-class women, the condition reflected a temporary response to immediate economic hardships, a pursuit taken up episodically and intending to be temporary. Males in a similar state understood pragmatic accommodations and often did not regard the activity as breaking any permanent taboos. The wartime expansion of this process shocked respectable women and middle-class men. "If all women were properly treated by their own sex, they would soon be by man; and thousands who sink in vice and misery to early and untimely graves, would live and grow in usefulness." Hardinge raised money across many cities.[54]

To a great extent, the spiritualist engagement with the freedmen represented an extension of what they had been attempting elsewhere on the home front, a secularization of the kind of relief that the churches lacked the strength to deliver. On the most pragmatic and immediate level, the *Banner of Light* began raising money to support the poor, particularly during the winter. Virtually every issue of the paper solicited for the local "bread fund." The fund-raisers thought it "behooves those who have a sufficiency of this world's goods, to render aid to the poor—no matter what the cause of their poverty." "We have been for some time past, and still are, aiding the destitute poor of this city by furnishing them with the requisite tickets wherewith they may be enabled to procure fresh bread from a bakery, each ticket entitling the holder to a ten-cent loaf." Through the *Banner,* the movement "already supplied to these needy ones, over six hundred loaves of bread," regardless of religious views or nationality. It recommended that "the Spiritualists of every city and town in the country, form a 'Provident Society.'" These societies would provide not only bread but also "the comforts and necessities of life to any who are unable to obtain them." The way for spiritualists to organize would be through "good works."[55]

In this respect, the goals of the movement had become remarkably modern. Woman's scope "needs growth and expansion; opportunities for the free employment and cultivation of all her faculties, and the freedom to exercise them untrammeled by such barriers as mistaken delicacy would raise." "Woman's sphere is anywhere where she can be of use—in legislation, on the bench, on the jury, in the field, in the nursery, or in the forum," declared one spiritualist in Boston. "Wherever she feels drawn to go, there is her place." The rise of such formations as the Workingwomen's Protective Union at New York City or the Working Women's Relief Association at Philadelphia suited the mainstream of the spiritualist response. As women's discontent became increasingly evident and the first meetings began to shape a common response, middle-class women, philanthropists, and clergymen rushed to shape their goals in what seemed to them the most constructive way. What resulted certainly involved job centers, fund-raising for poor relief, and the rhetoric of cooperation, which John Amos urged as "the embryo of health, happiness, progression, peace, and the millennium of harmony."[56]

\* \* \*

As civil war unfolded into a struggle for slave liberation, it also emancipated a radicalism in the Republican Party with a heavy dose of social radicalism and persistent calls for a thorough reconstruction of American civilization. Where Republicans backed away from such radicalism—which happened first in piecemeal form in local communities—the spiritualists persisted. One answer emerged in Maine, as local business interests muscled their way into power through the Republican coalition that discomforted some of the most prominent of its old leaders. Spiritualist and Republican Joseph Blake Hall saw no contradiction between editing the *Portland Daily Evening Courier* and serving as Maine's secretary of state and dabbling in spirit photography or supporting Portland's "Labor Reform Association." In the municipal election of March 1865, the Labor Reformers took up the radical rhetoric of the Republicans to challenge the often lackluster Republican practice. Wrote one of them, we "did not expect to cast over 300 votes, yet we actually cast 500 votes."[57] Periodic waves of such efforts swept the country for generations to come.

The Radical Republicanism that emerged represented no merely congressional response to the issues of Reconstruction. Even before the war's end, spiritualists—and surely many others—carried Republican ideas far enough to face not only slavery but also what they described as a pervasive prejudice "against abolitionists and free negroes," as well as Indians. As the spirit of a black patriot killed in Virginia reminded them, "A colored man is of as much account in the spirit-world, as a white man." They wondered why, as so many blacks regularly went to sea, none did so as navigators and masters. Spiritualists anticipated "the coming equality of the black races, who have so long been degraded, bound, fettered and abused by the white man."[58] War for liberty, they hoped, would foster the equality of nonwhites, women, and working people.

# 6

## Fraternity

*Reconstructing a Movement and the Nation*

As the nation strove to reconstitute itself, the spiritualist movement achieved a new level of national organization. Reminiscent of the Freemasons and Odd Fellows, their "Order of Eternal Progress" offered prospective members rituals, regalia, and standard mutual-aid benefits, while also overseeing "the necessary buildings for their meetings and all other purposes." However, it would be open to women as well as men. Nor did it replicate the color bar imposed by the white Masons. After all, it had as its goal nothing less than "the elevation of human character."[1] War not only destroyed existing structures, but also provided new standards for those that would be rebuilt.

As in the older revolutionary tradition, spiritualists saw equality as the root of genuine liberty and its only real safeguard a sense of fraternity, or solidarity, to use a term less gendered, as they intended. The struggle to maintain the mystical idea of the Union transformed the ideal of liberty, but actual material conditions provided these things with substance and meaning. In the course of the war and its immediate aftermath, spiritualists had to rebuild their own movement. At the same time, they and that movement became involved in broader efforts to reconstruct their communities in a more meaningful way. On the largest scale, of course, they sought to address the issues involved in the Reconstruction of the nation. On all of these levels, they formulated practical steps in hopes of moving into the real world their thoroughly unrealized vision of a fraternity of free and equal peoples.

## Reconstructing a Movement

The death and dislocations of war naturally expanded interest in spiritualism. Wrote Dr. Henry T. Child, "Letters from all parts of our country indicate an increasing interest, an earnest desire to know all that can be discovered of that unknown land towards which we all are hastening." By the middle of the war, some claimed five million spiritualists "in this country and the Canadian Provinces" and by the spring of 1864 six million. Less fancifully, the *Banner of Light* talked, the following fall, of two to five million spiritualists. "To the front, then, every one of us!" declared the *Banner,* using the language of military mobilization. It saw "legions under the lead of Ignorance to be met, grappled with, and overcome."[2]

Circumstances turned over much of the spiritualist leadership. "All mediums are constantly more or less susceptible to surrounding influences," declared Amanda M. Spence, "and those influences are constantly shaping their characters, their conduct, and the inspirations coming through them." The Fox sisters had never been particularly interested in a movement, and Andrew J. Davis had long moved to the margins, as had Thomas Gales Forster, the printer turned civil servant in Washington. Uriah Clark "did not know that a single one of the original twelve was now found actively and efficiently engaged in the field of spiritual progress." Chase ticked off S. B. Brittan, John Murray Spear, R. Ambler, Mattie Hulett, "and a host of others, less known," prominent before the war, but "lured out of the field by matrimonial retirement" or assailed by "the jealous and envious, and by rivals for public and private honors."[3]

Thomas L. Harris and James L. Scott had invested much of their credibility in building the Mountain Cove community in Virginia. After abandoning the colony and the colonists, Scott had already started distancing himself from the movement in general, during the "recantation" period of the late 1850s. After spelling out a "pantheistic" interpretation of spiritualism, Harris had gone overseas and denounced spiritualists as "gross sensualists and utterly immoral in their conduct in all the relations of life."[4]

Yet the war and wartime conditions had brought new leaders and spokespeople to the fore. Spiritualist ideas polarized the community of Seventh-Day Adventists at Battle Creek, Michigan, who hosted a debate between their minister, Moses Hull, and W. F. Jamieson in February 1863. Hull had already been experiencing six months of rethinking "in my 'faith'" and by the end of the year could "plead guilty of having but little left." He concluded that "the more a man knows the less faith he has; for as faith is based upon what a man does not know, an increase of knowledge must result in a decrease of faith."

By the fall of 1863, Hull had become an ardent spiritualist and, by spring of 1864, taken to the field himself as its advocate. A split among the Seventh-Day Adventists followed, but Hull went on tour and wound up speaking from Boston to Wisconsin on the issue.[5] A legion of other new leaders such as Leo Miller came out of the movement across the Midwest.

Local gatherings of spiritualists proliferated, though they often did so in ways virtually indistinguishable from those of "friends of progress" or coalitions around a "free platform." Activities in the Northeast reflected clear strivings toward organization. These included long-term gatherings, such as a three-day conference in Maine quarterly, annual conventions in Vermont, and a May 1864 convention at Boston, accompanied by outings and picnics. The networks at New York City brought out the believers like clockwork. Most famously, perhaps, were those at Dodworth's held twice weekly every Sunday, a regularity conducive to all sorts of activities, including funerals. Other regular gatherings took place at Clinton Hall.[6]

Organization in the Midwest may have been spotty, but in places it held its own with anything in the Northeast. The network of spiritualists became large enough in cities such as Cincinnati to sustain some sort of general society. Laura Cuppy at Dayton and locally important mediums across Ohio and Indiana anchored ongoing networks and communities. In the fall of 1863, a large spiritualist convention gathered at Evansville, near Madison. Over the following year, enough local organizations functioned to sustain quarterly meetings of a Northern Wisconsin Spiritualist Association. In late 1864, it brought in Moses Hull from Battle Creek as well as Mrs. Laura DeForce Gordon for a convention over which Colonel Abel B. Smedley—briefly back from the front—presided. Farther west, individuals such as Franz Widestrand worked on a movement in Minnesota. Associations in adjacent northern Illinois had held annual conventions through the war years at Oregon, but other conventions took place at McHenry and Belvidere. Even when Chase spoke at Cairo on the southern tip of the state, he reported lectures "crowded with earnest and interested listeners, and many came that could not get into the court house." The meetings particularly "brought out the ladies in respectable numbers." In October Chase announced he and his family had moved to southern Illinois. At Princeton in the summer of 1864, his path crossed that of James M. Peebles, who had returned from Tennessee broken in health, but resuming his lecture tour across the Midwest.[7]

The movement also coalesced, on a smaller scale, across much of the West. John B. Wolff, who had gone to Colorado from western Virginia, reported that the *Banner* circulated in Denver before the overland stage stopped running reliably and that a blind Illinois widow named Mrs. Briggs had begun holding meetings. At the start of 1865, Wolff attempted to start a quartz mining company "on a different basis from any extant here," in that it would divide the profits annually. Activities also took place in the West, not only in California but from the Nevada Territory right up into Oregon. The old New York radical William J. Young reported from central California that he had "never seen a place where the truths of the new religion were as cordially, spontaneously and universally received as in this valley." According to San Francisco's *American Flag*, local spiritualists had grown strong enough there to sustain a large meeting in defense of the Indians.[8] Permanent organizations, however, proved to be a different question.

Everywhere, the need for practical mutual aid goaded spiritualist spokespeople to attempt some kind of organization. As early as 1860, New York spiritualists had formulated plans for such a society that they could start among themselves and to which they could recruit everyone else. "Let every Spiritualist hand in his or her name, place of residence, business, trade, or profession, and let the same be recorded in a suitable book for convenient reference. Then when any of us are in want of merchandise, professional service, mechanical skill, etc., let us seek the supply from among those whose names are on this record."

As far as Ypsilanti, the spirits informed a woman about three orders of human development: the triangular Adam and Eve of the Old Testament, the right-angular square Adam and Eve of the New Testament, and the circular Adam and Eve of the New Dispensation. In this last, "woman's power shall be blended with the power of man, and love shall make the reign of unity and harmony."[9]

By the middle of the Civil War, several organizations had emerged. John M. Spear, his companion Caroline Hinckley, and others of the old Order of Pantarchs moved on to launch an explicitly secret Sacred Order of Unionists. It essentially regrouped their old organization with 147 spirits—including most of the founding fathers—as advisers. After 1863 Spear and Hinckley left for England, and the order continued, though losing its old community of Kiantone.[10]

In September 1863, Andrew Jackson Davis launched the oddly named Moral Police Fraternity at New York City. Christian "moral police" associations had long aimed at the eradication of prostitution, while the spiritualist group aimed at poverty, and its female members played key roles in this "fraternity." The spirits of departed Freemasons, Illuminati, and Brothers of the Rosy Cross participated, though insisting that "the absence of women" had crippled these earlier efforts. They hoped "to revolutionize the existing system of dealing with pauperism and crime," through "supplying the sick and destitute with food and clothing, and by kindly words of sympathy and encouragement might make them feel that they are children of the same Father-God and Mother-Nature—all striving for and nearing the love-lit sphere of the summer-land."[11] In short, it offered a kind of secularized church charity, as such presaging the idea of a modern social service agency.

The Children's Lyceums appeared as a by-product. These grew from Mary F. Davis's 1863 discussion on the education of children in the Summerland garden schools. That what amounted to spiritualist Sunday schools adopted the term used by contemporary adult education programs reflected a radical view of children. By 1871 the lyceums functioned in seventeen states, though their epicenter seemed to have become Philadelphia. Seldon J. Finney had brought the idea there, but Michael B. Dyott and his wife, Mary J. Dyott, built the first and largest of what became a half-dozen local lyceums with three hundred members.[12]

Perhaps the strongest and most stable spiritualist associations of the war coalesced at St. Charles, some fifty miles west of Chicago. Vermont-born lawyer Stevens S. Jones presided at a large convention held there in the summer of 1863. A resident of Kane County since the 1830s, he became one of the first attorneys in the area, a judge, and a railroad promoter. Jones's new son-in-law, Colonel John Curtis Bundy, returned from the war to assume responsibility for the group as well. Another transplanted Yankee, he served as a dry-goods clerk at St. Charles until he went to war, returning in broken health to study law and help lead the new Religio-Philosophical Society. This new association enlisted the skills of Chase, H. F. M. Brown, former Methodist elder Benjamin Todd, Leo Miller, and Warwick Martin. They proposed to offer "an example of the capability of man for self-government." They declared, "A mighty revolution has been wrought!"[13]

In his eclectic and homegrown "Rosicrucianism," Pascal B. Randolph argued the merits of hashish in helping to conjure visions. In general, movement leaders kept putting it to rest, asserting the importance of purity from drugs as well as alcohol. In late 1864, health reformer and old-time Free Democrat Dr. Russell T. Trall checked in against it, and A. J. Higgins wrote a serialized argument titled "Nature versus Drugs."[14] Yet it kept bobbing up, probably because those who tried it as an aid tended to agree with Randolph.

Nevertheless, the spread of spiritualism introduced or popularized innovations that even further decentralized the means of reaching the Other Side.

The wartime supply of mediums strained to meet the growing demand, and, as in other industries, necessity created new techniques, such as the planchette. The "little plank" provided a miniature table on which one or more persons could rest their fingertips, permitting the spirits to take possession of it. A pencil could be added to the planchette, permitting the movements to write, or, most popularly, it could be placed over markings with "yes" and "no" areas and an alphanumeric field, which permitted the planchette to spell its messages. By the 1880s, these became the "Ouija," a kind of take-home version of the séance.[15]

Along with the explosive interest in photography, some of its practitioners introduced a new kind of "spirit photography." William H. Mumler became particularly prominent in offering such photographs. The *Boston Investigator* infuriated the *Banner* by questioning the method, and the Adventists' *World's Crisis* jumped in to suggest that the images might really depict spirits, but possibly demonic ones. What had been demonstrations of animal magnetism resurfaced as theatrical magic. Spiritualists explored a kind of automatic painting, explained as similar to how cooks "infuse their magnetism into the food we eat, and make it more or less digestible." Others carried psychometry into the outright materialization of objects.[16]

## Reconstructing a Nation

War had pointed spiritualists to the possibility that a Radical Republican government could serve as a tool to abolish institutionalized injustices of all sorts. The more utopian had anticipated a condition where the country might abandon distinctions

> of color, caste, and fashion, now adored,
> Then perish, by no Angel-heart deplored;
> And North, and South, like twin-born children, rest,
> Drinking sweet life from one pure Mother's breast.

Yet government seemed an imperfect tool, as it existed, to bring heaven to earth. "All government, to my comprehension, is arbitrary, differing in degree only," wrote Benjamin N. Kinyon, "based on usurpation of consent, and not in quality or principle." The American government, he conceded, "arose out of consultation and agreement; but afterwards is upheld by acquiescence, the same as the Russian government." In the United States, he continued, "our boasted Republican form of Government falls but little behind that of Russia."[17] Civilization would have to reconstruct itself around the idea of universal liberty.

Yet everywhere the armies went—or recruited or taxed or employed—they seriously affected the largest part of the population. Though usually ignored by most historians of the conflict, the first modern war made massive numbers of refugees, and, in their wake, new communities pulled together. The process naturally revived the idea of planning and managing the process through intentional communities, the "Ácadias, New Atlantises, Edens and Elysiums." For several generations, Americans had toyed with utopian visions, "attempting to adapt them to the comprehension, apprehensions, tastes, prejudices, education, and temperaments of men in the lump." From the onset of the movement, spiritualists studied and experimented with innovative communities, from the Shakers or Iowa's Amana colonies to Fountain Home and secular colonies.[18] The Civil War opened the greatest unwritten chapter in the history of such utopian settlements.

The great overlap in constituencies and concerns between these early socialist ventures and spiritualism explained part of this. A key Illinois leader, Samuel Underhill grew up a Quaker before becoming convinced that the solution lay in "communism in some form." He wrote, "Nothing can be better proved than that success attends the Shakers; the monks of various orders who labor; the Rappites of Economy near Pittsburgh; the Zoaribs in Ohio; and the Swedes at Bishop's Hill, in Henry County, Ill." Underhill "passed three years of my life in one of the experiments which had its birth in the teachings of the noble philanthropist, Robert Owen, now gone to the spirit-land." Mrs. H. F. M. Brown described Underhill as "strong, stoutly built," a square-faced old man of about seventy, who became involved with M. M. Daniels of the *Rising Tide* at Independence, Iowa, but she knew him because of his work with her in the Religio-Philosophical Society.[19]

Chase, a founder of the old Fourierist Wisconsin Phalanx, returned as a spiritualist lecturer to his old home at Ripon. He looked out on "a beautiful amphitheatre valley of rich dry land, once the beautiful Ceresco home of the Wisconsin Phalanx, whose members composed the most moral, upright, honest, and intelligent inhabitants that ever lived in the town, but they are scattered and mostly gone." Still, he added, one of them currently represented the town in the legislature, "and several hold commissions in the army."[20] Among the latter was Major Alvan Earl Bovay, who had also presided over the first meetings there to protest the Kansas-Nebraska Act, from which a Republican Party had formed and grew across the country.

However, events had transformed the older notions of communitarianism. Early 1865 found Chase moving on through Philadelphia to new, less blueprinted kinds of communities in New York and New Jersey. Charles K. Landis drew settlers to Vineland "from nearly every Northern State, from Maine to Iowa." Women there went to polls symbolically in 1864, and contemporaries knew of its spiritualists and radicals. However, the newcomer destined to become its most famous resident combined dietary concerns with temperance to produce Thomas B. Welch's grape juice. Down the coast, spiritualists planning a healing institute and an industrial college settled at Hammonton.[21]

Another old radical, Alcander Longley had an eccentric penchant for finding niche markets at Cincinnati in the printing trades, and the war that moved thousands of men through the city heading south created an exceptional demand for playing cards. The son of Abner Longley, who had aided Owen's work in the Ohio Valley, Alcander had always fantasized about having the wherewithal to launch his own communitarian project. Early in 1864, he got more than a thousand across on the northern side of Black Lake near Crimea, Michigan, and announced the formation of "an association of cooperative labor, education, and a unitary home."[22] This last description reflected his debt to the New York City project launched by the pioneers of the Modern Times community on Long Island.

However, wartime conditions inspired a new and largely neglected set of communitarian theorists. One of them, Dr. A. B. Child, urged such a strategy in lieu of political action. Around the start of the war, some of the more radical thinkers, such as D. H. Hamilton or Benjamin N. Kinyon, had begun discussing cooperatives and communities. Former Universalist David J. Mandell recruited some entrepreneurial support to take up Child on his rhetoric in Missouri, rather bizarrely located "on the line of the Hannibal and St. Joseph Railroad."[23]

Henry P. Kidder founded the town when the railroad had reached that point in 1860. Patrick S. Kenney served as the storekeeper, postmaster, stationmaster, and freight agent, starting what the county history called "a one man hamlet." The arrival of the New Englanders supported a new hotel run by A. W. Rice and a one-room schoolhouse in 1862. Nannie Beaumont was a daughter of James Beaumont who came to Kidder in October 1860, when nothing was there but the depot and a start on the hotel. At the war's outbreak, Kenney and other locals, such as William Plumb, joined the Home Guards and eventually wound up in the Unionist Missouri State Militia Cavalry. Soldiers camped throughout the area, and Confederates raided nearby.[24] These military preoccupations generally depopulated the village and doomed the community, which was later opened for resettlement by others with different priorities.

Hamilton also contemplated a similar society "in Southern Kansas next spring" as part of his making the case for a sweeping national "Reconstruction." The *Banner* complained when it got his "large mass of MSS on the above subject—enough to make a dozen pamphlets, which the authors expect us to run through the columns of this paper, to the exclusion of other more valuable and interesting matter."[25] The approach sparked considerable controversy, as the more conservative spiritualists scoffed at the very notion that government could or should attempt a reconstruction of the entire society.

The war raised the prospect of doing something similar for the entire nation. Like some of the most respectable Republican officeholders, spiritualists understood that the longer the Confederacy persisted, "the more thoroughly will its spirit become subjected." They expected that "the barbarous organization that has taken the field for slavery, then we may expect that the final stroke will fall; and forever after the social and political atmosphere will be the purer." However, even the relatively conservative *Banner* wanted "not a war merely for victory but for principle" to be "firmly rooted in the new life of the nation." "This is a revolution—a war of ideas" that would require that "the great non-slaveholding class," including "emigration pouring in from the Free States—will gradually change their minds and become converted to freedom and the Union." Military victory alone would not do that. "There are months of bloody battles and years of wearying struggles on a diminished scale before the first steps to this revolution of the South are accomplished."[26] Unlike any conservatives of either party, though, spiritualists proposed that the people, through their government, take charge of the kinds of change the country needed.

Chase thought it "plain, also, to every observer, that the nation is drawing in its lines and tightening its coils around the heart of the rebellion, which, like the folds of an anaconda, must soon crush its victim." At that point, he added, "we must meet and saddle the great question of States Rights. Then we must decide whether a *State* can commit suicide; or by treason of its officers, and a majority of its voters, and forfeit all its rights as a state and become again a territory of the nation, to be readmitted as a state by a new Constitution." The Southern states, argued Chase,

> can and have forfeited *all* the rights they ever had as States, by using them all to destroy the National Government, of which they were a constituent part. If an individual forfeit his right to liberty, by using his liberty to destroy the

government, I see no reason why a combination, or organization of ten, or ten thousand, may not do the same; and certainly a state is no more nor less than an organization of individuals, without which it would be only national territory. If a plague had destroyed the lives of all the inhabitants of Florida, it would have been territory, subject to national law, till again settled, and re-admitted as a new State; and certainly treason is a plague, and it has killed South Carolina and other States.[27]

Conditions in the Confederacy had imploded. In desperation, Southern officials strove to militarize civilian functions and even tried such innovations as setting prices. Spiritualists understood the desperation as "an infamous fraud on the intelligence of the civilized world." Most important, the cycle of Federal victories and the loss of Confederate territory created an escalating problem of desertion. Some Confederate generals did express their fear of the impact of Lincoln's offer of amnesty to anyone leaving the rebellion, and thousands deserted from the Confederate armies, particularly from those of the western states, crossing over to the Federals "in large companies, in squads, and singularly." Even in Virginia, desertion was "no longer confined to solitary individuals, but large masses of men only wait for an opportunity to quit a service which they loathe." The *Banner*, like other Northern papers, reported such rumors as Sterling Price's withdrawal into Mexico. In part, the arrival of spiritualists such as Lincoln appointee Justice Joseph Williams at the U.S. District Court at Memphis, Tennessee, or Pascal B. Randolph and others at New Orleans brought these ideas of social reconstruction into the region.[28]

War brought spiritualism on a much larger scale into what had been the slaveholding South. At Hannibal, Missouri, where spiritualists could scarcely get a hearing before, "a Spiritual Association numbering some thirty members" formed part of "the great transition from slavery to freedom, through which we are passing." They brought in national speakers and began supporting a network of local mediums, including a young lady who could free herself from handcuffs, unlock doors, and converse with the spirits. Then, too, "a young widow lady from South" sought a career in opera because she became convinced that a departed diva had "advised me go upon the stage as a singer, I was a skeptic, but latterly my voice has astonished myself and friends. I can range a note as high as Jenny Lind in F, and can warble and thrill naturally." She assured her correspondent that she came from "the best blood of the South."[29]

Spiritualist congressman John R. Kelso of Missouri warned that the fate of loyal blacks and whites in the South would be inseparable, for "if the blacks be oppressed on account of their color the whites will be oppressed on account of their principles." He urged Republicans to confiscate and redistribute the property of the disloyal and to *"boldly* declare for *the equal rights of all men,"* mocking "hackneyed objections to negro suffrage." Southern blacks, he added, had "never faltered, though their fidelity to us subjected them to unheard of outrages and to death in a thousand terrible forms." Following the English model of Puritan Oliver Cromwell, he introduced resolutions for the impeachment of President Andrew Johnson as necessary "for the purpose of securing the fruits of the victories gained on the part of the republic during the late war, waged by rebels and traitors against the life of the nation, and of giving effect to the will of the people as expressed at the polls during the recent elections." He insisted on "the direct intervention of federal authority the right of franchise alike, without regard to color, to all classes of loyal citizens residing within those sections of the republic which were lately in rebellion."[30]

The scion of an old colonial Virginia family, William Emmette Coleman had not yet turned twenty when the war broke out. The native of Albemarle County attended school in Richmond, where he worked his way into a job at the local library. The bookish young Southerner had already become "interested in the various reformatory movements of the age, including the woman's rights, labor and other sociological reforms," including "rationalistic spiritualism." He quietly appreciated the possibilities of John Brown's raid on Harpers Ferry and thought of himself as the first and only Republican in the town. Likely associated with the estimated several hundred members of the Unionist underground in Richmond, he actively participated in Reconstruction, putting together the Republican Party and the Virginia State Woman's Rights Association.[31]

Spiritualists themselves had a firsthand view of the initial stages of this process in the Deep South. The Federal occupation transformed New Orleans, where Chase visited his son Milton in the army there. Laura De Force went there to be with her new husband, Captain Charles Howard Gordon, in a New England cavalry unit occupying the town. She found "its deserted warehouses and empty cotton-presses, formerly the repositories of Southern capital, are the saddest chapters yet written by the red hand of War against the traitorous enemies of our country, and the destroyers of Southern peace and prosperity, born and bred within her borders." Randolph, who had inconsistently identified his ethnicity, went overseas as the war began and showed every sign of staying there indefinitely. With emancipation, he returned, went to Louisiana, and became a new spokesman for the black American community there.[32]

Then, too, in the North, Cora L. V. Hatch had ascribed "slavery of thought and feeling, slavery of mind, slavery of soul, to principles that are not great slavery to things that are not true, and perfect, and religious." It left them "bondsmen and bondswomen to hard taskmasters—prejudices, superstition and bigotry." "All *slavery* is not *South*," insisted James M. Peebles. "The war," said Mrs. C. M. Stowe, "continues because the *North* is so much like the *South*! They are not all demons, nor the citizens of the North all saints and angels."[33]

Even at its most conservative, spiritualism recognized the material realities and saw the need for the entire nation, rather than just the Confederacy, to undergo a reconstruction. War posed the question for Chase of "whether an aristocracy or a democracy shall govern the country; and whether it shall be divided into little homesteads for the many or into cumbersome plantations for the few; whether wealth, education and the soil of the country shall be monopolized, or whether everything that man holds dear shall be free, including religion." In this content, he doubted that "this nation, or its great heart, the working classes has not been arrested—scarcely retarded." Through all the losses, Northerners had brought in their crops, maintained business, and assimilated immigrants. In contrast, the Southern ruling classes "monopolize the soil there, as they do not do in New England; and they have their labor done by persons whom they own; and the poor white population have no provision made for them. Thus they are kept poor, weak and ignorant. If you find school houses at the South, you will find them closed to the poor." Another described Kentucky as "owned and kept by a landed aristocracy," a place where "all property and power is in the hands of the landed proprietors."[34]

Reconstruction of the nation generally required resolving a power struggle between "aristocracy and democracy" on both sides of the Mason-Dixon line. Placed in merely sectional terms, "one class says, Cotton is king; the other says the mighty Dollar. God never made kings and rulers, but men and women." Slavery had been merely "the very cap-sheaf of the bottomless pit." "As we advance the interest of others we advance our own. Our armies have never been so successful as since the declaration of emancipation. If the ability of this nation was commensurate with its avarice, they would make a ladder to heaven and tear up the golden streets to sell in Wall Street." Another asked for "the apparent causes of your revolution; let us look at the chief ones. Look at the condition of society in your large cities." North, as well as South, "one class of society is allowed to live in luxury upon the unrequired labor of a weaker class—the effect being precisely that produced by Southern slavery, and slavery of all kinds and everywhere, viz., crime of every description is produced and cultivated by oppression." One of the departed returned to quip, through a medium, that "old Abraham Lincoln was smart when he instituted that plan that touched the pocket-books of the wealthy as a means of defraying the expenses of the war."[35]

Spiritualists found themselves in the vanguard of American thinkers exploring the possibilities of using government for the abolition of "slavery" in the broadest sense, which meant a return to what was believed to be, quite literally, fundamental. "When all other resources fail, then we may surely go back to our common mother—the earth." "Let the trades cease, and still the soil will support us. And, in this country, what a vast area we have to call our own! It stretches out, of virgin richness, almost limitless. It wants for labor, standing idle. There are not enough of us to properly take care of her. What a consoling fact is this for our future."[36]

The movement certainly had many adherents with serious social criticisms of the North as well as the South. War had also intensified spiritualist skepticism about Northern pretensions. Northern business interests, from colonial times, had fostered and profited from the development of plantation slavery. In the course of the war, spiritualists reported the Confederate dead coming back to complain of sectional responsibility for the injustice. In hindsight, spiritualists spoke of "so slim a basis of management, as we were apparently satisfied with before the final manifestation of our intestine troubles." "Our national and religious institutions are to be reconstructed," said J. S. Loveland. "The genius of the age is to be incarnated in forms corresponding and adapted to its power of use. And who shall do this but Spiritualists—those who possess the key of interpretation and the power of wise adaptation?" Politics "certainty to become spiritualized, or they must grow worse than they were before. The ward-room odor must give way to a purer one, and the coarse politician to the lead of higher and noble influences."[37]

These beliefs informed the approach most spiritualists took toward abolitionism and the promise of Union victory. As a movement, it believed "that humanity is one; and that, the experiences of all families, tribes and kindreds of men have helped to teach and demonstrate that *slavery,* in any and all of its *phases,* is at war with the best aspirations of the mind, the genius of civilization, and the philosophy of social reform."[38] That is, the movement insisted that abolition required an assault on social and economic hierarchy, on ignorance, and on the assumption that the issues of the war represented merely sectional differences.

In the end, the success of the antislavery movement cultivated a fuller flowering of Pascal B. Randolph's leadership abilities. Described as "a man of education, an author, an able writer, and . . . an example to our young men anxious for intellectual acquirements and literary distinctions," he plunged into the war effort, when it came, and headed south himself to play an important role in the attempted Reconstruction of Louisiana.[39] Nor had his contribution to spiritualist and occult history come to an end.

Wilfrid Wylley astutely warned that the central issue in the nation over "the next decade or two" would have to be race. "On the one side will be mustered all the forces and arguments that candid, earnest and enlightened minds can bring to bear; on the other, all the low-browed malice, all the slimy calumny and blind prejudice that partisan faction can call to its aid, will be marshaled in battle order by the demagogue and political quack."[40]

Success though, required an agenda identifying the issues on which the weight of spiritualists could be brought to bear. Toward the close of the war, Chase speculated that abolition would lead to "the political, social and religious equality of woman with man." Beyond that, he suggested "division of lands, security of homesteads, generality of labor and respectability of laborers, free schools and universal education, abolition of imprisonment for debt and repeal of laws for collecting debts; abolition of capital punishment, and other relicts of barbarism and Christianity combined, both of which are savage, because they have savage gods as bases of authority and law." Others pointed to issues like monetary reform and finances.[41] Establishing priorities would be another matter.

The result would carry the entire nation into a new "order of human development—the circle of unity, harmony and love," albeit with three divisions: Northern, Northwestern, and Southern. Perhaps it could raise a new flag that would be white with blue stars "in clusters of three each. The stripes can no longer be retained for the tears of the oppressed have washed them away. In place of the blue square on which are the stars of the old ensign, is a circle crowned with thirteen stars of the original States, under which is an eagle without the weapons of death in his talons, standing upon a world within the circle. In each corner is a new-moon crescent, in which there is the emblem of the All-Seeing Eye."[42] However worthwhile and interesting, the fantasies of a free nation carried some spiritualists far afield from the nasty realities of the conflict.

## Practical Steps to an Ideal Future

The dynamics of American development would increasingly mandate an acknowledgment of class. Already the conditions evident in London and other cities of the Old World had reappeared in American communities. Poverty represented the keystone of a set of problems associated with overcrowded housing, unemployment, sanitation, and crime. "The vagabond children of ten years ago in New York were the young rioters and fiends of last summer," noted one, commenting on the 1863 draft riots. "There is no way to suppress vice save to nip it in the bud." Egalitarians needed to address the new institutions of the police and prisons as the fruits of poverty. They also proposed to abolish capital punishment as a "brutal relic of a barbarous age" that fell disproportionately on "the diseased, the imbecile, the neglected, the failures of our social system." Then, too, wartime conditions had gendered poverty. "We estimate the forwardness of our civilization by the position of woman. Where she is compelled to labor as the beasts of the field, it is impossible that she should be other than degraded and down-trodden." As part of this, society should "fairly consider the intricate and exciting subject of marriage, which now agitates the people of this country."[43]

Yet many of these aspirations and assumptions grew from the belief that society would change in a rather organic way, as its components strained into a more just future. Uriah Clark talked of this in biblical terms as "the Nation's Jubilee." The triumph of republican government would represent, first and foremost, the success of the people, for "self-government, therefore, is nothing less than a process of self-humanization."[44]

"Spirits are endeavoring to unite mankind as a common brotherhood, and to sweep away all antagonisms existing among them," insisted Davis. "This can not be done until a change takes place in the conditions of society. We find that a few individuals claim to own the whole earth, while the rest of mankind are their slaves. Can there be such a thing as brotherhood where such a state of things exist." Thousands in New York City faced "the most degreating [sic] positions, and leading the most vicious lives, who are anxious to reform and be reunited to society, and yet there is no means by which their wishes can be gratified. What is Spiritualism worth to us, unless we can make it of some use in removing these evils?"[45]

One correspondent in the *Banner* insisted that the solution lay in education rather than radical social change. He declared Hamilton "wrong—right in spirit, I hope, but foolishly places his faith in externals." "Go back so far as history can carry us into all places and conditions of men, and we find only a reign of force." Force had "reigned, look, and behold the dangers and insecurity of human life!" "By our government of force another million of men, North and South, who have pursued safety through the dangers of force, have been maimed and crippled for the remnant of their earthly lives."[46] Of course, the argument made more sense to people who did not share a sense that the government had done any good in waging the war for Union and emancipation.

"People cannot grow refined and intelligent until they have first secured something to live on," declared the *Banner*, adding, "We never hear of a starving man exerting his energies for much of anything but food. Hence material wants must needs be provided for first; that is the law." Labor movements came from the "deranged condition of affairs." Spiritualists quoted one of its strike declarations: "We must consider whether our present social arrangements are satisfactory; and, if these things were changed, whether a better state of things would not result. Can there be anything more unfortunate, or more sorrowful to contemplate, than that masses of intelligent beings from childhood to old age, should toil in work in which they have no interest, and that between themselves and those for whom they toil, the attachment should be no more than that between a buyer and a seller?"[47]

Spiritualists looked at labor strife and strikes in that context. Joshua K. Ingalls freely discussed his ideas on "capital and labor" in the spiritualist press. "Often, too, that labor takes the form of downright and open conflict," declared the more moderate *Banner*. "When it comes to that—as it many a time has heretofore, in human history—that truth is forced to fight its way, instead of losing our strength in lamentations over the fact, we shall do better to rally to the side of the fact, and lend all possible aid and encouragement in helping it to secure final victory."[48]

At the same time, they discussed how strikes should become "*an agency toward an ameliorating change.*" They talked in terms of establishing "a *co-operation of labor and capital*—the most powerful instrument of social amelioration." The *Banner* expected that the labor movement would "lead to the final establishment of more just relations between Labor and Capital." Hardly the most radical voice among the spiritualists, it did object to "forcing their employers, who are under contract to the Government, to lie idle, they are directly hindering the operations of the Government itself, and at a time when it needs the whole service of all its men, to put to death this wicked rebellion. There is a rational limit even to the demands for justice." "Let the poor mechanic have every cent that belongs to him," it added.[49]

When striking printers launched the cooperative *Boston Daily Evening Voice*, the spiritualists reviewed it favorably as "devoted to the cause of moral, social and labor reform, published under the auspices of the Boston Printers' Union, and will favor the cause of the workingmen generally throughout the United

States." "Let not the hardy sons of toil of our own dearly beloved New England slumber at their posts. Still advocate and maintain the dignity of labor; and, if need be, rally to the polls and elect men to office who will second your noble endeavors."[50]

Like most of their contemporaries, spiritualism believed change would likely take place incrementally. The Fourierists—almost all of whom embraced spiritualism—had sought to foster anticapitalist communities across the Northeast and turned to forming cooperative protective unions after 1848. Their organizer at New York, Ira B. Davis, had organized a bakery to supply stores before explicitly declaring himself a spiritualist. Conversely, spiritualist publicist and manufacturer Charles Partridge employed "nearly 300 men, women, and children" in his operation off Thirty-Sixth Street near Seventh Avenue and found himself moved by the spiritualist critique of capitalism to develop profit-sharing arrangements.[51]

Spiritualists also publicized Josiah Warren's variant on cooperatives. Back at Cincinnati, he had developed a system of "Labor Stores," where customers purchased things with "Labor Notes," redeemable directly for their labor. This quickly evolved into an idea of regulating profit through social control of the money supply and the transformation of money into paper vouchers. "Why should we labor, and delve, and toil for gold to be used as a circulating medium, or as the basis thereof," declared one spiritualist, "when we have a better and more substantial one, without money and without price—one which can neither be stolen or adulterated." "This Republic is the first experiment of free government ever undertaken by an intelligent people who were capable of establishing and sustaining free institutions," wrote Warren. He favored social revolution "not to injure or destroy, but to purify and strengthen the Republic; and no fear whatever need be entertained of any other result. It is *no crisis,* but an *incident* in the progress of free institutions."[52]

These social critics had already developed remarkably detailed assessments of banking, money, and finance in the works of Warren, Andrews, William B. Greene, and Edward N. Kellogg. Other spiritualists expressed a similar preference for reforming the money supply through the government management of paper currency. One suggested that they "should be made redeemable not at their own counters only, but at the commercial counters of the country; not in gold and silver, but in current exchanges; and if they fail to do so, sell their securities and close them up."[53]

Significantly, although the record is less clear, a number of prominent early trade unionists also became spiritualists. Most important, South Carolina–born printer Thomas Gales Forster became a prominent leader in various locals of the Typographical Union. A founding member of the national union, he simultaneously took the platform on behalf of spirit communications and writing.[54]

So, too, many communitarians and cooperationists adhered to land reform. A Mr. Noe enumerated several immediate practical reforms: "the right of every individual to the land, or as much of it as will suffice for his sustenance"; women's equality "socially, politically, and morally"; and workers' right to "a higher destiny than to be bought and sold by the opulent as merchandise." The movement would eliminate the "ignorance, for which the more fortunate wealth classes are indirectly responsible," and the special role of spiritualism in addressing universal reform, for "it is useless to talk of reform in marriage, until the hungry are fed, the naked clothed, the ignorant educated, and the rights of every individual soul respected. That is the special mission of Spiritualism to reform these abuses, and to hasten the time when all men shall be free and *equal*."[55]

So, too, without radical land reform, the survivors would return home to nothing. "The social problem in the rebellions portion of the country will hereafter be, to raise up a class of middle men on the land, who shall constitute the bone and sinew, the stock and stability of the country." With the return of the soldiers, reform would ensure "the proper preservation of the people's peace, which is essential to the welfare of a community."[56]

Particularly in the South, where the war had reduced society to those basic elements, land reform would be essential. Spiritualists followed wartime experiments in areas with vast numbers of black refugees, where "wonderful things have already been done in that locality." At Newbern reports on the condition of the black refugees indicated that "the scheme for the occupation of abandoned plantations is working most favorably." Such projects offered "the real solution of this vexed problem of African Slavery on the continent." "An entirely new policy is yet to be adopted by the Government in this matter, which will profit us all alike."[57] This represented nothing short of the historic promise of "forty acres and a mule."

Their reactions to the economic crisis of 1857 transcended their moral responses to static inequalities, but their self-constructed spiritualist values remained the bedrock of their responses to social injustice. "The land abounds with everything. Flour and corn are plenty, and more than plenty," but "the prices are kept up without the least show of reason or justice." It "costs the poor man, who relies upon his daily labor to live, all he can earn to sustain his little family." Spiritualists urged the people to oppose "a class of men whose occupation is, and ever has been, to defraud them" or "a combination of men, who do not scruple to gamble in the very sustenance on which a nation depends for its life."[58]

To some extent, their critique of capitalism ran deeper, to raise issues about the nature of industrialization itself. Under capitalism even the large-scale introduction of sewing machines, which should reduce the burden of toil for needle women in particular, might well add an even greater burden. Despite "all our improvements in labor-saving machines," noted Davis, pauperism had grown exponentially. The state relieved 1 in every 123 inhabitants in 1831, 1 of 39 in 1841, 1 of 24 in 1851, and 1 in 17 in 1856.[59]

The same tradition and laws that gave capitalism and capitalists everything closely circumscribed and regulated what workers could have or do. "Did any person ever hear of a law limiting the price of houses or rents? Have we any laws limiting the price of beef, pork, flour, cotton cloth, or any other necessary of life? If this law is founded upon principle, why not carry it out?" In the end, "Laws are bought and sold, bartered, and gambled for, until humanity is made an outlaw, and men are cajoled into pliant instruments for their own oppression." Spiritualist predisposition tended to be for "a simpler and purer government" with very limited powers and low taxes. Understandably, spiritualists published Henry D. Thoreau's expression of "his unmeasured contempt of politics and government."[60]

In a series of articles in the *Rochester Express,* John T. Amos attributed the fundamental issue to "a problem in this matter of Capital and Labor . . . which it will take not one generation of inquiries and experiments only to solve." The *Banner* agreed enough to reprint the essays, declaring its rethinking of the common old assertions about mutual interests. "We might as well look for the friendly admixture of fire and water, and write about their identity of rights," they concluded. Amos urged workers "to try union, and see what result that will produce; but always to remember this fact, 'that Union, without Capitol [sic], will not give strength, and in America, to-day, Capital is Supreme Ruler.' These suggestions are worthy of careful consideration."[61]

Thomas Lake Harris lectured in the city morning and evening on Sunday about "three degrees of human development," sensuous and external, intermediate and intellectual, and spiritual and celestial. He added that "these three classes and their essential ideas, methods, and institutions, are represented among almost all religious sects, and that professed Spiritualists present these several phases of development."[62]

Spiritualism followed efforts to grope toward a scientific understanding of the human past. Spiritualists saw no problem in the idea that humans evolved from animal beginnings until a soul had appeared as a new kind of organ—or even that it would be infused later by divine will. This fitted the arguments of historian Henry Thomas Buckle, who proposed to measure humanity by the decline of superstition.[63]

* * *

D. H. Hamilton's long essay "Reconstruction" centered on recognizing the universal in its male and female dimensions. The system arrayed "capital against labor, brains against muscles." "Disintegration has nearly done its work. Combination must come next, and true Theocracy, where wisdom, Law and Justice, the godly elements in man shall rule and govern." The right of "every being that wears the human form, irrespective of complexion or capacity" would be the cornerstone of a new civilization. The most radical spiritualists spoke of the need to organize "Anti-Money-Clutching societies, and Anti-Look-Out-For-Yourself Societies, *ignorance, poverty, crime* and *contention* will continue to disgrace every opening page of the world's future history, as it has the past, clear down to the Revelator's great battle of Gog and Magog."[64]

"A system will be unfolded, sooner or later," declared one, "that will embrace in its fields Church and State, for the object of the two should be one and the same, ie., THE ELEVATION OF INDIVIDUAL MAN AND WOMAN." As did so many of his generation, Ira Porter, an old radical in the Religio-Philosophical Society, interpreted these hopes into a rhetoric insisting that "the true plan is the development of the individual." However, to them, this meant that "the laboring classes should have an opportunity to acquire mental wealth, (become enlightened) as well as a competence for physical support." Their hostility to political action reflected skepticism about "a Government of force" that served as a tool used "to get a living from some one else's labor." Porter distinguished between that and "a Government which recognizes the right of all men, strong and weak, rich and poor, black or white to 'life, liberty, and the pursuit of happiness.'"[65] Insofar as the war and emancipation offered an example of the latter, spiritualists contrasted the need to rethink their appreciation of government and the language used to discuss it.

## Epilogue

# Long Shadows

### *The Legacies of Civil War–Era Spiritualism*

> We declare that land, air, and water are the grand gifts of nature to all mankind, and the law or custom of society that allows any person to monopolize more of these gifts of nature than he has a right to, we earnestly condemn and demand shall be abolished.
> —Socialist plank in the Greenback-Labor Party platform, 1880

At the war's end, a Virginia newspaper recorded "a remarkable atmospheric phenomenon." As evening deepened, observers saw "shadow forms, like those of human beings—thousands upon thousands in number—moving through a deep valley, in clear view of the spectators, and finally ascending a steep mountain and disappearing."[1] What did these departing spirits of the Civil War era leave later Americans? The answer sometimes seems as wispy as the clouds in the haunting shimmer of the Virginia countryside.

Those who had posed the impertinent question meandered through the postwar years to various destinies. They sought a more coherent legacy through the establishment of organizations the significance of which proved ephemeral in its own right. Radical spiritualism perhaps left the most clear and discernible legacy, but its importance remains part of an ongoing negotiation among Americans. Some places where the spirits and the spiritualists eventually wound up are more identifiable.

\* \* \*

Since the American Revolution, the legitimacy of established religious institutions and ideologies had dwindled, creating a theological void that coincided with a similar crisis in medicine and healing, along with a revolution in scientific thinking. While surely some kinds of Protestantism proved more inclined to spiritualism than others, virtually all included some spiritualists, and the presence of freethinkers with the occasional Jew or Catholic among the spiritualists certainly represented something noteworthy. More important, perhaps, they reached back into pre-Christian pagan traditions, even attempting a rehabilitation of witchcraft at Salem. Whatever solace spiritualism offered a healing process had been real enough, as had been any therapeutic effects of that solace.

This same dynamic shaped a process of healing society. Spiritualism, like antislavery politics, started as loosely organized little networks of people skeptical of the dominant creeds. As we have seen, spiritualism overlapped significantly with the Free Democratic Party. They were present from the 1854 beginnings of the Republican Party, which proposed to intercede between the spirit of abolitionism and the practical realities of the political system. Under their mediumship, antislavery politics assumed mass proportions, even as the consolidation of an idea of mediumship shaped spiritualism into its true and massive form. Spiritualism argued that the grand common experience of mortality argued for an underlying mystical union of human spirits, while events drove the Republicans to embrace the inviolability of a grand mystical Union, rooted in the shared past and to-be-shared posterity.

All of which brings us to the importance of Abraham Lincoln. Everything we know about Lincoln's background, personality, and his belief in premonitions and dreams—and what William Herndon called his "fatalism"—often bears little relation to the iconic figure adulated as a particularly tall Whig railroad lawyer fond of spinning yarns. Beneath the veneer lathered on by Gilded Age Republicans and their successors, Lincoln actually retained a vast residue of folk beliefs, sharing many of the fundamental assumptions of spiritualism. Indeed, this almost personalizes why spiritualism could make such sweeping claims about the scale of its movement and the depth of its beliefs.

Belle Laurie Miller later passed on a lock of Abraham Lincoln's hair from her personal reliquary to the Chicago Historical Society. She had continued to maneuver for her husband's patent until 1869, though she had remarried three years before to a New York mechanic wounded in battle and working as a clerk for the quartermaster general. In 1873, a few years after they moved to Boston, he went missing, and what was said to be his body turned up two years later, after which Belle filed for the insurance over her brother-in-law's objections. It turned out that he had abandoned the family and gone west into the Black Hills. During the court proceedings, he showed up, and she scandalized reporters by looking him in the eye and claiming he was not her husband.[2]

Yet Belle's fate may have been preferable to that of the Fox sisters. Years later, Maggie actually demonstrated to a large New York audience how she had been using her toe joints to produce a rapping clearly audible through the entire theater. Long burdened with a guilty conscience over the deception, she said that Katie had first figured out how to do this with her fingers, and they then taught themselves to use their toes. When she found herself subsequently shunned by their old supporters, Maggie recanted her confession in November 1889, but her old friends did not come back. Feuding among the sisters continued until Maggie and Katie died a few years later, both in abject poverty.[3]

Nettie Colburn returned to New England, married, and enjoyed a full, if not entirely healthy, life. She returned to join Major George Chorpenning and his wife at the 1868 inauguration of President U. S. Grant and to talk at the new local hall for the spiritualists. There her path crossed with former Confederate general James Longstreet, who also turned up at the Chorpennings and had Nettie tell his fortune with cards. He playfully explained his clumsy handling of them by claiming that he had never played cards, and "neither have I ever tasted liquor nor tobacco in any form." The spirits, she replied in all seriousness, confirmed his story. Peace seems to have translated a vehicle for inspired insights into a respectable Victorian parlor game of mutual leg-pulling. Colburn waited to tell her story of wartime Washington until declining health forced her hand, writing *Was Abraham Lincoln a Spiritualist?* She had meticulously avoided answering the question in a simple affirmative or making any of the outrageous claims later attributed to her.[4]

Officiating at Nettie's funeral, Cora Lodencia Veronica Scott Hatch Daniels Tappan Richmond said that she rather understated rather than overstated the case in her book. She positioned herself for a key role in the final great political contribution of the movement, providing a greater coherence to a new Radical Republicanism, rooted in an insistence upon liberty and equality for all, regardless of race, gender, or class, as the prerequisite for a reformed national community. Cora herself arrived in Washington later in the war; married a former commander of a black regiment, Colonel Nathan W. Daniels; and began hosting séances. Giles B. Stebbins, Frances D. Gage, and other radical spiritualists participated. Senator Jacob M. Howard, Congressman George W. Julian, and at least a dozen other members of Congress associated with the Radicals regularly gathered at the séances, where the spirits of Theodore Parker and Abraham Lincoln advised their efforts to impeach President Andrew Johnson.[5] If Washington eclipses our understanding of Radical Republicanism in the wider society, what took place in Congress has certainly obscured what took place in the capital city.

The more radical Republicans, like many spiritualists, looked toward the idea of a complete reconstruction of the civilization. Southern Unionists, black and white, had already established a program for reconstruction of the old slave states and the former Confederacy.

However, the spiritualists also raised the prospect of carefully and coherently reconstructing the entire nation. Many embraced and used the language of "revolution" in discussing a war they hoped would become a completely transformative project. Ira B. Davis had bemoaned the movement's lack of focus: "Would the Spiritualists but bestow one-tenth part of the means and energy they now expend in the promulgation of the fact that man is immortal and that spirits communicate, upon the establishment of an order of mutual protection and brotherhood, the world would soon be attracted to them." War provided that focus and, at its peak, the 1864 national convention called upon spiritualists to organize "all progressive minds everywhere."[6]

The war's end proved to be the unmaking of spiritualism as a mass, pervasive preoccupation of people in the North, as it had of the kind of Republicanism that had seen the country through to victory. The course of events offered alternatives to the older movements. As the issues of secession and Union receded—with emancipation close behind them—partisan preferences turned less on ideology than demographics. In short, rural white Protestants tended to be Republican in the North and Democratic in the South, with urban whites inclining to the Democrats, particularly in ethnic enclaves of the large cities, while blacks tended to remain Republican almost everywhere.

So, too, the rapid expansion and proliferation of Christian denominations progressively stripped away the large numbers that had been investigating the claims of spiritualism. This tended to shift everything from Bible reading and prayer circles to séances from the parlor back into the more well-managed public space of the church. As church membership increasingly became a badge of virtue and respectability, it reframed spiritualism into something akin to a superstition. By the early twentieth century, this modern preoccupation with branding would later be called "traditional American values," an intensely politicized process deepened into a genuine dogma.

* * *

Three of the many organizations the spiritualists established after the war merit a brief description. In late 1867, Michael B. Dyott took the floor of the national convention at Cleveland. A pioneer in the movement—and in the development of streetlight technology—he had pressed for an association for nearly four years. He and his wife had formed the first of the children's lyceums, and he now suggested "that the Lyceums and Associations of Spiritualists should have some Emblem or sign by which they may recognize each other, and some Association or Society of the character of a beneficial institution, requiring an initiation fee to constitute membership, and a weekly or monthly payment of dues analogous to the Masons or Odd Fellows, entitling its members to a specific sum per week when sick or disabled from labor. By some such arrangement an income may be realized in every city sufficient to procure the necessary buildings for their meetings and all other purposes." The convention voted to pursue "a plan of organization of a society to be known and recognized by the name of 'THE UNITED ORDER OF SPIRITUAL PROGRESS,' or such other significant or appropriate name."[7] In the end, they adopted the paradoxical name of the Order of Eternal Progress (OEP).

The term had been used earlier. A quarter of a century before, John O. Wattles had spoken of principles rooted in "the unending career of eternal Progression" and a day when all people "will be elevated to the original standing, a little lower than the angels, and all tread the plains of Eternal Progression together." English novelist Edward Bulwer Lytton used the term, and religious thinkers wrote of the dutiful labor, whereby individuals might be "carried onward in the path of eternal progress." Another discerned a "holier joy, the saving and lovely spirit might have glided onward in the Eternal Progress." "A long and oftentimes a weary road it doubtless has to be, but still an eternal progress up to light and good." Others explicitly perceived "a ruin in eternal progress or one in which the soul is eternally involved."[8]

In the OEP, the spiritualists established a secret fraternal order of their own, of which there had been many predecessors, such as the Masons, Odd Fellows, and Knights of Pythias. These, however, had been "but *one-handed* instrumentalities" that benefited "but one half (and that the lest needy) of the human family." Promising its own "associative and co-operative" features as well as mutual aid, the OEP would admit "man and woman upon a perfect equality" and was "intended for every nation, kindred, people and tongue upon the face of this earth, so that wherever its members may be, they will find friends to cheer and assist, and the open hand of a brother or sister extended to greet them." Another Philadelphia member, Isaac Rehn, called the next spiritualist national convention to order in 1868 and actively discussed Dyott's report. The local group gained a feisty midwestern voice when Damon Young Kilgore moved to Philadelphia.[9]

Midwestern spiritualism drew itself together in the wake of the war. By the time Cora delivered her eulogy to Nettie, she had moved to Chicago. By the time of the great fire in October 1871, an estimated ten thousand spiritualists lived there, with an estimated thirty thousand after its rebuilding. At that point, the movement gathered periodically in the Madison Street Theatre, between State and Dearborn Streets, at which paid speakers addressed the audiences. At the time of the fire, Cora L. V. (at this point) Richmond had just published her poem "Hesperia," celebrating the spirit of Liberty having sought and found her home in America. Cora herself soon left on a six-month tour to England that grew to two years lecturing in England and Scotland, which she would periodically revisit. Finally, she married a supportive Chicago businessman and gave a speech on the shorter workday to the Knights of Labor, though she set aside her wartime memories to warn "the Knights to forbear from deeds of violence, as every deed in such a cause would retard it."[10]

The Chicago fire also consumed the *Religio-Philosophical Journal,* that powerful spiritualist publication that came out of the war. Stevens S. Jones and his son-in-law Colonel John C. Bundy launched and managed the publication through a series of reincarnations before it attained enough success to move to Chicago, where it lost everything once more. Jones managed to channel the dead publication into the chief spiritualist organ in the country. On March 15, 1877, at a peak in its success, an "insane phrenologist" barged into the *Journal*'s Dearborn Street office, where he shot and killed Jones. Bundy stepped into the breach and conjured yet another life for the periodical.[11]

Returning to New York from his role in investigating the Lincoln assassination, Henry S. Olcott enjoyed the financial security his expertise in insurance and revenue law earned. However, his continued interest in the occult took him to the Eddy farm in Vermont. As of 1864, the Eddys—who may have been cousins of some sort to the spouse of the founder of Christian Science—had been running something like the earlier spiritualist exhibition rooms. They had escape artists and various mechanisms to entertain visitors as one of them seemed to be "carried by unseen hands around the room above the heads of the skeptics."[12] In 1874 the *New York Sun* thought it worth sending Olcott to write about it.

While there Olcott met the remarkable Helena Petrovna Blavatsky. Born Helena von Hahn, she had been married off at an early age and made several attempts to escape the expectations of a woman of her class in czarist Russia, enjoying adventures from Odessa to Paris before reaching New York. Blavatsky told Olcott that she operated under the direction of invisible Mahatmas. In May 1875, Olcott received his first letter from one of the Masters and became a neophyte in the Brotherhood of Luxor, with instructions to learn from Blavatsky. By July 1875, Blavatsky announced orders "to establish a philosophico-religious Society and choose a name for it—also to choose Olcott." By November they proposed to uncover experimentally the hidden laws of nature, as the Theosophical Society, named for "the archaic Wisdom-Religion, the esoteric doctrine once known in every ancient country having claims to civilization."[13]

Theosophists did not, of course, originate the idea that the spirits would direct organizations in this world. Spiritualists regularly referred to societies of spirits such as the Zellabingen, "a vast German Association" identified in August 1855, existing somewhere in Summer Land, "located parallel with the rings of Saturn." Naturally enough, some wondered about their inspiration of societies among the living. "Was the organization known as the Order of Eternal Progress organized alone by mortals," asked one, "or did spirits out of the form favor and assist?" By the time Blavatsky set to work, though, the fickle spirits had moved on from the OEP. They hoped to subsume spiritualism into a broader paranormal current, which made sense to many, as did their plan to rigorously examine those claims. On the other hand, the idea that they should do so under the instructions or notes fluttering down from Blavatsky's ceiling tended to narrow the appeal of the project. Eventually, William E. Coleman, Andrew Jackson Davis, and many others explicitly repudiated the project.[14]

Nevertheless, the coherence of theosophy permitted it a much more measurable impact on the cultural history of the United States and the West. Olcott plunged back into his legal work to finance Blavatsky's work on what became *Isis Unveiled: The Key to Theosophy,* which appeared in 1877, and the two left for India at the end of 1878. He carried U.S. government credentials to explore trade possibilities, but by 1882 had taken up his new life as a healer. A few years later, Olcott resolved to separate theosophical goals from Blavatsky and her invisible helpmates and had personally already turned to Buddhism.[15]

\*  \*  \*

The experience of the antislavery movement and the war imbued spiritualism with a radical new kind of social empathy. "The shallower the man, so much the more isolated will everything appear to him, for on the surface all lies apart," declared William J. Young, quoting Friedrich Julius Stahl. "He will see in mankind, in the nation, aye even in the family, mere individuals, where the act of the one has no connection with that of the other. The deeper the man is, so much the more do these inward relations of unity, proceeding from the very center, force themselves on his notice."[16] Radical spiritualists, implicitly if not explicitly, embraced the assumption of Stephen Pearl Andrews's individual sovereignty, which challenged the assumptions of a secular salvation through success. Both the abolition of slavery and the survival of national identity raised the possibility that such a rethinking might inspire even broader circles of interested Americans.

In short order, though, the Republicans failed to pursue and implement a Radical agenda. The party's retreat from enforcement of the Constitution in the South had its parallel in its retreat from women's rights and the suffrage. Lincoln had raised woman suffrage in his first campaign for public office. Although the Republican old guard had been largely sympathetic, the postwar leadership pitted the issue's importance against that of black suffrage, opted for the latter, and then ultimately ignored both.

Missouri's spiritualist congressman John R. Kelso had been so confident in Radical Reconstruction that he had declined the renomination in 1866. The party's backtracking pulled him back into the race in 1868, though the far more moderate incumbent kept his place on the party's ticket. Now at St. Louis, Warren Chase sought to revive the social agenda of the Republican Party against the pragmatic managerialism of President Grant. Their new "liberal" faction began to win victories, but soon faced the same problems of the Frémont candidacy, as Democrats and conservatives eager to find a winning vehicle or to divide the Republicans came to predominate, eventually nominating the old radical and spiritualist Horace Greeley for president, though little remained of what he once had been.[17]

A more distinct dynamic took place on the East Coast. Some of the émigré veterans of Colonel Hugh Forbes's antebellum International Association reorganized under General Gustav Cluseret to promote the presidential nomination of John C. Frémont, though the weight of the spiritualist movement had helped anchor American radicals to Lincoln. By 1870 the International

Workingmen's Association (IWA)—the misnamed "First International," led by Karl Marx and others at London—began assimilating many of them. The Cosmopolitan Conference Ira B. Davis had launched a decade before joined as Section No. 9. People associated with the spiritualists such as Josiah Warren, Andrews, John Murray Spear, James S. Loveland, and William B. Greene also became more or less associated with American sections of the IWA. So did old land reformers and socialists associated with spiritualism such as William West, John H. Keyser, and Joshua K. Ingalls. Notable members of the Philadelphia section of the IWA included Eternal Progressives Rehn and Kilgore. To the south, William E. Coleman organized alongside Dick Hinton, whose wife, Isabelle, was a popular medium in her own right.[18] By late 1871, though, part of the German sections cited spiritualism, with other differences—real and imagined—to justify their essentially ethnic purge of the American and French sections. Nevertheless, the premises of spiritualism made it easier for adherents to see disembodied labor in material substance of capital.

The flamboyant Victoria Woodhull dominated the course of the American Internationalists. The National Women's Suffrage Association scheduled a convention for May 1872 at New York's Steinway Hall, where Elizabeth Cady Stanton, Susan B. Anthony, and Matilda Joslyn Gage veered away from their earlier threat to launch a third party. Woodhull led those unwilling to do so over to Apollo Hall and launched the new Equal Rights Party, with her heading the national ticket and offering the vice presidential slot to Frederick Douglass. Supporters sang "Victory for Victoria," which promised to

> raise the dead.
> Then around them let us rally
> Without fear or dread.

Among the many other spiritualists in the movement from beyond the IWA were Moses Hull and Juliet Severance. Kelso also endorsed the movement, as did Alfred H. Love, who had long urged action beyond emancipation "to remove the great burdens that rest upon the colored race on account of their color merely, and that more justice and freedom must exist before suffering can cease."[19] The campaign itself, though, passed over before its time.

The IWA never developed a large English-speaking following in Boston, partly because Ezra Hervey Heywood's organizations filled that niche. He, Love, Elihu Burritt, and others started the Universal Peace Union to prevent anything like the Civil War from breaking out again. As the IWA declined in the United States, Heywood's New England Labor Reform League expanded into an American Labor Reform League that included many spiritualists. From New York, these included Andrews, Albert Brisbane, Andrew Jackson Davis, Ira B. Davis, Horace H. Day, Edward Newberry, Albert L. Rawson, Cora A. Syme, John H. W. Toohey, and Woodhull, as well as the old land reformers Henry Beeny, Ingalls, Keyser, and Lewis Masquerier. William B. Greene, B. M. Lawrence, John Orvis, and Josiah Warren participated from New England, while midwesterners and westerners included Hull, Lois Waisbrooker, William Denton, Kersey Graves, and John B. Wolff.[20]

As they moved on from the IWA to a series of new socialist parties, spiritualists continued to turn up. In addition to many of those mentioned, Rawson joined the American section at New York. From the wilds of Minnesota, spiritualist Franz Herman Widstrand began making suggestions. The former Swedish civil servant had gone to Minnesota in 1855 and became an early Republican, eager to promote spiritualism and all "advanced" ideas. He attempted several times to take his ideas into politics after the war and encouraged the birth of a Socialistic Labor Party in the later 1870s.[21]

Across the line in Wisconsin, veteran spiritualists launched Morris Pratt's Institute at Whitewater. Juliet H. Worth Stillman, who had officered the local convention that had sent Damon Y. Kilgore to war, married Dr. Anson B. Severance and studied medicine herself. She spent her time between Whitewater and Milwaukee, where she devoted her efforts to bringing medical care to working women. Hull, the self-defrocked Seventh-Day Adventist, became her key collaborator at Whitewater. Both increasingly took up the causes of the discontented farm folk of the upper Midwest and the emergent labor movement. The two had a hand in every third-party movement that passed through the region, and, shortly before he died, Hull ran for Congress in 1904 on the Socialist Party ticket.[22]

Spiritualism had inspired much in terms of political action but proved markedly less adept at forging a coherent, practical leadership. Nevertheless, it made one notable attempt to retrace the steps that had taken a small and relatively marginalized Free Democratic Party to a mass Republican movement. In June 1880, the Greenback-Labor insurgency drew many of these veteran spiritualists to the Exposition Building in Chicago—the present site of the Art Institute. In entering the hall, socialists and other convention-goers quite literally occupied a space just vacated by the Republicans. More prominent veterans of the earlier third-party movement such as Warren B. Chase attended, but hardly a delegation present did not number spiritualists among them. The Socialistic Labor Party, formulating the most radical statement adopted by the convention, came up with a more concise version of the 1858 "land, air, and water" resolutions of the Rutland Free Convention.[23] So it was that the spirits of the dead, as communicative or uncommunicative as we imagine them, always seem to have had their say in the present.

Of course, the ongoing advocacy of any kind of reconstruction had long begun to blink out of the vision of the movers and shakers in an exclusively self-congratulatory postwar American self-perception. Gage, who addressed the 1880 convention on behalf of woman suffrage, had already become well known for her persistent defense of Indian rights. Later, her son-in-law L. Frank Baum drew upon the themes of destiny and magic for his series on the Wizard of Oz.[24] Others had long recognized the importance of smoke and mirrors and the need to tug at the curtain to upset those pulling the levers behind it.

The movement more broadly continued to provide some of lower social standing a rare voice. At the height of the war, Adeline Eliza Nichols, a former Ohio domestic who had borne a child out of wedlock at seventeen, remade herself as Lois Waisbrooker. Another perennial advocate of "labor reform" issues, she probably became most famous for her 1893 novel, *A Sex Revolution*. Like Severance, Waisbrooker studied under the Yankee-born Dr. Russell T. Trall, whose medical institute focused on reproduction and sexuality.[25] Their views led to a series of escalating run-ins with federal authorities, who had authorized a crusade against obscenity, as defined by the lowest-possible Calvinist denominator.

\* \* \*

Near the start of the twentieth century, radical spiritualism underwent yet another of its reincarnations. Firmly rooted in the author's small-town Victorian experience, Edward Bellamy's *Looking Backward, 2000–1887* offered a striking utopian novel on the irrationality of capitalism. It moved the spiritualists, including some theosophists, to form "Nationalist Clubs" to promote the abolition of capitalism, not through workers' revolution but through a general social enlightenment. Then, too, the rise of the People's Party had drawn these clubs into a kind of socialist component of the populist insurgency, the eldest among them certainly hoping for a reprise of their success in the 1860 insurgency.

The new century brought the emergence of an American capitalism pervasive and wealthy enough to allow comforting subcultures among those who had either made their peace with power or, at the very least, would never be able to threaten it directly. One could already see this taking form in the decades after the Civil War when the railroads, mining, and agriculture settled the West and finally carried the line of western settlement to the Pacific Coast. The same process that stifled the last hopes for Native peoples and established the foundations for a global expansion also established cultural niches of all sorts, including a spiritualism requiring no policing beyond the demands of the marketplace.[26] At the very edge of the continent, the spirits found a place in the sun where anarchists and socialists ran vineyards and orchards.

The discovery of gold in California had inspired something of an international gold rush among those discontented with their societies and their place within them. John A. Collins, the old abolitionist and spiritualist, after some time in Nevada, settled in California. With the war's end, the French-born spiritualist Laura Cuppy headed for the coast, where she retained her views, though feeling less impelled to take the public platform so often on their behalf. The same happened to Benjamin M. Lawrence when he went to San Bernardino and to Hannah F. M. Brown when she settled at National City, near San Diego.[27]

Laura E. A. De Force Gordon, who had been with her husband in New Orleans during the war, took a wagon train west after the war. An early leader of the suffrage movement, she was nominated to the state legislature in 1871 and entered the newspaper business. In addition to collaborating with Elizabeth Cady Stanton, Susan B. Anthony, and others on their massive multivolume *History of Woman Suffrage,* Gordon also wrote a tourist guide, *The Great Geysers of California and How to Reach Them*. She also fought her way into the legal profession at the age of forty-one, establishing a reputation as a defense attorney and winning admission to practice before the U.S. Supreme Court in February 1885.[28]

Former congressman John Kelso abandoned Missouri for Modesto, where he taught school while lecturing on spiritualism and challenging local ministers. Noting that he had "sacrificed my little fortune, my health—everything but my life" in "our late civil war," he had come to see it as "a vast conspiracy of the capitalists of Europe and America" and regretted his own involvement in the "butchery" of the war. "Had we made those people really free," he wrote of black Americans, "our act might have been regarded as the one redeeming feature of the war. Even then, however, it would have been, not the *object* of the war, but simply a non-intended *incident*." In his last years, Kelso hoped to see a "full socialistic, or rather communistic anarchism" emerge in the United States.[29]

Some came with extant credentials from the government. After the collapse of Reconstruction in Virginia, William E. Coleman took a military position in Kansas and, later, at San Francisco. There he "published hundreds of articles on psychic and occult matters" and built a private library of more than eight thousand volumes. At the time William Denton visited the La Brea Tar Pits, his sister and brother-in-law Anne and Alfred Cridge had settled in Oregon. James M. Peebles, after serving President Grant as U.S. counsel at Trebizonde and on the Congressional American Indian Peace Commission, toured the world and visited Olcott in India before settling at Los Angeles, where he died in 1922, just shy of one hundred years of age.[30]

One of the radical theosophists, Katherine Augusta Westcott Tingley, had been a mere infant when the Fox sisters had their first encounter. She had been working in a New York settlement when she first encountered the theosophists, but, by the mid-1890s, she had assumed its leadership. At Point Loma outside San Diego, she established a series of schools and institutes aimed at reviving the lost mysteries of antiquity and the teaching of yoga, capping it all with the Theosophical University.[31]

Spiritualism in the promised land of California was long destined for the tourist trade. In 1862 Sarah Pardee—likely related to the family of spiritualists—married William Wirt Winchester, even as the war profits enriched the Winchester Repeating Arms Company. After his death, Sarah moved to California and bought an unfinished farmhouse near San Jose in 1884. The spirits, it was said, warned her never to stop building or renovating it because of the violent source of her fortune, and work never stopped on it until her death in 1922.[32] Representing something like rooms of Tippie or Koons, the house became something of a mecca for paranormal tourism of all sorts.

More important, before Sarah Winchester had shuffled off the mortal coil, an entirely new industry had already set up operations in southern California. Early on, Hollywood learned how to feed the public taste for ghosts, fairies, and the paranormal in ways that nobody would ever really take seriously. As early as 1906, *Dream of a Rarebit Fiend* used pioneering special effects to portray hallucinations and visions. A new commercialized genre could bring the sensibilities of the Winchester House or Koons's spirit rooms to the nearest cinema or into one's own home. It brought commercialized entertainment without any genuine enlightenment. This has evolved into new kinds of television documentaries that burn our time and leave us not only philosophically unchallenged but artfully uninformed and not even very entertained. Nothing is left beyond the commercial exchange that acquires the unseen.

On the West Coast, spiritualism and its legacy found their fit in what Christopher Lasch later called "the culture of narcissism." That is, the willfully subjective spiritualist sense of self came to fit modern American values, once it could shed that sense of social responsibility and political outrage.[33]

Within a self-conscious celebration of the theatrical, coupled with an obsessive drive for private wealth, at least some of the spirits found their place. The explosively expansive capitalism of the coast found ways to absorb and commoditize spiritualism. To a great extent, it found that even the abandonment of old orthodoxies and the pluralistic embrace of tailor-made—even personalized—views of the cosmos can supply the same conservatizing influence of the ancient religions.

* * *

Time may have cultivated some aspects of spiritualism (or the Republican Party), while other features of the movement withered, but the record can still bring its original features into sharper focus. In the early days, all shades of spiritualism addressed the extent to which a properly Republican government could do and made it entirely more reasonable than ever to discuss racial equality, women's rights, and economic justice. Brandishing antebellum ideas of cooperation and land reform, they challenged the unspoken assumptions equating virtue and merit with wealth and power. These represented the American seeds of fundamentally radical—even working-class, socialist, and anarchist—alternatives. In the broadest sense, spiritualists envisioned a future allowing for continued moral and political growth, a process of "eternal progress." This, not the segregationist Democrats or the Gilded Age Republicans, represented the real foundation of any genuine Left in American history.

More broadly, though, spiritualists discerned patterns when they peered into what had seemed a fearsome and unknowable future. It diffused a much-needed level of confidence among a distinctly parochial population on the edges of Western civilization. It did so particularly among the oppressed and exploited, who needed that confidence. History may have domesticated aspects of spiritualism, but the idea inspired an essential conversation with the ubiquitous bump in the night. In an age pervaded by forebodings, spiritualism distilled those fears into a belief that the people could make the world over again. In the process, they demonstrated how ideas move history even when spoken with many voices, including those seemingly disembodied of power. Perhaps, too, it provided an example of how an ultimately mistaken understanding of the world can nonetheless have something of a generally positive impact.

The original impulse that inspired spiritualism survives intact. When Allen Ginsberg asked when America will look at itself through the grave, he certainly channeled the old spiritualist desire to confront the civilization with the same kind of memento mori it had so needed in the middle of the nineteenth century. We individually understand the power of that unsettling private voice in our heads that reminds us in the night of our own mortality to foster reflection and reorientation. Mid-nineteenth-century spiritualism demonstrated how that impulse, on the level of society, could do much the same, as sectional strife underscored the mortality of a nation. Developments such as global warming and robotic war pose mortality on an even larger scale, despite the 24-7 hucksterism to distract from and rationalize these things. Perhaps the greatest legacy of spiritualism should be our realization that beneath the societal din lies a quiet space to imagine other worlds and conjure better, more human possibilities.

# Notes

## Abbreviations

BoL     *Banner of Light,* a weekly journal published in Boston between 1857 and 1907

MAS     Emma Hardinge, *Modern American Spiritualism: A Twenty Years' Record of the Communion between Earth and the World of Spirits* (New York: the author, 1870)

STP     These represent the republication and most readily accessible contents of New York's *Spiritual Telegraph* (1853–55), although WorldCat indicates that a digital version of the publication has been made online and is currently available through select subscribing German libraries

WALS     Nettie Colburn Maynard, *Was Abraham Lincoln a Spiritualist? or, Curious Revelations from the Life of a Trance Medium* (Philadelphia: R. C. Hartranft, 1891)

## Prologue

1. See E. W. Capron and Henry D. Barron, *Singular Revelations,* 2nd ed. (Auburn, N.Y.: Finn and Rockwell, 1850), 10–11, 12–18; E. W. Capron, *Modern Spiritualism: The Facts and Fanaticisms* (Boston: Bela Marsh, 1855), 32–56; *MAS,* 28–36, 36–42; and A. Leah Underhill, *The Missing Link in Modern Spiritualism* (New York: Thomas R. Knox, 1885), 5–29.

2. Ernest Isaacs, "The Fox Sisters and American Spiritualism," in *The Occult in America: New Historical Perspectives,* edited by Howard Kerr and Charles L. Crow (Urbana: University of Illinois Press, 1986), 79–110; Barbara Weisberg, *Talking to the Dead: Kate and Maggie Fox and the Rise of Spiritualism* (San Francisco: Harper San Francisco, 2004);

David Chapin, *Exploring Other Worlds: Margaret Fox, Elisha Kent Kane, and the Antebellum Culture of Curiosity* (Amherst: University of Massachusetts Press, 2004); Warren Chase, "The Lybian Sibyl; or, Sojourner Truth," *BoL*, February 11, 1865, 8. In terms of occult beliefs, as Jon Butler correctly notes, the emergence of spiritualism was "almost anticlimactic" in the context of preexisting occult beliefs. Butler, *Awash in a Sea of Faith* (Cambridge, Mass.: Harvard University Press, 1990), 252–53.

3. Capron and Barron, *Singular Revelations*, 12–18; Underhill, *Missing Link*, 273–76, 455.

4. Davis's comments under "The New York Conference," in *STP*, n.s., 9 vols. (New York: Partridge and Brittan, 1853–57) vol. 4 (February, March, April 1854): 3:577, 579, 4:42; Capron, *Modern Spiritualism*, 99; *MAS*, 19–29; Sir Arthur Conan Doyle, *The History of Spiritualism*, 2 vols. (1926; reprint, New York: Arno Press, 1975), 1:83. See also E. E. Lewis's brief tract *A Report on the Mysterious Noises Heard in the House of Mr. John D. Fox: In Hydesville, Arcadia, Wayne County, Authenticated by the Statements of the Citizens of That Place and Vicinity* (Canandaigua, N.Y.: E. E. Lewis, printed on the power press of Shepard and Reed, 1848); and "Mr. I. B. Davis—His Explanation," *Christian Spiritualist* 1 (September 16, 1854): 2.

5. Robert Owen, "The Permanent Happy Existence of the Human Race; or, The Commencement of the Millennium of 1855," *Christian Spiritualist* 1 (December 30, 1854): 2; "Robert Owen and the World's Convention," *Christian Spiritualist* 1 (April 14, 1855): 2; Robert Owen, "Spiritual Manifestations in London," *Christian Spiritualist* 2 (November 17, 1855): 2–3. The best source on the movement is Carl Guarneri, *The Utopian Alternative: Fourierism in Nineteenth-Century America* (Ithaca, N.Y.: Cornell University Press, 1991); "Spiritualism and Socialism," *Christian Spiritualist* 2 (May 16, 1855), 2; "North American Phalanx," *Christian Spiritualist* 1 (September 16, 1854), 1.

6. Capron and Barron, *Singular Revelations*, 38–39, 45–47, 59–60, 60–62, 75; *MAS*, 40, 41; Capron, *Modern Spiritualism*, 57–99; Underhill, *Missing Link*, 30–73, 100–114; W. F. Bailey, *History of Eau Claire County, Wisconsin: Past and Present* (Chicago: C. F. Cooper, 1914), 265; *The Bench and Bar of Wisconsin History and Biography* (1882), 103; *Biographical Dictionary and Portrait Gallery of Eminent and Self Made Men—Wisconsin* (1877), 628; Underhill, *Missing Link*, 251.

7. Doyle, *The History of Spiritualism*, 1:81; *MAS*, 23–27. The Fourierist *Harbinger* reviewed Davis's *Principles of Nature, Her Divine Revelations, and a Voice to Mankind* (Boston, 1871 [rev. ed. of New York, 1847]), finding "no standard of comparison, with which to estimate its value, as a statement of objective truth" and hoping it would "make a profound impression on a large portion of the community." Review, *Harbinger, Devoted to Social and Political Progress* 5 (August 28, 1847): 177, 184.

8. John B. Buescher, *The Other Side of Salvation: Spiritualism and the Nineteenth-Century Religious Experience* (Boston: Skinner House Books, 2004), 102–4, 106; "Harmonial Convention," *STP*, 4:49–58; Uriah Clark, *Plain Guide to Spiritualism* (Boston: William White, 1863); Underhill, *Missing Link*, 250; *MAS*, 60, 80; Capron and Barron, *Singular Revelations*, 96; *MAS*, 60, 77–79, 87–88.

9. Robert W. Delp, "Andrew Jackson Davis: Prophet of American Spiritualism," *Journal of American History* 54 (June 1967): 46–47; Robert W. Delp, "A Spiritualist in

Connecticut: Andrew Jackson Davis, the Hartford Years, 1850–1854," *New England Quarterly* 53 (September 1980): 345–62; Mrs. J. R. Mettler from Hartford, October 17, 1853, "Psychometrical Portrait of W. Chase," *STP,* 3:79; Capron and Barron, *Singular Revelations,* 39, 41, 42–43, 73, 81–82, 96; William T. Coggeshall, *The Signs of the Times: Comprising a History of the Spirit-Rappings, in Cincinnati and Other Places, with Notes of Clairvoyant Revealments* (Cincinnati: by the author, 1851), 88; *MAS,* 60, 80, 81, 203, 264–65, 269–70, 270–71, 272, 164–66; Capron, *Modern Spiritualism,* 132–71, 204–5; Underhill, *Missing Link,* 115–21, 121–27, 250, 251, 325; "Siege of Troy by the Spirits" and "Epistle from a Friend," *STP,* 5:268–69, 269–71. See also Warren Chase, "Letter from Winsted," October 17, 1853, *STP,* 3:40–42; "The Spirits at Stamford," *STP,* 4:255; and G. W. Lascell, "Progress of Spiritualism in Vermont," *BoL,* April 25, 1863, 3.

10. Capron and Barron, *Singular Revelations,* 96; *MAS,* 60, 273–76. On Burr, see 1860, 1870, 1880, 1900 Census, Newton, Middlesex, Mass. Parents: Heman Merrick Burr, b. June 30, 1785, in Bridgewater, Plymouth, Mass., and Nelley Tucker, b. April 22, 1793, in Milton, Norfolk, Mass. "The New York Conference," *STP,* 4:145; *MAS,* 279–80, 281–83; Underhill, *Missing Link,* 235, 219–49. See also John B. Campbell, *Pittsburgh and Allegheny Spirit Rappings, Together with a General History of Spiritual Communications throughout the United States* (Allegheny, Pa.: Purviance, 1851); Sarah G. Bagley, "Signs of Progression," written from Philadelphia, *Spiritual Philosopher* 1 (July 1850): 14.

11. John Benedict Buescher put together an excellent essay, "Who Was Kersey Graves?" (November 15, 2004), http://www.spirithistory.com/kgraves.html, based on local histories and "Funeral of Kersey Graves," *Richmond (Ind.) Evening Item,* September 6, 1883, 3, col. 2; "An Early Anti-slavery Record of Wayne County," *Radical* (Richmond, Ind.), May 5, 1870, 1, which reproduces the original constitution of the Richmond Society and a list of its signatories; Thomas D. Hamm, *God's Government Begun: The Society for Universal Inquiry and Reform, 1842–1846* (Bloomington: Indiana University Press, 1995), 133; *MAS,* 60, 346–53; Coggeshall, *Signs of the Times,* 27, 29, 42, 107, 108–10; John S. Haller, "Buchanan's Feuds and Fads," in *Medical Protestants: The Eclectics in American Medicine, 1825–1939* (Carbondale: Southern Illinois University Press, 1994), 94–124. See also Haller, *A Profile in Alternative Medicine: The Eclectic Medical College of Cincinnati* (Kent, Ohio: Kent State University Press, 1999).

12. W. W. Williams, *History of the Firelands* (Cleveland, Ohio: Press of Leader Print, 1879); *Cleveland Plain Dealer,* January 1, 1851, quoted in Coggeshall, *Signs of the Times,* 237; Underhill, *Missing Link,* 221–33; "New York Conference of Spiritualists," *STP,* 3:14; *MAS,* 295–98, 298–306; John C. Spurlock, *Free Love: Marriage and Middle-Class Radicalism in America, 1825–1860* (New York: New York University Press, 1988), 143–44.

13. Capron and Barron, *Singular Revelations,* 82; *MAS,* 245–46, 293–95, 298, 309–18, 319–24, 325–26, 393–99, 402; Underhill, *Missing Link,* 223–24, 225, 227–28, 230, 232–34, 234–35, 243, 250, 253, 273–76, 453–54; "Father Woolsey and Necromancy," *STP,* 5:256–58; "Br. Jonathan Koons' Rooms" and "Letter from Jonathan Koons," *Christian Spiritualist* 1 (February 3, 1855): 2; "A Visit to J. Koons Spirit-Room" (from *Spirit Advocate*), 4; Going to the West, "A Letter from Jonathan Koons," *Christian Spiritualist* 1 (April 21, 1855): 2; "Spirit Manifestations in Ross County, Ohio" (from *Spiritual Telegraph*), *Christian Spiritualist* 2 (July 21, 1855): 4; Charles A. Dana, "Spiritual Manifestations in Ohio" (to

*New York Tribune), Christian Spiritualist* 2 (July 28, 1855): 4; response, "Mr. Dana's Last Issue on Spiritualism," *Christian Spiritualist* 2 (July 28, 1855): 2; "The Wonders at Mr. Koons' Rooms," *Christian Spiritualist* 2 (August 18, 1855): 2; "Visit to the Spiritualists of Ohio," *Christian Spiritualist* 2 (August 18, 1855): 4; Jonathan Koons in "Correspondence," *Christian Spiritualist* 1 (September 2, 1854): 3; J. H. Fowler charges over manifestations, "The Manifestations at the Rooms of Mr. Koons," *Christian Spiritualist* 2 (September 15, 1855): 2; Jonathan Koons, "Spiritualism and Reform" (from *Lockport [Pa.] Messenger*), *Christian Spiritualist* 2 (October 6, 1855): 4; "Proposition in Behalf of Brother J. Koons," *Christian Spiritualist* 1 (January 6, 1855): 2; "Jonathan Koons and Daughter Coming to New York," *Christian Spiritualist* 2 (January 5, 1856): 2; "The Koons Family in New York," *Christian Spiritualist* 2 (February 9, 1856): 2; "Memnonia Institute," *Nichols Monthly* (October 1856): 199–202; "Antioch College, Word from a Student," *Nichols Monthly* (September 1856): 180–82; "Address to the Friends, Officers, and Students of Antioch College," *Nichols Monthly* (October 1856): 233–44.

14. "The New York Conference," *STP*, 3:570–71; Finney's challenge noted in J. W. Daniels, *Spiritualism versus Christianity; or, Spiritualism Thoroughly Exposed* (New York: Miller, Orton, and Mulligan, 1856), 245–46. According to Olcott, "Three gentlemen developed as healing mediums, including Mr. Finney and other's name is Steele." "The New York Conference," *STP*, 3:570–71. By 1856 Olcott wrote at least a half-dozen articles as "Amherst" in the *Spiritual Telegraph*. See also Stephen Prothero, "From Spiritualism to Theosophy: 'Uplifting a Democratic Tradition,'" *Religion and American Culture* 3 (Summer 1993): 200. See also Mrs. J. R. Mettler, "Portrait of S. J. Finney: Psychometrically Delineated," *Journal of Progress* 2 (October 1853): 89–90; "Mr. S. J. Finney—His Labors and Lectures," *Christian Spiritualist* 2 (April 12, 1856): 2.

15. *MAS*, 241–42, 249–55, 381, 388–89, 358–59 (on El Paso), 324 (on Koons). Two individuals named Seth Paine in the 1850 Illinois Census, one in Lake and the other in Lasalle County. *MAS*, 377–79, 379–80, 383; "The Bank of Chicago," *New York Times*, February 24, 1853, 7; "Liberation of Mr. Eddy, the Chicago Banker" and untitled item *New York Times*, July 20 (p. 1), 22 (p. 6), 1853; Warren Chase, *The Life-Line of the Lone One; or, Autobiography of the World's Child* (Boston: Bela Marsh, 1857), 190; "An Ineffectual Attempt to Place a Spiritualist under Guardianship for Insanity," *Boston Herald*, August 19, 1861, 2. See also Dr. O. H. Wellington, "Insane Mediums—No. 2," *BoL*, November 21, 1863, 3; an account of a water-cure establishment, Marcia Worth, "Local History: South Orange Water Drew New Yorkers," *South Orange (N.J.) Patch*, September 7, 2011, http://southorange.patch.com/articles/local-history-south-orange-was-destination-for-water-cures; Troy Taylor, "The Haunted Museum: The Koons' Spirit Room; How Athens County, Ohio Became So Haunted!," *American Hauntings*, http://www.prairieghosts.com/koons.html; Capron and Barron, *Singular Revelations*, 50–53, 96; *MAS*, 387–90, 309–18, 319–24, 399; and "Land Reform Meeting," *Spiritual Philosopher* 1 (November 2, 1850): 110–11.

16. *MAS*, 80, 82–83, 165–78, 179–96, 197–205, 263, 381, 389 (on Iowa).

17. Underhill, *Missing Link*, 222–23, 225–27, 235–38; *MAS*, 60, 401–2, 438–43, 443–58, 477, 479–80; Capron and Barron, *Singular Revelations*, 96.

18. J. S. Loveland, *Mediumistic Experiences of John Brown, the Medium of the Rockies, with Introduction and Notes by Prof. J. S. Loveland*, 3rd ed. (San Francisco: Philosophical

Journal, 1897), iv. See also LeRoy R. Hafen, ed., *The Mountain Men and the Fur Trade of the Far West,* 10 vols. (Glendale, Calif.: A. H. Clark, 1965–72), 7:46–47, 55–56; Bill Cunningham, "The Life of John Brown—Mountain Man," *Smoke Signals* (November–December 2010), http://nafsmokesignals.tripod.com/2010/nov-dec10_issue/smoke signalpg7.htm; P. C. Ewer, "Spiritualism in California: The Eventful Nights of August 20 and 21," *Christian Spiritualist* 1 (November 18, 1854): 1.

19. Warren B. Chase, *Forty Years on the Spiritual Rostrum* (Boston: Colby and Rich, 1888), 79; John Patrick Deveney, *Paschal Beverly Randolph: A Nineteenth-Century Black American Spiritualist, Rosicrucian, and Sex Magician* (Albany: State University of New York Press, 1997), 35–37, 44–45; series on "Ghost Land" in *Boston Western Star* (1872); Emma Hardinge Britten, *Autobiography,* edited by Margaret Wilkinson (Manchester: J. Heywood, 1900); Emma Hardinge Britten, *The Place and Mission of Woman: An Inspirational Discourse, Delivered by Miss Emma Hardinge, at the Melodeon, Boston, Sunday Afternoon, Feb. 13, 1859, Phonographically Reported by James M. W. Yerrington* (Boston: H. W. Swett, 1859); *MAS;* Emma Hardinge, *Nineteenth Century Miracles* (Manchester: William Britten, 1884); Capron, *Modern Spiritualism;* Clark, *Plain Guide to Spiritualism;* Underhill, *Missing Link;* Frank Podmore, *Modern Spiritualism: A History and a Criticism,* 2 vols. (London: Methuen, 1902), republished as *Mediums of the Nineteenth Century,* 2 vols. (New Hyde Park, N.Y.: University Books, 1963); Campbell, *Pittsburgh and Allegheny Spirit Rappings.* These quasi-official histories continued through Doyle's influential book *The History of Spiritualism.*

20. Ann Taves, *Fits, Trances, and Visions: Experiencing Religion and Explaining Experience from Wesley to James* (Princeton, N.J.: Princeton University Press, 1999); Robert S. Cox, *Body and Soul: A Sympathetic History of American Spiritualism* (Charlottesville: University Press of Virginia, 2003).

21. For Swedenborgianism, see S. Maker, "Courtney on 'The Interior Sense,'" *STP,* 5:352–54. See also Isaac Rehn, "Has Spiritualism a Basis," *BoL,* December 16, 1865, 4; J. K. Ingalls, "The Abasement of Labor," "The Idea of Immortality: Its Development and Progress," and "The Divine Gift, Impartial and Immutable," *Univercoelum,* January 8, 22, March 4, 1848, 90–91, 209–12; Buescher, *Other Side of Salvation,* 193; F. W. Evans, "A Free Lecture on Shakerism," *Christian Spiritualist* 2 (February 2, 1856): 2; "Shakerism," *Christian Spiritualist* 2 (February 9, 1856): 1.

22. Capron and Barron, *Singular Revelations,* 39, 41, 42–43, 73, 81–82, 96; David Allen Johnson, *Founding the Far West: California, Oregon and Nevada, 1850–1890* (Berkeley: University of California Press, 1992), 195–97.

23. Capron and Barron, *Singular Revelations,* 40–41, 64–72, 96; Capron, *Modern Spiritualism,* 101–11, 119–27, 129–30, 131; Buescher, *Other Side of Salvation,* 77–79. James Leander Scott wrote *A Journal of a Missionary Tour through Pennsylvania, Ohio, Indiana, Illinois, Iowa, Wisconsin and Michigan* (Providence, R.I.: by the author, 1843). His career as a Seventh-Day Baptist missionary is described in Cathy Luchetti, *Under God's Spell: Frontier Evangelists, 1772–1915* (San Diego: Harcourt Brace Jovanovich, 1989). See also Herbert Wallace Schneider and George Lawton, *A Prophet and a Pilgrim, Being the Incredible History of Thomas Lake Harris and Laurence Oliphant: Their Sexual Mysticisms and Utopian Communities, Amply Documented to Confound the Skeptic* (New York: Columbia University Press, 1942).

24. Delp, "Andrew Jackson Davis," 43–56; Buescher, *Other Side of Salvation*, 20, 21–22, 25, 29–30, 30–31, 78; Catherine L. Albanese, "On the Matter of Spirit: Andrew Jackson Davis and the Marriage of God and Nature," *Journal of the American Academy of Religion* 60 (Spring 1992): 9. For background, see Craig James Hazen, *The Village Enlightenment in America: Popular Religion and Science in the Nineteenth Century* (Urbana: University of Illinois Press, 2000); and Taves, *Fits, Trances, and Visions*. Andrew Jackson Davis, *The Great Harmonia, Being a Philosophical Revelation of the Natural, Spiritual, and Celestial Universe*, 5 vols. (Boston and New York: B. B. Mussey / J. S. Redfield, 1850–61), though his copious material includes *The Principles of Nature*; Delp, "Andrew Jackson Davis," 46. Catherine L. Albanese described this as a version of "nature religion" in "On the Matter of Spirit," 1–17. See also R. Laurence Moore, "Spiritualism and Science: Reflections on the First Decade of the Spirit Rappings," *American Quarterly* 24 (October 1972): 478.

25. Coggeshall, *Signs of the Times*, 7, 15; "Clairvoyance—Davisism," *Evangelical Magazine and Gospel Advocate* 19 (May 12, 1848): 150. On John Patterson Cornell, see William Cornell, *History of Seneca County, Ohio* (Chicago: Warner, Beers, 1886), 291, 308, 310; Spurlock, *Free Love*, 89–90, 107–8, an elaboration of his "The Free Love Network in America, 1850 to 1860," *Journal of Social History* 21 (Summer 1988): 765–79; Lizzie Carley on "Capital and Labor, and the Inconsistency and Evils Resulting Therefrom," David H. Shaffer, "Spiritualism in Cincinnati," *BoL*, January 14, 1865, 3; "Physicians and Surgeons: Practicing without License, Spiritualism," *Michigan Law Review* 16 (November 1917): 53–54; Cora L. V. Hatch, "Does Science Conflict with the Bible? Subject Chosen by a Committee, . . . before the Lyceum Society of Spiritualists, in Lyceum Hall, Boston, Sunday, July 6, 1863," *BoL*, September 26, 1863, 3–4; Alexander Wilder, *New Platonism and Alchemy: A Sketch of the Doctrines and Principal Teachers of the Eclectic or Alexandrian School; Also an Outline of the Interior Doctrines of the Alchemists of the Middle Ages* (Albany, N.Y.: Weed, Parsons, 1869); very favorable review of "Equitable Commerce," *Christian Spiritualist* 2 (August 25, 1855): 2.

26. Capron and Barron, *Singular Revelations*, 96; *MAS*, 60, 354–60, 361, 371–75, 376–77, 376; "A Friendly Letter," "Discussion in St. Louis," "Rev. N. L. Rice and the Spiritualists," and "R. P. Ambler in St. Louis," *STP*, 2:502, 4:187, 479–82, 7:226–27. On Fishback, see Buescher, *Other Side of Salvation*, 121; and Thomas Gales Forster, "Healing Mediums," *Christian Spiritualist* 2 (December 8, 1855): 2.

27. Dr. S. W. Corbin, "An M.D. on Human Magnetism," *STP*, 5:357–59. See also Annetta Gertrude Dresser, *The Philosophy of P. P. Quimby, with Selections from His Manuscripts and a Sketch of his Life* (Boston: George H. Ellis, 1895); Horatio W. Dresser, ed., *The Quimby Manuscripts, Showing the Discovery of Spiritual Healing and the Origin of Christian Science* (New York: Thomas Y. Crowell, 1921); and James John Garth Wilkinson, *The Human Body and Its Connection with Man, Illustrated by the Principal Organs* (Philadelphia: Lippincott, Grambo, 1851).

28. "Sojourner Truth, the Libian Sybil," *BoL*, May 2, 1863, 4; *Narrative of Sojourner Truth, a Northern Slave* (1850; reprint, Mineola, N.Y.: Dover, 1997); Paul E. Johnson and Sean Wilentz, *The Kingdom of Matthias: A Story of Sex and Salvation in 19th-Century America* (New York: Oxford University Press, 1994); William Leete Stone, *Matthias and His Impostures; or, The Progress of Fanaticism* (New York, 1835); Margaret Washington,

*Sojourner Truth's America* (Urbana: University of Illinois Press, 2009); for a very critical view of this, see Gilbert Vale, *Fanaticism: Its Source and Influence Illustrated by the Simple Narrative of Isabella, in the Case of Matthias, Mr. and Mrs. B. Folger, Mr. Pierson, Mr. Mills, Catherine, Isabella, &c. &c.* (New York, 1835); Carleton Mabee with Susan Mabee Newhouse, *Sojourner Truth: Slave, Prophet, Legend* (New York: New York University Press, 1993); Nell Irvin Painter, *Sojourner Truth: A Life, a Symbol* (New York: W. W. Norton, 1996); Erlene Stetson and Linda David, *Glorying in Tribulation: The Lifework of Sojourner Truth* (East Lansing: Michigan State University Press, 1994); Christopher Clark, *The Communitarian Moment: The Radical Challenge of the Northampton Association* (Ithaca, N.Y.: Cornell University Press, 1995); Christopher Clark and Kerry W. Buckley, eds., *Letters from an American Utopia: The Stetson Family and the Northampton Association, 1843–1847* (Amherst: University of Massachusetts Press, 2004).

29. John Lardas Modern, *Secularism in Antebellum America* (Chicago: University of Chicago Press, 2011); Robert Green Ingersoll, "A Tribune to Horace Seaver, at Paine Hall, Boston, August 25, 1889," in *The Works of Robert G. Ingersoll*, 12 vols. (New York: Dresden, 1907–11), 12:459–66, http://www.infidels.org/library/historical/robert_ingersoll/tribute-seaver.html. See also *Occasional Thoughts of Horace Seaver: From Fifty Years of Free Thinking. Selected from the "Boston Investigator"* (Boston: J. P. Mendum, 1888). Davis from "Harmonial Convention," *STP*, 4:57; item from *Boston Investigator* in *STP*, 2:51. See also A. Peabody, "A Missourian on Spiritualism," *Farmers' Cabinet*, September 28, 1865, 1; untitled item, *STP*, 8:275–76; Davis from "The New York Conference," *STP*, 3:575; and Seaver "an old warrior," "The *Boston Investigator*, Again," *Spiritual Eclectic* 1 (May 26, 1860): 52.

30. Peter Lamont, "Spiritualism and a Mid-Victorian Crisis of Evidence," *Historical Journal* 47 (December 2004): 897–920. Lamont pointed out that where conjurers and entertainers could see through the "manifestations," the test of science frequently tended to validate the experience by not offering an explanation.

31. Capron and Barron, *Singular Revelations*, 96; Underhill, *Missing Link*, 165–78, 179–96, 197–205; Doyle, *The History of Spiritualism*, 1:85; *MAS*, 152, 153–55, 155, 255–57, 286–92; John B. Buescher, *The Remarkable Life of John Murray Spear: Agitator for the Spirit Land* (Notre Dame, Ind.: University of Notre Dame Press, 2006), 200. See Heman Burr, *Knocks for the Knockings* (New York: by the author, 1850), refuted in *MAS*, 93, and outright assailed in Underhill, *Missing Link*, 221–23, 224–25, 228, 235, 238–39, 258, 382. On Burr, see *New York Daily Tribune*, November 2, 1855; Joel Tiffany, *Spiritualism Explained* (New York: Graham and Ellinwood, 1856). Partridge and Brittan published his *Tiffany's Monthly: Devoted to the Investigation of Spiritual Science* from 1856 to 1859. Also present was "Captain" James M. Turner, a *Tribune* reporter associated with the land-reform agitators, the National Reform Association through the citywide Industrial Congress.

32. "The New York Conference," *STP*, 4:198; "The Progressive Union: Third Report of the Central Bureau," *Nichols Monthly* (August–September 1855): 193–97.

33. Underhill, *Missing Link*, 475.

34. R. Laurence Moore, "The Spiritualist Medium: A Study of Female Professionalism in Victorian America," *American Quarterly* 27 (May 1975): 200–221. Though based on

contemporary spiritualism, see Carol Lois Haywood, "The Authority and Empowerment of Women among Spiritualist Groups," *Journal for the Scientific Study of Religion* 22 (June 1983): 157–66. See also the observations on contemporary mediumship in Michael P. Richard and Albert Adato, "The Medium and Her Message: A Study of Spiritualism at Lily Dale, New York," *Review of Religious Research* 22 (December 1980): 186–97. See Judith R. Walkowitz, "Science and the Séance: Transgressions of Gender and Genre in Late Victorian London," *Representations* 22 (Spring 1988): 3–29. For a wider context, see Jill Galvan, *The Sympathetic Medium: Feminine Channeling, the Occult, and Communication Technologies, 1859–1919* (Ithaca, N.Y.: Cornell University Press, 2010).

35. *MAS*, 157–64, 246–47, 304–6, 326–27, 327–28, 329–33, 447.

36. Untitled, *STP*, 3:386; "New York Conference," *STP*, 3:571; Peter Lamont, *The First Psychic: The Extraordinary Mystery of a Notorious Victorian Wizard* (London: Abacus, 2005, London: Little, Brown, 2005); Daniel Dunglas Home, *Incidents in My Life* (New York, 1864), with D. D. Home, "Incidents of My Life," *BoL*, April 4, 1863, 8; *MAS*, 1365, 309–18, 319–24, 325–26; Underhill, *Missing Link*, 273–76; Coggeshall, *Signs of the Times*, 92, 99; Dale Cockrell, ed., *Excelsior: Journals of the Hutchinson Family Singers, 1842–1846* (Hillsdale, N.Y.: Pendragon Press, 1989), 204–6; George F. Root, "'Tramp, Tramp, Tramp,'" *BoL*, September 23, 1865, 3; George F. Root, "Rosedale," in J. B. Packard and J. S. Loveland, *The Spirit Minstrel: A Collection of Hymns and Music, for the Use of Spiritualists, in Their Circles and Public Meetings*, 2nd ed. (Boston: Bela Marsh, 1856); Jesse Hutchinson Jr., "The Hutchinson Family," *Spiritual Philosopher* 1 (October 19, 1850): 81–82; E. W. Hazard and Jesse Hutchinson letters, "Case of Justin Hutchinson," *Spiritual Philosopher* 1 (November 9, 1850): 113–14.

37. "Different Kinds of Manifestations" (from the *Sacred Circle*), *Christian Spiritualist* 2 (October 20, 1855): 4; *MAS*, 361.

38. "Spiritual Convention" (from *Journal*) and "Affairs about Home," *Boston Herald*, August 7, 1852, 2, 4; "Why Should Religion and Science Quarrel? Lectures by Rev. Adin Ballou, before the Lyceum Society of Spiritualists, in Lyceum Hall, Boston, Sunday, March 15, 1863" and "Evening Discourse: Stumbling Blocks in the Way of Human Progress," *BoL*, March 28, 1863, 8; "The Supreme Authority of Divine Principles: A Lecture by Rev. Adin Ballou, before the Lyceum Society of Spiritualists, in Lyceum Hall, Boston, Sunday, Sept. 20, 1863," *BoL*, October 3, 1863, 8; "Marriage at Hopedale," *Christian Spiritualist* 1 (October 14, 1854): 2.

39. Buescher, *Remarkable Life of John Murray Spear*, 177–78, 190–91, 205–6; Capron, *Modern Spiritualism*, 221–24; *MAS*, 166–68, 228–29, 229–39; N. S. Emerson, *The History of Dungeon Rock* (Boston: Adams, 1856); "Benjamin Franklin a Spiritualist," *Christian Spiritualist* 2 (January 26, 1856): 2.

40. Clark in "National Spiritualist Convention, Oswego, N.Y., Aug. 13 to 18, 1861," *BoL*, September 7, 1861, 3; Chase annually delivered 184 lectures (1860), 170 (1861), 136 (1862), 170 (1863), 158 (1864), 121 (1865), and 147 (1866), according to his *Forty Years*, 81, 84, 87, 91, 95, 99, 101. On Watertown, see *MAS*, 381.

41. For estimates of the movement's size, see Mr. & Mrs. U[riah and Eliza] Clark, comps., *The Spiritualist Register, with a Counting House & Speaker's Almanac: Containing Facts and Statistics of Spiritualism, for 1857* (Auburn, N.Y.: U. Clark, 1857); and Mr. & Mrs.

U[riah and Eliza] Clark, comps., *The Fourth Annual Spiritual Register, with a Calendar and Speakers' Almanac, for 1860: Facts, Philosophy, Statistics of Spiritualism* (Auburn, N.Y.: U. Clark, 1860). See also Werner Sollors, "Dr. Benjamin Franklin's Celestial Telegraph; or, Indian Blessings to Gas-Lit American Drawing Rooms," *American Quarterly* 35 (Winter 1983): 469. Estimate of 996,500 spiritualists in America by "an editor and itinerant who had surveyed and gone over the ground." These included 300,000 in New York and 120,000 each in Ohio and Indiana. "The Religion of Revolution: Every Man His Own Evangelist," *New York Herald,* July 5, 1858, 5.

42. William J. Young, New York, April 2, "Spiritual Pictures in a Washtub," *BoL,* April 18, 1863, 8. See also "Cautions against 'Defective Mediums,'" *Christian Spiritualist* 2 (September 8, 1855): 3.

43. Another eighty during the Civil War and forty-two after the war.

44. *MAS,* 350–51. See also Coggeshall, *Signs of the Times.*

45. Chase, *Forty Years,* 81, 87, 91, 95, 99, 101. From the start of 1860 through 1865, he gave a total of 1,086 talks on spiritualism. (Ordinarily, these annual totals would have been higher, but, during these years, he also gave frequent lectures on the politics of the war.)

46. "The Conference at the Office," *STP,* 6:373.

47. "The Convention System," *BoL,* September 3, 1859, 4; "From J. E. Snodgrass," *Liberator,* October 22, 1852, 171; *MAS,* 364, 284–85.

48. Capron, *Modern Spiritualism,* 111–17; *MAS,* 207, 436–37; Buescher, *Other Side of Salvation,* 79–80. On Mountain Cove, see Robert S. Fogarty, *Dictionary of American Communal and Utopian History* (Westport, Conn.: Greenwood Press, 1980, 197), which mistakenly describes the location of the community as unknown, and John Comstock, ed., *The West Virginia Heritage Encyclopedia,* 25 vols. (Richwood, W.Va.: Jim Comstock, 1976), 16:3387, and in the 1974 supplemental volume 16:50–51. See also Calvin Blanchard, *The Life of Thomas Paine* (New York: Calvin Blanchard, 1860), 89–90; I. S. H., "Movements at Mountain Cove: Results of Fanaticism," *Journal of Progress* 1 (June 11, 1853): 107.

49. Elizabeth Sweet, *The Future Life: As Described and Portrayed by Spirits, through Elizabeth Sweet* (Boston and New York: W. White, 1870), 3; Chase, *Forty Years,* 81; *MAS,* 414, 435–36, 416–18; "Departure of Mr. Harris for the South," *STP,* 3:471–72; W. A. Simpson, Stockton Valley, Louden, Tenn., "East Tennessee," *BoL,* October 15, 1864, 2; Richmond, Va., Palladium on spiritualism and progress, "Controversies on Spiritualism," *Christian Spiritualist* 2 (May 3, 1856): 2; Harris in Houston and Galveston area, "Rev. Thomas L. Harris, in Texas," *Christian Spiritualist* 2 (April 26, 1856): 2.

50. For Hootee, see "Washington and the South," *STP,* 5:136; John R. Kelso, "Autobiography of John Russell Kelso, 1882, Ukiah, Calif.," in "Complete Works in Manuscript, Written for His Beloved Son John R. Kelso, Junior, and His Posterity, 1873–1882," Huntington Library, Huntington, Calif., 670, 672, 673, 674, 675–76, 677, 687, 696, 697, 702–4, 709; John R. Kelso, *Government Analyzed,* edited by Etta Dunbar Kelso (Longmont, Colo.: by the author, 1892), 4; Wiley Britton, *The Civil War on the Border,* 2 vols. (New York: G. P. Putnam's Sons, 1899, 2:204, 205, 207; George E. MacDonald, *Fifty Years of Freethought: Being the Story of the Truth Seeker, with the Natural History of Its Third Editor,* 2 vols. (New York: Truth Seeker, 1929, 1931), 1:539; William Neville Collier,

*Ozark and Vicinity in the Nineteenth Century* (Long Beach, Calif.: by the author, 1946), 9–10; E. L. Rudolph, "Another Discordant Harmony," *Arkansas Historical Quarterly* 3 (Autumn 1944): 211–16; Kim Allen Scott and Robert Myers, "The Extinct 'Grass Eaters' of Benton County: A Reconstructed History of the Harmonial Vegetarian Society," *Arkansas Historical Quarterly* 50 (Summer 1991): 140–57. Appointed from Missouri, there were references to spiritualist activities not only in Brookville, Missouri, but also in Wilmington, North Carolina; Memphis, Tennessee; and Mobile, Alabama. *MAS*, 60, 205, 357, 375–76, 433, 407–16.

51. Buescher, *Other Side of Salvation*, 195–97, 197–98. Also Mrs. Ostrander, now Mrs. Bliss, John P. Harvey, F. F. Lewis, and George Redman toured there. *MAS*, 60, 407–16, 205, 430–33, 437; "Remarkable Developments: By Poetic Spirits," *STP*, 6:120; "Interesting from Texas," *STP*, 7:103–15; J. B. Ferguson, "Spiritualism—Its Antiquity," *Christian Spiritualist* 1 (February 3, 1855): 4; J. B. Ferguson, "God Will Teach His Creatures," *Christian Spiritualist* 1 (May 5, 1855): 1; "Brother J. B. Ferguson in the Tennessee Legislature" *Christian Spiritualist* 2 (November 10, 1855): 2; J. B. Ferguson, "Immortality; or, We Live in God," *Christian Spiritualist* 2 (January 19, 1856): 2; and "The Late 'Miracle' at Rev. J. B. Ferguson's," *Christian Spiritualist* 2 (February 23, 1856): 2.

52. "Spiritual Manifestation," *Southern Literary Messenger: Devoted to Every Department of Literature* 19 (July 1853): 385, 386. See also Sollors, "Franklin's Celestial Telegraph," 477. For curious poltergeist incidents, see "Mysteries in Charleston 35 Years Ago," *STP*, 8:296–98.

53. "Miracles in New Orleans," *STP*, 8:254, 255, 256–57. On Catholic hostility, see Rev. Dr. Patrick Eugene Moriarty, "Catholic View of Spiritualism," *STP*, 5:288–89, but see also Sheri Abel, *Charles Testut's "Le Vieux Salomon": Race, Religion, Socialism, and Freemasonry* (Lanham, Md.: Lexington Books, 2009).

54. *MAS*, 205, 419–30; Joseph Barthet, "Miracles in New Orleans," *STP*, 8:254–57; "Miracles in New Orleans," *STP*, 9:1–12; "Letter from New Orleans," *BoL*, October 22, 1859, 7. For Coonley's 1860 visit to the city and his encounter with the healing medium Valmore, "a colored man, living in the French part," see "Mediums in New Orleans," *BoL*, April 30, 1864, 5; and, on Colonels Wright and Fouke, "Colonel Fouke," *BoL*, September 3, 1864, 6; http://listsearches.rootsweb.com/th/read/LAORLEAN/2000-06/0960846604.

55. Orestes Augustus Brownson, *The Spirit-Rapper: An Autobiography* (Boston: Little, Brown / London: Charles Dolman, 1854), 46, 68.

56. R. H. Brown, "The Signs of the Times," *STP*, 8:261. 260–64; John Weiss, ed., *The Life and Correspondence of Theodore Parker* (London: Longman, Green, 1863), 1:428, quoted in R. Moore, "Spiritualism and Science," 475. These represent the republication and most readily accessible contents of New York's *Spiritual Telegraph* (1853–55), although WorldCat indicates a digital version of the publication has been made online and is currently available through select subscribing German libraries. "Theodore Parker," *Christian Spiritualist* 1 (October 7, 1854): 3.

## Chapter 1. Free Democrats to the Republicans

1. *The History of Fond DuLac County, Wisconsin* (Chicago: Western Historical, 1880), 886; Frank A. Flower, *History of the Republican Party, Embracing Its Origin, Growth and Mission* (Springfield, Ill.: Union, 1884), 148–68; John R. Commons, "Horace Greeley and

the Working Class Origins of the Republican Party," used as an introduction to vols. 7–8 of *A Documentary History of American Industrial Society,* edited by J. R. Commons et al., 10 vols., 2nd ed. (New York: Russell and Russell, 1958), 7:36–37. See also the Wisconsin Phalanx reference materials posted on the Ripon College website, https://web.archive .org/web/20120327223137/http://www.ripon.edu/library/archives/exhibits/phalanx .htm. Clashes around Ripon and members of Ceresco Union making the press: *Nichols Monthly* (August–September 1855): 145–46.

2. See also Allan Nevins, *Ordeal of the Union,* 2 vols. (New York: Charles Scribner's Sons, 1947), 2:322–23; *New York Daily Tribune,* June 17, 1856, 4. The essential titles on antislavery politics remain Richard H. Sewall's *Ballots for Freedom: Antislavery Politics in the United States, 1837–1860* (Oxford: Oxford University Press, 1976); Eric Foner's *Free Soil, Free Labor, Free Men: The Ideology of the Republican Party before the Civil War* (Oxford: Oxford University Press, 1970); William E. Gienapp, *The Origins of the Republican Party, 1852–1856* (New York: Oxford University Press, 1987); Hendrik Booraem V, *The Formation of the Republican Party in New York: Politics and Conscience in the Antebellum North* (New York: Oxford University Press, 1983); Roy F. Nichols, *The Disruption of American Democracy,* 2nd ed. (New York: Collier Books, 1962); Michael Holt, *The Political Crisis of the 1850s,* 2nd ed. (New York: W. W. Norton, 1983); and Joel H. Silbey, *The Partisan Imperative: The Dynamics of American Politics before the Civil War* (New York: Oxford University Press, 1985).

3. "Meetings," *National Era,* August 5, 1852, 176; "The Free Democratic Party," *Spirit of the Age* 1 (September 29, 1849): 203–4; Kaulback present at Boston's Spiritual Conference, *BoL,* May 18, 1861, 8.

4. "Grand Mass Meeting of the Free Soilers in Faneuil Hall," *Boston Herald,* October 14, 1852, 2; "Meetings," *National Era,* August 5, 1852, 176; "The Hale Dinner," "Free Democratic Convention," and "Our Fall Elections," *Boston Herald,* May 6 (p. 2), September 15 (p. 4), 21 (p. 2), 1853.

5. "Meeting in Philadelphia," *National Era,* July 15, 1852, 114; "Free Soil State Convention at Pittsburgh," *New York Tribune,* August 11, 1852, 5; "Pennsylvania," *National Era,* October 14, 1852, 165. See also Coggeshall, *Signs of the Times* (see prologue, n. 9). Freda Postle Koch's *Colonel Coggeshall: The Man Who Saved Lincoln* (Columbus, Ohio: Poko Press, 1985), a genealogical account erroneously claiming him as an orthodox Christian. First annual convocation of supreme circle, "Brotherhood of the Union," *Spiritual Philosopher* 1 (October 19, 1850): 92; "Brotherhood of the Union" (from *Family Journal*), *Spiritual Philosopher* 1 (December 7, 1850): 152–53.

6. [John Bell Bouton], *The Life and Choice Writings of George Lippard* (New York: H. H. Randall, 1855), 7–10, 70, 72, 83, 121; "Editorial Department," in *White Banner* 1 (1851): 150; Frederick S. Frank includes a good recent bibliography in "George Lippard," in *Gothic Writers: A Critical and Bibliographical Guide,* edited by Douglass H. Thomson, Jack G. Voller, and Frederick S. Frank (Westport, Conn.: Greenwood Press, 2002), 70–72; George Lippard, "A Great Man" and "The Other World," *BoL,* July 6 (p. 4), November 2 (p. 2), 1861.

7. *Cleveland Daily True Democrat,* June 5, 1849, 2; "Free Democracy of Vt.," *Cleveland Daily True Democrat,* June 11, 1849, 2; *New Lisbon Aurora,* July 26 (or 28), 1849; "Peace Convention at Painesville," *Cleveland Daily True Democrat,* June 11, 1849, 3; "Mr. Brisbane

on European Socialism," *Salem Anti-Slavery Bugle*, June 29, 1849, 4; "The Convention—Legislation for Classes—Banking," *Lancaster Ohio Eagle*, June 6, 1850, 3; Capron and Barron, *Singular Revelations*, 96 (see prologue, n. 1); and Buescher, *Other Side of Salvation*, 150.

8. John W. Edmonds to Abraham Lincoln, June 1, 1863.

9. Chase, *Life-Line of the Lone One* (see prologue, n. 15) and *Forty Years*, 85–86 (see prologue, n. 18); records of the Wisconsin Phalanx in Ripon College Archives; Ceresco, "A National History Day Resource," http://www.uwosh.edu/archives/NHD/ceresco/; Chase, *Forty Years*, 85–86.

10. "The Industrial Congress," *Univercoelum*, May 12, 1849, 377. In general, see Mark A. Lause, *Young America: Land, Labor, and the Republican Community* (Urbana: University of Illinois Press, 2005), 98, 104–5, 113, 107–8 (on 1851), but see also "Cooperative Brotherhood," *Spirit of the Age*, 2:56–57; "Appeal to Reformers from the Fifth Industrial Congress" with "Constitution of the Industrial Reform Association of ——," *Spiritual Philosopher* 1 (October 26, 1850): 102.

11. "The National Industrial Congress," *Baltimore Sun*, May 26, 1852, 4; the memorial of the National Industrial Congress filed June 8, SEN32A-H20, Box 141, f.6/7–8/52; Michael Frank, "Events in the Life of Charles Dukee," *Collections of the State Historical Society of Wisconsin* 6 (1872): 123–35.

12. "Free Soil National Convention," *Pittsburgh Evening Chronicle*, August 10, 1852, 2; "Free Soil National Convention," with untitled update giving officers of the convention, *Pittsburgh Evening Chronicle*, August 11, 1852, 2; "Free Soil National Convention," *Pittsburgh Evening Chronicle*, August 12, 1852, 2; John R. Irelan, *The Republic; or, A History of the United States of America*, 18 vols. (Chicago: Fairbank and Palmer, 1888), 13:330–31. James H. Collins, S. M. Booth, John Sheddon, George F. Gordon, Samuel Lewis, Gerrit Smith, James H. Paine, J. E. Snodgrass, as well as J. B. Alley and Frederick Douglass.

13. Chase, *Life-Line of the Lone One*, 170, 185; *MAS*, 381; "Facts in Wisconsin," *STP*, 2:57.

14. Chase, *Life-Line of the Lone One*, 191, 194–97, 197–201; Chase, *Forty Years*, 70–71, 179; Henry D. Barron, "The Past, Present, Future," *Spiritual Philosopher* 1 (November 16, 1850): 121–22.

15. Allan Nevins and Milton H. Thomas, eds., *The Diary of George Templeton Strong* (New York: Macmillan, 1952), 2:244–45, quoted in R. Moore, "Spiritualism and Science," 475 (see prologue, n. 24).

16. Capron and Barron, *Singular Revelations*, 96; *MAS*, 509–10; Underhill, *Missing Link*, 128–42, 431–33 (see prologue, n. 1); Coy F. Cross II, *Go West, Young Man! Horace Greeley's Vision for America* (Albuquerque: University of New Mexico Press, 1995); Suzanne Schulze, *Horace Greeley: A Bio-Bibliography* (Westport, Conn.: Greenwood Press, 1992); Robert C. Williams, *Horace Greeley: Champion of American Freedom* (New York: New York University Press, 2006).

17. Spiritualists attributed significance to the fact that Emma Hardinge could still publicly reduce Rynders to tears. R. Moore, "Spiritualist Medium," 208–9 (see prologue, n. 34); "Spiritualists Convention," *New York Herald*, August 8, 1852, 4; *MAS*, 148. New York had meetings on Twenty-Sixth Street from 1852 to 1854, at Irving Hall on Fif-

teenth Street from 1854 to 1855, No. 1 Ludlow Street until 1858, and then back to West Thirty-Seventh Street. Underhill, *Missing Link*, 252. Spiritualists held larger meetings across the city, though sometimes at Taylor's Hotel, 555 Broadway, a site shared with the radicals, including the "free love" that created such a scandal in the mid-1850s.

18. On the New York Circle, see Capron, *Modern Spiritualism*, 172–97; Doyle, *The History of Spiritualism*, 1:86 (see prologue, n. 4); *MAS*, 128–34, 266–67, 509–10; Buescher, *Other Side of Salvation*, 41, 71, 142; John Worth Edmonds, *Spiritualism* (New York: Partridge and Brittan, 1853). Brittan had published the *Shekinah, a Quarterly Review* at Bridgeport before launching the *Spiritual Telegraph* and, after its demise, attempted the short-lived the *Spiritual Eclectic* at Boston in 1860.

19. "The Spiritualists," *New York Times*, November 25, 1856, 1, mistakenly saying "some four years ago" rather than three. *The New Testament of Our Lord and Saviour Jesus Christ, as Revised and Corrected by the Spirits* (New York: by the proprietors, 1861); Alexander Smyth, *The Occult Life of Jesus of Nazareth*, rev. ed. (Chicago: Progressive Thinker, 1905).

20. "Meeting of Independent Democrats at the Chinese Building," *New York Tribune*, August 2, 1852, 5; "Free Democratic Convention at Syracuse," *New York Herald*, September 30, 1852, 1; "The Free Democracy," *New York Times*, October 1, 1852, 8. On Watertown, see *MAS*, 381. "Free Democratic State Convention," *New York Herald*, February 24, 1853, 1; "The Free Democratic State Convention," *New York Herald*, February 25, 1853, 1; "Gerrit Smith's Platform," *Jubilee Harbinger for 1854* (Philadelphia: Jubilee Association, [1854]),144–45; "The Origins of the Republican Party," *Historical Magazine* 20 (December 1873): 330, 331 (for resolutions), 333; "The Free Democratic League," *New York Times*, October 26, 1853, 5; Harriet Beecher Stowe, "The Dead" (from the *Independent*), *Christian Spiritualist* 2 (March 15, 1856): 3.

21. Jean L. Silver-Isenstadt, *Shameless: The Visionary Life of Mary Gove Nichols* (Baltimore: Johns Hopkins University Press, 2002); T. B. Aldrich, "Good Night," *BoL*, Feb. 28, 1863, 8. "The Spirit Had Departed," *BoL*, November 7, 1863, 8; Marie Howland, *Papa's Own Girl: A Novel* (New York: Bost, 1874) and her *The Familistere*, 3rd ed. (Boston: Christopher, [1918]), with a new edition, introduced by Robert S. Fogarty (1975); Madeleine B. Stern, *The Pantarch: A Biography of Stephen Pearl Andrews* (Austin: University of Texas Press, 1968); "H. W. Ballard at Thompson's Station, Long Island" and "All Sorts of Paragraphs," *BoL*, July 27, 1861, 5; Spurlock, *Free Love*, 114–17, 123–25, 127–29, 131–39 (see prologue, n. 12); Roger Wunderlich, *Low Living and High Thinking at Modern Times, New York* (Syracuse, N.Y.: Syracuse University Press, 1992); Blanchard, *Life of Thomas Paine*, 89–90 (see prologue, n. 48); MacDonald, *Fifty Years of Freethought*, 1:207–8 (see prologue, n. 50); Walt Whitman, *Notebooks and Unpublished Prose Manuscripts* (New York: New York University Press, 1984), 250; Underhill letters as "The Unitary Household: Letter from the Proprietor in Reply to the Times" and "The Unitary Household: Letter from Mr. Underhill in Reply to the Article in the Times" as well as "Edward F. Underhill Dead," *New York Times*, June 25, 1858 (p. 2), September 26, 1860 (p. 2), and June 19, 1898 (p. 7); "Mary Lyndon," *Nichols Monthly* (August–September 1855): 198–200; Hesperus, "'Leaves of Grass,'" *Christian Spiritualist* 2 (November 3, 1855): 1.

22. Capron and Barron, *Singular Revelations*, 96; Underhill, *Missing Link*, 149, 287; *MAS* (Lamartine Hall), 149, 509; and, on the public séances, see Underhill, *Missing Link*, 261–63. For the citywide numbers, see *MAS*, 151–52; "Conference of Dec. 29," *STP*, 3:428–29. See Sollors, "Franklin's Celestial Telegraph," 469 (see prologue, n. 41).

23. "New York Conference," *STP*, 3:51; "New York Conference of Spiritualists," *STP*, 3:14–24, 21; "New York Conference," *STP*, 3:55; "A. J. Davis' Lectures in New York," *STP*, 5:294–300; "The New York Conference," *STP*, 4:72–73; "The New York Conference," *STP*, 4:214–17; Delp, "Andrew Jackson Davis," 48 (see prologue, n. 9); *MAS*, 61–62; "New York Conference," *STP*, 5:34; Underhill, *Missing Link*, 258; *MAS*, 186. On Ingalls, see *MAS*, 62, 63–65, 66, 73, 74–75, 85, 93–94, 103. On the NRA, see Lause, *Young America*.

24. "The Spiritualists," *New York Times*, November 25, 1856, 1; Buescher, *Other Side of Salvation*, 169; Chase, *Forty Years*, 79–80.

25. Chase, *Forty Years*, 70; First Congressional District, *Free Democratic Extra: For President, John P. Hale* (n.p.: Free Democratic Press, [1852]); "Departure of Gov. Tallmadge," *STP*, 5:202–3; Tallmadge to Partridge and Brittan, October 11, 1854. See also "Interesting from Wisconsin," *STP*, 6:446–47. Chase, letter on "Facts in Wisconsin," *STP*, 2:57–59; H. O. B. letter, March 6, 1854, "The Spirits of Fond du Lac," *STP*, 4:533–34; *MAS*, 284; "Washington and the South," *STP*, 5:109–111; "Washington and the South," *STP*, 5:263–65; Capron and Barron, *Singular Revelations*, 39, 41, 42–43, 73, 81–82, 96; Coggeshall, *Signs of the Times*, 99.

26. "Spiritualism in Washington" and quote on Laurie from "The Revolutions in the Old World," *STP*, 30, 111.

27. "Washington and the South," *STP*, 5:136, 137; Charles H. Cragin, "The Genealogy of the Cragin Family, Being the Descendants of John Cragin, of Woburn, Massachusetts, from 1652 to 1858" (Washington: for the author, 1860); W. L. Montague, ed., *Biographical Record of the Alumni of Amherst College, 1821–1871* (Amherst, Mass.: n.p., 1883), 136–37; *Obituary Record of the Graduates of Amherst College* (Amherst, Mass., 1874), 164; Cunningham's obituary from the *Washington, D.C., Evening Star*, June 16, 1871 is posted at congressional cemetery site, where he is buried, and his *Oration before Trade Unions, July 4, 1834, Containing a Short Account of Their Formation, with Constitution and By-laws* (Washington, D.C., 1834). See also "Mr. Redman at Washington," *Christian Spiritualist* 2 (April 5, 1856): 2.

28. "Spiritualism in Washington," *STP*, 3:531–34, and, under the same title, 4:28–30.

29. "Letter from Hon. N. P. Tallmadge," *STP*, 3:310–16; "Washington and the South," *STP*, 5:37, 110; and "Distinguished Investigators," *STP*, 5:203; several under the title "Washington and the South," *STP*, 5:35–36, 137, 138. On Doubleday, see "Washington and the South," *STP*, 5:264. On Hootee in Missouri, see above. On Preuss, see "Washington and the South," *STP*, 5:136, and on Queensbury, "An Evidence of Spirit Presence," "Washington and the South," "Washington and the South," and "The Case of the 'Lost Note' Discovered by Spirits," *STP*, 5:265–67, 345–46, 419–20, 420–21; "Governor N. P. Tallmadge's Reply," *Christian Spiritualist* 2 (March 1, 1856): 2; Tallmadge, Harris, Edmonds at Broadway Tabernacle, "Great Spiritual Meeting. Address by Gov. Tallmadge, Rev. T. L. Harris, and Judge Edmonds," *Christian Spiritualist* 1 (February 24, 1855): 2–3.

30. "Washington and the South," *STP*, 5:35, 37; "The Revolution in the Old World," *STP*, 4:111–16.

31. "The Revolution in the Old World," *STP,* 4:112, 113, 114; "New York Conference," *STP,* 3:53; "Wave-Motion" (from *Portland Eclectic*), *STP,* 6:360–61. See also Hudson Tuttle, "Military Instincts of Insects," *BoL,* July 5, 1862, 2.

32. *Journal of the House of Representatives of the United States, 1853–1854* (February 20, 1854, 402, May 30, 1854, 950); "A Memorial: To the Honorable the Members of the Senate and House of Representatives of the United States, in Congress Assembled," *STP,* 3:386; "Presentation of the Memorial," *STP,* 4:525–27.

33. "Presentation of the Memorial," *STP,* 4:520, 523, 524. See also *Journal of the Senate of the United States of America, 1789–1873* (April 17, 1854, 321). For the complete wording, see "A Memorial: To the Honorable, the Members of the Senate and House of Representatives of the United States, in Congress Assembled," *STP,* 3:382–86; "Presentation of the Memorial," *STP,* 4:525–27, 527, 528–32, with commentary by the editor of *STP;* "Washington and the South," *STP,* 5:35–36; Joshua K. Ingalls, *Reminiscences of an Octogenarian in the Field of Industrial and Social Reform* (New York: M. L. Holbrook, 1897), 155, 156; *MAS,* 132, 134, 135, 140, 141; Doyle, *The History of Spiritualism,* 1:135, 120, 121, 134–35; E. J. Dingwall's "New Introduction" to *MAS,* xi, 146; Britten, *Nineteenth Century Miracles,* xvii (see prologue, n. 19). Also, Linton, a blacksmith, wrote *The Healing of Nations.*

34. "The Memorial," *STP,* 3:472–73.

35. For some discussion of the secret-society tradition in spiritualism, see Mary A. Lowell, "The Red Cross Knight" (fiction), "Freemasonry," "Odd Fellowship and Secession," Emma Hardinge, "The Rosicrucians," "Brotherhood," A. W. Fenno, "Who and What Were the Rosicrusians," untitled Odd Fellows' festival, *BoL,* April 25 (p. 3), May 28 (p. 2), 1857, May 25, 1861, (p. 5), May 24 (p. 4), July 2 (p. 4), 1862, March 7 (p. 8), Oct. 31 (p. 4), 1863.

36. "Washington and the South," *STP,* 5:263–65; F. L. Burr, "The 'Double-Mind' Theory," *STP,* 5:234–39.

37. *MAS,* 261; S. B. Brittan's "The Tribune's Objections," "The Tribune's Assaults," his letter to "C. A. Dana, the Tribune, and Ghostology,'" and his "Conduct of the Tribune," *STP,* 5:214–20, 6:225–28, 356–57, 8:217–19. Also, from the same publication, see "The 'Telegraph' and the 'Tribune,'" "The *Tribune*'s False Report: Spiritualist 'Benefit at Hope Chapel,'" 7:27–28, 8:227–29. See also "Spiritual Manifestation," *Southern Literary Messenger: Devoted to Every Department of Literature* 19 (July 1853): 386–87; "Spiritualist Convention at Providence, R.I.," *BoL,* August 11, 1860, 4; Spiritualist Relief Association, 1858, *MAS,* 539–40; William B. Greene, *The Blazing Star* (Boston: A. Williams, 1872); Deveney, *Paschal Beverly Randolph,* 89–90, 90–92 (see prologue, n. 19); "Organization," *Christian Spiritualist* 2 (April 19, 26, 1856): both 1. See also SDSK on "'Free Love,'" *Christian Spiritualist* 2 (September 1, 1855): 2; "Mr. Warren Chase and His Accusers,'" *Christian Spiritualist* 2 (September 22, 1855), 2; Spoke at Dodsworth, Daniel Webster and Davy Crockett, "Mr. Randolph," *Christian Spiritualist* 1 (April 21, 1855): 2; and "Lecture by the Hon. Warren Chase, Stuyvesant Institute," *Christian Spiritualist* 1 (April 7, 1855): 2.

38. "Organization of Spiritualism" and "Address of the Society for the Diffusion of Spiritual Knowledge to the Citizens of the United States," *STP,* 5:304–5, 305–10; "Address of the Society for the Diffusion of Spiritual Knowledge to the Citizens of the United States" and "Organization of Spiritualism," *STP,* 5:310; *MAS,* 150–51. See also

Sweet, *Future Life*, 5 (see prologue, n. 49). General Bullard, "Popery and Republicanism, Spiritualism Christianity and Politics: The Future of Nations," *Christian Spiritualist* 1 (April 28, 1855): 1; Hume in Florence, "Spiritualism in Italy," *Christian Spiritualist* 2 (February 23, 1856): 2.

39. S. B. B., "The New Organization," *STP,* 5:291, 292.

40. J. K. I., "The New Organization," *STP,* 6:73, 75–76. Ingalls also had likely mistrusted Edmonds because of his earlier mistreatment of the upstate Antirenters. *Voice of Industry* (November 7, 1846).

41. Buescher, *Remarkable Life of John Murray Spear,* 156, 178–79, 226–31, 236–49, 253–54 (see prologue, n. 31), and his *Other Side of Salvation,* 200–201, 202–3; Deveney, *Paschal Beverly Randolph,* 15–16, 16–17, 17–19, 29, 31–33, 48–51, 51–59, 77–88, 67–71; and an exposé by John Shoebridge Williams, *The Patriarchal Order; or, True Brotherhood* (Cincinnati: Longley Brothers, for the author, 1855).

42. *Congressional Globe,* 33rd Cong., 1st sess., 1321. See also Charles Sumner, "The Law of Human Progress," *Journal of Progress* 1 (June 25, 1853): 130–31.

43. For Howard's ubiquitous presence in the circles at Washington, see John B. Buescher, "Across the Dead Line: Lincoln and the Spirits during the War and Reconstruction Era Washington," http://spirithistory.iapsop.com/jb_buescher_across_the_dead_line.pdf.

44. *The History of Fond du Lac County, Wisconsin* (Chicago: Western Historical, 1880), 314–19, 400–408, with portrait and biographical sketch of Bovay, 523, 886. See also David P. Mapes, *History of Ripon, and of Its Founder, David P. Mapes* (Milwaukee: Cramer, Aikens, and Cramer, 1873), 67–72, 79–95, 142–43; the Wisconsin Phalanx Reference Materials posted on the Ripon College website; and Buescher, "Across the Dead Line," 56, 57–59, 63–64. See also Alan W. Farley, "Annals of Quindaro: A Kansas Ghost Town," *Kansas Historical Quarterly* 22 (1956): 305; Carl Magnuson, "The Town of Quindaro: From Community Narrative to Public Debate," *Mid-America Folklore* 2 (1990): 91–107; Jeff R. Bremer, "'A Species of Town-Building Madness': Quindaro and Kansas Territory, 1856–1862," *Kansas History* 26 (Autumn 2003): 156–71; Larry Schmits, "Quindaro: Kansas Territorial Free-State Port on the Missouri River," *Missouri Archaeologist* 49 (1988): 89–145. See also *Quindaro, Kansas on the Underground Railroad,* an online exhibit, Kansas Collection at the Kansas City, Kansas, Library, 2000. Max Greene's book *The Kansas Territory* reviewed in "Books on Our Table," *Christian Spiritualist* 1 (November 11, 1854): 2.

45. *MAS,* 324; "Distinguished Investigators," *STP,* 5:203; Coggeshall, *Signs of the Times,* 29, 30–31, 46–48, 123; Hamm, *God's Government Begun* (see prologue, n. 11); Mark A. Lause, *Race and Radicalism in the Union Army* (Urbana: University of Illinois Press, 2009).

46. MacDonald, *Fifty Years of Freethought,* 1:539; Kelso, "Autobiography," 672, 702–4, 709–10; *Biographical Directory of the U.S. Congress;* Return I. Holcombe, ed., *History of Greene County, Missouri. Written and Compiled from the Most Authentic Official and Private Sources, Including a History of Its Townships, Towns and Villages* (St. Louis: Western Historical, 1883), 476. Martin Hancock, who apparently died in 1911, was the only source of "John R. Kelso" from the *Republic,* probably published in late 1891 after "nearly 30 years of peace," a clipping of which is in the Garland Carr Broadhead Scrapbook, f. 4,

Western Historical Manuscript Collections, University of Missouri–Columbia; Collier, *Ozark and Vicinity,* 9–10 (see prologue, n. 50).

47. "Never has a vote for president been so sectional." *Nichols Monthly* (November 1856): 199–245.

48. "Miscellaneous," *New York Times,* September 20, 1858, 2; "Emma Hardinge in New Brighton, Pa.," "Vermont State Spiritual Convention," and "Spiritual Convention in Illinois," *BoL,* September 17 (both p. 5), October 1 (p. 8), 1859.

49. "Berlin Heights, Ohio: The Convention and the Socialists," *BoL,* September 10, 1859, 7; "Meeting of Progressive Friends," *BoL,* June 13, 1859, 3.

50. *Proceedings of the Free Convention Held at Rutland, Vt., June 25th, 26th, 27th, 1858* (Boston: J. R. Yerrington, 21 Cornhill, 1858); "Harmonial Convention," *STP,* 4:54. See also "The Religion of Revolution—Every Man His Own Evangelist," *New York Herald,* July 5, 1858, 5; "A Case for the Underground Railroad.—Slavery of Women.—Mrs. Julia Branch," *New York Times,* June 28, 1858, 4; "'The Cause and Cure of Evil,'" *New York Times,* September 2, 1858, 4; William Goodell, "The Rutland Convention," *Radical Abolitionist* 3 (July 1858): 89; and Stephen H. Branch, Birth: About 1830 Williamsburg, Kings, New York. Spouse: Margaret Schenck 11 JAN 1834 Middlebush, Somerset, New Jersey. Marriage: 18 DEC 1851 Readington, Hunterdon, New Jersey.

51. "A Second Edition of the Rutland Convention," "The Philanthropic Convention at Utica," with untitled item under "News of the Day" and "'Overcoming Evil with Good'—Convention," "The Free-Love Convention," "The Free-Love at Utica," untitled item, "The Free-Lovers at Utica," "Harmonial Convention," "A Variety of State Conventions," "Another Reformatory Convention," and "News by Telegraph: Abolition, Free Love, Infidel and Women's Rights Convention," *New York Times,* August 7 (p. 4), September 11 (pp. 1, 4, 5), 13 (p. 1), 15 (p. 4), 17 (p. 4), 21 (p. 4), 1858, September 9 (p. 4), 19 (p. 1), 1859; "'Overcoming Evil with Good'—Convention" and "Overcoming Convention," *New York Tribune,* September 11, 13, 1858, both 5; "Utica Philanthropic Convention: Its Organization—Few Philosophers Present," *New York Herald,* September 12, 1858, x; "First Anniversary of Philanthropic Convention" and "Religious Reform Convention at Ellensville, N.Y.," *Liberator,* August 12 (p. 127), September 30 (p. 29), 1859.

52. "The Convention System," *BoL,* September 3, 1859, 4; "The Proposed National Convention," *BoL,* August 27, 1859, 8; "The Proposed National Convention," *BoL,* October 29, 1859, 5; "Spiritualist Convention at Providence, R.I.," *BoL,* August 11, 1860, 4.

53. Harrison Delivan Barrett, *Life Work of Mrs. Cora L. V. Richmond* (Chicago: Hack and Anderson, 1895) (for Garrison and T. W. Higginson) xv, (Abby Heywood) xvi, (Robert Dale Owen). On George Luther Stearns, see his "The Age of Virtue . . . Second Section," *BoL,* March 21, 1863, 2; "The Age of Virtue," *BoL,* April 25, 1863, 2–3; Ralph W. Emerson's "Tribute to George L. Stearns Delivered in the First Parish Church of Medford on the Sunday Following Major Stearns's Death, April 9, 1867," printed in the *Boston Commonwealth,* April 20, 1867.

54. *The National Cyclopaedia,* 63 vols. (New York: James T. White, 1892–1907), 5:20; John Brown under "Summary of News," *Spiritual Age,* n.s., October 9, 1859, 5.

55. David S. Reynolds, *John Brown, Abolitionist: The Man Who Killed Slavery, Sparked the Civil War, and Seeded Civil Rights* (New York: Alfred A. Knopf, 2005), 194, 245; Michael

Gora, *Lake Erie Islands: Sketches and Stories of the First Century after the Battle of Lake Erie* (Bloomington, Ind.: Demand, 2004), 195. On Forbes, see Barrett, *Life Work of Mrs. Cora L. V. Richmond*, 131. Langston certainly sensed the change. "I never thought that I should ever join in doing honor to or mourning for any American white man," he said. But he hailed John Brown as "a lover of mankind—not of any particular class or color, but of all men." Brown had fearlessly warred on "the religion, the priests, the God of slaveholders, and their 'aiders and abettors.'" *Tribute of Respect, Commemorative of the Worth and Sacrifice of John Brown, of Osawatomie* (Cleveland: For the Benefit of the Widows and Families of the Revolutionists of Harpers Ferry, 1859), 17–18, 20, also 8–9. Professor J. M. Vincent donated a copy to the Johns Hopkins University Library.

56. "A New John Brown Party in Massachusetts" (from *Boston Traveller,* May 30), *New York Herald,* June 2, 1860, 10. Referring to professional prizefighter John C. Heenan, one of them later quipped that he "would rather see to day a negro Heenan than a negro Frederick Douglass."

57. *Tribute of Respect,* 51–52. A newspaper account of a spiritualist political speech in 1860 described him dwelling on "the immunity with which Walker and other filibusterers had been allowed by our Government to disturb the peace of neighboring nations; dwelt upon the Kansas outrages; the Republic stood sponsor of them." "Twentieth Ward Wide-Awakes," *New York Times,* October 26, 1860, 1.

58. "Spiritual Lyceum and Conference," *Herald of Progress,* July 7, 1860, 3.

59. "Social Equality," *Herald of Progress,* July 7, 1860, 5; "Social Equality," *Herald of Progress,* July 14, (p. 5), July 21 (p. 5), 1860; "Spiritual Lyceum and Conference," *Herald of Progress,* June 3, 1860, 3; "Spiritual Lyceum and Conference," *Herald of Progress,* June 16, 1860, 3; "Spiritual Lyceum and Conference," *Herald of Progress,* June 30, 1860, 3; letter by "T." under "Social Equality," *Herald of Progress,* July 21, 1860, 8; "Social Equality," *Herald of Progress,* August 11, 1860, 5; "Social Equality," *Herald of Progress,* August 25, 1860, 5; "The Infidel Convention," *Herald of Progress,* October 20, 1860, 5; "The Platform of Infidelity: Skeptical Positions Defined," *Herald of Progress,* November 10, 1860, 2–3.

60. "The Industrial Congress," *Herald of Progress,* November 17, 1860, 5; "The Industrial Congress," *Herald of Progress,* December 1, 1860, 4; "The Industrial Congress," *Herald of Progress,* December 22, 1860, 5. Dr. Snodgrass, of this city, presided. The principal speakers were A. T. Dean, I. B. Davis, Mrs. E. L. Rose, Mrs. Spence, Miss Johnson, S. P. Andrews, Wm. White, S. T. Thompson, and others. For other names, see "An Industrial Congress," *BoL,* November 10, 1860, 7.

61. "Boston Spiritual Conference," *BoL,* July 28, 1860, 4; "Boston Spiritual Conference," *BoL,* August 4, 1860, 5; Young in "Spiritual Lyceum and Conference," *Herald of Progress,* June 30, 1860, 3.

62. "What an Army—Its Future," *BoL,* April 18, 1863, 4.

## Chapter 2. The Mystical Union

1. Chase, *Forty Years,* 175; "Spiritual Lyceum and Conference," *Herald of Progress,* July 7, 1860, 4.

2. "To Such as Understand," *BoL,* June 13, 1863, 5.

3. A. B. Child, *Whatever Is, Is Right* (Boston: Berry, Colby, 1860), 17, 31, 19, 26, 37, 64, 83, 108, 109, 119–20, 135, 139, 150, 162, 178–79; "War for an Idea: A Lecture by Cora L. V.

Hatch at Dodworth's Hall, New York, Sunday Evening, April 21st, 1861," *BoL,* May 11, 1861, 8; "The Good of War," *BoL,* February 28, 1863, 4; A. B. Child, "Punishment of Children," *BoL,* January 28, 1865, 2; "Spiritual Lyceum and Conference," *Herald of Progress,* June 16, 30, 1860, both 3; A. B. C., "Causes of Riches and Poverty," *BoL,* Nov. 8, 1862, 3.

4. Hudson Tuttle, "The Social Relation of Spiritualists," *BoL,* May 24, 1862, 2. See also "Datus Kelley requests statistical report on working conditions." "Labor," *BoL,* March 2, 1861, 6.

5. Waite's letters, "The War Cry of Abolitionism," *BoL,* January 4, 1862, 3; "The Slave Question," *BoL,* July 12, 1862, 3.

6. "Education of the Negro," *BoL,* April 13, 1861, 6; "Spiritualism in Vermont," *BoL,* July 27, 1861, 6; "The Free Negroes," *BoL,* April 20, 1861, 4; "Is Not American Slavery Unconstitutional?," *BoL,* April 20, 1861, 5; "Thomas Jefferson on the Declaration of Independence: A Lecture by Cora L. V. Hatch, at Dodworth's Hall, New York, Sunday Evening, April 14th, 1861," *BoL,* May 11, 1861, 3.

7. "Criticisms by Mr. Hacker," *BoL,* July 2, 1864, 3.

8. "National Convention of Spiritualists, at Oswego, N.Y., Aug. 13 to 18, 1861," *BoL,* September 21, 1861, 8. Also interesting are Hudson Tuttle, "Military Instinct of Insects," *BoL,* July 5, 1862, 2; C. D. Griswold, "Power," *BoL,* August 31, 1861, 7; and "The Great Rebellion," *BoL,* May 11, 1861, 5. See also Hudson Tuttle, "The War," *BoL,* Sept. 14, 1861, 3; A. B. Child, "The Good of Suffering," *BoL,* February 22, 1862, 4; "The Great Rebellion," *BoL,* May 11, 1861, 5; and "Reform and Reformers," *Spiritual Eclectic* 1 (June 2, 1860): 60.

9. C. D. S., "A Congress of Nations," *STP,* 5:442, 440–43; "Cora L. V. Hatch: At the Music Hall, Boston, Sept. 4th, 1859," *BoL,* October 8, 1859, 6; Delp, "Andrew Jackson Davis," 47–48 (see prologue, n. 9); "The Burial of the Sword: A Hymn of the Future," *Herald of Light* 3 (October 1859): 373. "Heaven is peace, and hell is war. How much wrong do we find in the world? Our opposition, our warlike faculties are active in proportion to our discovery of wrong, and our heaven is commensurate with our peace; harmony in the soul with all things. A heavenly condition of the soul does not see or resist any wrong." Child, *Whatever Is, Is Right,* 12.

10. "Two Confederacies," *BoL,* April 6, 1861, 4; "The Great Rebellion," *BoL,* May 4, 1861, 4; "Spiritualism in Vermont," *BoL,* July 27, 1861, 6; "The Union: A Lecture by Cora L. V. Hatch, at Dodworth's Hall, New York, Sunday Evening, March 24, 1861," *BoL,* April 13, 1861, 8; "Slave Insurrections," *BoL,* June 1, 1861, 4; "A Slave Insurrection," *BoL,* June 15, 1861, 4; "The Government Policy," *BoL,* April 13, 1861, 5; "An Old Subscriber," "A Protest from the South," with editorial reply, *BoL,* May 11, 1861, 4; "John McRae, Wilmington NC, May 13: The New Time," *BoL,* June 15, 1861, 5; "Moderation," *BoL,* February 8, 1862, 4.

11. John O. Wattles, "Communication," *Spiritual Philosopher* 1 (October 19, 1850): 82; "National Spiritualist Convention, Oswego, N.Y., Aug. 13 to 18, 1861," *BoL,* September 7, 1861, 3.

12. Warren Chase, "Whatever Is, Is Right," *BoL,* December 14, 1861, 3; Chase, *Forty Years,* 81, 82–83.

13. "Lecture by Dr. Cheever, in New York City, Dec. 1st, 1861," *BoL,* December 14, 1861, 6.

14. Chase in "Spiritualism in Vermont," *BoL*, July 27, 1861, 6; Chase, "Our Country," *BoL*, August 17, 1861, 5; "Secession and Its Consequences: A Lecture by Cora L. V. Hatch, at Dodworth's Hall, New York, Sunday Evening, March 31, 1861," *BoL*, April 20, 1861, 8; S. B. Brittan, "The Argument for Secession: Examined and Refuted," *BoL*, February 15, 1862, 4; "The Secession Nation," *BoL*, July 26, 1862, 4. See also defense of "Free Speech," *BoL*, June 8, 1861, 4. Copy of the *Banner* returned from Virginia. "Ha! Ha!," *BoL*, June 8, 1861, 4.

15. Smith, Lyceum Hall, Boston, December 28, 1862, "Charity for One Another," *BoL*, January 10, 1863, 8; F. L. Crane, "Nostradamus's Prophecies in 1500," *BoL*, May 6, 1865, 3. Six years ago in Buffalo, "The War Predicted by Andrew Jackson in 1856," *BoL*, November 8, 1862, 6.

16. "'Spiritualism and the War': Judge Edmonds on 'The Times, and Our Duty in Regard to Them,'" *BoL*, May 18, 1861, 6. See also "Benjamin Franklin," *BoL*, July 25, 1863, 4.

17. "The Prospects," *BoL*, May 18, 1861, 4; "The Great Rebellion," *BoL*, May 4, 1861, 4; "A Brave Virginian," *BoL*, June 8, 1861, 5, as well as the following from the *BoL*: "All Sorts of Paragraphs," *BoL*, June 22, 1861, 5; "War Items," *BoL*, May 25, 1861, 8; "Preparations," *BoL*, May 25, 1861, 4; "The Great Rebellion," *BoL*, May 4, 1861, 5; "Old Kentucky," *BoL*, September 7, 1861, 4; Warren Chase, "Our Country," *BoL*, August 17, 1861, 5; "All Sorts of Paragraphs," *BoL*, June 22, 1861, 5; the title was "The Present Crisis of American Affairs" in Warren Chase, "The Rebellion—Its Cause and Cure," given September 22, *BoL*, October 5, 1861, 5.

18. For these other publications, see "The Progressive Age," "A New Paper in California," and "The Fifth Annual Festival of the Religio-Philosophical Society, at St. Charles, Ill.," *BoL*, September 5 (p. 4), 1863, July 30 (p. 4), August 20 (p. 3), 1864. Also Frances H. McDougal, *A Tiny Footfall within the Golden Gate: By the author of "The Fountain of Living Waters"* (New York: by the author, 1863).

19. From the *BoL:* "Rev. J. S. Loveland," "Western Lecturers' Conference," "The West and Our Cause," "All Sorts of Paragraphs," W. K. Ripley, "Grove Meeting in Bradford, Me.," "Celebration of the 4th at St. Charles, Ill.," and "Mediums Wanted in California," May 18 (pp. 4, 6), June 15 (p. 6), July 27 (pp. 5, 7), August 10 (pp. 3, 5), 1861.

20. "National Spiritualist Convention, Oswego, N.Y., Aug. 13 to 18, 1861," *BoL*, September 21, 1861, 8.

21. "National Spiritualist Convention, Oswego, N.Y., Aug. 13 to 18, 1861," *BoL*, August 31 (p. 8), September 7 (p. 3), 14 (p. 4), 1861, 8. The former reported that Elmira clergyman Thomas Kinnicut Beecher—one of the Beecher siblings that included Lyman Beecher, Henry Ward Beecher, and Harriet Beecher Stowe—had invited him to teach a class on spiritualism.

22. "National Spiritualist Convention, Oswego, N.Y., Aug. 13 to 18, 1861," *BoL*, September 14, 1861, 4.

23. "National Spiritualist Convention, Oswego, N.Y., Aug. 13 to 18, 1861," *BoL*, August 31 (p. 8), September 14 (p. 4), 1861.

24. "National Convention of Spiritualists, at Oswego, N.Y., Aug. 13 to 18, 1861," *BoL*, September 14 (p. 4), 21 (p. 8), 1861.

25. "The Three Days' Festival at St. Charles, Ill.: A Brief Synopsis of the Exercises, Reported for the *Banner of Light* by L. K. Coonley," *BoL,* October 19, 1861, 3.

26. "National Convention of Spiritualists, Oswego, N.Y., Aug. 13 to 18, 1861," *BoL,* September 14, 1861, 4.

27. "National Spiritualist Convention, Oswego, N.Y., Aug. 13 to 18, 1861," *BoL,* August 31 (p. 8), September 7 (p. 3), 14 (p. 4), 21 (p. 8), 1861.

28. "The Three Days' Festival at St. Charles, Ill.: A Brief Synopsis of the Exercises, Reported for the *Banner of Light* by L. K. Coonley," *BoL,* October 12, 1861, 3.

29. "A Spiritual Telegraph," *BoL,* April 27, 1861, 5; "Incidents of the Battle," *BoL,* August 17, 1861, 4; Randall in "Report of the Meeting Held at Reynoldsville, Schuyler Co., New York," *BoL,* June 15, 1861, 6; "The Great Rebellion," *BoL,* April 27, 1861, 5. See also "The Great Rebellion," *BoL,* May 11, 1861, 5.

30. "The Old Constitution," *BoL,* September 21, 1861, 5; "The Great Rebellion," *BoL,* May 4, 1861, 4–5; "Spiritualism in Vermont," *BoL,* July 27, 1861, 6; "Secession—War—Cotton—Rumors," *BoL,* April 20, 1861, 4; "The Great Rebellion," *BoL,* April 27, 1861, 5; response to "An Old Subscriber" and "A Protest from the South," *BoL,* May 11, 1861, 4; "War," *BoL,* April 27, 1861, 4; "The Times," *BoL,* May 18, 1861, 4.

31. Lizzie Doten, "A Song for the Army" (from the *BoL*), *New Hampshire Sentinel* 46 (September 22, 1864): 38.

32. From the *BoL,* see "Identification of the Soldiers Killed at Baltimore," "'Spiritualism and the War': Judge Edmonds on 'The Times, and Our Duty in Regard to Them,'" "Col. Ellsworth's Presentiment of Death" with Butler's report "The Affair at Great Bethel," "Patriotic Envelope" with "New Publications," "Thanksgiving Day," Leo Miller on "The Great Conflict; or, The Cause and Cure of Secessionism," E. W. H. Beck, Third Indiana Cavalry, December 6, 1861, as "From the Field of War," letter of "Young Dearborn," "Relics from Virginia," May 11 (p. 6), 18 (p. 6), June 22 (pp. 5, 8), September 14 (p. 5), November 23 (p. 4), December 28 (p. 5), 1861, January 4 (p. 7), September 20 (p. 4), 1862, 4. From the same source, the following pieces were published under "The Great Rebellion," April 27, May 11, 18, 1861, all p. 5; "All Sorts of Paragraphs," April 27 (p. 5), June 22 (p. 5), July 20 (p. 4), 1861; and "Our War Roster," December 13 (p. 8) and 20 (p. 4), 1862. These include references to members of the Typographical Union listed in the *Printer,* but see also *BoL,* October 4, 1862, 5.

33. "'Spiritualism and the War': Judge Edmonds on 'The Times, and Our Duty in Regard to Them,'" *BoL,* May 18, 1861, 6; "Visions of the War," *BoL,* September 6, 1862, 6; "Guardian Spirits," *BoL,* January 31, 1863, 5.

34. Untitled piece and "The Battle of Manassas" (from the *New York World*), "The Great Battle," "Gone to the Wars," and "News from the War," *BoL,* August 3 (pp. 5, 8), 1861, 10 (p. 4), 17 (pp. 4, 6), 1861.

35. Colonel Abel B. Smedly letter from near Holly Springs, Mississippi, quoted in E. Warner, "An Interesting Letter from the Army," *BoL,* April 11, 1863, 3.

36. "The Regiment of Spiritualists," *BoL,* November 2, 1861, 4, which describes the major as a veteran of the wars in Germany and Hungary. This is possibly referring to the Fourteenth Massachusetts of Colonel William B. Greene, Lieutenant Colonel Nathaniel Shatswell, and Major Horace Holt. "Provided a whole regiment is recruited

in Massachusetts, a great objection will be overcome, which is in the way of those who are not willing to enlist in a New York regiment." "The Spiritualist Brigade," *BoL*, November 9, 1861, 5.

37. S. B. Brittan, "Letter from Prof. S. B. Brittan," *BoL*, December 14, 1861, 4. See also "Letter from Prof. S. B. Brittan," *BoL*, November 16, 1861, 5; "Death of S. B. Brittan, Jr.," *BoL*, February 22, 1862, 4, much from "A Young Hero," *New York Times*. See also Auclare Ritchie, "To the Memory of S. B. Brittan, Jr., U.S.N.," *BoL*, March 29, 1862, 5. Selling likenesses of him, "'Boy Brittan,'" *BoL*, July 12, 1862, 4. On Fox, see *infra*.

38. Sullivan Ballou, July 14, 1861. Washington found among Sullivan Ballou's effects when Governor William Sprague of Rhode Island traveled to Virginia to retrieve the remains of his state's sons who had fallen in battle. *Brown University in the Civil War: A Memorial* (Providence, R.I.: Providence Press, 1868), 107, letter on 105–8. Treatment of bodies of Major Ballou and Colonel Cameron after Bull Run, "Barbaric Tendencies," *BoL*, April 12, 1862, 4.

39. Find a Grave; Cunningham, "Life of John Brown" (see prologue, n. 18). For this and the following paragraph, see Kelso, "Autobiography," 712, 713–14 (the last referring to "Maybry"), 716–17, 718–19, 720–21, 726–31, 732, 734–38, 748–50, 762–64; Britton, *Civil War on the Border*, 2:204, 206–7 (see prologue, n. 50); *Biographical Directory of the U.S. Congress*; Holcombe, *History of Greene County, Missouri*, 476–7 (see chap. 1, n. 46); Ward L. Schrantz, *Jasper County, Missouri, in the Civil War* (Carthage, Mo.: Carthage Press, 1923, reprinted by Carthage, Mo.: Missouri Kiwanis Club, 1988, 1992), 161–62, 162–64; and Collier, *Ozark and Vicinity*, 10 (see prologue, n. 50); *The War of the Rebellion: A Compendium of the Official Records of the Union and Confederate Armies, Published under the Direction of the . . . Secretary of War . . .*, 70 vols. (Washington, D.C.: Government Printing Office, 1880–1901), (ser. 1) 22 (pt. 1) 314, 761–62, 762–63, (pt. 2) 330, hereafter cited as *O.R.*; Britton, *Civil War on the Border*, 2:204, 206, 205; Collier, *Ozark and Vicinity*, 10; Britton, *Civil War on the Border*, 2:206, 207–8, 205–6, 208; Holcombe, *History of Greene County, Missouri*, 477; *O.R.* (ser. 1), 13:164; "Speech Delivered at Mt. Vernon, Mo., April 18, 1864," 9, in the bound eight-hundred-page "Complete Works in Manuscript, Written for His Beloved Son John R. Kelso, Junior, and His Posterity, 1873–1882" (Huntington Library, San Marino, Calif.); Kelso on "Reconstruction," *Congressional Globe: Containing the Debates & Proceedings of the First Session of the Thirty-Ninth Congress (39th) 1865–66*, 5 vols., pts. 1–5 and appendix (Washington, D.C.: Congressional Globe Office, 1866), 733. For his collaboration with "Wild Bill," see James Butler "Wild Bill" at http://www.angelfire.com/md/saddlesandspurs/wildbill4.html. See Isaac Kelso, *The Stars and Bars; or, The Reign of Terror in Missouri* (Boston: A. Williams, 1863).

40. K. Scott and Myers, "Extinct 'Grass Eaters' of Benton County," 140–57 (see prologue, n. 50).

41. "Wilfrid Wylley," "Letter from a Soldier," Gauley Bridge, November 15, 1861, *BoL*, December 14, 1861, 6; wrote earlier from the Kanawha at Charleston, Wilfrid Wylleye, "From the National Army," *BoL*, January 18, 1862, 6–7. He identified the United States as "the land of my adoption." Wilfred Wylleye, "A Voice from the Army," *BoL*, October 25, 1862, 8. Most likely, Wilfred Wylie, christened June 18, 1843, Holy Trinity, Whitehaven, England. John B. Wolff, "From Colorado" under "Correspondence in Brief," *BoL*, June 25, 1864, 8.

42. From the *BoL:* "War News," "Coming Home," "Real Riches," July 20, August 24, 1861, March 1, 1862, all 4. See also "An Army Crossing a River," Remus Robinson, "A Soldier's Farewell," letter on "The Banner in the Army," *BoL,* July 20 (p. 4), 1861, January 11 (p. 3), July 19 (p. 3), 1862. See also the obituaries of Myron Bennett, William N. Call, Nelson Roland Stevens, Captain John L. Hackstaff late of Eleventh Michigan and editor of the newspaper *Coldwater Union,* Frederick L. N. Willis, "Abstract of a Discourse Delivered at the Funeral of Capt. John L. Hackstaff, of Coldwater, Mich.," *BoL,* March 1 (p. 8), 15 (p. 7), April 26 (p. 8), 1862. Also *BoL,* June 14 (p. 5), July 12 (p. 3), 1862. Also, those of the last weeks of the war for Colonel Charles A. May of Palo Alto fame, James W. Wallack, David Roberts. Samuel Barry, "Obituaries," Henry T. Child, "Obituaries," L. K. Coonley, "Vision of a Funeral in Dixon, Ill.," Samuel Davis the father of Andrew Jackson Davis and Israel Herrick, "From a Venerable Subscriber," *BoL,* January 7 (p. 4), February 18 (p. 7), April 29 (p. 2), May 6 (pp. 7, 8), 1865.

43. Reports on the woes of the Confederacy from the *BoL:* "The Great Rebellion," "Western Virginia," "All about War" and "Rebellious Religion," "John Bell," untitled items with "Parson Brownlow" and "The Dying Rebellion," L. K. Coonley, "Notes by Dr. Coonley," "The Fever in North Carolina," "Emancipation in Virginia," "A Slaveholder on Slavery," "Arming the Slaves," "Southern Governors," May 11 (p. 5), 25 (p. 5), 1861, April 19 (p. 4), May 31 (p. 4), June 14 (p. 4), April 4 (p. 3), August 29 (p. 4), 1863, March 19 (p. 5), 26 (p. 5), November 19 (p. 4), 1864, February 11 (p. 4), 1865, 4. See also "Aid for the People of Savannah," "In Savannah," and "Savannah," January 21 (p. 4), 28 (p. 5), February 11 (p. 4), 1865. Davis, *Death and the After-Life: Eight Evening Lectures on the Summer-Land* (Rochester, N.Y.: Austin, 1911).

44. Buescher, "Across the Dead Line," 53–55; "Life in the Tented Field," "Army Nurses," "Mr. Mansfield in California, etc.," *BoL,* May 24 (p. 3), 31 (p. 4), 1862, March 28 (p. 3), 1863. See also J. Bomber Jr. "Pestilence is King! A Yellow Fever Reminiscence," "To Correspondents," "The Hospitals" with Mrs. Anna H. Webb poem for Banner, "The Dying Soldier," "Hospital Life in the Army," "Dying in Hospital," C. D. Griswold, M.D., "Human Progress," H. F. M. Brown, "Persons and Places.—No. 10," *BoL,* June 1 (p. 2), 1861, June 7 (p. 5), 28 (pp. 4, 7), 1862, August 16 (pp. 6–7), 1862, January 31 (p. 4), September 12 (p. 2), December 12 (pp. 2–3), 1863. Finally, see the following by Henry T. Child: "A Week in a Camp Hospital after a Battle," "Something That Spiritualism Has Done. Number Seven. Haunted Houses," "Compensation: A Lecture by Henry T. Child, M.D., Delivered at the Phoenix Street Church, Philadelphia, Nov. 8th, 1863," "Narrative of George Montieth, Giving Some of His Experiences in the Spheres," "The Davenport Boys in Philadelphia," "Notes of a Sermon Delivered through H. T. Child, M.D., of Philadelphia Pa., at the First Spiritual Church, Thompson Street below Front, on Sunday, March 6, 1864," "Scenes after the Great Battle of the War," letter to "The National Convention of Spiritualists," "Letter from Dr. Child of Philadelphia," and "Narrative of a Spirit Who Entered Spirit-Life at the Age of Three Months," *BoL,* August 22 (pp. 5, 8), October 31 (pp. 2–3), November 28 (p. 8), 1863, January 9 (p. 1), March 5 (p. 3), April 16 (p. 2), June 25 (p. 8), October 8 (p. 4), 15 (p. 4), November 5 (p. 3), 1864, 3. Note too Kay Larson, *Great Necessities: The Life, Times, and Writings of Anna Ella Carroll, 1815–1894* (Philadelphia: Xlibris, 2004).

45. "Death of Lieut. William Berry," *BoL*, October 4, 1862, 4; "Our War Roster," *BoL*, December 20, 1862, 4; "Arthur B. Fuller," *BoL*, January 3, 1863, 4; S. B. B., "A Deserving Officer," *BoL*, January 17, 1863, 4; W. F. Jamieson, "Obituaries," *BoL*, July 30, 1864, 7.

46. "Reform Convention at Evansville, Rock Co. Wisconsin," *BoL*, September 19, 1863, 8, 1864; *Journal of the Executive Proceedings of the Senate of the United States of America*, 13:372, War Department, December 31, 1864. Nominations to be assistant quartermaster with the ranks of captain. Damon Y. Kilgore, of Wisconsin, July 30, 1863; Kilgore to Joseph Osgood Barrett, January 1, 1871, in Osgood Barrett's *The Spiritual Pilgrim: A Biography of James M. Peebles* (Boston: William White, 1872), 88–89. For the two authorized biographies of James Martin Peebles: J. O. Barrett, *Spiritual Pilgrim* (1871), and Edward Whipple, *A Biography of James Martin Peebles* (Battle Creek, Mich.: for the author, 1901); J. M. Peebles, "My Spirit Guide," *BoL*, January 28, 1865, 2; J. M. Peebles, "Thoughts on the Wing: Number Five," *BoL*, April 22, 1865, 3.

47. On Randall and Allen: "Western Lecturers' Conference," "A Traveler's Note," "Recruits! Recruits!," "The Return of J. H. Randall," "J. H. Randall in the Field," "Physical Manifestations by the 'Boy Medium,'" "The Allen Boy Séances," "Test Séance with the Boy-Medium Henry R. Allen," "Physical Manifestations in Boston," "The Séance of Henry B. Allen, the Boy Medium," "The Randall and Allen Boy Séances Again" with "Henry B. Allen, the Boy-Medium," *BoL*, May 18 (p. 6), 25 (p. 7), 1861, August 9 (p. 5), 1862, September 3 (p. 4), 24 (p. 3), October 22 (p. 3), December 31 (p. 4), 1864, January 7 (p. 4), 21 (p. 4), 28 (p. 4), February 18 (pp. 3, 5), 1865. On White, "From the Seat of War," "N. Frank White," *BoL*, March 29 (p. 5), 1862, June 18 (p. 4), 1864. On Blood: "Address of the Society for the Diffusion of Spiritual Knowledge to the Citizens of the United States," "Organization of Spiritualism," *STP*, 5:310; Theodore Tilton, *Biography of Victoria C. Woodhull* (Kansas City, Mo.: Times Steam, 1874), 11.

48. Martin Henry Blatt, *Free Love and Anarchism: The Biography of Ezra Heywood* (Urbana: University of Illinois Press, 1989), 21, 28–29, 33–34, and his spiritualism, 84–88. Also, Blatt's introduction to *The Collected Works of Ezra H. Heywood*, with introductions by Martin Blatt (Weston, Mass.: M&S Press, 1985). See also Spurlock, *Free Love*, 218–20 (see prologue, n. 12).

49. "Spiritualism in Vermont," *BoL*, July 27, 1861, 7. Expectation that "soundness and simplicity" would emerge. "Change in Trade," *BoL*, August 17 (p. 4), 1861, 4.

50. See also John Brown, Belchertown, Massachusetts via Mrs. A. R. Worcester, "'His Soul's Marching On,'" *BoL*, March 14, 1863, 3.

51. "Origin of Great Ideas," *BoL*, August 29, 1863, 4; "Relation of Spiritualism to the Times," *BoL*, September 12, 1863, 5; "Relation of Spiritualism to the Times," *BoL*, September 12, 1863, 5; "Daniel Webster," *BoL*, August 23, 1862, 6; "Henry Clay," *BoL*, November 29, 1862, 6; "Message from John Quincy Adams," *BoL*, September 13, 1862, 6–7. See also "The War Predicted by Andrew Jackson in 1856," *BoL*, November 8, 1862, 6; "Stephen A. Douglas," *BoL*, January 31, 1863, 6; "John C. Calhoun," *BoL*, August 23, 1862, 6; "More Thoughts from Mr. Calhoun," *BoL*, November 1, 1862, 6; "John C. Calhoun," *BoL*, November 22, 1862, 6; "Sam Houston," *BoL*, February 13, 1864, 6; "General Zachary Taylor," *BoL*, April 13, 1865, 6.

52. "Nancy T. Brown," *BoL,* August 16, 1862, 6; "Rebecca Price," *BoL,* September 20, 1862, 6; "Lucy Lee," *BoL,* May 14, 1864, 6; "Alice Grover," *BoL,* May 16, 1863, 6; and, for the daughter, "Caroline Taylor," *BoL,* June 4, 1864, 6.

53. "Gen. Ben McCulloch," *BoL,* August 2, 1862, 6; "General Ben. McCulloch," *BoL,* October 11, 1862, 6; "Feliz K. Zollicoffer," *BoL,* January 24, 1863, 6, and, under "Gen. Felix Zollicoffer," *BoL,* August 6, 1864, 6, and January 7, 1865, 6. "Gen. T. J. Jackson," *BoL,* July 4, 1863, 6; and under "General 'Stonewall' Jackson," *BoL,* March 5, 1864, 6, and July 2, 1864, 6–7; "Relation of Spiritualism to the Times," *BoL,* September 12, 1863, 5; and also "Frances A. Grosseland," *BoL,* February 11, 1865, 6; "The Spirit of Gen. Beauregard," *BoL,* October 31, 1863, 6. For other Confederates, see "Message from a Rebel," *BoL,* October 11, 1862, 6; "Rebel Desertions," *BoL,* September 19, 1863, 4; "Dr. Ebenezer Emmons," *BoL,* December 26, 1863, 6; "Colonel Jones," *BoL,* August 30, 1862, 6; "Major Henry L. Crawford," *BoL,* February 11, 1865, 6; "Stephen T. Dustin," *BoL,* March 21, 1863, 6.

54. "Albert Gould," *BoL,* July 23, 1864, 6; "Reverend William Arnold," *BoL,* July 30, 1864, 6; "Sergeant Robert M. Ridick," *BoL,* January 14, 1865, 6; "Clarissa Oldney," *BoL,* September 3, 1864, 6.

55. Untitled letter, L. Armstrong, Sacramento, February 23, *BoL,* April 4, 1863, 5. N to E. B. H. at Chattanooga. Untitled notice, shall answer but Henry C. Gilbert belongs to 19th Michigan not the Ninth. *BoL,* January 28, 1865, 5. On Henry C. Gilbert, "Explanatory," *BoL,* February 4, 1865, 4; "William Madigan," *BoL,* August 16, 1862, 6; "Marian Elizabeth Kinderfield," *BoL,* April 1, 1865, 6. For prisoners, "Clarence Bowen," *BoL,* April 23, 1864, 6; "Moses Dwight," *BoL,* October 17, 1863, 6; "Horace Brown," *BoL,* December 31, 1864, 6; "Robert Taylor," *BoL,* April 8, 1865, 6; "John N. Hanley," *BoL,* April 29, 1865, 6.

56. L. Armstrong, "Correspondence in Brief," *BoL,* April 4, 1863, 5; "Are the Spirits in Favor of War?," *BoL,* January 24, 1863, 6; "David Grafton," *BoL,* March 12, 1864, 6; A. B. C., "Bromfield Street Conference," *BoL,* September 26, 1863, 5.

57. "Major Christian," *BoL,* April 15, 1865, 6; "Relation of Spiritualism to the Times," *BoL,* September 12, 1863, 5. "Benjamin—a Slave," *BoL,* March 21, 1863, 6; "James Williams," *BoL,* September 20, 1862, 6; "Sam Bolton," *BoL,* December 27, 1862, 6; "Leoni—a Slave," *BoL,* January 9, 1864, 6; "Joe Baxter (Colored)," *BoL,* July 30, 1864, 6; "Prince. (A Slave.)," *BoL,* October 15, 1864, 6; "Peter Gross. (Colored.)," *BoL,* December 24, 1864, 6. Also "George Sheldon (Colored)," *BoL,* March 5, 1864, 7, "Lafayette (Colored)," *BoL,* April 16, 1864, 6, "Phil (a Colored Boy)," *BoL,* October 1, 1864, 6, "William Apel (Colored)," *BoL,* January 28, 1865, 6. See also "Walter Grosse," *BoL,* December 24, 1864, 6.

58. "William Sampson. (Colored.)," *BoL,* November 19, 1864, 6; "James Peer," *BoL,* October 17, 1863, 6; "Archibald Lewis (Colored)," *BoL,* April 30, 1864, 6; "William Culneuigh (Colored)," *BoL,* May 28, 1864, 6; "Isaac Poole," *BoL,* September 26, 1863, 6–7. Killed at Fort Pillow. Free for two years. "George L. Josselyn," *BoL,* June 25, 1864, 6.

59. Indians "Phillip of Narragansett," *BoL,* November 8, 1862, 6; S. C. Simonds on "The Indians," *BoL,* October 10, 1863, 6; "An Indian Council in Spirit Land," *BoL,* October 10, 1863, 6. Also "Little Crow," *BoL,* October 1, 1864, 6. References to "Allah" interfered, and some discussion of the Hindus. A Chinese migrant in California tried

to get the floor once, but found that the language barrier had survived death as well. "Invocation," *BoL*, May 28, 1864, 6; "Is Allah a Hindoo God?," *BoL*, September 10, 1864, 6; "Foo-Chow," *BoL*, May 9, 1863, 6.

60. "Something to Think Of," *BoL*, May 25, 1861, 5; "The Times," *BoL*, May 18, 1861, 4. "Astrologers tell us that certain martially inclined planets happen to be in conjunction just at this time, which certainly *ought* to be true, if it be not" in "War," *BoL*, June 1, 1861, 4; "Possessed," *BoL*, September 14, 1861, 4. Also "A New National Hymn," *BoL*, June 15, 1861, 5.

61. "A Lecture by Mrs. M. M.[?] Macomber(?), at Alston Hall, Boston, on Sunday Evening, May 19th, 1861," *BoL*, May 25, 1861, 6. W. S. A. communications from Washington, printed as Messages from John Quincy Adams, 1859. J. D. Stiles, medium. Writings commended August 1854, continued to March 1857. "Prophecy on the Present Crisis," *BoL*, April 27, 1861, 4. See also Joseph D. Stiles, *Twelve Messages from the Spirit of John Quincy Adams through Joseph D. Stiles, Medium, to Josiah Brigham* . . . (Boston: B. Marsh, 1859), xxiii. Quoting Garrison's *Liberator* as to skepticism about war leading to the end of slavery. "War and Peace," *BoL*, June 22, 1861, 5; response to "An Old Subscriber." "A Protest from the South," *BoL*, May 11, 1861, 4; "The Country's Crisis," *BoL*, May 4, 1861, 4.

62. Warren Chase, "Our Country," *BoL*, August 17, 1861, 5; "The Prospects," *BoL*, May 18, 1861, 4; Mrs. M. S. Townsend of Taunton, Mass, formerly of Bridgewater, Vermont spoke on "Our National Crisis" at L. K. Coonley, "Fourth of July Celebration," *BoL*, August 10, 1861, 3.

63. "Boston Spiritual Conference," *BoL*, May 18, 1861, 6; "War," *BoL*, August 24, 1861, 6.

64. Kaulback quoted in "Boston Spiritual Conference," *BoL*, May 18, 1861, 6; "The War, as It Progresses," *BoL*, July 27, 1861, 5; D. J. Mandell, "A Card, and a Problem for the People," *BoL*, September 28, 1861, 6.

65. "The Political Revolution," *BoL*, April 13, 1861, 3.

66. "The National Struggle, and Its Effect upon the Principles of Truth and Progress Throughout the World. Subject Chosen by a Committee. A Lecture by Cora L. V. Hatch, before the Lyceum Society of Spiritualists, in Lyceum Hall, Boston, Sunday, July 12, 1863," *BoL*, October 17, 1863, 8; John McRae, Wilmington NC May 13. "The New Time," *BoL*, June 15, 1861, 5; Confederate government's discussion of adopting a "Coat of Arms," *BoL*, November 22, 1862, 3.

## Chapter 3. Father Abraham

1. *MAS*, 301–2; William Herndon and Jesse W. Weik, *Abraham Lincoln: The True Story of a Great Life*, 3 vols., consecutively paged (Springfield, Ill.: Herndon's Lincoln, [1889]), on *Vestiges*, 3:437–39, on change, 2:339, 1:167, 3:527–29; *The Collected Works of Abraham Lincoln*, edited by Roy P. Basler, 9 vols. (New Brunswick, N.J.: Rutgers University Press, 1953–55), 2:405–6. For the influence of Chambers's anticipation of Darwin upon James G. Birney of the abolitionist Liberty Party, see Clement Eaton, *The Freedom of Thought Struggle in the Old South*, rev. ed. (New York: Harper and Row, 1964), 313, 326.

2. For quotes in this and the following paragraph, see Herndon and Weik, *Abraham Lincoln*, 1:12; and John L. Scripps, *Life of Abraham Lincoln*, edited by Roy P. Basler and

Lloyd A. Dunlap (Bloomington: Indiana University Press, 1961), 13. See also Robert L. Miller, *The Early Years, Birth to Illinois Legislature* (Mechanicsburg, Pa.: Stackpole Books, 2006) and *Prairie Politician, 1834–1843* (Mechanicsburg, Pa.: Stackpole Books, 2008).

3. Lloyd Ostendorf and Walter Oleksy, eds., *Lincoln's Unknown Private Life: An Oral History by His Black Housekeeper Mariah Vance, 1850–60* [recorded by Adah Sutton, 1900–1904] (Mamaroneck, N.Y.: Hastings House, 1995), 158; Winifred E. Garrison and Alfred T. DeGroot, *The Disciples of Christ: A History* (St. Louis: Bethany Press, 1948); Robert Richardson, *Memoir of Alexander Campbell* (Cincinnati: R. W. Carrol, 1872); William E. Tucker and Lester C. McAlliston, *Journey in Faith: A History of the Christian Church (Disciples of Christ)* (St. Louis: Bethany Press, 1975); Winifred E. Garrison, *Religion Follows the Frontier: A History of the Disciples of Christ* (New York: Harper and Row, 1931). For the Lincolns' affiliations, see Herndon and Weik, *Abraham Lincoln*, 1:14–15, 11–12; Harold L. Lunger, *The Political Ethics of Alexander Campbell* (St. Louis: Bethany Press, 1954); David E. Harrell Jr., "The Sectional Origins of the Churches of Christ," *Journal of Social History* 30 (August 1964): 261–77. Of course, one by-product of the Elizabethtown revivals early in the century was Kentucky's largest Shaker community. Quoting two Baltimore Presbyterians. "The President's Religious Feelings," *BoL*, December 12, 1863, 2; *Collected Works of Lincoln*, edited by Basler, 6:536; Herndon and Weik, *Abraham Lincoln*, 1:125, 3:439–40, and see also 3:440–46, 538, 582, confirmed by the testimony of John Hill in *The Hidden Lincoln: From the Letters and Papers of William H. Herndon* (New York: Viking Press, 1938), 283; *WALS*, 191.

4. John E. Remsburg, "Abraham Lincoln," in *Six Historic Americans* (New York: Truth Seeker, 1906). The local storekeeper at New Salem "snatched the manuscript from [Lincoln's] hands and thrust it into the stove. The book went up in flames and Lincoln's political future was secure."

5. Ervin Chapman, *Latest Light on Abraham Lincoln and War-Time Memories* (New York and London: Fleming H. Revell, 1917), 505; Jennifer Fleischner, *Mrs. Lincoln and Mrs. Keckly: The Remarkable Story of the Friendship between a First Lady and a Former Slave* (New York: Broadway Books, 2003), 288. Early in 1861, Mary Lincoln laughed it off when an old Washington slave woman, said to be a native African, predicted war, but her warning impressed the president. Fleischner, *Mrs. Lincoln and Mrs. Keckly*, 260. N. G. Ordway, Sergeant-at-Arms of the House of Representatives, see William T. Coggeshall, *Lincoln Memorial* (Columbus: Ohio State Journal, 1865), 140, 175. The Walter Ordway who lived in Springfield did not move there from Kansas City until the war broke out. J. C. Power, *History of Springfield, Illinois* (Springfield: Illinois State Journal Print, 1871), 75; Harry C. Blair, *Dr. Anson G. Henry: Physician, Politician, Friend of Abraham Lincoln*, 19 (Portland, Ore.: n.p., 1950).

6. Ostendorf and Oleksy, *Lincoln's Unknown Private Life,* 159–60.

7. Paul M. Angle, *"Here I Have Lived": A History of Lincoln's Springfield* (Springfield, Ill.: Abraham Lincoln Association, 1935), 140–41; Bret E. Carroll, "The Religious Construction of Masculinity in Victorian America: The Male Mediumship of John Shoebridge Williams," *Religion and American Culture* 7 (Winter 1997): 29; 1845–46 Socialist Community. Integral Phalanx absorbing the Sangamon Association, earlier OH. Fogarty, *Dictionary of American Communal and Utopian History,* item #93 (see prologue, n. 48);

Carroll, "Religious Construction of Masculinity," 27–60; Fogarty, *Dictionary of American Communal and Utopian History*, 191.

8. Dr. John W. Field, "Spiritualists' Meeting," *BoL*, September 14, 1861, 3; *WALS*, 92–93.

9. "Seth Paine," *Chicago Daily Tribune*, July 7, 1872, 5. Cridge's son Alfred Denton Cridge later wrote *Utopia; or, The History of an Extinct Planet* (Oakland, Calif.: for the author by Winchester and Pew, 1884), an early science fiction novel that unfolds because of the psychometric reading on a meteorite, reading the earth from a destroyed utopia. See also Michael J. Kline, *The Baltimore Plot: The First Conspiracy to Assassinate Abraham Lincoln* (Yardley, Pa.: Westholme, 2008). Dr. David Cory letter from Waukegan, *Journal of Progress* 1 (June 4, 1853): 890; Alfred Cridge channeling "The Fate of Sir John Franklin," *Christian Spiritualist* 1 (October 28, 1854): 2.

10. Chase, *Forty Years*, 56, 72, 79, 81, 82 (see prologue, n. 18).

11. *MAS*, 301–2. One wonders if this represented the work of Chase, who had continued on from Philadelphia to Berlin Heights. Chase, *Forty Years*, 176. William H. Herndon, Springfield Ill., December 4, 1885, "Letter from Lincoln's Old Partner," *Religio-Philosophical Journal* (December 12, 1885), from John Buescher, "Unlocking the Mystery of a Lincoln Relic," long posted at the author's website, http://www.spirithistory.com; A Citizen of Ohio [David Quinn], *Interior Causes of the War: The Nation Demonized and Its President a Spirit-Rapper* (New York: M. Doolay, 1863); "Abraham Lincoln's Ghost," http://dcpages.com/Events/Holidays/Halloween/Abraham_Lincoln.shtml.

12. Quoted in Jason Emerson, *The Madness of Mary Lincoln* (Carbondale: Southern Illinois University Press, 2007), 36; Ostendorf and Oleksy, *Lincoln's Unknown Private Life*, 159.

13. William H. Herndon, Springfield, Ill., December 4, 1885, "Letter from Lincoln's Old Partner," *Religio-Philosophical Journal* (December 12, 1885): 5, from Buescher, "Unlocking the Mystery of a Lincoln Relic." It is simply not true that "William Herndon, flatly denied it." Joseph Trainor, "1863: The President's Psychic," posted at *Pete's Journal* (2007), http://seekeronline.info/journals/y2007/jan07part2.htm.

14. Princess Felix Salm-Salm, *Ten Years of My Life* (New York: R. Worthington, 1877), 45. See also Doris Kearns Goodwin, *Team of Rivals: The Political Genius of Abraham Lincoln* (New York: Simon and Schuster, 2005), 422; Ernest B. Furgurson, *Freedom Rising: Washington in the Civil War* (New York: Alfred A. Knopf, 2004), 244.

15. William O. Stoddard, *Inside the White House in War Times*, edited by Michael Burlingame (New York Charles L. Webster, 1890), 32. See also David H. Donald, *"We Are Lincoln Men": Abraham Lincoln and His Friends* (New York: Simon and Schuster, 2003).

16. William O. Stoddard, *Lincoln's White House Secretary: The Adventurous Life of William O. Stoddard*, edited by Harold Holzer (Carbondale: Southern Illinois University Press, 2007), 134, 142–42, 143–44.

17. Francis L. Capen to Abraham Lincoln, March 29, April 25, 1863, with Lincoln's annotation of April 28. For a Mrs. S. R. Capen of Sharon. *Massachusetts Progressive Annual* for 1862, 1863, and 1864; I. B. Conklin to Abraham Lincoln, December 28, 1861; "Premonitions," *BoL*, Nov. 16, 1861, 4. One wonders if this could be "L. K. Coonley" of Vineland, N.J., listed in the *BoL*, August 17, 1878, February 1, 1879, and July 31,

1880; *WALS*, 92; Chase, *Forty Years*, 96; Stoddard, *Inside the White House in War Times*, White House Sketches, No. 4, 157, from William Stoddard, *White House Sketches*, No. 4; Fleischner, *Mrs. Lincoln and Mrs. Keckly*, 259; "Abraham Lincoln's Ghost"; "The President's Bereavement," *BoL*, March 8, 1862, 4.

18. *WALS*, 192–93; David Homer Bates, *Lincoln in the Telegraph Office: Recollections of the United States Military Telegraph Corps during the Civil War* (New York: Century, 1911), 210. For reappearances of "Willie Lincoln," *BoL*, December 13, 1862, 6, April 23, 1864, 6, June 4, 1864, 6.

19. Susan B. Martinez, *The Psychic Life of Abraham Lincoln* (Franklin Lakes, N.J.: New Page Books, 2007), 38–39, 40, 41–42, a work that combines serious digging with minimal critical reflection. On exempting the Shakers, Daniel Boler et al. to Abraham Lincoln and William H. Seward, August 12, 1862, the Abraham Lincoln Papers at the Library of Congress, posted at http://memory.loc.gov/ammem/malquery.html; "Horace H. Day's India-Rubber Breech-Piece," *Scientific American* 9 (October 19, 1863): 228.

20. *WALS*, 40–41, 41–42, 43, 91, 93–94, 128–29, 129–31, 131–32, 190, 154, 157, 160. Robert Dale Owen, *Footfalls on the Boundary of Another World* (Philadelphia: J. B. Lippincott, 1860); Robert Dale Owen, *The Debatable Land between This World and the Next, with Illustrative Narrations* (New York, 1872); Fleischner, *Mrs. Lincoln and Mrs. Keckly*, 259; "Remarkable Case of Pre-vision and Mental Telegraphing," *BoL*, January 14, 1865, 3; Alfred Horton, "Letter from Washington," *BoL*, May 16, 1863, 2–3; J. C. "Jack" Laurie. Sworn to and subscribed before me this 1st day of November 1885. Theodore Munger, U.S. commissioner. From Cyrus Oliver Poole, "The Religious Convictions of Abraham Lincoln: A Study," *Religio-Philosophical Journal* (November 28, 1885), well discussed in Buescher, "Unlocking the Mystery of a Lincoln Relic," long posted at the author's website, http://www.spirithistory.com.

21. Buescher, *Other Side of Salvation*, 141; "Personal," *BoL*, September 21, 1861, 5; "The Birthday of John Pierpont," *BoL*, April 27, 1861, 3. For materials by Pierpont, see *Airs of Palestine* (Baltimore: B. Edes, 1816); *The National Reader* (Boston, 1828); *The Burning of the Ephesian Letters* (Boston: Ford and Damrell, 1834); *New Heavens and a New Earth* (Boston: Tuttle, Weeks, and Dennett, 1837); *Moral Rule and Political Action* (Boston: James Munroe, 1839); *A Discourse on the Covenant with Judas* (Boston: C. C. Little and J. Brown, 1842); *Phrenology and the Scriptures* (New York: Fowler and Wells, 1850). See also Franklin B. Dexter, *Biographical Sketches of the Graduates of Yale College*, vol. 5, 1792–1805 (New York, 1911), 692–704.

22. Professor Henry Cowles of Oberlin to John Pierpont, March 6, 1863. Abraham Lincoln Papers; *WALS*, 66n; "Western Lecturers' Conference" and, with J. R. Rouse, Belle Scougall, H. F. M. Brown, C. M. Stowe, and G. W. Holliston, "National Conference of Spiritualists," *BoL*, May 18 (p. 6), and July 27 (p. 5), 1861; Lewis Masquerier, *Sociology; or, The Reconstruction of Society, Government, and Property, upon the Principles of the Equality, the Perpetuity, and the Individuality of the Private Ownership of Life, Person, Government, Homestead, and the Whole Product of Labor* (New York: by the author, 1877), 125. See also John Neal, "John Pierpont," *Atlantic Monthly*, December 1866, 649–65; J. E. M. Latham, *Search for a New Eden: James Pierrepont Greaves (1777–1842), the Sacred Socialist and His Followers* (Madison, N.J.: Fairleigh Dickinson University Press, 1999).

23. Lewis C. Perry, *Childhood, Marriage, and Reform: Henry Clarke Wright, 1797–1870* (Chicago: University of Chicago Press, 1980).

24. Buescher, "Across the Dead Line," 46–47, 50, 56, 60–61, 62–63, 64, 65, 68.

25. John W. Edmonds to Abraham Lincoln, June 1, 1863.

26. *WALS*, 9–11, 13–15, 18n, 22, 36–37, 177; Chase, *Forty Years*, 96; Nettie Colburn Maynard listed in *BoL*, August 28, 1869, June 18, 1870; *Yearbook of Spiritualism* (1871); *BoL*, July 12, 1873, July 18, 1874, August 7, 1875, July 15, 1876, August 4, 1877, August 17, 1878, February 1, 1879, July 31, 1880; *WALS*, 37–38; Wash. A. Danskin, "The 'Herald of Progress' and 'Banner of Light' on the Civil War," *BoL*, June 15, 1861, 4; Wash. A. Danskin, "Meeting for the Indians," *BoL*, May 2, 1863, 3–4; obituary of Rosalie Danskin, 23-year old wife of Lt. Washington A. Danskin, Jr., *BoL*, March 15, 1862, 7. On Baltimore, see also "The Davenport Brothers in Baltimore," *BoL*, April 23, 1864, 3; "Charles H. Foster in Baltimore," *BoL*, May 7, 1864, 4; "Lecturers Wanted in Baltimore" *BoL*, September 24, 1864, 4; Alfred Horton, "Spirit Message Tested," *BoL*, September 24, 1864, 4; Wash. A. Danskin, "Spiritualism in Baltimore," *BoL*, October 22, 1864, 8; and Warren Chase, "Circles in Washington D.C.," *BoL*, February 18, 1865, 4.

27. *WALS*, 37–38, 41–43, 44–45n; "Personal," *BoL*, September 21, 1861, 5; 1850 Census. Cincinnati, Ward 8, Hamilton County OH, G. A. B., "Our Washington Letter," *BoL*, October 29, 1864, 4. "Mr. Foster's Séances," *BoL*, December 31, 1864, 4.

28. See also Kathlyne, "Medium's Message May Have Moved Lincoln to End Slavery." http://www.omplace.com/articles/Lincoln_Medium.html.

29. "Abraham Lincoln's Ghost"; J. C. "Jack" Laurie. Sworn to and subscribed before me this 1st day of November 1885. Theodore Munger, U.S. commissioner. From Poole, "Religious Convictions of Abraham Lincoln," in Buescher, "Unlocking the Mystery of Lincoln Relic." Careless accounts say, "The medium was playing the instrument when it began to rise off the floor." Not Colburn's memoir and almost surely story from Belle Miller, the pianist. Simon P. Kase, *The Emancipation Proclamation: How, and by Whom, It Was Given to Abraham Lincoln in 1861* (Philadelphia: by the author, [1900?]); *WALS*, 90–91.

30. 1880 U.S. Census. Washington, Washington, District of Columbia. Laurie Cranstoun; A Bill for the relief of Cranstoun Laurie, S561, February 6, 1857. Mr. Rusk from Committee on the Post Office and Post Roads. Congress requires postmaster general to pay Cranstoun Laurie "a just and reasonable compensation for the extra duties performed" http://memory.loc.gov/ammem/amlaw/browse/llsb_034_keyw.html; *WALS*, 53–55, 64–65; Prof. W. H. Chaney, Portland, Ore., "Was He a Spiritualist? Reminiscences of President Lincoln," *Religio-Philosophical Journal* (January 16, 1886), in Buescher, "Unlocking the Mystery of a Lincoln Relic." Belle had a rather nasty divorce with Colonel Miller. *WALS*, 84, 92; F. B. Carpenter artist of singing of emancipation. "A Touching Incident at the White House," *BoL*, May 13, 1865, 4. See also Jean H. Baker, *Mary Todd Lincoln: A Biography* (New York: W. W. Norton, 1987).

31. Lydia Smith to Abraham Lincoln, October 4, 1862; *WALS*, 124–26.

32. "The Prospects," *BoL*, May 18, 1861, 4; "The President," *BoL*, July 26, 1862, 4.

33. *Diary of Orville Hickman Browning,* edited by Theodore Calvin Pease and James Garfield Randall (Springfield: Illinois State Historical Library, 1925) (January 1, 1863), 1:609–10; Trainor, "1863: The President's Psychic." See also Kathlyne, "Medium's Message May Have Moved Lincoln to End Slavery"; and Martinez, *Psychic Life of Lincoln*, 29, 262n11.

34. Chaney, "Was He a Spiritualist?," in Buescher, "Unlocking the Mystery of a Lincoln Relic." Margaret Laurie asks Lincoln for the full release of Elbert F. Turner, December 19, 1864 (Abraham Lincoln Papers at the Library of Congress: search keywords "Laurie" and "Turner"); Buescher, "Unlocking the Mystery of a Lincoln Relic."

35. *WALS,* 71–72, 72–76, 115–16, 117–18, 153, and for a January meeting, 168–70; J. C. "Jack" Laurie. Sworn to and subscribed before me this 1st day of November 1885. Theodore Munger, U.S. commissioner. From Poole, "Religious Convictions of Abraham Lincoln," posted on http://seekeronline.info/journals/y2007/jan07part2.htm; Trainor, "1863: The President's Psychic." See also Kathlyne, "Medium's Message May Have Moved Lincoln to End Slavery."

36. *WALS,* 99–101, 163–64, 165–66.

37. Joshua F. Speed to Abraham Lincoln, October 26, 1863, Lincoln Papers.

38. *WALS,* 64–68, 80–81; "The Dome of the Capitol," *BoL,* December 17, 1864, 4; "Matters at Washington," *BoL,* February 27, 1864, 4; Just in from Washington, D.C., "Dr. L. K. Coonley," *BoL,* March 5, 1864, 5; Alfred Horton, "Charles H. Foster, the Medium in Washington," *BoL,* March 12, 1864, 3; Alfred Horton, "Spiritual Manifestations at Washington," *BoL,* March 26, 1864, 3; "Foster and Spiritualism in Washington," *BoL,* April 16, 1864, 5; Thomas Gales Forster, "Spiritual Meetings in Washington," *BoL,* April 23, 1864, 4; G. A. B., "Our Washington Letter—Bro. Pardee, &c.," *BoL,* June 11, 1864, 4.

39. "Incident of the War," *BoL,* Oct. 15, 1864, 4; *WALS,* 146–52. Hootee became an assistant surgeon, Field and Staff, Second DC Infantry, in the Civil War.

40. "The War—What It Has Done—What It Is Doing—and What It Is to Do for the Nation," *BoL,* October 31, 1863, 4.

41. "Our Washington Letter: New Committees—Miss Netti Coburn's Lectures—a Wedding Among Spiritualists, etc.," *BoL,* January 14, 1865, 8; Washington A. Danskin, "Thomas Gales Forster in Baltimore," *BoL,* January 16, 1864, 5.

42. "Personal," *BoL,* September 21, 1861, 5; Napoleon Bonaparte Wolfe, *Startling Facts in Modern Spiritualism* (Chicago, 1875); "Health of the Army," *BoL,* August 24, 1861, 4.

43. "Who Shall Be Mayor?," "The Metropolitan Police Question," "Peace and War: A Lecture by Mrs. Cora L. V. Hatch, before the Lyceum Society of Spiritualists, in Lyceum Hall, Boston, Sunday, May 17, 1863," "John Brough, of Ohio," "New York as a City," "The Cities and Exemption," "U. Clark's Itinerary Etchings," "The Suppression of the Papers," "Miscegenation," *BoL,* December 7 (p. 5), 1861, April 25 (p. 4), June 6 (pp. 3–4), July 4 (p. 4), August 8 (p. 4), September 19 (p. 4), November 14 (p. 8), 1863, June 4 (p. 4), 1864, December 3 (p. 4), 1864.

44. H. A. W., "The War—Its Causes and Uses," "Letter from Horace Dresser: The Vice of the Constitution," advertisement for his *The Battle Record of the American Rebellion,* "Mr. Greeley on Mr. Sumner," Warren Chase, "What Next?," "Abuse of Habeas Corpus,"

*BoL*, April 4 (p. 3), July 18 (p. 1), 25 (p. 8), October 17 (p. 2), 24 (p. 4), 1863, July 30 (pp. 2–3), 1864.

45. "The 'Man on Horseback,'" *BoL*, May 24, 1862, 4. See also Dr. C. S. Griswold, "Shall This Republic Live?," *BoL*, November 22, 1862, 8.

46. David E. Long, *The Jewel of Liberty: Abraham Lincoln's Re-election and the End of Slavery* (Mechanicsburg, Pa.: Stackpole Books, 1994).

47. "President Making," *BoL*, February 27, 1864, 4; "The President's Message," *BoL*, December 13, 1862, 4; "Political Spiritualism" with untitled items, *BoL*, June 11, 1864, 4, 5. Some of the arguments Wayne C. Temple made in *Abraham Lincoln: From Skeptic to Prophet* (Mahomet, Ill.: Mayhaven, 1995) fit contemporary views of spiritualist prophecy more than those of orthodox Christianity.

48. "The Great Spiritualist Convention in Boston," "The Great Spiritualist Convention in Boston: First and Second Days' Proceedings," *BoL*, March 5, 12, 19, 1864, all 8, but see also "The National Convention," "The Spiritual Convention," "The Great Spiritualist Convention in Boston: The Last Day's Speeches and Proceedings," "Spiritualist Convention," "The Spiritualists National Convention" and "Three Days' Spiritualist Convention at Clinton Hall, New York," "The Spiritual National Convention," and "The New York Convention," "Spiritual National Convention at Clinton Hall, New York," "The Spiritual National Convention," "The National Spiritualist Convention," "First Grand National Convention of Spiritualists," "The National Convention of Spiritualists," *BoL*, March 12 (p. 4), 19 (pp. 4, 8), 26 (p. 5), April 2 (p. 5), 23 (p. 4), May 14 (p. 4), June 4 (p. 5), 11 (p. 4), July 30 (p. 8), October 8 (p. 3), 1864. Note that the "Three Days' Spiritualist Convention at Clinton Hall, New York," April 30, 1864, 5, is repeated into May. "The New York City Convention—Notice to Speakers and Others," *BoL*, May 7, 1864, 4.

49. "Warren Chase in Chicago" [on Byran Hall], "The Great Spiritualist Convention in Boston: First and Second Days' Proceedings," *BoL*, September 21, 1861, 8.

50. "Spiritualist National Convention Byran Hall, Chicago, Illinois, August 9th, 10th, 11th, 12th, 13th, and 14th, 1864," and "National Convention," *BoL*, August 20 (pp. 4, 5), with "Official Report of the National Convention of Spiritualists, Held in Chicago, Ill., August 9th to 14th, 1864," August 15, 27, September 3, 10, 17, 24 (all p. 8), with the final session reported October 1 (pp. 5, 8), with Henry T. Child, "The National Convention of Spiritualists," October 8, 1864, 3. For preliminaries, see "National Convention of Spiritualists, at Oswego, N.Y., Aug. 13 to 18, 1861," "The Great Spiritualist Convention in Boston" [February 24, 25, 26, 1864], "Warren Chase in Chicago" [on Byran Hall], "The Great Spiritualist Convention in Boston: First and Second Days' Proceedings," Alcinda Wilhelm, "The Convention—'Rising Tide'—Reformers, etc.," *BoL*, September 21 (p. 8), 1861, March 5 (p. 8), 12 (p. 4, 8), September 3 (p. 3), 1864. For persistence of anti-Lincoln conservatives, "Annual Meeting," [for Progressive Spiritualists of Cincinnati], D. Tarbell, "'The Suffering Poor,'" A. G. W. Carter, "A Western Lecturer," *BoL*, January 21 (p. 8), 28 (p. 8), April 1 (p. 3), 1865.

51. *Religio-Philosophical Journal* (November 11, 1865); "Formation of the Religio-Philosophical Society, 1864," *Friend of Progress* (December 1864): 37. Its officers were as follows: S. S. Jones, Chairman, St. Charles, Ill.; Warren Chase, Battle Creek, Mich.;

Henry T. Child, M. D., 634 Race Street, Philadelphia; W. F. Shuey, Elkhart, Ind.; Mary F. Davis, Orange, N.J.; Selden J. Finney, Plato P.O., Ohio; M. M. Daniels, Independence, Iowa; H. B. Storer, Boston, Mass.; Milo O. Mott, Brandon, Vt.; and F. L. Wadsworth, secretary, National Executive Committee of Spiritualists.

52. See also "Assaults on the Chicago Convention," A. G. Parker, "Facts of Spiritual Convention," "Spiritual Organization," "The Foundation of Governments, and Ownership of Property: A Lecture Delivered before the 'Religio-Philosophical Society of Des Moines, Iowa, Sunday, May, 1864, by B. N. Kinyon," *BoL,* September 10 (p. 4), 24 (p. 3), April 1 (p. 3), May 6 (p. x), 1865; E. E. Gibson, "Self-Reform the Centre of All Reform," *Christian Spiritualist* 2 (November 10, 1855): 1; E. E. Gibson, "Soul Marriage,'" *Christian Spiritualist* 2 (September 22, 1855): 1; E. E. Gibson, "Soul Marriage,'" *Christian Spiritualist* 2 (October 6, 1855): 1.

53. "The Position of Spiritualism in Its Relations to Slavery and the Rebellion," *Liberator* 34 (August 26, 1864): 140; "The Spiritualist Convention," *BoL,* April 22, 1865, 4; "Presidential Nomination," *BoL,* June 18, 1864, 4.

54. "Letter from Henry T. Child, M.D.," *BoL,* November 19, 1864, 8; R. A. Beck to Abraham Lincoln, November–December 1864.

55. *WALS,* 175–76; "The Fall Elections," *BoL,* October 22, 1864, 4; "Election," *BoL,* November 5, 1864, 4. See also "Mrs. Beecher's Lecture," "Congress" with "The President's Message and Presents to Public Men," *BoL,* November 26, December 17, 1864, all 4.

56. Holcombe, *History of Greene County, Missouri,* 476, 477 (see chap. 1, n. 46); E. Underhill from Medora, "From Missouri," *BoL,* April 1, 1865, 8. Ignoring this division among the Republicans, Collier asserts the Republican Kelso won the election "as a result of that ticket sweeping the state." Collier, *Ozark and Vicinity,* 10 (see prologue, n. 50). *The Tribune Almanac for 1865* (New York: Tribune, 1865), 66.

57. *WALS,* 179–80, 181. Also H. T. C., "Colonel John W. Crosby," *BoL,* April 29, 1865, 3; "The End of the Rebellion," *BoL,* April 15, 1865, 4. "This removal by the President takes out of public view the last civilian general known to our armies." "Removal of Gen. Butler," *BoL,* January 21, 1865, 4. War had "virtually ended." "The Great Event," *BoL,* April 22, 1865, 4; "Dissolution of the Union," *BoL,* April 15, 1865, 6; "The End of Rebellion," *BoL,* April 29, 1865, 4; "Capture of Fort Fisher," *BoL,* January 28, 1865, 5; "Over Fort Sumter," *BoL,* April 15, 1865, 4; "Gen. Sheridan," *BoL,* April 15, 1865, 4; Fell, "Mobile," *BoL,* May 6, 1865, 4.

58. "Terrible National Calamity! Murder of President Lincoln!," *BoL,* April 22, 1865, 5; "The National Tragedy," *BoL,* April 29, 1865, 4; Emma Hardinge, *The Great Funeral Oration of Abraham Lincoln, Delivered Sunday, April 10, 1865, at Cooper Institute, New York, before Upwards of Three Thousand Persons* (New York: American News, 1865), 3, 17; Chase, *Forty Years,* 95–96. A few days later, Philadelphia. Henry T. Child, Isaac Rehn, S. J. Finney. "Funeral Solemnities by the Spiritualists of Philadelphia," *BoL,* May 6, 1865, 3; Sarah Belle Dougherty, "Remembering H. S. Olcott," "The Attempted Assassination of Secretary Seward," *BoL,* April 29, 1865, 4; "The Assassins," *BoL,* April 29, 1865, 4; "The President's Assassin," *BoL,* May 6, 1865, 4. On Steele, see *MAS,* 500.

59. *Through Five Administrations: Reminiscences of Colonel William H. Crook,* edited by Margarita Spalding Gerry (New York and London: Harper and Bros., 1910), 69–70;

Harry E. Pratt, "Dr. Anson G. Henry, Lincoln's Physician and Friend," *Lincoln Herald* 45 (October 1943). See J. Emerson, *Madness of Mary Lincoln*, 35–38.

60. Jay Monaghan, "Was Abraham Lincoln Really a Spiritualist?," *Journal of the Illinois State Historical Society* 34 (June 1941) 214; Ward Hill Lamon, *Recollections of Abraham Lincoln, 1847–1865*, edited by Dorothy Lamon Teillard (Washington, D.C.: for the editor, 1911), 121; John G. Nicolay to Jesse W. Weik, November 25, 1894, in *The Real Lincoln: A Portrait*, edited by Michael Burlingame (Lincoln: University of Nebraska Press, 2002), 370; Carl Sandburg, *Abraham Lincoln: The Prairie Years and the War Years*, 394; Herndon and Weik, *Abraham Lincoln*, 3:537, 479, 1:116; Hanks from Emanuel Hertz, *Hidden Lincoln*, 282, 281; Jay Monaghan, *The Lincoln Bibliography, 1839–1939*, 2 vols. (Springfield, Ill.: State Historical Library, 1943, 1945), 1:411; Fleischner, *Mrs. Lincoln and Mrs. Keckly*, 258–59; Martinez, *Psychic Life of Lincoln*, 30.

61. Tilton, *Biography of Woodhull*, 11 (see chap. 1, n. 47); "Colonel Blood & the Fogg Women," http://www.victoria-woodhull.com/blood.htm. His three wives were Mary Ann Clapp Harrington, Victoria Claflin Woodhull, and Isabell Morrill Fogg.

62. Hardinge, *Great Funeral Oration*, 26–27; "The New President," *BoL*, May 6, 1865, 4; F. V. P., "Radicalism," "Conservative," *BoL*, February 7 (p. 5), 14 (p. 4), 1863.

## Chapter 4. Liberty

1. Henry C. Wright to Lincoln, December 16, 1863, *Collected Works of Abraham Lincoln*, edited by Basler, 7:81 (see chap. 3, n. 1).

2. "Wisconsin, Marriages, 1836–1930," index, FamilySearch, https://familysearch.org/pal:/MM9.1.1/XRD3-KWX, Anson B. Severance and Juliet H. Stillman, M.D., May 12, 1869; "The Poor Man's Wife," *BoL*, April 25, 1857, 4. Also account Correspondence with Dr. Joanne Passet, Indiana University East (January 30, 2012). View more information elsewhere at http://www.wisconsinhistory.org/dictionary/index.asp?action=view&term_id=15573&term_type_id=1&term_type_text=People. "Juliet Severance, Radical Victorian," March 17, 2010, http://www.wisconsinhistory.org/odd/archives/002054.asp. For more on Trall, see Spurlock, *Free Love*, 9, 148 (see prologue, n. 12).

3. Coggeshall, *Signs of the Times*, 115–17, 144 (see prologue, n. 9); *MAS*, 147, 166, 200. See also Sollors, "Franklin's Celestial Telegraph," 459–80, esp. 464–65 (see prologue, n. 41). Franklin quoted from the *Daily Magnet*, February 24, 1850; untitled item, *Louisville (Ky.) Daily Journal*, December 13, 1858, 1; *MAS*, 273, 276, 278. See also *STP*, November 18, December 9, 1854, March 3, 1855.

4. William T. Coggeshall, *Poets and Poetry of the West, with Biographical and Critical Notes* (New York: Follett, Foster, 1864); William Denton, *Radical Discourses on Religious Subjects: Delivered in Music Hall, Boston, Mass.* (Boston: for the author, 1872); Spurlock, *Free Love*, 143–44, 147, 165, 218; Doyle, *The History of Spiritualism*, 2:165, 1:148 (see prologue, n. 4); James J. Martin, *Men against the State: The Expositors of Individualist Anarchism in America, 1827–1908* (DeKalb, Ill.: Adrian Allen Associates, 1953), 116. Also Blatt, *Free Love and Anarchism* (see chap. 1, n. 48). See also "Lectures on Geology," *BoL*, April 4, 1863, 4; Denton lecture "Geology," *BoL*, April 11, 1863, 4; "Prof. William Denton in Lyceum Hall," *BoL*, June 13, 1863, 5; William and Elizabeth Denton, from

*Progressive Age,* "'The Soul of Things,'" *BoL,* December 12, 1863, 4; Denton, "Physical Manifestations," *BoL,* December 31, 1864, 4; William Denton, *The Soul of Things* (Boston: Walker, Wise, 1863); *Is Spiritualism True?* (Boston, 1871); and *Radical Discourses on Religious Subjects* (Boston: for the author, 1872); Buescher, "Across the Dead Line," 56, 57–59, 63–64. See also his sister's work Annie Denton Cridge, *Man's Rights; or, How Would You Like It? Comprising Dreams* (Wellesley, Mass.: Mrs. E. M. F. Denton, 1870); J. C. Merriam, "The Fauna of Rancho La Brea," pt. 2, "Canidae," *Memoirs of the University of California* 1, no. 2 (1912): 201–13; "Genesis and Geology," *Christian Spiritualist* 2 (February 2, 1856): 1; "The Earth in Motion; or, The Movements of Continents" (from *Putnam's Monthly*), *Christian Spiritualist* 1 (March 3, 1855): 4.

5. "Professor Hare," *STP,* 5:288; M. Faraday, "Michael Faraday's Researches in Spiritualism," *Scientific Monthly* 83 (September 1956): 145–50; Robert Hare, *Experimental Investigation of the Spirit Manifestations* (New York: Partridge and Brittan, 1855). See also R. Moore, "Spiritualism and Science," 493 (see prologue, n. 24); James A. Secord, *Victorian Sensation: The Extraordinary Publication, Reception, and Secret Authorship of Vestiges of the Natural History of Creation* (Chicago: University of Chicago Press, 2001), 259; Don C. Rawson, "Mendeleev and the Scientific Claims of Spiritualism," *Proceedings of the American Philosophical Society* 122 (February 15, 1978): 1–8; Michael Gordin, *A Well-Ordered Thing: Dmitrii Mendeleev and the Shadow of the Periodic Table* (New York: Basic Books, 2004); Secord, *Victorian Sensation,* 494–95; Malcolm Jay Kottler, "Alfred Russel Wallace: The Origin of Man, and Spiritualism," *Isis* 65 (June 1974): 146–47, 149, 150–56, 170, 171; William S. Keezer, "Alfred Russel Wallace: Naturalist, Zoogeographer, Spiritualist, and Evolutionist," *Bios* 36 (May 1965): 66–70; "Prof. Hare's Letter to the Clergy of the Episcopal Convention," "Prof. Hare's Letter" (from *Fitzgerald's City Item*), *Christian Spiritualist* 2 (June 2, 1855): 2; Robert Hare, "Spiritualism in the Tabernacle: A Descriptive and Philosophical Lecture by Professor Robert Hare," *Christian Spiritualist* 2 (December 1, 1855): 2–3; "Dr. Hare's Lecture at the Tabernacle," *Christian Spiritualist* 2 (November 24, 1855): 2; and "The Lesson of Professor Hare's Lecture," *Christian Spiritualist* 2 (December 1, 1855): 2.

6. *MAS,* 173–83; "The American Scientific Association," *STP* 5 (May, June, July 1854): 112–13, 201; Buescher, *Other Side of Salvation,* 143; R. Moore, "Spiritualism and Science," 494–95, 474–500; "Free Meetings in New York," *BoL,* March 26, 1864, 5. Lieutenant (probably William David) Porter of the navy attended the May gathering of the Washington Conference.

7. "Union of Labor and Capital," *STP,* 4:263; "Spiritual Lyceum and Conference," *Herald of Progress,* June 3, 1860, 3; Mrs. Sara A. Horton of Brandon in "Spiritualism in Vermont," *BoL,* July 27, 1861, 6. In fact, while some saw spiritualism as "the first blow at the gigantic evils of modern Socialism," meaning secularism, Orestes A. Bronson, the repentant radical freethinker turned conservative Catholic, saw spiritualism as a stalking horse for "modern philanthropy, visionary reforms, socialism, and revolutionism." J. M. A., "The Foundation Stone of Reconstruction," *BoL,* January 30, 1864, 2; O. A. Bronson, *The Spirit-Rapper: An Autobiography* (Boston, 1856), vi.

8. Delp, "Andrew Jackson Davis," 44–45 (see prologue, n. 9). On Brisbane, see Blanchard, *Life of Thomas Paine,* 89 (see prologue, n. 48).

9. On Davis, see Dodworth Hall for January 17, 1854. On Brisbane, "A New Work on the Social Sciences," *Nichols Monthly* (August 1856): 283–85.

10. "Spiritual Lyceum and Conference," *Herald of Progress*, June 3, 1860, 3; "Spiritual Lyceum and Conference," *Herald of Progress*, June 16, 1860, 3.

11. "The New York Conference," *STP*, 3:579. On Hamilton, see "'The Spirit of Reformers,'" *BoL*, October 1, 1859, 7.

12. S. B. Brittan, "The Gospel of Harmony," Warren Chase, October 17, 1853, "Letter from Winsted," and "Harmonial Convention," *STP*, 2:331–35, 3:40, 4:53, 58.

13. R. H. Brown, "The Signs of the Times," *STP*, 8:262, 260–64.

14. Davis in "Spiritual Lyceum and Conference," *Herald of Progress*, June 3, 1860, 3, and "Spiritual Lyceum and Conference," *Herald of Progress*, June 30, 1860, 3; Thompson in "Spiritual Lyceum and Conference," *Herald of Progress*, July 7, 1860, 3; from the *Regenerator*, in *Young America*, February 14, 1846, and, for Davis, "Curious Infidel Movement in the United States" (from *Spirit Messenger*), *New York Daily Herald*, June 10, 1851, 3. Born 1801, native of Dracut, Middlesex, Massachusetts, married in Vermont

15. "Reconstruction—Religious, Political and Social: A Lecture Delivered through and by L. Judd Pardee, at Lyceum Hall, Boston, Sunday Evening, July 17th, 1864," *BoL*, August 6, 1864, 2; "Infidelity and Fidelity," *BoL*, February 28, 1863, 8; "Lectures by Leo Mille, Esq.," *BoL*, March 7, 1863, 4; "Progressive Convention: An Interesting Session of Three Days," *BoL*, October 10, 1863, 3; [The spirit of George Washington,] "A Warning Voice," *STP*, 4:203–4; "Cora L. V. Hatch: At the Music Hall, Boston, Sept. 4th, 1859," *BoL*, October 8, 1859, 7. Union soldier in Chicago heard Leo Miller's lecture on the Sabbath. "Daily in contact with rebel prisoners of war at Camp Douglas." H. S., "Suggestions from a Soldier," *BoL*, July 9, 1864, 3.

16. "Col. Cowdin Turned Slave-Catcher," *BoL*, July 20, 1861, 4; "Lecture by Dr. Cheever, in New York City, Dec. 1st, 1861," *BoL*, Dec. 14, 1861, 6. From Port Royal letter, "de Lord would bress dese damned Yankees." He had never heard them referred to differently. "The Negro's Prayer" under "All Sorts of Paragraphs," *BoL*, March 8, 1862, 5.

17. "The President's Message," *BoL*, April 5, 1862, 4; C. D. Griswold, "Intolerance," *BoL*, April 12, 1862, 2. 2. Baltimore American complains of the institution's demise owing to the war. "Slavery in Maryland," *BoL*, April 26, 1862, 5.

18. Objections to this, "Sending Back the Slaves," *BoL*, June 14, 1862, 4; "Smoked Out," *BoL*, June 14, 1862, 4. Congress discussing the recognition of Haiti, untitled, *BoL*, June 14, 1862, 5. Praises Lincoln for repudiating Hunter's emancipation, "The Hunter Proclamation," *BoL*, May 31, 1862, 4; Horace Dresser, "Letter to Secretary Seward: Rights Belonging to National Citizenship," *BoL*, November 8, 1862, 3. See also "Emancipation Proclamation," *BoL*, October 4, 1862, 8; "The Emancipation Proclamation," contrasting it with the British, "Civil War," *BoL*, October 25, 1862, 5; "Our Country," *BoL*, December 13, 1862, 4; "The President's Emancipation Proclamation," *BoL*, January 10, 1863, 8. Henry C. Wright to Abraham Lincoln, December 16, 1863, return care of Wendell Phillips. See also Wright, *Defensive War Proved to Be a Denial of Christianity and of the Government of God* (London: C. Gilpin, 1846).

19. "Charity for One Another," *BoL*, January 10, 1863, 8.

20. "Emancipation" and "Fraternity Lecture," *BoL,* April 11, November 21, 1863 (both p. 4).

21. The paper gave various spellings of this writer's name, but see Wilfrid Wylley, "The Terrible Contest in Virginia," Wilfred Wylleye, "A Voice from the Army," Wilfrid Wylleye, poem "Farewell, Monitor," Wilfrid Wylleys, "From an Unpublished Poem," and Wilfrid Wylleys (from Milan, Ohio), "The Canadians and the United States" *BoL,* September 13 (p. 8), October 25 (p. 8), 1862, January 24 (p. 3), March 28 (p. 3), September 5 (p. 8), 1863.

22. C. D. S., "A Congress of Nations," and S. B. Brittan, "Who Rules the World?," *STP,* 5:443, 440–43, 8:103–6; "The Nobleness of Labor," "The Danger to Liberty," Frederick Robinson on "The True Benefactors of Humanity," "Progressive Convention, an Interesting Session of Three Days [Concluded]," and untitled item, *BoL,* October 29 (p. 3), 1859, March 15 (p. 4), 1862, December 13 (p. 5), 1862, October 17 (p. 3), 1863, January 2 (p. 5), 1864.

23. "Gen. Grant," "Gen. Grant's Campaign," "Grant's Victory," "A Lieutenant-General," "Lieut. General Grant," "Gen. Grant," "Grant with the Troops," "'Fight It Out,'" "The Morning Battle," "Something That Is Real," "Gen. Grant's Work," "Grant's Operations," "Grant's Movements," "The Lieutenant General," *BoL,* July 18 (p. 4), November 28 (p. 4), December 12 (p. 4), 1863, February 27 (p. 4), March 19 (p. 4), 26 (p. 5), April 9 (p. 4), May 28 (p. 4), June 18 (p. 4), 25 (p. 4), July 2 (p. 5), 9 (p. 4), October 22 (p. 4), 1864, February 25 (p. 4), 1865.

24. William H. De Camp [Michigan Engineers and Mechanics Regiment], "White Slaves of the South," *BoL,* September 19, 1863, 4.

25. Wilfrid Wylleys, "Thoughts for the Times," *BoL,* October 10, 1863, 2.

26. "The War in Florida," "The Colored Regiment," Elizur Wright in *New York Post,* "Troops for the Tropics," "The Negro as a Soldier," "Black Regiments," "Negro Cavalry," and noting John M. Langston's working with Major Stearns to recruit "Colored Soldiers," "A New Plan for Volunteers," *BoL,* February 21, April 18, May 16, June 6, September 19, October 10, 31, 1863, December 12, 1863, all 4.

27. "Negro Intelligence," the discussion from the *Mobile Register,* as given in an untitled item, "Rebel Bloodhounds," "The Black Troops," "The Fort Pillow Massacre," *BoL,* August 15 (p. 4), November 28 (p. 5), December 19 (p. 4), 1863, April 16 (p. 5), 30 (p. 4), 1864; Hardinge, *Great Funeral Oration,* 17 (see chap. 3, n. 58).

28. "Reconstruction—Religious, Political and Social: A Lecture Delivered through and by L. Judd Pardee, at Lyceum Hall, Boston, Sunday Evening, July 17th, 1864," *BoL,* August 6, 1864, 2; Ira B. Davis and Fowler from "Spiritual Lyceum and Conference," *Herald of Progress,* respectively June 3 (p. 3), 16 (pp. 3, 4), 1860.

29. W. S. Courtney, "Individual Sovereignty," *Journal of Progress* 1 (April 30, 1853): 3–4.

30. O. W. Holmes, "The Autocrat at War," *BoL,* September 28, 1861, 4.

31. "Haunted," "The New Mania," "The Rich Man and the Disinherited Hero?," "No Speculation," *BoL,* May 30 (p. 4), October 17 (p. 4), 1863, January 2 (p. 1), October 1 (p. 4), 1864.

32. Warren Chase, "Hard Times," *BoL,* October 5, 1861, 8; "Labor and Prices," *BoL,* January 17, 1863, 4.

33. "The Danger to Liberty," *BoL,* March 15, 1862, 4; *New York Herald* quoted; "'Shoddy' in the Park," *BoL,* November 7, 1863, 4.

34. "'Shoddy in the Park,'" "The Use of Shams," "The Bondage of Debt," *BoL,* November 7, 14, 1863, May 7, 1864, all 4. Andrew Barrows, taking leave of son in the cavalry, mentioned "the bigotry, ingratitude and self shoddy of earth, but arrayed in the bright and beautiful garments of spiritual life." "Spiritual Faith and Patriotism," *BoL,* January 28, 1865, 8.

35. Sarah Belle Dougherty, "Remembering H. S. Olcott," Theosophical Society, posted at http://www.theosociety.org/pasadena/sunrise/46-96-7/th-sbdo.htm.

36. "The Foundation of Governments, and Ownership of Property: A Lecture Delivered before the Religio-Philosophical Society of Des Moines, Iowa, Sunday, May, 1864, by B. N. Kinyon," *BoL,* May 6, 1865, x.

37. "Conspiracy against Society," *BoL,* November 21, 1863, 4; "Speculators at Work," *BoL,* May 21, 1864, 4. Also "Gold Speculation," *BoL,* April 18, 1863, 4.

38. "The Poor," *BoL,* January 19, 1861, 4; "Description of a Coal Mine," *BoL,* April 14, 1860, 4; "Town's-Poor," *BoL,* January 10, 1863, 4; "The Poor," *BoL,* November 19, 1864, 2.

39. "Real Riches," "Labor and Prices," "Compensation: A Lecture by Henry T. Child, M.D., Delivered at the Phenix Street Church, Philadelphia, Nov. 8th, 1863," "Wealth and Riches," *BoL,* March 1 (p. 4), 1862, January 17 (p. 4), November 28 (p. 8), 1863, December 31 (p. 4), 1864.

40. Noe in "Spiritual Lyceum and Conference," *Herald of Progress,* June 3, 1860, 3; "Wages and Want," *BoL,* April 14, 1860, 4; Partridge in "Spiritual Lyceum and Conference," *Herald of Progress,* June 23, 1860, 3.

41. Kinyon's "The Poor," *BoL,* July 16, 1864, 2; "The Poor: Number Two," *BoL,* November 12, 1864, 2.

42. "The Rights of Labor," *BoL,* April 18, 1863, 4.

43. "Concerning Maternity," *BoL,* June 27, 1863, 4. See also Juliet H. Stillman, "Hints on Dress," *BoL,* January 28, 1865, 2

44. Lizzie Doten, "A Plea for the Working Women," E. W., "The Maternity Question," Warren Chase, "Woman's Work and Woman's Wages," *BoL,* May 10 (p. 4), 1862, January 16 (p. 3), 1864, April 22 (p. 4), 1865. See also Sarah A. Southworth, "The Two Sisters; or, The Little Match Girl," *BoL,* January 24, 1863, 1; and "Aged Indigent Females," *BoL,* April 8, 1865, 5.

45. Buescher, *Remarkable Life of John Murray Spear,* 235, 237–38, 240–42 (see prologue, n. 31); "Sewing Machines," two pieces entitled "The Sewing Women" and two entitled "The Laboring Women," *BoL,* August 30, 1862, December 12, 1863, January 30, April 23, June 18, 1864, all on 4. For a statement of those wages, see "Women and Work," *BoL,* December 5, 1863, 4. See also Bella Bush, "A Song for the Army of Knitters," *BoL,* December 20, 1862, 4, poem.

46. Lizzie Doten, "A Plea for the Working Women," Bella Bush poem, "A Song for the Army of Knitters," "The Sewing Girls," "Proceedings of the Yearly Meeting of Progressive Friends," H. F. M. Brown, "A Few Questions," "The Working Women's Relief

Association," *BoL*, May 10 (p. 4), December 20 (p. 4), 1862, November 28 (p. 4), 1863, July 9 (p. 3), 23 (p. 3), September 17 (p. 4), 1864. See also "Boston Spiritual Conference," "The Marriage Question," "Libertinism and Licentiousness," "Free Love," "Dr. A. B. Child's Letter," D. S. Hamilton, "True Marriage—the Hope of the World," "Unhappy Families," "Versatility of Employment," "The Working Women's Relief Association: An Acknowledgement," Horton, "From Another Washington Correspondent," Cora Wilburn, "The Wrongs of Needle Women," *BoL*, May 11 (p. 6), December 28 (p. 5), 1861, February 8 (p. 5), May 3 (p. 4), 1862, January 10 (p. 3), February 7 (p. 2), July 4 (p. 4), December 5 (p. 4), 1863, November 5 (p. 4), December 24 (p. 3), 1864, February 11 (p. 8), 1865, 8. Warren Chase noted C. S. Woodruff's book *Legalized Prostitution*. "A pioneer in the great social and Harmonial regeneration and reformation of society," "Legalized Prostitution," *BoL*, April 11, 1863, 5, and on through June 20, 1863, 7; "Andrew B. Smolnikar," *Christian Spiritualist* 1 (August 26, 1854): 2.

47. "The Labor Question," *BoL*, November 15, 1862, 4; B. N. Kinyon of Des Moines, June 9, "The Poor," *BoL*, July 16, 1864, 2. "The Poor: Number Two," *BoL*, November 12, 1864, 2. "The Rich Man and the Disinherited Hero?," *BoL*, January 2, 1864, 1. See also B. N. Kinyon, "Spiritualism in Des Moines, Iowa," *BoL*, November 19, 1864, 3; and "Discussion at Des Moines, Iowa," *BoL*, December 17, 1864, 8; *The History of Polk County, Iowa* (Des Moines, Iowa: Union Historical, Birdsall, Williams, 1880), 967.

48. "National Spiritualist Convention, Oswego, N.Y., Aug. 13 to 18, 1861," *BoL*, Sept. 7, 1861, 3; Andrews, "Spiritual Lyceum and Conference," *Herald of Progress*, June 16, 1860, 3; "The Question for the Future," *BoL*, December 31, 1864, 4.

49. "Rich Poor People," "Property in All Things," *BoL*, October 19 (p. 4), 1861, April 25 (p. 4), 1863.

50. Warren Chase, "Political," *BoL*, July 25, 1863, 4; Chase, *Forty Years*, 81, 82–87, 88, 89–95, 99 (see prologue, n. 18). For reports of Chase's activities in the *BoL*, see Chase, "The Union and Its Parties," two lectures in Boston called "The Present Rebellion and Its Results," and "Lecture by Hon. Warren Chase," "Picture of Our Future," "Letter from a Sick Soldier," "Out in the Cold," "A Trip to the Cities," "Why?," "Political," and H. F. M. Brown, "Persons and Places—No. 6," "Ohio," "Reform Convention at Evansville, Rock Co. Wisconsin," "What Next?," "Mediums and Lectures," "Elkhart, Ind.," and Chase, "The Rebellion," J. N. Wilson, "Spiritualism in Bloomington, Ill.," "Cairo, Ill.," *BoL*, June 22 (p. 7), 1861, September 21 (p. 5), December 13 (p. 4), 27 (p. 3), 1862, February 21 (p. 4), March 7 (p. 4), June 27 (p. 3), July 25 (p. 4), August 22 (p. 3), 29 (p. 3), September 19 (p. 8), October 24 (p. 4), November 7 (p. 3), 14 (p. 3), December 5 (p. 4), 12 (p. 3), 1863, January 9 (p. 3), 1864.

## Chapter 5. Equality

1. "The Times," *BoL*, May 18, 1861, 4; "The Foundation of Governments, and Ownership of Property: A Lecture Delivered before the Religio-Philosophical Society of Des Moines, Iowa, Sunday, May, 1864, by B. N. Kinyon," *BoL*, May 6, 1865, x; Cora L. V. Tappan, *Boston Standard*, May 29, 1869, quoted in Kerber, "Abolitionist Perception of the Indian," 295, cited in Elliot West, "Reconstructing Race," *Western Historical Quarterly* 34, no. 1 (2003): 47.

2. Accounts of the "Spiritual Lyceum and Conference," *Herald of Progress*, June 16, July 7, 1860, both 3; Wattles from "Conference at the Telegraph Office," *STP,* 6:181.

3. I. Rehn, "What Is Spiritualism?," *BoL,* April 29, 1865, 3. See also "Spiritual Phenomena: Translations from the 'Revue Spirite,'" *BoL,* November 7, 1863, 3.

4. Fishbough quoted in "The New York Conference," *STP,* 4:104; "The New York Conference," *STP,* 4:294; Gerald Massey, "The Kingliest King," *BoL,* February 16, 1861, 5; "Gerrit Smith," *BoL,* September 24, 1859, 4.

5. Spiritualists made the involvement of freethinkers easier by confirming that some of the most prominent of those who had died had returned to confirm the spiritualist view of an afterlife. See also the series "The First Experience of Voltaire as a Spirit," *BoL,* starting in February 1865.

6. Harvey A. Jones, "Report of the Third Annual Convention of the Illinois State Spiritual Association," *BoL,* August 15, 1868, 3; Wilder, *New Platonism and Alchemy* (see prologue, n. 25). General Ethan Allen Hitchcock, the longtime superintendent of the U.S. Military Academy at West Point and an associate of Pascal B. Randolph, became more famously known as the father of American alchemy.

7. Buescher, *Other Side of Salvation,* 63–64, as well as his *Remarkable Life of John Murray Spear* (see prologue, n. 31). On Smolnikar, see Jon Alexander and David Williams, "Andreas Bernardus Smolnikar: American Catholic Apostate and Millennial Prophet," *American Benedictine Review* 35 (March 1985): 50–63. See also Andrew B. Smolnikar, *Secret Enemies of True Republicanism* (Springhill, Pa.: R. D. Eldridge, 1859). For John H. W. Toohey's reply to Mr. Matthias, arguing for the compatibility of spiritualism with Christianity, see "New York Conference," *STP,* 8:160.

8. *MAS,* 248 on Spence, and 242–43. See also Hugh B. Urban, *Magia Sexualis: Sex, Magic, and Liberation in Modern Western Esotericism* (Berkeley: University of California Press, 2006).

9. Parker Pillsbury, "Faith and Patience," in *The Liberty Bell by Friends of Freedom* (Boston: National Anti-Slavery Bazaar, 1858), 204–5. Takes issue with Louis Agassiz over diverse human origins. "Origin of Man," *Spiritual Philosopher* 1 (July 1850): 12.

10. "National Spiritualist Convention, Oswego, N.Y., Aug. 13 to 18, 1861," *BoL,* August 31, 1861, 8; Giles Badger Stebbins, *Chapters from the Bible of the Ages* (Detroit, 1872).

11. Delp, "Andrew Jackson Davis," 45 (see prologue, n. 9). In addition to the sources cited above, see, for the slavery issue, John R. McKivigan, *The War against Proslavery Religion: Abolition and the Northern Churches, 1830–1863* (Ithaca, N.Y.: Cornell University Press, 1984), esp. 27, 50.

12. Quoted in Deveney, *Paschal Beverly Randolph,* 2, 5, 3–4. 8, 101, 373n1, 374n5 (see prologue, n. 19); Chase, *Life-Line of the Lone One,* 217; "Harmonial Convention," *STP,* 4:52; Deveney, *Paschal Beverly Randolph,* 8, 12–13, 16, 22, 25, 19–21, 26, 99–100. See also Stephen Pearl Andrews, *Discoveries in Chinese* (New York: Charles B. Norton, 1854); Barbara White, *The Beecher Sisters* (New Haven, Conn.: Yale University Press, 2003), 12–13, 15–21, 29, 31–33, 48–59, 62–65, 67–71, 77–88, 89, 92–99; Buescher, *Remarkable Life of John Murray Spear,* 132; "The Three Days' Festival at St. Charles, Ill.: A Brief Synopsis of the Exercises, Reported for the *Banner of Light* by L. K. Coonley," *BoL,* Oct. 19, 1861, 3; "Boston Spiritual Conference," *BoL,* November 10, 1860, 5; A. W. Sprague, "Abuse of Exhilarating Gas in Surgery," *Scientific American* 9 (December 5, 1863): 358;

C. M. P., "Spirit-ous vs. Spiritu-al," *Herald of Progress,* November 24, 1860, 4; Achsa White Sprague, *The Poet, & Other Poems* (Boston, 1864); Leonard Twynham, "Achsa W. Sprague," *Proceedings of the Vermont Historical Society* 9 (December 1941): 271–79; "Selections from Achsa W. Sprague's Diary and Journal, Ed. Twynham," *Proceedings of the Vermont Historical Society* 9 (September 1941): 131–84.

13. Chase letter December 5, 1853, "Letter from Troy," *STP,* 3:358; "A Good Fact," *STP,* 5:400–401; Deveney, *Paschal Beverly Randolph,* 101–2; *Tribute of Respect, Commemorative of the Worth and Sacrifice of John Brown . . . by the Citizens of Cleveland,* 23–24; "The New Catholic Church" and "Letter from Dr. Child, of Philadelphia," *BoL,* March 28 (p. 4), 1863, December 3 (p. 3), 1864.

14. "Spiritual Lyceum and Conference," *Herald of Progress,* June 3, 1860, 3.

15. Warren B. Chase, "1861," Chase, "Hospital, Camp M'Kim," "Letter from Savannah, Ga.," Cora Wilburn, "Western Sanitary Fair," "Spiritualism and the Sanitary Fair," "The Boston Sanitary Commission," "The Western Sanitary Fair," *BoL,* January 11 (p. 8), February 22 (p. 4), 1862, January 14 (p. 8), April 1 (p. 3), 15 (p. 4), 22 (p. 4), 29 (p. 4), 1865. Service record for Milton Chase.

16. Professor Henry Cowles of Oberlin to John Pierpont, March 6, 1863, Lincoln Papers; "The Chances of Slavery" and M. J. Wilcoxsen, "Among the Freemen," *BoL,* December 12, 1863, July 9, 1864, both 4.

17. *WALS,* 144–45, 198–200.

18. A. Horton, "Letter from Washington," G. A. B., "Our Washington Letter—Warren Chase's Lectures—Finances, etc.," "Letter from Dr. Child of Philadelphia," and Warren Chase, "The Lybian Sibyl; or, Sojourner Truth," *BoL,* September 17 (p. 3), 1864, February 11 (p. 8), 1865.

19. Robert Dale Owen, head of committee reporting to president. Reports recommendation, "The Case of the Freedmen," *BoL,* August 22, 1863, 4; Robert Dale Owen, "The Claims to Service or Labor," *Atlantic,* July 1863, 116–25, with notice of "Robert Dale Owen," *BoL,* July 11, 1863, 4, and, later, Owen's *The Wrong of Slavery, the Right of Emancipation, and the Future of the African Race in the United States* (Philadelphia: J. B. Lippincott, 1864); *WALS,* 128, 135; G. A. B., Washington, "The *Banner*—the Spiritual Cause—Colored Schools, etc.," A. J. Higgins, "Nature vs. Drugs," and "First Semi-annual Report of the Association of Volunteer Teachers of Washington and Vicinity," *BoL,* April 9 (p. 4), 1864, January 14 (p. 2), 28 (p. 5), 1865.

20. Alfred Horton, "Letter from Washington," *BoL,* May 16, 1863, 2–3.

21. Two of Horton's under "Letter from Washington," *BoL,* May 21 (p. 4), 1864, January 7 (p. 3), 1865. One wonders what it meant to say, "Monazolappa is the only exclusively African realm that I have ever seen in the spirit-world." A. J. Davis, *Death and the After-Life,* 66 (see chap. 2, n. 43); L. K. Coonley, "Notes by Dr. Coonley," *BoL,* April 4, 1863, 3.

22. Mary Todd Lincoln to Abraham Lincoln, November 2, 1862. For more on the relationship between Keckley and Mary Lincoln, see Baker, *Mary Todd Lincoln* (see chap. 3, n. 30); and Elizabeth Keckley, *Behind the Scenes; or, Thirty Years a Slave and Four Years in the White House* (New York: G. W. Carlton, 1868); Mary Todd Lincoln to Abraham Lincoln, November 3, 1862.

23. Dresser, "Letter to Secretary Seward: The Vice of the Constitution," *BoL,* May 31, 1862, 2.

24. Sollors, "Franklin's Celestial Telegraph," 461, 480 (see prologue, n. 41), naming Black Hawk, Osceola, King Philip, Red Jacket, Logan, Powhatan, Samoset, Coacoochie, Ke-che Bezhe-kee (Big Buffalo), Spotted Tail, Great Turtle, Pocahontas, and "Arrowhead the Terrible," 5; William M. Johnston's letter (August 6), "Indian Chees-a-kees; or, Spiritualists," *BoL,* November 5, 1859, 3. See also A. Irving Hallowell, *The Rôle of Conjuring in Salteaux Society* (Philadelphia: University of Pennsylvania Press, 1942). The *Banner* praised Mary Langdon's new novel, *Agnes,* for having made Indians essential characters, *BoL,* Oct. 9, 1858, 4. Louis Alphonse Cahagnet, *The Celestial Telegraph* (New York and Rochester: D. M. Dewey, J. S. Redfield, 1851). Translated from the original French *Magnétisme: Arcanes de la vie future dévoilés* (Paris: L'Auteur, 1848).

25. J. M. Peebles, "Notes in and Out of New York," *BoL,* August 6, 1864, 3; John Beeson, "Are the Indians to Be Exterminated?," *BoL,* August 15, 1863, 2.

26. Quote from J. M. Peebles, "From Whence the Indians," *BoL,* October 24, 1863, 2–3, but see also "The Indians' Influence in Spirit Life," "Father Beeson and the Indians," Cora Wilburn, "Thanksgiving at Beeson's," "The Indians," "Spiritualism and the Indians," A. Quails, "An Incident of the Minnesota War," *BoL,* June 22 (p. 6), October 5 (p. 5), December 14 (p. 6), 1861, August 23 (p. 4), October 18 (p. 3), 1862, January 31 (p. 1), 1863.

27. Cora Wilburn, November 28, 1861, "Thanksgiving and Beeson in Philadelphia," *BoL,* December 14, 1861, 6; "Going Back to Barbarism," *BoL,* April 5, 1862, 4. "Dishonest is evidently in majority," declared the *Banner,* adding, "No doubts the Old Abe is honest. The less one knows of official matters here the better, if he would retain a good opinion of all parties and persons concerned in the Government." Warren Chase, "Washington, D.C.," *BoL,* February 11, 1865, 3.

28. "The Indian Movement," letter of size in *BoL,* November 20, 1858, 5.

29. Ibid.; letter on Indians, *BoL,* December 11, 1858, 8.

30. "Vermont State Spiritual Convention," "Meeting on Behalf of the Indians on the Western Frontier," "The Indians," John Beeson, "An Address to the People of the United States in Behalf of the Indians," "The Causes of the Indians," *BoL,* September 17 (p. 5), October 1 (p. 4), 22 (p. 5), 29 (p. 7), 1859, September 29 (p. 2), 1860, 2.

31. Several pieces under the heading "Spiritual Conference at Clinton Hall, New York," *BoL,* April 27 (pp. 6–7), May 18 (p. 6), September 28 (p. 6), 1861; "Thanksgiving and Beeson in Philadelphia," *BoL,* December 14 (p. 6), 1861.

32. Annie Heloise Abel, *The American Indian as Participant in the Civil War,* 225; *Journal of the Senate of the United States of America, Being the First Session of the Thirty-Eighth Congress, Begun and Held at the City of Washington, December 7, 1863* (Washington, D.C.: Government Printing Office, 1863), 269–70, 318.

33. "A Plea for the Red Man," *BoL,* December 17, 1864, 3.

34. "The Indians' Influence in Spirit Life," *BoL,* June 22, 1861, 6; "Communication from Tecumseh," *BoL,* December 12, 1863, 3.

35. A. Quails, "An Incident of the Minnesota War," two entitled "The Indians," "Free Spiritual Meetings in Washington Proposed," "Are the Indians to Be Exterminated?," with H. Bronson, "Indian Remedy," J. M. Peebles, "From Whence the Indians?," "The

Indians," *BoL,* January 31 (p. 1), February 7 (p. 4), 21 (p. 4), May 2 (p. 3), August 15 (pp. 2, 8), October 24 (p. 2), November 7 (p. 4), 1863.

36. Wilburn, "Visit to Starved Rock," two by Beeson as "Religion of the Savages, a Reality," "Religion of the Savages a Reality," Beeson to "The National Convention," Wilburn, "The Convention—Spiritual Séance.—A Plea for the Indians" with "The Indians," Jane M. Jackson, "A Few Words for the Indians," F. L. Hildreth, "A Plea for the Red Man," "The Indians," and "Soul Harmony between the Sexes," *BoL,* May 14 (p. 3), June 11 (p. 3), 18 (p. 3), July 30 (p. 4, 8), September 3 (p. 3), November 12 (p. 2), December 17 (p. 3), 1864, January 28 (p. 4), February 25 (p. 3), 1865.

37. "Meeting in Behalf of the Indians," "The Meeting in Behalf of the Indians: Held in U.S. House of Representatives," and "The Wrongs of the Indians," *BoL,* March 26 (p. 5), April 2 (pp. 2–3), 23 (p. 3), 1864. Investigations of Special Agents Augustus Wattles and George E. H. Day, negotiations with the Chippewa Indians, accounts of Agent Alexander H. McKisick of the Wichita Agency, claim of Henry Glowacki for compensation for service as special agent for the Tonawanda Indians of New York, loyalty of Indians in the Southern Superintendency and assistance to refugee Indians, and application for appointment of Elijah White, 1857–63. Special Files of the Office of Indian Affairs, 1807–1904, M574 (1965), 85 reels.

38. "The Meeting in Behalf of the Indians: Held in U.S. House of Representatives," *BoL,* April 2, 1864, 3.

39. Untitled item, *BoL,* January 21, 1865, 5; City Hall at San Jose, Beeson, J. J. Own, ed. Mercury; "The Indians," *BoL,* January 21, 1865, 5.

40. Excerpt from Daily Mail appended to "Spiritualists Convention," *New York Herald,* August 8, 1852, 4. Or "Spiritualists Convention," *New York Herald,* August 8, 1852, 4.

41. Barrett, *Life Work of Mrs. Cora L. V. Richmond,* 2 (see chap. 1, n. 53); "The Old Spiritualist.—No. 11. Mrs. Hatch," *BoL,* June 11, 1859, 5; R. Moore, "Spiritualist Medium," 212–13, 215–17 (see prologue, n. 34); "B. F. Hatch, M.D., in His Own Defense," *BoL,* January 19, 1859, 6; John F. McClymer, "Who Is Mrs. Ada T. P. Foat? And Why Should Historians Care? An Historical Reading of Henry James' *The Bostonian,*" *Journal of the Gilded Age and Progressive Era* 2 (2003): 191–217.

42. On Underhill, see the sources cited in Mark Lause, *The Antebellum Crisis and America's First Bohemians* (Kent, Ohio: Kent State University Press, 2009), 29–30, 48–49, 65–67, 123–26; "Let Them Be Heard," *STP,* 2:286, 285–86.

43. "Spiritual Convention" [from *Journal*], *Boston Herald,* August 7, 1852, 2; "Affairs about Home" and "Spiritual Convention," *Boston Herald,* August 7, 1852, 2, 4; and less either. Excerpt from *Daily Mail* appended to "Spiritualists Convention," *New York Herald,* August 8, 1852, 4; or "Spiritualists Convention," *New York Herald,* August 8, 1852, 4. Henry Clay's spirit, speaking through a young woman, said that her mediumship "is unknown, but she will be known." Dodworth Hall for February 14, 1854, "The New York Conference," *STP,* 4:150.

44. On Owen, see Spurlock, *Free Love,* 29–30, 39–41 (see prologue, n. 12). See also "Reformatory: Speech of Rev. William B. Greene, of Brookfield, in the Constitutional Convention of Massachusetts, on the Question of Allowing the Women of the Commonwealth

to Vote on the Amended Constitution," *Liberator* 23 (August 19, 1853): 132. See also Alexander Wilder, *Plea for the Liberal Education of Women* (New York: Judson, 1884).

45. Letter by "J." under "Social Equality," *Herald of Progress*, August 4, 1860, 2–3; "Woman's Rights," *Christian Spiritualist* 1 (October 14, 1854): 4; "Good Resolutions," *Spiritual Philosopher* 1 (November 2, 1850): 111.

46. "A Move in the Right Direction," *BoL*, September 17, 1864, 4; "Homes for the Laboring Class," *BoL*, December 17, 1864, 4.

47. "A Spiritual Villain," *Boston Herald*, January 4, 1862, 2; untitled item [from *Exchange*], *New Orleans Daily Picayune*, August 23, 1862, 2.

48. Albanese, "On the Matter of Spirit," 9–10 (see prologue, n. 24); James A. Clay, "'As a Man Thinketh, So Is He'" [from *Northern Home Journal*], *Christian Spiritualist* 1 (September 9, 1854): 4.

49. Molly McGarry, "Spectral Sexualities: Nineteenth-Century Spiritualism, Moral Panics, and the Making of U.S. Obscenity law," *Journal of Women's History* 12 (Summer 2000): 8–29; "Morals and Legislation," *BoL*, June 2, 1860, 4; Buescher, *Other Side of Salvation*, 154–55, 157. See also Spurlock, *Free Love*, 142–43, 157–58, 173–74, 209, 219–20; Barrett, *Life Work of Mrs. Cora L. V. Richmond*, 4, 5–6, 6–7, 24, 30–31, 47–48, 51; R. Moore, "Spiritualist Medium," 212–13, 215–17. See also A. T. Andreas, *History of Chicago: From the Earliest Period to the Present Time, in Three Volumes*, vol. 3, *From the Fire of 1871 until 1885* (Chicago: A. T. Andreas, 1886), 831–32; "The Old Spiritualist.—No. 11. Mrs. Hatch," *BoL*, June 11, 1859, 5; Barrett, *Life Work of Mrs. Cora L. V. Richmond*, xvii, 7–8; Andreas, *History of Chicago*, 3:831–32; Buescher, *Other Side of Salvation*, 154–55, 157, 159; Tatiana Kontou, *Spiritualism and Women's Writing: From the Fin de Siècle to the Neo-Victorian* (Houndmills, Basingstoke, Hampshire: Palgrave Macmillan, 2009).

50. Quoted in Albanese, "On the Matter of Spirit," 11. For the *Banner*'s drive for respectability in marriage, Hal D. Sears, *The Sex Radicals: Free Love in High Victorian America* (Lawrence: University Press of Kansas, 1977), 21–22.

51. Lucius A. Hine, "Relation of Marriage to Greatness" [from *Phrenological Journal*], *Spiritual Philosopher* 1 (December 21, 1850): 189–91. See also "A Scandal in Bohemia: Free Love and the Antebellum American Culture Wars," chapter 2 in *The Antebellum Political Crisis & the First American Bohemians*, by Mark Lause (Kent, Ohio: Kent State University Press, 2009).

52. Urban, *Magia Sexualis*; Françoise Basch, "Women's Rights and the Wrongs of Marriage in Mid-Nineteenth-Century America," *History Workshop*, no. 22 (Autumn 1986): 29–32; John Spurlock, "The Free Love Network in America, 1850 to 1860," *Journal of Social History* 21 (Summer 1988): 765–79.

53. Child, *Whatever Is, Is Right*, 19, 73. In short, overwork shortens the life that enslaves us to the material world.

54. Discussion of Hardinge's project, "A Spicy Correspondence," "Miss Hardinge's Enterprise in Behalf of Homeless and Outcast Females," "The Home for Outcast Females," "A Real Lady," Warren Chase, "Abandoned Women," "A Vision of Emma Hardinge," "Emma Hardinge, to Her Friends in America," "Emma Hardinge," Warren Chase, "The Fugitive Wife," "Emma Hardinge," "Fallen Women: Lecture by Mrs. Emma Hardinge," *BoL*, May 5 (pp. 2–3), August 11 (p. 3), 1860, April 13 (p. 1), June 15 (p. 8), 1861, May 10

(p. 4), 1862, January 3 (p. 2), April 4 (p. 3), September 19 (p. 8), October 17 (p. 4), 1863, January 30 (p. 2), September 10 (p. 4), 1864, April 13 (pp. 1–2), 1867; "The Lost Ones of the Cities," *New York Times*, February 25, 1862, 2. She at Cincinnati, untitled item, *Louisville (Ky.) Daily Journal*, December 13, 1858, 1. Hardinge's project involved not only out-of-town spiritualists, such as Isaac Rhen and Henry T. Child, but also such prominent endorsers as James Russell Lowell, Mrs. Julia Ward Howe, James Freeman Clark, and Henry Wadsworth Longfellow.

55. "The Widow's Mite," "Starve, Steal or Beg," "True Benevolence," "Bread Ticket Fund," "Bread for the Destitute Poor?," "Bread for the Poor," "The Poor," "Winter and the Poor," "The Suffering Poor," *BoL*, October 17 (p. 4), November 7 (p. 8), December 5 (p. 4), 1863, April 2 (p. 4), September (p. 3), October 15 (p. 4), November 19 (p. 2), December 17 (p. 4), 31 (p. 4), 1864.

56. "Boston Spiritual Conference," "The Woman Question," "Women and Work," "The Sewing Women," "The Laboring Women," "Not the Way to Save a Country," "The Laboring Women," "The Working Women's Relief Association," Cora Wilburn, "The Wrongs of Needle-Women," *BoL*, May 11 (p. 6), 1861, July 18 (p. 4), December 5 (p. 4), 1863, January 30 (p. 4), April 23 (p. 4), May 21 (p. 4), June 18 (p. 4), November 5 (p. 4), December 24 (p. 3), 1864, as well as Judge Boardman's challenge to the "old mosaic dispensation" that left women "classed with idiots and Negroes." "The Three Days' Festival at St. Charles, Ill.: A Brief Synopsis of the Exercises, Reported for the *Banner of Light* by L. K. Coonley," *BoL*, October 19, 1861, 3.

57. "The Allen Boy Medium," *BoL*, April 1, 1865, 4; Joseph Griffin, ed., *History of the Press of Maine* (Brunswick: Press, 1872), 209–10, 212, 63. Also Edward H. Elwell, *Portland and Vicinity, with a Sketch of Old Orchard Beach and Other Maine Resorts*, rev. ed. (Portland, Maine: Loring, Short and Harmon, 1881), 33; Joseph Williamson, *A Bibliography of the State of Maine from the Earliest Period to 1891*, 2 vols. (Portland, Maine: Thurston Print, 1896), 1:534; Joseph Williamson, "Spirit Photographs," *Photographic News: A Weekly Record of the Progress of Photography* 7 (January 9, 1863): 20; "Charter Elections," *New York Daily Times*, March 8, 1865, 4; "The Portland Election: Working Reform Matters in That City," *Fincher's Trades' Review* (April 1, 1865): 71. Joseph B. Hall. Also mentioned were R. B. Bean and L. P. Ingree, as well as candidate Albert H. Waite. See also Emma Hardinge, "The New Party," *BoL*, July 11, 1863, 3.

58. "Old Age in the Negro," "The Present Crisis: Its Causes and Probably Results: A Lecture by Mrs. Laura Cuppy, before the Lyceum Society of Spiritualists, in Lyceum Hall, Boston, Sunday, Nov. 8, 1863," Warren Chase, "Egypt and Egyptians, Illinois," "Peter Marsh (Colored)," "The Freedmen," *BoL*, July 5 (p. 5), 1862, November 21 (p. 8), 1863, January 16 (p. 3), 1864, January 14 (p. 6), February 25 (p. 4), 1865.

## Chapter 6. Fraternity

1. "Fourth National Convention of Spiritualists, Held at Cleveland, Ohio, September 3rd, 4th, 5th, and 6th, 1867," *BoL*, October 19, 1867, 1; *MAS*, 275, 276, 278.

2. Henry T. Child, letter "From Dr. Child, of Philadelphia," "What an Army—Its Future," "The Great Convention," "At the Front," "The Danger of the Present House, and How to Avert It: A Discourse Delivered by J. S. Loveland, in Lyceum Hall, Boston,

Oct. 30, 1864," *BoL*, February 7 (p. 3), April 18 (p. 4), 1863, March 5 (p. 4), August 6 (p. 4), 1864, November 5 (p. 8), 1864.

3. "National Spiritualist Convention, Oswego, N.Y., Aug. 13 to 18, 1861," *BoL*, September 7 (p. 3), 14 (p. 4), 1861; Warren Chase, "Mediums and Lectures," *BoL*, November 7, 1863, 3; "Death of Hon. N. P. Tallmadge," *BoL*, November 26, 1864, 4; "Letter from the Davenport Brothers," *BoL*, December 10, 1864, 8; "U. Clark's Itinerary Etchings," *BoL*, November 14, 1863, 8. In 1881, to launch his First Harmonial Association. Delp, "Andrew Jackson Davis," 52 (see prologue, n. 9).

4. "Spiritualism Abandoned by the Rev. T. L. Harris" [from the *London Advertiser*], *Appleton (Wisc.) Motor*, March 1, 1860. Scott wrote *The Anti-Pantheist: False Metaphysics Exposed, and Theopneusty Defended* (Dayton, Ohio: Stephen Deuel, 1856) and became a traveling missionary for the Seventh-Day Baptists. He also penned *Scenes beyond the Grave: Trance of Marietta Davis, from Notes by Rev. J. L. Scott* (Dayton, Ohio: Stephen Deuel, 1859), sixteenth edition, describing a somnambulist and visionary he encountered while he was pastoring in Berlin, New York. He edited *The Calendar*, a religious newspaper, in Hartford, Connecticut, from July 1853 through June 1854.

5. The running debate with the Adventists can be followed through the *Banner* from February 1863 into April 1864 and beyond. See also Daniel Hull, *Biography of Moses Hull* (Wellesley, Mass.: Maugus Printing, 1907), also posted at http://stevepearson.org/moseshull; Sears, *Sex Radicals*, 21–22, 88–89, 231–32 (see chap. 5, n. 50), with Spurlock, *Free Love*, 220–22, 225–26 (see prologue, n. 12); Edwin S. Gaustad, ed., *The Rise of Adventism: Religion and Society in Mid-Nineteenth-Century America* (New York: Harper and Row, 1974); and Moses Hull, *The Question Settled: A Careful Comparison of Biblical and Modern Spiritualism* (Boston: William White, 1869); W. F. Jamieson, "Spiritualism in Grand Rapids, Mich.," *BoL*, December 12, 1863, 3.

6. Captain Adams at "The Spiritual Conference at Clinton Hall, New York," "Notices of Meetings," "Great Spiritualist Mass Meeting: Held at Oshtemo, Kalamazoo County, Michigan, on Saturday and Sunday, June 26th and 27th, 1863," "An Address by Mrs. Hatch," F. L. H. Willis lecturing at Dodworth noted in untitled item, "Excommunication of a Spiritualist," "Yearly Meeting of Friends of Progress, at Richmond, Indiana," "Mass Convention," Sarah E. Weyburn, "Spiritual Progress in Kalamazoo," M. K., "The Clergymen vs. Spiritualism, at Toledo, Ohio" with "Spiritual Grove Meeting at Three Rivers Point—Twenty-Five Hundred to Three Thousand People in Council," "Quarterly Meeting at Cadiz, Ind., 9th, 10th, and 11th of Sept.," "U. Clark's Western Itinerant Michigan," "A Free Platform," the Dodsworth Hall, "Funeral of Mrs. [Eliza W.] Farnam," *BoL*, November 2 (pp. 6–7), 1861, April 11 (p. 5), August 8 (p. 3), October 17 (p. 4), 24 (p. 4), November 14 (p. 3), 28 (p. 3), 1863, May 14 (p. 5), June 4 (p. 3), September 3 (p. 3), October 15 (p. 8), November 26 (p. 8), December 3 (p. 4), 31 (p. 4), 1864.

7. "E. Whipple," "Cottage Home," "Reform Convention at Evansville, Rock Co., Wisconsin," *BoL*, July 25 (p. 5), September 12 (p. 8), 19 (p. 8), 1863. See also Caferay in "Obituary Notices," "Spiritualism at the West," "Third Annual Convention of Spiritualists, at Oregon, Cole Co., Ill.," "Convention of Spiritualists: Held in Belvidere, Boon County, Ill., September 19th and 20th," Warren Chase, "Cairo, Ill.," "Spiritual Convention: A Report of the Spiritual Convention Held at McHenry, Illinois, on the 2d, 3d and 4th

of October, 1863," A. G. W. C., "Spiritualism in Cincinnati," "Convention at Lockport, N.Y.," "The Meeting in Cincinnati," "Quarterly Meeting of the Northern Wisconsin Spiritualist Association," J. L. Potter of Albert Lea, Minnesota, "Spiritualism in the Far West," *BoL,* March 14 (p. 4), September 19 (p. 4), October 3 (p. 2), 10 (p. 8), 1863, January 9 (p. 3), 30 (p. 3), May 14 (p. 3), July 23 (p. 3), October 15 (p. 5), November 26 (p. 3), 1864, April 29 (p. 4), 1865. See also "Globe Trotter at 91: Dr. Peebles Does Things Instead of Talking of By-Gones," *New York Times,* June 17, 1913; and "How to Live One Hundred Years: Dr. J. M. Peebles Appears before Octogenarian and Centenarian Clubs; Occasion Was His 98th Birthday Anniversary—He Formerly Lived Here—First Spiritualist Pastor," *Battle Creek Enquirer and News,* June 19, 1920.

8. "Mr. Mansfield in California, Etc.," William J. Young, "A Wolf from California," William C. Yorrey, "Mrs. Stowe's Arrival in California, &c.," C. F. O'Brion, "A Note from California" with D. H. Hender of Portland, "A Word from Oregon," L. Armstrong, "Spiritualism in Sacramento, Cal." with "Voices from Oregon," "Meeting for the Protection of the Indians," John B. Wolff, "From Colorado," J. V. Mansfield, J. K. Jones, Nevada City, "Colorado Territory," *BoL,* March 28 (p. 3), 1863, April 9 (p. 3), October 29 (p. 3), December 17 (p. 8), 24 (p. 8), 1864, January 14 (p. 8), February 4 (p. 8), April 29 (p. 4), 1865.

9. "Spiritual Lyceum and Conference," *Herald of Progress,* July 7, 1860, 3; "The New America," *BoL,* November 16, 1861, 8.

10. Deveney, *Paschal Beverly Randolph,* 19–20 (see prologue, n. 19); Buescher, *Remarkable Life of John Murray Spear,* 225 et seq. (see prologue, n. 31). See also Neil Burkhart Lehman, *The Life of John Murray Spear: Spiritualism and Reform in Antebellum America* (Columbus: Ohio State University Press, 1973), 418.

11. "Brotherhood," "The Rosicrucians," Mrs. F. A. Logan under "Correspondence," J. S. Loveland, "New York: Friends of Progress—Moral Police Fraternity—Progressive Lyceum—Mr. Davis, etc.," *BoL,* July 5 (p. 4), 1862, March 7 (p. 8), 1863, November 19 (p. 3), 1864, February 25 (p. 3), 1865, 3; *MAS,* 539; Delp, "Andrew Jackson Davis," 49–50. "Let no none call God, Father, who calls not Man, Brother." "So natural and fraternal," 119. "Unlike many self-protective and beneficial societies, this plan did not exclude Woman from any of its departments, privileges, or benefits," 119–20. "A mighty lever for accomplishing good among the millions," 120. *Arabuola; or, The Divine Guest, Containing a New Collection of Gospels* (Boston: William White / New York: Banner of Light Branch Office, 1868).

12. L. K. Coonley, "Notes by Dr. Coonley," "Free Meetings in Philadelphia," "Philadelphia Progressive Lyceum," Mary F. Davis, "The New York Children's Lyceum," *BoL,* April 4 (p. 3), 1863, September 17 (p. 4), 1864, January 21 (p. 4), April 8 (p. 2), 1865; Delp, "Andrew Jackson Davis," 48–49; *MAS,* 538–39; A. J. Davis, *Death and the After-Life,* 67 (see chap. 2, n. 43); Hy. T. Child, M.D., "Spiritualism in Philadelphia," in *The Year-Book of Spiritualism for 1871,* edited by Hudson Tuttle and J[ames] M[artin] Peebles (Boston, 1871). In 1833 Thomas W. Dyott described his *An Exposition of the System of Moral and Mental Labor Established at the Glass Factory of Dyottville,* in which he claimed to have created a complete "system of combining mental and moral with Manual Labor."

13. S. S. Jones, "Spiritualism in the Northwest—Local Organization, etc.," *BoL,* December 10, 1864, 3; Buescher, *Other Side of Salvation,* 143, 173; Lawyers Who Practiced

In Kane County, Illinois, http://freepages.genealogy.rootsweb.ancestry.com/~ilkane/LawyersPracticed.htm; Andreas, *History of Chicago*, 3:832–33 (see chap. 5, n. 49); "Mrs. Mary E. Bundy, 94, Claimed by Death," *Wilmette Life*, September 28, 1933, 12; "Wilmette Newspaper Index," http://news.wilmette.lib.il.us/details.asp?NewsID=284206. For the child mediums there, in particular the Bangs children, see Todd Karr, "David P. Abbott and the Notorious Bangs Sisters," http://www.miraclefactory.net/mpt/view.php?id=195&type=articles; Mrs. H. F. M. Brown, "Annual Festival of the Religio-Philosophical Society at St. Charles, Ill.," H. F. M. Brown, "Persons and Places.—No. 6," Mrs. Matteson, "Crimes and Chats," "St. Charles, Ill.," Ira Porter, "Self-Sustaining Industrial Colleges," S. S. Jones, "Religio-Philosophical Association: Circular," *BoL*, August 1 (p. 8), 22 (p. 3), 1863, September 3 (p. 3), November 19 (p. 8), 1864, February 25 (p. 2), April 1 (p. 3), 1865.

14. A. J. Higgins, "Nature versus Drugs.—No. Two," *BoL*, September 17, 1864, 3, "'Nature versus Drugs,'" *BoL*, November 19, 1864, 3, and "Nature versus Drugs," *BoL*, December 10, 1864, 3; Randolph entranced and reading newspaper from 3356. "A Spiritual Glimpse of the Future," *Age of Progress* (February 9, 1856): 274–75.

15. See the "Museum of the Talking Board" website at http://www.museumoftalkingboards.com/. Epes Sargent, *Planchette; or, The Despair of Science; Being a Full Account of Modern Spiritualism, Its Phenomena, and the Various Theories Regarding It; With a Survey of French Spiritism* (Boston, 1869); anonymous [Kate Field, "ed."] *Planchette's Diary* (New York: J. S. Redfield, 1868) (fiction). See also Sargent's *Peculiar: A Tale of the Great Transition* (New York: Carleton, 1864), and his *The Proof Palpable of Immortality: Being an Account of the Materialization Phenomena of Modern Spiritualism; With Remarks on the Relations of the Facts to Theology, Morals, and Religion* (Boston, 1876).

16. J. W. Monroe, "Cartes de Visite from the Other World: Spiritism and the Discourse of Laicisme in the Early Third Republic," *French Historical Studies* 26 (2003): 119–53; Georgiana Houghton, *Chronicles of the Photographs of Spiritual Beings and Phenomena* (London: E. W. Allen, 1882); R. Dixon, "'Where Are the Dead?' Spiritualism, Photography, and the Great War," *History of Photography* 28 (2004): 247–60. Many articles in the *Banner*, of course.

17. "The Higher Law," *Herald of Light* 4 (November 1859): 63; "The Foundation of Governments, and Ownership of Property: A Lecture Delivered before the Religio-Philosophical Society of Des Moines, Iowa, Sunday, May, 1864, by B. N. Kinyon," *BoL*, May 6, 1865, x.

18. E. V. Wilson, "The Fountain Home," "Associated Interest in Farming," "Feverish Reformers," "The Adelphian Institute," "Correspondence in Brief" [on North Union Shaker village], "Coming Home" with "A Peculiar Institution in Iowa" [on Amana], "Local Co-operation and Organization," *BoL*, October 2 (p. 7), 1858, August 10 (p. 3), 1861, January 18 (p. 4), 1862, December 13 (p. 4), 1862, October 10 (p. 4), 1863, January 9 (p. 4), 1864, April 1 (p. 4), 1865; John Humphrey Noyes on "The Spiritualist Communities," in his *History of American Socialisms* (Philadelphia: J. B. Lippincott, 1870), 564–76.

19. Samuel Underhill, "Farming Associations," "Annual Festival of the Religio-Philosophical Society at St. Charles, Ill.," H. F. M. Brown, "Persons and Places.—No. 6," "In the Field Again," "Letter from Dr. Underhill," *BoL*, March 15 (p. 3), 1862, August 1 (p. 8), 22 (p. 3), 1863, December 3 (p. 4), 1864, February 18 (p. 4), 1865.

20. Warren Chase, "Oshkosh and Ripon, Wis.," *BoL,* October 10, 1863, 3.

21. Chase, *Forty Years,* 96 (see prologue, n. 18); Samuel E. Nichols, Hammonton, "The Settlement at Hammonton, N.J.," "Sketch of A. C. Stiles," "The Hammonton Settlement," "Tribute to the Memory of Lieut. David R. Newbold," H. F. M. Brown, "Places and Persons—No. 12" [Vineland NJ], "Progressive Spiritualists of Hammonton, N.J.," Warren Chase, "Vineland, N.J.," *BoL,* January 19 (p. 3), June 22 (p. 4), September 28 (p. 3), 1861, April 18 (p. 3), 1863, June 18 (p. 3), 1864, February 11 (p. 8), April 1 (p. 4), 1865.

22. Untitled note on Long's project and "Black Lake Co-operative Association," *BoL,* January 11, June 11, 1864, both 5. Pierre-Joseph Proudhon, *Spiritual Philosopher* 1 (December 28, 1850): 205.

23. Buescher, *Other Side of Salvation,* 173; A. B. Child, "Plan for a Farming Community" and "Farming Corporations: A Plan for the Private Residence and Gardens, Corporation Block, Ornamented Grounds and Streets," *BoL,* July 27 (pp. 2–3), September 14 (p. 8), 1861, with responses "Thoughts on Recent Topics: Dr. Child's 'Corporation' and Miss Hardinge's Complaint" and S. W. Ellis's "Farming in the West," August 24 (p. 8), 1861, May 24 (pp. 6–7), 1862, and the writings of D. J. Mandell, "Thought to Recourse," "The Grand Aurola of Northern Triumph and Liberty" with "Pictures in a Wash-Tub," and "The 'Generous Proposition' Again," August 24 (p. 8), 1861, April 25 (pp. 2, 4), 1863, June 18 (p. 3), 1864.

24. "Farming Corporation in Operation," "Profits of Farming over Trade" (an excerpt from *A Plea for Farming and Farming Corporations*), S. W. Ellis's "Farming in the West," and "Organization, By-Laws, etc. of the New England Agricultural Company," *BoL,* March 22 (p. 5), May 3 (p. 8), 24 (pp. 6–7), 1862, June 21 (p. 3), 1862; Crosby Johnson, *An Illustrated Historical Atlas of Caldwell County, Missouri* (Philadelphia: Edwards Brothers, 1876). In 1934 Nannie Beaumont recalled "The First Days of Kidder" at Kings Cross Farm, Caldwell County, Missouri, posted at http://kingscrossfarm.tripod.com/interviews/first_days_of_kidder_missouri.htm. Patrick S. Kenney was in the home guard and joined First MSM Cavalry at nearby Cameron.

25. Long article from D. H. Hamilton on "Reconstruction," "Social Reform 'Communities,'" *BoL,* January 28, 1865, 4.

26. Susie A. Hutchinson, "Letter from Mrs. Hutchinson," "The Destruction of Slavery," "A War of Ideas," *BoL,* December 26 (p. 3), 1863, June 4 (p. 4), 1864, August 13 (p. 5), 1864.

27. Warren Chase, "The Rebellion," *BoL,* December 5, 1863, 4.

28. "Duty Done," "Circulating the Documents," "Rebel Re-enlistments," "Gone to Mexico" and "Rebel Desertions," "Rebel Finances," *BoL,* October 4 (p. 4), 1862, February 6 (p. 5), 13 (p. 3), March 5 (p. 4), November 5 (p. 4), 1864; "Distinguished Investigators," *STP,* 5:203.

29. N. O. Archer, "Hannibal, Mo.," *BoL,* April 22, 1865, 3; letter of Mrs. M. A. Swelt, Brooklyn, to Maretzek, February 7, 1864; Max Maretzek, *Sharps and Flats: A Sequel to "Crotchets and Quavers"* (New York: American Musician, 1890), 46–47.

30. Kelso, Speech Delivered at Walnut Grove, September 19, 1865 in the eight-hundred-page "Complete Works in Manuscript," 24, 27 (see prologue, n. 50); Kelso on "Reconstruction," *Congressional Globe* (39th), 730–31, 732–33; *Journal of the House of*

*Representatives,* January 7, 1867, 118–19, January 14, 1867, 163, and February 4, 1867, 320. See also Britton, *Civil War on the Border,* 2:204 (see prologue, n. 50); and MacDonald, *Fifty Years of Freethought,* 1:538 (see prologue, n. 50).

31. *Who Was Who in America,* 1:243; *The National Cyclopaedia,* 5:20 (see chap. 1, n. 54).

32. Chase, *Forty Years,* 79, 84; "P. B. Randolph," "Police Regulation," "The Kingdom on Earth: Lectures by Mrs. Laura De Force Gordon, before the Lyceum Society of Spiritualists, in Lyceum Hall, Boston, March 1, 1863," "Afloat," advertisement for *Pre-Adamite Man,* advertisement for *Dealings with the Dead!,* "Letter from Laura De Force Gordon," "Departed" (Randolph's obituary for his doctor), "Dr. P. B. Randolph," Laura DeForce Gordon, "From New Orleans," "'My Religion,'" "A New Work by Warren Chase," Laura DeForce Gordon, A.B., "Spiritualism in New Orleans," *BoL,* September 7 (p. 3), 1861, August 23 (p. 5), 1862, March 14 (p. 4), April 11 (p. 3), June 6 (p. 8), 20 (p. 7), 1863, February 27 (p. 3), 1864, March 5 (p. 3), 26 (p. 5), June 18 (p. 3), September 10 (p. 4), 1864, May 6 (p. 4), 13 (p. 2), 1865.

33. "Cora L. V. Hatch: At the Music Hall, Boston, Sept. 4th, 1859," "Annual Festival of the Religio-Philosophical Society at St. Charles, Ill.," "The Present Crisis: Its Causes and Probably Results: A Lecture by Mrs. Laura Cuppy, before the Lyceum Society of Spiritualists, in Lyceum Hall, Boston, Sunday, Nov. 8, 1863," *BoL,* October 8 (pp. 6–7), 1859, August 1 (p. 8), 1863, November 21 (p. 8), 1863, 8.

34. "The Present Crisis of American Affairs" in Chase, "The Rebellion—Its Cause and Cure," "The World's Crisis," "The New Union," Warren Chase, "The Rebellion," "Kentucky," *BoL,* October 5, (p. 5) 1861, September 27 (p. 4), 1862, September 12 (p. 4), December 5 (p. 4), 1863, April 16 (p. 4), 1864.

35. "The Duration of the War," "Reform Convention at Evansville, Rock Co. Wisconsin," "An American Woman" writing "A Burning Shame—Reform It," "John N. Hanley," *BoL,* May 2 (p. 6), September 19 (p. 8), 1863, April 8 (p. 4), April 29 (p. 6), 1865.

36. "The Soil Our Best Friend," *BoL,* January 24, 1863, 4. For the antebellum land-reform movement, see Lause, *Young America* (see prologue, n. 9), which includes references to the rest of the scholarship. Another name for this movement, "Young America," was hinted at in John S. Adams, "Young Earth," *BoL,* March 26, 1864, 5.

37. "Captain Timothy Welton," *BoL,* May 30, 1863, 6; "Major Andrew Burnett," *BoL,* September 24, 1864, 6; "Politics and Politicians," "A Better Class of Public Men," "The Great Struggle in This Country," "The Elections," "The Genius of the Age, as Manifested in American Civilization: A Discourse Delivered by J. S. Loveland, in Lyceum Hall, Boston, Oct. 23, 1864," "Glimpses of the Spirit-World: A Sermon by Henry T. Child, M.D., 634 Race Street, Philadelphia," *BoL,* August 9 (p. 4), 1862, August 29 (p. 4), October 10 (p. 4), 31 (p. 4), 1863, November 12 (p. 8), 1864, February 4 (p. 8), 1865.

38. "Progressive Convention: An Interesting Session of Three Days [Concluded]," *BoL,* October 17, 1863, 3.

39. David C. Rankin, "The Origins of Negro Leadership in New Orleans during Reconstruction," in *Southern Black Leaders of the Reconstruction Era,* edited by Howard N. Rabinowitz (Urbana: University of Illinois Press, 1982), 161–62.

40. Wilfrid Wylleys, "Thoughts for the Times," *BoL,* October 10, 1863, 2.

41. "Humanity, Truth and Justice: What We as Spiritualists Should Do," Warren Chase, "Change of Base," *BoL*, July 25 (p. 1), 1863, September 10 (p. 3), 1864

42. "The New America," *BoL*, November 16, 1861, 8.

43. Lee Blewett, "Spiritualism and Crime," *Columbia Law Review* 22 (May 1922): 439–49; "The Lost Ones of the Cities," J. S. Loveland, "Crime and Its Cure," "Women and Work," S. Dayton, "Incidents of City Rambles," [on Chicago], "Self-Reliance," H. S. Brown, "How to Prevent Crime" [from Milwaukee] with "Vagabond Children," "The Case of Green" [on capital punishment], *BoL*, March 8 (p. 2), December 27 (p. 8), 1862, December 5 (p. 4), 1863, January 2 (p. 8), April 2 (p. 4), May 7 (pp. 2, 4), July 16 (p. 4), 1864; W. S. Courtney's commentary, particularly "The Cause and Cure of Crime," in *STP*, 2:204–20, 3:81–90, with "Individual Sovereignty," "The Despotism of Opinion," "Clairvoyance and Psychometry," "God," "The New Theology," and "The Interior Memory," 2:296–308, 3:227–37, 275–79, 363–71, 404–13, 4:245–55, 5:164–73, as well as B. W. Richmond, "God: Reply to W. S. Courtney," 4:8–13. See also "The Cause and Cure of Crime," and Charles Partridge, "Our Prisons," *STP*, 2:277–78, 5:373, 374–75. See also W. S. Courtney, *The Gold Fields of Santo Domingo* (New York: Anson P. Norton, 1860).

44. U. Clark, "Startling Prophesy Fulfilled: The Nation's Jubilee at Hand," Samuel Melvin, "Thoughts on Harmonial Progression," "Self-Government," *BoL*, August 22 (p. 8), September 12 (p. 2), October 18 (p. 4), 1862.

45. "The New York Conference," *STP*, 4:201; "New York Conference," *STP*, 9:39.

46. A. B. Child, "Are We Safe without a Government of Force?," T. Hance, "Human Governments," W. A. C., "Governments of Force," "'Reconstruction': A Reply," *BoL*, January 7 (p. 2), 28 (p. 8), February 18 (p. 3), 25 (pp. 2–3), 1865.

47. "Wages and Want," "Rights of Labor," *BoL*, April 14, 1860, March 14, 1863, both 4.

48. J. K. Ingalls, "Capital and Labor," *Journal of Progress* 1 (June 4–11, 1853): 85–86, 100–101; "The Perpetual Conflict," *BoL*, November 19, 1864, 4.

49. "Rights of Labor," "Strikes," "Women and Work," *BoL*, March 14, November 21, December 5, 1863, all 4.

50. "The Daily Evening Voice," *BoL*, December 17, 1864, 4.

51. Davis in "Spiritual Lyceum and Conference," *Herald of Progress*, June 16, 1860, 3; "Union of Capital and Labor," *New York Tribune*, February 22, reprinted in "Union of Labor and Capital," *STP*, 4:260–62, part of the larger article on 257–66; "Protective Unions," *Spiritual Philosopher* 1 (November 9, 1850): 118.

52. Hitchcock in "Spiritual Lyceum and Conference," *Herald of Progress*, July 7, 1860, 3; "Banking and Currency" by "W." and "A Few Remarks on 'True Civilization'," review by "W." *BoL*, December 4, 1858, 5, May 16, 1863, 2.

53. "Spiritual Lyceum and Conference," *Herald of Progress*, July 7, 1860, 3. See also the argument over with Warren's blanket endorsement of the idea of "rebellion." "A Few Remarks on 'True Civilization as Immediate Necessity, and the Last Ground of Hope for Mankind, by Josiah Warren, Counsellor in Equity,'" and "W." [probably Josiah Warren], "Finance, Banking and Currency," *BoL*, May 16, 1863, 2, and February 13, 1864, 2.

54. *BoL*, November 26, 1858; "The West," *BoL*, October 8, 1859, 7. Among other trade unionists associated with the movement were C. H. Crowell, the printer at Cambridgeport, and the Henry Van Dorn at Chicago may be the leader of the shoemakers there.

55. "Spiritual Lyceum and Conference," *Herald of Progress*, June 3, 1860, 3.

56. "The Confiscated Lands," *BoL*, January 9, 1864, 4; "The Present Crisis: Its Causes and Probably Results; A Lecture by Mrs. Laura Cuppy, before the Lyceum Society of Spiritualists, in Lyceum Hall, Boston, Sunday, November 8, 1863," *BoL*, November 21, 1863, 8. Also, "The Future of America: A Lecture by Mrs. Cora L. V. Hatch, before the Lyceum Society of Spiritualists, in Lyceum Hall, Boston, Sunday, May 10, 1863," *BoL*, May 30, 1863, 3–4.

57. "A New Labor System," *BoL*, February 6, 1864, 4; "Homesteads," *BoL*, March 12, 1864, 4. See also "The Free Plantation," *BoL*, January 30, 1864, 3. But also Horace Dresser, "Suburban Homes," *BoL*, April 25, 1863, 3, and "Homes for the Laboring Class," *BoL*, December 17, 1864, 4.

58. "Speculation," *BoL*, Sept. 17, 1857. "If every man would wear the wool, nor work in silken stuff. / Society—the king—be satisfied with well enough; / Then each might help the fallen one, and kiss from off the rod / A holy balm for earthly strife, and win the love of God— / But where the great world rolled in peace, 'neath Fortune's smile so sunny. / Now nations hide, each terrified, at people's cry for money!" "The People's Cry for Money," *BoL*, October 31, 1857.

59. "Spiritual Lyceum and Conference," *Herald of Progress*, June 23, 1860, 4; "Sewing Machines," *BoL*, August 30, 1862, 4.

60. "Union of Labor and Capital," *STP*, 4:259, 260; "A Touch of Political Economy,' *BoL*, December 3, 1864, 4; Cora L. V. Hatch, "Direct Taxation—Its Fruits: A Lecture by Mrs. Cora L. V. Hatch, at Dodworth's Hall, New York, Sunday Evening, Feb. 23, 1862," *BoL*, March 15, 1862, 3; "Henry D. Thoreau at Music Hall, Sunday, October 9th," *BoL*, October 22, 1859, 5. "Little Economies," *BoL*, October 4, 1862, 4. Like an inheritance, developed as a habit and passed.

61. Amos, "The Rights of Labor," *BoL*, April 18, 1863, 4.

62. "Lectures at Dodworth's Academy," *STP*, 7:121.

63. Russell H. Hvolbek, "Being and Knowing: Spiritualist Epistemology and Anthropology from Schwenckfeld to Bohme," *Sixteenth Century Journal* 122 (February 15, 1978): 97–110; Henry Steel Olcott recalled information confirming the historicity of the Iliad, "Homer, and the Siege of Troy," *STP*, 5:380–81. See also Hudson Tuttle, *The Origin and Antiquity of Physical Man Scientifically Considered* (Boston: William White, 1866), 49–50.

64. D. H. Hamilton, "Reconstruction," *BoL*, February 4, 1865, 2–3.

65. Porter quoted in Mrs. H. F. M. Brown, "Annual Festival of the Religio-Philosophical Society at St. Charles, Ill." and in "Two Days' Meeting at Alpine, Mich., on Saturday and Sunday, Sept. 12th and 13th," *BoL*, August 1 (p. 8), October 3 (p. 2), 1863, but see also "Concert of Action among Spiritualists," May 7, 1864, 4. Another of the class-oriented Fourierists, Kaulback "surely beneficial so far as it compels the admission of rights to one class, which they have demanded from another, who have withheld them." John G. Kaulback, "Boston Spiritual Conference," *BoL*, May 18, 1861, 6. For a genuinely conservative view, though, see "The Helpless Poor," *BoL*, July 12, 1862, 4.

## Epilogue

1. Untitled item, *BoL*, January 21, 1865, 5. See also "What an Army—Its Future," *BoL*, April 18, 1863, 4.

2. Following from the *New York Times* of 1880–81: "Mr. Youngs or Not Mr. Youngs," October 21; "Mr. Theophilus Youngs's Case," October 22; "A Mystery to Be Solved," November 30; "Youngs and His Daughter," December 1; "Theophilus Youngs's Story," January 30, 1881; "Theophilus Youngs in Court," February 12; "Identifying Theophilus Youngs," February 19; "The Alleged Theophilus: Mrs. Youngs Repudiates Him after an Examination," March 2; "Theophilus Youngs Again," March 17; "Not the True Theophilus," April 19; "The Theophilus Youngs Case," May 3; "City and Suburban News," May 11; "The Disputed Theophilus," May 18; "Theophilus Youngs's Bald Spot," May 24; "City and Suburban News," May 27. See also the 1882 articles: "Mrs. Theophilus Youngs Dead," March 14; "Not Solved by Mrs. Youngs's Death," March 19; "Theophilus Youngs Again," August 12. See also John B. Buescher, "Unlocking the Mystery of a Lincoln Relic" (see chap. 3, n. 11).

3. Earl Wesley Fornell, *The Unhappy Medium: Spiritualism and the Life of Margaret Fox* (Austin: University of Texas Press, 1964); Nancy Rubin Stuart, *The Reluctant Spiritualist: The Life of Maggie Fox* (New York: Harcourt, 2005); Underhill, *Missing Link* (see prologue, n. 1); Daniel Cottom, *Abyss of Reason: Cultural Movements, Revelations and Betrayals* (Oxford: Oxford University Press, 1991).

4. *WALS*, 201–3. See Jeffry D. Wert, *General James Longstreet: The Confederacy's Most Controversial Soldier* (New York: Simon and Schuster, 1993).

5. Buescher, "Across the Dead Line," 28–32, 33–39, 43–45, 46–48, 65, 67, 68–60, which also mentions William Lawrence, George Lawrence, Glenni Scofield, Charles Upson, Ferndando Beaman, Rowland Trowbridge, and five others (49).

6. "Spiritual Lyceum and Conference," *Herald of Progress*, June 3, 1860, 3; *Religio-Philosophical Journal* (Chicago) (November 11, 1865); "Formation of the Religio-Philosophical Society, 1864," *Friend of Progress* (December 1864): 37.

7. "Fourth National Convention of Spiritualists, Held at Cleveland, Ohio, September 3rd, 4th, 5th, and 6th, 1867," *BoL*, October 19, 1867, 1; *MAS*, 275, 276, 278.

8. John O. Wattles, "Art. V.—The Crisis.—Universal Unity," *Herald of Truth: A Monthly Periodical, Devoted to the Interests of Religion, Philosophy, Literature, Science and Art* 1 (January 1847): 43, 47; "How Shall Life Be Made the Most Of?," *American Whig Review* 1 (April 1845): 423; Edward Bulwer Lytton, *"My Novel"; or, Varieties in English Life*, 2 vols. (Longon: G. Routledge, 1856), 1:172–73. Also in many serialized versions, including "My Novel; or, Varieties in English Life," *Living Age* 29 (April 12, 1851): 74; "The Christmas Fires" (from *Sharpe's*), *Living Age* 36 (March 26, 1853): 577; "Immortality: The Argument from Scripture," *New Englander and Yale Review* 14 (May 1856): 196. It might be significant that the use of the phrase as indicating a collective process discussed "female authors," *North American Review* 72 (January 1851): 171. "But faith the dark hiatus can supply— / Teaching eternal progress still shall reign; / Telling (as these things aid her to espy) / In higher worlds that higher laws obtain; / Pointing, with radiant finger raised on high, / From life that still revives, to life that cannot die!" "Immortality," *Living Age* 1 (July 20, 1844): 591, reprinted in Epes Sargent, ed., *The Testimony of the Poets* (Boston: Benjamin B. Mussey and Abel Tompkins, 1854), 312.

9. M. B. Dyott, *Explanatory Treatise upon the Construction, Objects and Purposes of the Order of Eternal Progress* (Philadelphia: for the organization, 1869), 5, 7, 9–10; Benjamin Todd quoted in "Reform Convention at Evansville, Rock Co. Wisconsin," *BoL*, September 19, 1863, 8; *Charge Book for Subordinate Sanctuaries of the Children of Light, of the Order of Eternal Progress* (Philadelphia, 1867); and Dyott's report on the change of name to the "Fifth National Convention of Spiritualists, Held at Cleveland, Ohio, September 3rd, 4th, 5th, and 6th, 1867," *BoL*, September 12, 1868, 3; Dyott, *Explanatory Treatise;* "Sixth National Convention of Spiritualists, Held at Kremlin Hall, Buffalo, N.Y., Commencing Tuesday, Aug. 31, 1869," *BoL*, September 11, 1869, 8, also September 18, 25, 1869, both on 4.

10. Andreas, *History of Chicago*, 831–32 (see chap. 5, n. 49); "Stead Sends Spirit News, Says Medium," *New York Times*, April 29, 1912, 3; Buescher, *Other Side of Salvation*, 143, 173. Cora remained a spokesperson for the movement over decades. After writing a novel, she represented spiritualism at the Congress of Religions held at the 1893 World's Fair. In 1912 she received the spirit of W. T. Stead into her Rogers Park home, where he reported his death on the *Titanic*. She herself did not cross over until 1923. "Cora L. V. Richmond on the Eight-Hour Movement," *Chicago Tribune*, April 5, 1886, 1.

11. History of Washington County, http://www.rootsweb.ancestry.com/~vermont/WashingtonCoHistory14.html. See also "Minard House (Jones House, Farson House)," 504 East Main Street, St. Charles Public Library, http://www.st-charles.lib.il.us/history/farson.htm.

12. William H. Eddy, "Spiritualism in Eddyville, N.Y.," *BoL*, April 9, 1864, 5; William Eddy and A. J. Sargeant, M.W.D., "Wonderful Manifestations in Rutland, Vt.," *BoL*, July 30, 1864, 8; "Truth Making Its Way," *BoL*, October 29, 1864, 4; from Burlington family, R. M. Adams, "The Eddy Family in Vermont," *BoL*, May 6, 1865, 8. Asa Gilbert Eddy, the sewing machine salesman from Vermont who married Mary Baker at Lynn. Mary Baker Eddy did successfully translate the mysticism of the healer Phineas Parkhurst Quimby into a full-blown denomination, the Church of Christ Scientist.

13. The literature by and about Madame Blavatsky is extensive, but good starting points would include Gertrude M. Williams, *Priestess of the Occult: Madame Blavatsky* (New York: Alfred A. Knopf, 1946); Marion Meed, *Madame Blavatsky: The Woman behind the Myth* (New York: G. P. Putnam's Sons, 1980); Sylvia Cranston, *H. P. B.: The Extraordinary Life & Influence of Helena Blavatsky, Founder of the Modern Theosophical Movement* (New York: Tarcher Books, 1993); and K. Paul Johnson, *The Masters Revealed: Madame Blavatsky and the Myth of the Great White Lodge* (Albany: State University of New York Press, 1994).

14. A. J. Davis, *Death and the After-Life*, 63 (see chap. 2, n. 43), also crediting it with the origins of the Children's Lyceum Society. L. K. Coonley, "Notes by Dr. Coonley," *BoL*, April 4, 1863, 3. For the quote on the OEP, see Allen Putnam, *Flashes of Light from the Spirit-Land, through the Mediumship of Mrs. J. H. Conant*, compiled by Allen Putnam (Boston: William White, Banner of Light Office, 1872), 146; Delp, "Andrew Jackson Davis," 50 (see prologue, n. 9).

15. Prothero, "From Spiritualism to Theosophy," 197–216 (see prologue, n. 14).

16. "Spiritual Lyceum and Conference," *Herald of Progress*, June 30, 1860, 3; Friedrich Julius Stahl, *Die Philosophie des Rechts*, 3rd ed., 3 vols. (Heidelberg, 1833), vol. 2, pt. 1,

99 et seq., quoted in Hermann Olshausen, *Biblical Commentary on the New Testament, Adapted Especially for Preachers and Students* (Edinburgh: Clark, 1849), 186n. Paul must also have had a glimpse. See Cor. 7:29–35. "Spiritual Lyceum and Conference," *Herald of Progress,* June 16, 1860, 4.

17. *Biographical Directory of the U.S. Congress; Missouri Weekly Patriot,* November 8, 1866, 3, August 8, 1867, 3, July 9, 1870. See also Gregory A. Borchard, *Abraham Lincoln and Horace Greeley* (Carbondale: Southern Illinois University Press; 2011); Walter A. McDougall, *Throes of Democracy: The American Civil War Era, 1829–1877* (New York: HarperCollins, 2008); Erik S. Lunde, "The Ambiguity of the National Idea: The Presidential Campaign of 1872," *Canadian Review of Studies in Nationalism* 5, no. 1 (1978): 1–23; Bernard A. Weisberger, "Horace Greeley: Reformer as Republican," *Civil War History* 23, no. 1 (1977): 5–25.

18. Timothy Messer-Kruse, *The Yankee International: Marxism and the American Reform Tradition* (Chapel Hill: University of North Carolina Press, 1998). For its predecessors, see Mark A. Lause, *A Secret Society History of the Civil War* (Urbana: University of Illinois Press, 2011), 21–50. Colonel Greene defending spiritualism, but not Davenports. *BoL,* April 8, 1865, 5.

19. Barbara Goldsmith, *Other Powers: The Age of Suffrage, Spiritualism and the Scandalous Victoria Woodhull* (New York: HarperPerennial, 1999); J. M. Peebles, "Thoughts on the War, Number Two," *BoL,* January 7, 1865, 4. See also Eliza Woodson Burhans Farnham, *The Ideal Attained* (New York: C. M. Plumb, 1865) (fiction). See also for her "gynocentric" views Sears, *Sex Radicals,* 234–35 (see chap. 5, n. 50). For Kelso, see *Woodhull & Claflin's Weekly,* May 4, 1872; and *BoL,* July 27, 1872, July 12, 1873, July 18, 1874, August 7, 1875; Holcombe, *History of Greene County, Missouri,* 521 (see chap. 1, n. 46).

20. Blatt, *Free Love and Anarchism,* 34–35, 43, 84–88. See also *The Collected Works of Ezra H. Heywood,* with introductions by Martin Blatt (Weston, Mass.: M&S Press, 1985); *Word* 1 (July 1872): 1, cited in Spurlock, *Free Love,* 218 (see prologue, n. 12); Martin, *Men against the State,* 116 (see chap. 4, n. 4). "The Healing of the Nations, Published by the Society for the 'Diffusion of Spiritual Knowledge,'" *Christian Spiritualist* 1 (May 5, 1855): 2; Charles Linton, author and engraver; Buescher "Who Was Kersey Graves?" (see prologue, n. 11).

21. For Widstrand, "Organization," *BoL,* April 18, 1863, 2; "Republican State Convention," *Winona Daily Republican,* September 6, 1861, 2; untitled item, *Winona Daily Republican,* April 22, 1873, 2; "Mr. Widstrand's Bid for the Senatorship," *Winona Daily Republican,* February 19, 1875, 2; "Widstrand," *Socialist* (December 21, 1878): 5; "What Is Said," *Winona Daily Republican,* March 6, 1894, 3; Franklin Curtis Wedge, *History of Wright County Minnesota,* 2 vols. (Chicago: H. C. Cooper, 1915), 872. Particularly after his son's severe wounding at Antietam, "Address of the Society for the Diffusion of Spiritual Knowledge to the Citizens of the United States," "Organization of Spiritualism," *STP,* 5:310.

22. "Reform Convention at Evansville, Rock Co. Wisconsin," *BoL,* September 19, 1863, 8; "Itinerant Etchings of U. Clark," *BoL,* February 18, 1865, 8; J. P. Gallup, "The Northern Wisconsin Spiritualist Association," *BoL,* February 25, 1865, 8.

23. On these particular Greenbackers, see "Recruits! Recruits!," *BoL,* August 9, 1862, 5; for E. H. Chapin, "Mercantile Library Lectures," *BoL,* January 21, 1865, 4. In addition to the census material, see *Boston City Directory, 1890* (Boston: Sampson, Murdock,

1890); and Jacob Edson, "Hymn," *BoL,* January 14, 1865, 2. See chapter 3 of Mark A. Lause, *The Civil War's Last Campaign: James B. Weaver, the Greenback-Labor Party, and the Politics of Race and Section* (Lanham, Md.: University Press of America, 2001), 65–88.

24. Mathilda Josyln Gage, "Is Woman Her Own?," *Revolution,* April 9, 1868, 215–16, and her concise summary of witchcraft in *Woman, Church and State* (Chicago: Charles Kerr, 1893), 260–61; Joanne Ellen Passet, *Sex Radicals and the Quest for Women's Equality* (Urbana: University of Illinois Press, 2003), 204.

25. Lois Waisbrooker, "Things as I See Them," *BoL,* April 16, 1864, 3; Sears, *Sex Radicals;* Joanne E. Passet, *Sex Radicals and the Quest for Women's Equality* (Urbana: University of Illinois Press, 2003).

26. Kevin Starr, *Americans and the California Dream, 1850–1915* (Oxford: Oxford University Press, 1973), and his *Inventing the Dream: California through the Progressive Era* (Oxford: Oxford University Press, 1985).

27. In general, see Mark A. Lause, "Progress Impoverished: The Origins of Henry George's Single Tax," *Historian* 52 (May 1990): 394–410. For Collins, see D. Johnson, *Founding the Far West,* 197–98 (see prologue, n. 22); H. F. M. Brown, "Places and Persons.—No. 8," *BoL,* November 14, 1863; "Mrs. Laura Cuppy," *BoL,* November 21, 1863, 4; Laura Cuppy Smith, "How One Woman Entered the Ranks of Social Reform; or, A Mother's Story," *Woodhull & Clafflin's Weekly,* March 1, 1873, 3, 4, 5; David H. Shaffer, "How the Cause Progresses in Cincinnati," *BoL,* April 16, 1864, 3; "Mrs. Laura Cuppy," *BoL,* December 24, 1864, 4; A. G. W. C. "Spiritualism in Cincinnati," *BoL,* May 14, 1864, 3.

28. "National Spiritualist Convention, Oswego, N.Y., Aug. 13 to 18, 1861," *BoL,* September 21, 1861, 8.

29. MacDonald, *Fifty Years of Freethought,* 1:287, 301–2, 416, 538–39 (see prologue, n. 50); *Biographical Directory of the U.S. Congress;* but listings in the *BoL* do not give Modesto addresses for several more years, viz., issues of July 15, 1876, August 4, 1877; and J. R. Kelso, *Government Analyzed,* 101, 277 (see prologue, n. 50); comment in "On Picket Duty," *Liberty,* February 28, 1885, 1. For the dismissal of Kelso, see Victor Yarros in *Liberty* (December 3, 1892): 2–3, with Tucker's comments in "On Picket Duty," *Liberty* (December 3, 1892): 1; J. R. Kelso, *Government Analyzed,* 48, 106, 277, 298, 299.

30. *Who Was Who in America,* 1:243; *The National Cyclopaedia,* 5:20, 21 (see chap. 1, n. 54); G. Williams, *Priestess of the Occult,* 194, 112, 294–95, 337–38; Meed, *Madame Blavatsky,* 158–59, 379, 380, 416–17, 453, 501; Barrett, *Spiritual Pilgrim,* 211 (see chap. 1, n. 46); Whipple, *Biography of Peebles* (see chap. 2, n. 46); J. M. Peebles, *The Christ Questioned Settled; or, Jesus, Man, Medium, Martyr: A Symposium by W. E. Coleman, J. S. Loveland, H. Tuttle, M. Hull, J. R. Buchanan, B. B. Hill, I. M. Wise, Col. Ingersoll, and What the Spirits Say about It* (Boston: Banner of Light, 1899).

31. *The Wisdom of the Heart: Katherine Tingley Speaks,* compiled and edited by W. Emmett (San Diego: Point Loma, 1978). In general, see Everett W. MacNair, *Edward Bellamy and the Nationalist Movement, 1889 to 1894: A Research Study of Edward Bellamy's Work as a Social Reformer* (Milwaukee: Fitzgerald, 1957).

32. Born Sarah Lockwood Pardee was the daughter of Leonard Pardee and L. Judd Pardee.

33. Christopher Lasch, *The Culture of Narcissism: American Life in an Age of Diminishing Expectations* (New York: W. W. Norton, 1979).

# Index

abolitionism and abolitionists: antiwar resistance among some, 59; convergence with sectionalization of interest in, 16, 18–19, 146; interest in spiritualism 5, 7, 9–10; politicization of alongside rise of spiritualism, 24, 27; posthumous embrace of, 137, 125, 156; relations with emergent Republican Party, 38–40, 68; resistance to among some spiritualists, 45; spiritualism in wartime labors for, 48, 57, 72, 81, 89, 94–95; wider struggle for labor reform and equality, 98, 103, 106–9, 124
Adams, John Quincy, 48, 59
African-Americans: influences on antebellum reform, 26–27; influences on spiritualist, 18–19; mediumship of, 19
Africans, 10, 45, 46, 61, 95, 106, 114, 121, 142; Afro-Creole, 18
Allegheny, PA, 5, 49
Ambler, Russell P., 4, 5, 31, 32, 126
Andrews, Lewis Feuilleteau Wilson, 17, 18
Andrews, Stephen Pearl, 30, 36, 81, 92, 98, 104, 141, 152, 154
Anthony, Susan B., 153, 156
Arcadia, NY, 2, 11
Auburn, NY, 4, 9, 16

Bacon, George A., 73, 78, 112
Baker, Edward D., 70, 83
Ballou, Adin, 13, 119
Ballou, Sullivan, 54, 55
Baltimore, 16, 54, 68, 73, 97
*Banner of Light*, 15, 16, 43, 47, 49, 53, 59, 63, 75, 78, 84, 99, 106, 111, 115, 117, 122, 126
Barron, Henry D., 4, 8, 27, 28, 93
Battle Creek, 6, 126, 127
Baumfree, Isabella. *See* Truth, Sojourner
Beeson, John, 114–18
Bible, 2, 66, 67, 69, 91, 148
Blood, James H., 10, 58, 85
bohemians and bohemianism, 10, 30, 31, 110
Bonaparte, Napoleon, 33, 79
Boston, 13, 16, 37, 80, 112, 115, 116, 123, 127, 146, 153
*Boston Herald*, 25, 120
*Boston Investigator*, 11, 130
Boston Printers' Union, 140
Branch, Julia, 14, 39
Brisbane, Albert, 91, 92, 93, 154
Brittan, Emma Hardinge, 8, 15, 17, 18, 30, 33, 84, 85, 97, 119, 122
Brittan, Samuel Byron, 9, 29, 48, 55, 126
Brooklyn, 30, 31
Brotherhood of the Union, 5, 15, 25, 30, 38, 41
Brown, Hannah F. M., 40–41, 103, 129, 131, 156
Brown, John, 7, 40–41, 47, 53, 55, 59, 100, 110, 135

Brown, John (of California), 7–8
Browning, Orville H., 75, 76
Brownson, Orestes Augustus, 19, 45
Buchanan, Joseph Rodes, 6, 9
Buffalo, 2, 11, 39
burned-over district, 6, 8
Burr, Charles Chauncey, 11, 25, 26

Calhoun, John C., 59, 60
Calvinism and Calvinists, 3, 155
Canada and Canadians, 50, 96, 126
Cannon, Le Grand B., 70–71
Capron, Eliab W., 3, 4, 8, 28, 32, 34, 93, 119
Caribbean, 18–19
Carter, Albert G. W., 81, 82
Charleston, SC, 17, 79
Chase, Milton, 111, 135
Chase, Warren B., 10, 23, 91, 129; postwar radicalism of, 154; as radical and socialist agitator, 26, 27–28, 36, 38, 99, 120, 131–32; Republicanism as vehicle for radical change, 44, 47–48, 68, 84, 103–5, 133, 136, 138, 152; as spiritualist missionary, 14, 15, 17, 31; on spiritualist organization, 82, 110, 126–27; wartime activities, 111, 112, 135
Chicago, 7, 26, 52, 70, 81, 121, 129, 146, 154; Great Fire of 1871, 150
Child, Asaph Bemis, 45, 52, 132
Child, Dr. Henry T., 5, 58, 79, 81, 83, 126
Chinese, 1, 106
Chorpenning, George, 73, 77, 78, 111, 147
Christianity, 12, 19, 25, 61, 72, 96, 114, 119, 138; Adventists, 90, 126, 127, 130; Catholics and Catholicism, 18, 107, 108, 146; Christian Science, 10, 150; Disciples of Christ, 66; Free-Will Baptists, 66; Methodists, 2, 35, 91, 112, 129; Mormons and Mormonism, 8, 103, 113; Presbyterians, 32, 66; Progressive Friends, 3, 38; Protestants, 18, 148; Quaker, 5, 8, 58, 90, 131; Seventh-Day Adventist, 154; Unitarians and Unitarianism, 8, 9, 11, 72; Universalists and Universalism, 4, 8, 13, 17, 31, 108, 132
*Christian Spiritualist*, 17, 33, 49, 50
Cincinnati, 6, 9, 15, 26, 28, 35–36, 38, 68, 73, 82, 91, 95, 111, 116, 127, 132, 141
Clapp, Henry, 10, 30
Clark, Uriah, 4, 8, 14–15, 50–51, 126, 139

Cleveland, OH, 11, 12, 26, 39, 40, 68, 80, 121, 149
Coggeshall, William Turner, 9, 38, 68
Colburn, Nettie, 72–78, 83, 84, 85, 111, 112, 147
Colchester, Charles J., 70, 75, 78
Coleman, William E., 40, 73, 135, 151, 153, 156
Collins, John A., 9, 27, 93, 156
Columbus, OH, 6, 12, 17
communities and utopian experiments: Berlin Heights, 38, 121; Bishop Hill, 131; Black Lake, 132.; Ceresco, 7, 23, 26, 37, 131; Fountain Home, 131; Harmonial Healing Institute, 17; Harveysburg, 5; Highland Home (Zanesfield), 5–6; Hopedale community, 119; Kiantone, 13, 39, 128; Modern Times, 8, 30, 132; Northampton Association, 10; Rappites, 131; Ripon, WI, 23, 37, 131; Shakers, 9, 12, 71, 131; Skaneateles, NY, 9; Union Home, 5; Utopia, 9; Vineland, NJ, 132; Zoar, 131
Coonley, L. K., 50, 51
Cooper Institute, 84, 115
cooperatives and cooperativism, 7, 9, 25, 132, 140, 141; Labor-for-Labor Stores, 9, 141. *See also* Warren, Josiah
Cornell, John P., 9, 28
Cosby, Mrs., 77
Cridge, Alfred, 6, 68, 91, 157
Cridge, Anne Denton, 6, 37, 68, 91
Cuppy, Laura, 127, 156

Daniels, Cora L.V. Scott Hatch. *See* Richmond, Cora Lodencia Veronica Scott Hatch Daniels Tappan
Daniels, Edward, 37, 50, 85, 131, 147
Daniels, Nathan W., 78, 97, 121, 147
Danskin, Washington A., 16, 73
Davis, Andrew J., 11, 47, 92–93; and emergence as leader, 5, 9, 13, 39, 151; involvement with the New York City movement, 28, 29, 31; and organization, 126, 128; relation to radicalism, 63, 92–93, 154; and women's rights, 118, 121
Davis, Ira B., 3, 11, 41–42, 93, 107, 139, 141, 143, 148, 153–54
Davis, Jefferson, 60, 81
Davis, Mary Fenn Love, 121, 129
Dawes, Henry l., 73, 83

Day, George E. H., 116, 117
Day, Horace H., 29, 33, 71, 91, 154
Dayton, OH, 6, 78, 127
Democratic Party and Democrats, 37, 38, 68, 80, 84, 121; development after the war, 148, 152, 158; general hostility to spiritualism and to antislavery, 36; party of the cotton South, 53, 79, 114; sectional rift in the party, 1–2, 23, 24; spiritualists among, 6, 26, 73, 114
Denton, Anne. *See* Cridge, Anne Denton
Denton, William, 6, 37, 68, 91, 154, 157
Dodworth Hall circle (New York City), 31, 48, 107
Doten, Lizzie, 53, 81, 83, 102
Douglass, Frederick, 27, 30, 39, 97, 109, 153
draft riots, 79, 139
Dresser, Horace, 30, 79, 113
Durkee, Charles, 27, 28
Dyott, Michael B. and Mary Jane, 129, 149, 150

Eddy, Ira B., 7, 85
Edmonds, John W., 4, 17, 26, 29, 31, 34, 35, 54, 73
Emerson, Ralph Waldo, 8, 28
England, 9, 12, 68, 91, 128, 150. *See also* London
Europe, 1, 23, 96, 156; French influences, 12, 18, 100, 153, 156

Ferguson, Jesse Babcock, 17, 18
Finney, Seldon J., 6–7, 129
Fisk, Theophilus, 5, 32
Floyd, Emma. *See* Brittan, Emma Hardinge
Forbes, Hugh, 30, 40, 152
Forster, Thomas Gales, 10, 73–75, 78, 121, 126, 141
Fort Sumter, 47, 52
Fourier, Charles, 3, 9, 28, 91
Fourierists and Fourierism, 4, 7, 9, 26–29, 36, 37, 41, 45, 63, 67, 92–93, 131, 141
Fox sisters, 7, 11–12, 25–30, 118, 119, 126, 157; Katie, 2, 4, 11, 29, 32, 147; Margaret (Maggie), 2, 3, 4, 5, 11, 29, 30, 32, 147; popping of toes, 2, 11, 147. *See also* Underhill, Leah Fox
Franklin, Benjamin, 12, 13, 32, 86, 90, 108, 113

Free Conventions: Ellensville, 39; "land, air and water" resolution, 154–55; Kiantone, 39; Rutland, 30, 39, 87; Utica, 39; Worcester, 39
Free Democrats and Free Democratic Party, 23–28, 30, 37–38, 41, 129, 146, 154
Freemason and Masonic orders, 18, 125, 128, 149
Free-Soilers and Free Soil Party, 2, 23
Fremont, John C., 38, 80, 152

Galveston, TX, 7, 17, 18
Garrison, William Lloyd, 9, 13, 30, 39, 82, 109
Georgia, 17, 34, 57, 60
Gettysburg, 58, 79
Giddings, Joshua R., 26, 27, 32, 80
Glover, John J., 7, 85
Gordon, Laura E. A. De Force, 127, 135, 156
Grant, U.S., 147, 152, 157
Graves, Kersey, 5, 154
Greeley, Horace, 3, 4, 6, 23, 28, 29, 35, 80, 91, 152
Greenbackers, Greenbackism, and Greenback-Labor, 84, 145, 154
Greene, William Batchelder, 120, 141, 153, 154
Griswold, C. D., 58, 79

Hacker, Jeremiah, 5, 46
Hamilton, D. H., 132, 133, 139, 144
Hannibal, MO, 17, 134
Hannum, Parnie R., 71–73, 76, 78
Hardinge, Emma. *See* Brittan, Emma Hardinge
harmonial, 82, 90, 93
Harpers Ferry, 7, 39–40, 135
Harris, Thomas Lake, 4, 9, 16, 17, 29, 31, 32, 56, 92, 126, 143
Hartford, CT, 5, 7
Hatch, Benjamin F., 119, 121
Hatch, Cora L. V. Scott. *See* Richmond, Cora Lodencia Veronica Scott Hatch Daniels Tappan
Henry, Anson G., 67, 85
*Herald of Progress*, 41, 42, 49, 111
Herndon, William H., 65, 67–69, 75, 146
Heywood, Ezra H., 59, 153
Higgins, A. J., 51, 129
Higginson, Thomas Wentworth, 25, 39, 92, 97
High Rock, Lynn, 13, 91

Hinckley, Caroline, 14, 128
Hinton, Richard J., 40, 153
Hitchcock, Ethan Allen, 10, 71
Hootee, Lewis C., 17, 33, 78
Horton, Alfred, 71, 112–13
Hull, Moses, 126–27, 153–54
Hutchinson Family, 13, 103
Hydesville, NY, 2–4

Indians and Indian rights, 6, 32, 56, 62, 111, 113–18, 155, 157; as spirit guides, 12, 86. *See also* Indian Territory; Ojibwa
Indian Territory, 56, 62, 111, 115, 117
Ingalls, Joshua K., 31, 36, 140, 153, 154
International Workingmen's Association (IWA), 152–54
Iowa, 7, 33, 37, 38, 42, 50, 72, 90, 131, 132
Irish, 79, 108

Jackson, Andrew, 52, 59
Jefferson, Thomas, 13, 46, 59
Jefferson County, MO, 7, 17
Johnson, Andrew, 17, 85, 135, 148
Jones, Stevens Sanborn, 50, 52, 82, 110, 129, 150
*Journal of Man*, 6, 10
Julian, George W., 27, 148

Kane, Elisha Kent, 30, 110, 129
Kansas, 7, 23–24, 35, 37–39, 43, 47–48, 116, 133, 156
Kansas-Nebraska Act, 23, 35–37, 131
Kellogg, Edward N., 30, 141
Kelso, John R., 17, 38, 55–56, 83–84, 134, 152–53, 156
Keyser, John H., 153, 154
Kilgore, Damon Y., 58, 150, 153–54
Kinyon, Benjamin N., 101, 103, 106, 130, 132
Kneeland, Abner, 10, 11
Koons, Jonathan, 6–7, 13, 157

labor movements, 140; free labor ideology, 24; Labor Reformers break from Republicans, 123–24. *See also* land reformers and land reform
Lamartine, 109
land reformers and land reform, 9, 25, 27, 42, 45, 120, 142, 153, 154, 158
Laurie, Cranston, 32–33, 35, 74–76, 78, 85

Laurie, Isabel. *See* Miller, Isabelle Laurie
Lawrence, Benjamin M., 154, 156
Lincoln, Abraham, 26, 43, 65–66, 136, 146, 147, 148; passing of, 84–89; philosophical predispositions, 66–69; presidential re-election, 82–84, 152; spiritualist proclivities and involvement, 70 75, 75–77
Lincoln, Mary Todd, 70–72, 74–77, 85, 113
Lincoln, Robert Todd, 70, 85
Lippard, George, 5, 25, 28
London, 8, 31, 36, 99, 120, 138, 153; East End, 8
Loveland, J. S., 137, 153
Lynn, MA, 13, 38, 91

Madison, WI, 27, 127
Mandell, D. J., 63, 132
Marx, Karl, 90, 104, 153
Mason-Dixon, 18, 109, 136
Masquerier, Lewis, 31, 72, 154
mediums and mediumship, 2, 6, 53, 94; emergence of as a profession, 10, 12–16, 27; gender and, 12–13, 118; and the Lincolns, 67–70, 73–77, 86, 113, 136–37; local variations, 18–19; and photography, 130; and public lectures, 31–32, 43; race and, 16, 18–19, 35, 61–62, 109–10, 111–13; spread of as organizing concept, 39, 51, 126–27, 134, 146; and the war, 54–55, 58–59. *See also* séance; spirit guides
Mid-Atlantic: New York, 2–18, 28–36, 40–43, 50, 67–68, 79–80, 84, 90–91, 94, 100–103, 107–23, 127–28, 132, 139, 141, 146–57; Pennsylvania, 5, 42, 50, 66, 79, 83, 90, 112. *See also specific communities*
Midwest, 5–6, 24, 26, 50, 127, 154; Illinois, 6–7, 17, 34, 42, 45, 50, 52, 67, 73, 84–85, 111, 115, 127–28, 131; Indiana, 5, 6, 42, 66, 83, 119–21, 127; Ohio, 6–7, 12–13, 17, 24, 26, 34, 37–38, 42–43, 57, 67, 81, 83, 91, 96, 111, 121, 127, 131–32, 155; Wisconsin, 7, 14, 24, 26–27, 32, 36–37, 42–43, 68, 90, 119–20, 127, 154. *See also specific communities*
Miller, Isabelle Laurie, 33, 74, 146–47
Miller, Leo, 81, 129
Milwaukee, 7, 27, 90, 103, 154
Mississippi River and Valley, 18, 111
Mumler, William H., 90, 91, 130

National Industrial Congress, 108; radicalization of, 26–27; last antebellum (1860), 42, 108
National Typographical Union, 61, 73; Boston Printers' Union, 140
New England, 5, 8, 24, 29, 43, 47, 50, 55, 74, 85, 111–15, 135, 136, 141, 147, 153, 154; Connecticut, 5, 7, 16, 42, 72, 73; Maine, 5, 42, 46, 76, 123, 127, 132; Massachusetts, 5, 10, 11, 13, 16, 24, 34, 42, 54, 62, 72, 73, 94, 119; New Hampshire, 5, 28, 32, 33, 42, 67, 121; Vermont, 5, 24, 37, 38, 39, 42, 45, 72, 81, 115, 127, 129, 150. *See also specific communities*
"New Motive Power," 13, 91
New Orleans, 16–18, 109, 120, 134–35, 156
Newton, Alonzo E., 13–14, 29, 75, 79
New York City, 28, 31, 35, 40–42, 84, 103, 119, 121, 123, 127–28, 132, 139
*New York Herald*, 28, 79, 118
*New York Tribune*, 4, 6, 29, 35, 91, 100
Nichols, Adeline, 155
Nichols, Thomas L., 6, 30

Odd Fellows, 125, 149
Ojibwa, 111, 114
Olcott, Henry S., 6, 13, 73, 84, 91, 100, 150–51, 157
Ordway, Nehemiah, 67, 68, 74
Orvis, John, 14, 36, 93, 154
Owen, Robert, 3, 9, 36, 119, 121, 131
Owen, Robert Dale, 40, 71, 112, 119, 120

Paine, Seth, 7, 68, 70
Paine, Thomas, 6, 10, 17, 66
Paris, 1, 18, 99, 120, 151
Parker, Theodore, 13, 19, 148
Partridge, Charles, 11, 12, 29, 101, 141
Peebles, James Martin, 58, 114, 127, 136, 157
Philadelphia, 5, 25, 32, 58, 68, 78, 103, 116, 123, 129, 132, 150, 153
Pierpont, John, 40, 72, 75, 78, 103, 109
Pinkerton, Allan, 68, 73
Pittsburgh, 5, 27, 32, 131
*Pleasure Boat*, 5, 46
Plymouth, 5, 39
Poe, Edgar Allan, 30–31, 92
Porter, Ira, 7, 144
Portland, ME, 5, 123, 124

Post, Amy, 3, 119

race, 61, 114
Radical Republicans and Radical Republicanism, 79, 124, 148, 152
Randall, John H., 52, 58
Randolph, Pascal B., 35–36, 42, 93, 109–10, 129, 134–35, 137
Rawson, Albert Leighton, 110, 154
Reconstruction, 130–38
Rehn, Isaac, 90, 107, 150, 153
Republicans and Republican Party, 158; in the 1860 election and secession crisis, 42, 44, 57, 135; in the 1864 election, 81; origins, 23–24, 26, 37; radicalization of, 123–24, 152, 158; and republicanism in antiquity, 64; rise and overlap with spiritualism, 14, 31, 35–38, 43, 68, 71, 85, 119, 131, 146–48, 154; spirits advising, 60, 61–62, 79
revolution, 1, 52, 62, 64, 66, 129, 133, 136, 141, 146, 148, 155; of 1848, 1, 41–42
Richmond, Cora Lodencia Veronica Scott Hatch Daniels Tappan, 27, 46, 47, 64, 85, 118, 119, 121, 135, 136, 147, 150
Richmond, VA, 32, 40, 57, 84, 121, 135, 150
Rochester, 2–4, 6, 9, 11, 25, 29, 70, 102, 119, 143; Corinthian Hall, 4, 11; "Rochester rappings," 2, 9, 29
Rosicrucians and Rosicrucianism, 34, 35, 93, 109–10, 128–29
Russia, as compared to the U.S., 130–31
Rynders, Isaiah, 28, 29, 30

San Francisco, 7, 73, 128, 156
Sanitary Commission, 57, 110
Scott, Cora L. V. *See* Richmond, Cora Lodencia Veronica Scott Hatch Daniels Tappan
Scott, James Leander, 9, 16, 126
séance, 2, 6, 70, 73, 92, 112, 113–14; emergence, importance, and popularity of 12, 15, 16, 17; importance among Radical Republicans, 147–48; later retreat of movement into, 118; Lincolns and, 67, 68–69, 74–76; 85; Ouija, 130; prohibition of in some Southern states, 17; utility of in spread of movement, 29–30; table, riding, 13, 74. *See also* mediums and mediumship; spirit guides

secession, 38, 48, 56, 57, 59, 62, 64, 75, 81, 114, 118, 148
Seneca Falls, 1, 2, 119
Sennett, New York, 4, 5
Severance, Anson B., 90, 154
Severance, Julier H. Worth Stillman, 90, 102, 153–55
Seward, William H., 37, 43
sewing machines, 13, 103
Sheddon, John, 25, 27
Shields, James A., 34, 35, 36
Shiloh, 58, 79, 95
Sickles, Daniel, 72, 112
slaves and slavery: Emancipation Proclamation, 78; as feature of the entire social order, 103, 106–7, 124, 133–37, 152; few spiritualists equivocal on the issue, 18, 44–45, 46; former slaves in the movement, 10; innate hostility of spiritualism towards, 19, 23–24, 24–25, 26–27, 40, 42, 47–48, 91, 142; wartime emancipation, 49, 51, 57, 59–63, 72, 79–83, 89, 94–98, 111–15, 117; in the western territories, 33, 36–38
Smith, Elizabeth Oakes, 119
Smolnikar, Andrej Bernard, 103, 108
Snodgrass, J. E., 16, 27
socialism and socialists: appeal of spiritualism among, 3, 5, 8–9, 45, 91, 92, 119; communities of, 23, 26–28, 30, 38–39, 131; in electoral politics, 27; reemergence after the Civil War, 103, 108, 145, 153–56, 158; regarded in South as kindred to abolitionism and spiritualism, 18–19; as scientific understanding of society, 90, 98, 108
Somes, David E., 71, 76, 77
South and slaveholding states: Alabama, 17, 34, 49, 57; Arkansas, 17, 56, 115; Florida, 34, 134; Maryland, 17, 49; Missouri, 17, 33, 37, 38, 49, 55, 56, 58, 78, 83, 132, 134, 152, 156; North Carolina, 57; South Carolina, 17, 32, 61, 72, 73, 134, 141; Tennessee, 17, 49, 55, 57, 127, 134; Texas, 7, 16, 73; Unionists in, 49, 60, 148; Virginia, 16, 17, 32, 34, 40, 53, 56, 57, 66, 100, 124–27, 134, 135, 145, 156. *See also specific communities*
Spear, John Murray, 13–14, 36, 91, 93, 103, 110, 126, 128, 153
Spence, Amanda M., 46, 51, 81, 108, 126

spirit guides, 12, 71–72, 78, 84, 86, 90, 111, 113. *See also* mediums and mediumship; séance
*Spirit of the Age*, 24, 28
spiritualists and spiritualism:
—communities of: Kidder, 132, 133; Mountain Cove, 16, 17, 56, 57, 126. *See also* communities and utopian experiments
—diversity of, 107–23; blacks in, 108–11, 113; and campaign for "fallen women," 122; Catholics in, 107; Civil War as revolution, 58; and free love, 120–22; Indians and Indian reform, 113–18; Jews in, 41, 108; and racial equality, 111–13, 114, 122, 12; and radicalism, 138–44; visions of the war and battlefields, 58, 145; and wartime Labor Reform Party, 123–245; and women's rights, 118–23; and working women, 122–23
—as a movement: "missionaries," 15, 27; origins and growth of 4–8; sectional character of, 16–19; size of, 14–16, 19, 31–32, 43; theological roots. 8–11, 146
—national conventions: origins of, 39, 40; of 1861, 49–52; of 1864, 82–84, 114; of 1867, 149
—organizations and related organizations: Apostolic Circle, 4, 9; Association of Electrizers, 13; Brotherhood of Luxor, 151; Brothers of the Rosy Cross, 128; Children's Progressive Lyceums, 129, 149; Commonwealth Association, 42; Harmonial Society, 17; Harmonial Vegetarian Society, 56; Massachusetts Association of Spiritualists, 13; Memnonia Institute, 6; Moral Police Fraternity, 128–29; Morris Pratt's Institute, 90, 154; Northern Wisconsin Spiritualist Association, 127; Order of Eternal Progress (OEP), 125, 149–50, 151; [E.C.] Posten Circle, 6; with *Religio-Philosophical Journal*, 5, 110, 150; Religio-Philosophical Society, 52, 82, 129, 131, 144; Sacred Order of Unionists, 36, 128; Society for the Diffusion of Spiritual Knowledge, 33–34, 35–36; Spiritual Brotherhood or True Brotherhood, 9, 26, 35, 91; in wartime Washington, 77–79; Washington Conference, 33, 34. *See also* Brotherhood of the Union

—political dimensions: U.S. Congress and, 33–35; in Kansas struggle, 37–38; in the Civil War 53–59; insights from spirits of the war dead, 59–63; support for Lincoln administration, 79–85; post-war reconstruction of the movement, 126–30
—social reform and radicalism, 19, 45–47, 92–94, 152–53, 156–57, 158–59; capitalism and, 98–105, 142–44; capital punishment, 19; diet, 18, 38; emancipation, 94–98; and First International, 152–53; free-love, 35, 38, 59; and Greenback-Labor, 154; and Labor Reform League, 153–54; race and, 45–46, 79; and Socialistic Labor, 145, 154–55. *See also* abolitionism; socialism; women's rights
Stanton, Elizabeth C., 119, 153, 156
St. Charles, IL, 52, 82, 129
Stearns, George Luther, 39, 97
Stebbins, Giles B., 10, 109, 147
Stillman, Juliet H. Worth. *See* Severance, Julier H. Worth Stillman
St. Louis, 10, 13, 16, 17, 58, 85, 152
Sturgis, MI, 6, 50
Sunderland, LeRoy, 5, 13
Swedenborg, Emmanuel, 8, 9
Sweet, Theophilus, 35, 67
Syme, Cora A., 46, 51, 154

Tabor, Stephen J. W., 72, 103
Tallmadge, Nathaniel P., 32, 34, 35, 36
Tappan, Cora L.V. Scott Hatch Daniels. *See* Richmond, Cora Lodencia Veronica Scott Hatch Daniels Tappan
Taylor, Zachary, 52, 60
Tecumseh, MI, 6, 62, 117
Testut, Charles, 18, 109
theosophists and theosophy, 12, 150–51, 157
Tiffany, Joel, 11, 26
Tippie, John, 6, 13, 37, 157
Toohey, John Henry Watson, 33, 40, 47, 50, 79, 104, 108, 110, 154
Trall, Russell T., 30, 90, 129, 155
Truth, Sojourner, 10, 109, 112

Underhill, Edward F., 30, 119

Underhill, Leah Fox, 3, 4, 8, 11, 12, 29, 30
Union and Unionism: mystical idea of, 44, 52–53, 146; revolutionary potential of, 63–64; war for as spiritual regeneration, 47–49, 53–59, 63
Utica, NY, 35, 39, 110

Van Buren, Martin, 1, 23, 24
Vance, Mariah, 66–67
*Vestiges of the Natural History of Creation*, 65, 91
Vicksburg, 18, 58

Waisbrooker, Louis, 154, 155
Waite, William Smith, 45–46
War Department, 74, 78, 82, 100
Warren, Josiah, 9, 30, 93, 141, 153–54
Washington, D.C., 16, 24, 27, 31–35, 41, 55, 62, 65–77, 84, 92, 103, 111–13, 116, 126, 147–48
Wattles, Augustus, 6, 38, 107, 116, 117
Wattles, John Otis, 5, 6, 9, 38, 47, 91
Waukegan, IL, 7, 13, 52
Webster, Daniel, 59, 76
West: California, 12, 38, 42, 55, 91, 128, 156, 157; California Gold Rush, 8, 32; Minnesota, 116, 117, 127, 154; Nebraska, 7, 33, 35, 37; Oregon, 7, 67, 115–17, 127, 128, 157; Pacific Coast, 7, 156. *See also* Indian Territory; Kansas; *and specific communities*
Wheeling, WV, 16, 57
White, Elijah, 116, 117
Williams, John Shoebridge, 34, 67, 68
Williams, Joseph, 33, 134
Williamsburg, NY, 13, 30
Willis, Frederick L. N., 57, 92
Wilson, Henry, 27, 72
Wolff, John B., 16, 57, 127, 128, 154
women's rights, 1, 10, 19, 72, 85, 91, 107–8, 119–21, 158; suffrage, 18, 26, 120, 152–53, 155; working women, 123
Woodhull, Victoria, 10, 58, 85, 153, 154
Workingmen's party, 24, 25
Wright, Henry C., 51, 72, 81, 89, 109
Wylley, Wilfrid, 56, 96–97, 138

Young, William J., 14, 42, 116, 128, 152

MARK A. LAUSE is a professor of American history at the University of Cincinnati and the author of numerous books, including *Free Labor: The Civil War and the Making of an American Working Class*; *A Secret Society History of the Civil War*; *Price's Lost Campaign: The 1864 Invasion of Missouri*; and *Race and Radicalism in the Union Army*.

The University of Illinois Press
is a founding member of the
Association of American University Presses.

---

Composed in 10.25/14 Adobe Chaparral Pro
with Archer display
at the University of Illinois Press
Manufactured by Sheridan Books, Inc.

University of Illinois Press
1325 South Oak Street
Champaign, IL 61820-6903
www.press.uillinois.edu